LEGACY
OF A
WAR

LEGACY OF A WAR

The American Soldier in Vietnam

Ellen Frey-Wouters

Robert S. Laufer

M. E. SHARPE, INC.
ARMONK, NEW YORK
LONDON, ENGLAND

Available in the United Kingdom and Europe from M. E. Sharpe,
Publishers, 3 Henrietta Street, London WC2E 8LU.

Library of Congress Cataloging in Publication Data

Frey-Wouters, Ellen
    Legacy of a War.

    Includes bibliographical references and index.
    1. Vietnamese Conflict, 1961–1975—United States. I. Laufer,
Robert S. II. Title.
DS558.F73   1986   959.704 '33 '73   85-10913
ISBN 0-87332-354-8

Printed in the United States of America

CONTENTS

Part Three: Perceptions of the Conduct of the War

Part Four: Vietnam and Beyond

LIST OF TABLES

FOREWORD

Frances Fox Piven

Large-scale wars make a deep and lasting imprint on the societies that participate in them. The memory of death and pillage may recede, but wars leave in their wake organizational and cultural changes generated by military mobilization that usually endure. These include new patterns of political centralization initiated by ruling regimes in the effort to extract military resources from civil society. Economic life is also permanently changed by the new forms of production, as well as changes in economic organization and technology stimulated by military expansion. In just this way, America's wars have left us with an engorged military sector that continues to dominate our economic and political life.

War, especially modern war, also leaves its mark on the political culture. Victorious wars sustain and strengthen the identification of ordinary people with the military state. This is at least partly a result of the exigencies of war making. Just because the terrible toll that even victorious wars take of civil society rarely makes sense from the perspective of common people, rulers with military aspirations confront difficult problems of domestic mobilization. Somehow, men and women have to be induced not to do what makes sense, not to shirk or hide or desert, but to collaborate, for the resources of war are ultimately their lives and limbs and livelihoods. Invariably in the modern world this collaboration is promoted by extravagances of nationalist propaganda through which people are urged to identify their own well-being with that of the Nation, and to transfer to a distant and abstract state their natural attachment to kin and kind and place. Once this transfer is accomplished, people are rendered helpless to interpret their reality, for now the impulse to defend one's concrete community is activated in the name of an unknowable abstraction engaged with other unknowable abstractions in unseen contests which are said to threaten security and honor in unknowable ways.

This is the essence of the nationalist myth. And if the myth serves the war-making purposes of state leaders, war in turn generates a dynamic that may memorialize that myth, or perhaps weaken it. In victorious conflicts, the triumphs and horrors of the fighting, the celebrations of victories and the making of heroes, may sear the nationalist myth into the consciousness of peoples. Long after the guns are quiet, the excitement remains in the masculine images that see triumph as military triumph and find personal self-respect by identifying with national power. And, of course, these images continue to influence political life, for they are always available for the next military mobilization.

But the experience of war, especially the experience of defeat, can also weaken the myth. This is not always to the good, for the disappointment, even anguish, at the tarnished nationalist myth can fester among people who are accustomed to find the meaning of their personal lives in the strange and awesome idea of the Nation. This appears to have happened in Germany after World War I, and it may also be evident in the growth of militaristic right-wing groups in the contemporary United States. But sometimes defeat discredits the militaristic myth and the mythmakers and makes possible the restoration of a measure of popular common sense, of wisdom, in evaluating the meaning of war. Something like this seems to have occurred in much of Western Europe and Japan in the aftermath of World War II. And there is reason to think Americans may have benefited from the Vietnam War in a similar way.

It is true that the memories of death and pillage in Southeast Asia receded quickly, and that was perhaps inevitable, for most of the destruction was visited on other peoples and other lands. But the war left our myth of national greatness, and the military prowess associated for us with national greatness, deeply scored and tarnished. The importance of this scarcely needs saying. When the nationalist myth weakens, the authority of leaders who speak in the name of the Nation erodes, and their latitude for action domestically and abroad in the name of national necessity contracts. Small wonder, then, that still today, a dozen years after the American withdrawal from Southeast Asia, the "war at home" continues, as government leaders and right-wing intellectuals exert themselves to find scapegoats for the defeat in Vietnam, and to restore confidence in American military strength. It is a tough and serious effort because on its outcome hinges the strength of the nationalist myth. And the myth in turn is critical to the ability of state leaders and their military and business allies to impose on us the domestic costs of their military policies abroad.

As the authors of this study point out, the Vietnam War was the first war rejected while it was being fought by a substantial portion of Americans. Moreover, surveys conducted in the years after the end of the Vietnam conflict showed a majority of Americans thought the United States should have stayed out of the fighting in Vietnam, and that the war's lasting effects were harmful. In other words, majorities of Americans remain in stubborn disagreement with crucial state policies. It is difficult to overstate the significance of these opinions, for they represent widespread dissent with state policies, and a challenge to state authority.

The great value of this book is that it adds detail and depth to our understanding of the impact of the Vietnam War on public opinion, and therefore to our
understanding of why the war at home goes on. Ellen Frey-Wouters and Robert
Laufer eschew the excesses of rhetoric that have come to be associated with
reflections on the Vietnam War in favor of a careful empirical inquiry into the
attitudes of the generation that came of age during the war. This is a detailed
examination of the attitudes of the men who in a sense fought on both sides of the
war, for this was the generation from which the men who fought in Vietnam were
drawn, and from which the antiwar protestors in the United States were also
drawn. And whichever side they found themselves on, this generation's experiences, and the ideas formed by those experiences, were key to the wider public
disaffection with a military nationalism that the Vietnam War produced. Taken as
a whole, the study provides a thorough documentation of the opinions that
emerged as the nationalist myth eroded, and an analysis of the specific experiences associated with those opinions.

The basis of Frey-Wouters and Laufer's findings is a careful survey, including in-depth interviews, of 1,159 men in the "Vietnam generation," over half of
whom were veterans, and a substantial proportion of whom were veterans of the
war in Vietnam. The survey was conducted in ten communities around the
country in the late 1970s, several years after the war had ended, and thus
represents the retrospective attitudes of these men toward the war. But if wars
mark societies by the way military mobilization shapes enduring social myths,
then this inquiry is more rather than less significant for being retrospective, for it
reveals the attitudes men continue to have toward the war at some remove from
the events themselves.

The exclusion of women from the survey requires some comment. It is a
drawback, as the authors themselves acknowledge, because we are thus prevented
from knowing what women of that generation think about the war, or how they
came to think it. Moreover, the poll data of the past five years have made it clear
that the attitudes of women, particularly on matters of war and peace, diverge
sharply from the attitudes of men. That said, however, the remarkable findings of
this study are findings about how a generation of young men, including those who
fought the war, turned against the war, and the complexity of the experiences and
ideas that led them to turn against the war. While it would surely be interesting to
have comparable information about women, it seems safe to say that militaristic
nationalism has always been the domain of men more than women. For that
reason, scrutiny of the attitudes of the men of the generation that turned against
the war is in fact more to the point.

Several instructive conclusions emerge from this detailed scrutiny. One is
the extent of opposition to the war among the generation as a whole. Another,
more striking fact is the extent of opposition even among the men who actually
fought in Vietnam. A plurality of these respondents came over the course of the
war, or more precisely over the course of their experience of the war, to oppose

American involvement. It is the circumstance of the respondents that makes this particular finding so striking and revealing. For opposition to the fighting to emerge among soldiers it must surmount not only the definitions provided by national and military leaders, but also the ordinary human impulse to justify one's own actions, whatever the train of events that led to those actions. Thus it has often been said (incorrectly in my view) that civilian antiwar protestors in the United States opposed the war out of self-interest because they did not want to go to Vietnam. But this surely cannot be said of the men who were already in Vietnam. Indeed, their self-interest would if anything lead them to support the war, if only to give sense and meaning to their situation. Yet these veterans offer few of the invocations to flag and nation and honor that might justify the war and lionize their own role. The tone is different, the views more troubled. It must have been difficult for a veteran to reach the conclusion that the war "seemed like a classic example of bullying, you know . . . for ideological reasons." Or for another veteran who served as an army cannoneer to conclude "Somebody was getting rich on it" and then go on to speculate perceptively on just who it was that was getting rich and how. Or for a Marine Corps lieutenant to conclude that the war was a complete betrayal "of everyone who thought he was doing what his country asked of him and found that he was contributing not at all to this country's welfare or to the welfare of South Vietnam. We were made party to a deception. . . . When leadership is that corrupt, that dishonest, then it bodes ill for the country." Or for another white army infantryman to say, simply and eloquently, that he was ashamed to be an American. These sorts of views on the part of the men who actually fought the war represent a wisdom that must have been only painfully attained, for opinions like this can only be formed when a ruling ideology is penetrated, and when self-interested rationalization is surmounted.

Because the nationalist justification for the war disintegrated for many of this generation, they were able to develop perspectives that were remarkably thoughtful, complex, and finely shaded. Most of the veterans, for example, scorned the corruption and timidity of their erstwhile allies in the Army of the Republic of South Vietnam (ARVN) and actually felt more positive toward the enemy, whether the Vietcong or the North Vietnamese. At the same time, some of them also pondered the reasons for what they perceived as the poor performance of the men of the ARVN, and did so with sensitivity and empathy, as when an army helicopter pilot reflected: "The average soldier . . . strongly wanted to keep their country Vietnamese. They must have had a hell of a conflict, the guys getting caught up in the ARVN, you know." And another veteran said: "We couldn't win the war because these were people who were fighting for the land and their lives and everything that they held dear to them."

Most remarkable of all, I think, most of these respondents eschew easy solutions. They reflect on the brutality of the war, on the American treatment of enemy soldiers and Vietnamese civilians, on the devastating weaponry employed. They wonder how much of the cruelty was necessary or justified, and they do not offer simple answers, nor the same answers. Some of the respondents, veterans and nonveterans, even reach the tormented conclusion that both sides were in fact brutal and inhumane. As one of the generation who was not a veteran but was an antiwar activist observed: "The South Vietnamese were trying to make a living with a corrupt government on one hand and a bunch of marauding people's army soldiers on the other hand, and they were just caught in the middle." Whoever the winners, ordinary people are the losers in such a war.

Whether you agree with this judgment or not, it has, like so many of the statements offered by the Vietnam generation, the ring of independence and thoughtfulness. And independent and thoughtful opinions about these matters are only possible when the mystifying myth of nationalism is overcome. In the pages that follow, the authors try to identify the conditions that made that possible. They probe the bearing of the different backgrounds of the men of the generation, and of their different experiences during the war, on the opinions they formed of war in general and of this war in particular, and the opinions they formed of specific aspects of this war that may have made it particularly ethically repugnant. And the authors also explore the bearing of background, experience, and judgments of the Vietnam War on attitudes toward possible future military intervention in the Third World by the United States. They are guided by the supposition that exposure to the war influenced perceptions of its conduct. And they think that is especially the case in the Vietnam War because "translated into human terms, the war and the military strategies used turned an entire nation into a target and shattered a whole society. In the end, the conflict became a battle against the civilian population." The fact that the war was both a civil war and a guerrilla war meant that the awesome destruction visited upon civilians and civil society was more nearly continuous and total.

Was it an especially cruel and destructive war that produced the revulsion of the Vietnam generation? Was it the mistreatment of civilians, or the abuse of POWs that the difficult circumstances of a guerrilla war encouraged? Was it the actual experience of heavy combat, or of witnessing or even participating in particular acts of abusive violence? It seems reasonable to think so, and the authors carefully examine the relationship between these diverse experiences and the diverse opinions of respondents. Still, what struck me was not the diversity in attitudes, but the fact that 90 percent of the entire sample, whatever their experience, opposed military action against individual citizens, that 75 percent opposed the bombing and shelling of cities to terrorize the population, and that 90 percent of nonveterans and 70 percent of veterans would not support future military action by the United States in the Third World.

In fact, the Vietnam War was not unique in making the entire society the target of destruction. All major wars are brutal, and all are at least indirectly battles against the civilian populations who provide the economic and personnel resources that make the continuation of the war possible. Even in World War II, the "Good War" where there seemed to be a right side and a wrong side, the

American firebombing of German and Japanese cities and the devastation of Hiroshima and Nagasaki were not aimed at military targets. They were intended rather to wreak such havoc with the civilian population as to crush their morale. The Vietnam War was neither our first brutal war nor our first ethically ambiguous war. But it was the first war that Americans, especially the young, and including even the men who fought it, came to denounce with spirit and intelligence.

All wars are rotten. Wars kill, they maim, they poison the fields and shatter the cities. For common people there are no gains commensurate with this desolation except perhaps the successful resistance of a military power even more destructive than their own. If men are nevertheless induced to fight, and women to weep and cheer, it is because the myth of nationalism befuddles their common sense by supplanting the reality they can see and hear and assess with the abstractions of flag and state, and by infusing those abstractions with the sentiments of community. Nationalism as the preeminent modern ideology is often said to date from the French Revolution, from the glorious moment when men and women rose up to call themselves citizens and assert their right to participate in state power. There was a dark side to the glory, for this new identification with the state made it possible only a few short years later for Napoleon to march across Europe, wanton with the lives of his own men because the ranks were continually replenished with multitudes of new recruits, their enthusiasm newly fired by the idea of the Nation.

Perhaps what made the Vietnam War different was not that it was brutal, but that some of the people of the Vietnam generation described in this book somehow found the courage to say it was, and to say it loudly and defiantly. Their dissenting voices were at first few, and their protests modest, even sedate. But as the war escalated, so did the marches and demonstrations and the rhetoric. The antiwar movement challenged first the legitimacy of the war, then the authority of the leaders who perpetrated it, and finally the interpretation of Nation and national interest that justified it. The growing defiance helped to create the political space through which the actual horror and brutality of the war could be recognized and become part of the American consciousness of what was happening in Vietnam. It was inevitable that as the war continued and the movement grew, and spread even to the armed forces, the movement's condemnation of the war would begin to affect perceptions by men in Vietnam of their experience of combat.

Just as important, those men came home. They came home to a society whose lust for glory had been tempered by defeat, and whose understanding of the war had now been formed perhaps as much by the protestors as by state authorities. They came home to a public that, because of the antiwar movement, did not cheer them as returning warriors are always cheered. Instead, as the veterans themselves report in the pages that follow, they felt isolated and even shunned. That was sad for them, of course, and a good deal has since been said about the unfairness of it all. But it was good for the country, for it was a necessary consequence of the widespread revulsion toward the war. More important, by denying the returning men the ritual celebration for returning heroes, we rejected at least for the time being the pride of place that goes to warriors in the nationalist myth. If as a result masculine and military nationalism was not eradicated—and subsequent events show of course it was not—it was nevertheless weakened. That is a good thing for Americans. And it may turn out to be some protection for the people of Central America too.

PREFACE

The decision to undertake the writing of a book about the meaning of the Vietnam War from the perspective of the generation that bore the brunt of the fighting abroad and at home evolved out of a complex of events that started in 1973 and culminates with this volume. Originally, the book began as part of a larger project, *Legacies of Vietnam*, which produced its findings in 1981. This study included some data on political attitudes, but most of the information on the political implications of the war was relegated to future analysis. Our task at that time was to address the social and psychological consequences of the war, and the analysis of the political consequences remained something of a stepchild. The funding available for the political aspect of the study has been more difficult to obtain than for subsequent analysis of the psycho-social issues. Nonetheless, we received support from both the Rubin and Hazen foundations, and without the original support from the National Institute of Mental Health (NIMH) and the Veterans Administration (VA) for *Legacies of Vietnam*, the data would not have been available for analysis. Subsequent support by NIMH for mental health analysis was critical in allowing that work to go forward.

Financial support for research, though vital, was only one part of the support required to complete this book. Professional colleagues, research assistants and associates, secretaries, and editors all made an important contribution. The list of people who have played a role in the project is too long to mention each one by name. We hope that those we do not cite understand that we gratefully recognize their contribution to the final product.

There are, however, a number of people whose support over the years has been continuous and vital and whom we wish to acknowledge with special thanks. S. Maxwell Finger, former director of the Ralph Bunche Institute, Graduate Center C.U.N.Y., has for the last four years been a constant source of support and has facilitated our work in whatever way he could. Nancy Okada, the administrator of the Institute, took care of many details, including financial, with grace.

We have had the support of several colleagues over the years who encouraged us to persevere, contributed their thoughts, invited us to present sections of the manuscript at professional meetings, or read drafts of early versions of the chapters. In this regard we wish to thank Roberta Sigel, Richard Falk, Maurice Richter, John P. Wilson, Richard Hough, Patricia Gongla, Glen Elder, Elizabeth Brett, William Eaton, Bessel van der Kolk, Arthur Blank, and Steven Sonnenberg.

The actual production of a study also takes many hands. We are especially indebted to Mark Gallops, our research associate, who did a great deal of programming and other computer work and who participated in many hours of discussion involved in interpreting the findings. His contribution was invaluable and working with him was always a pleasure. Kathy Stenbeck and Joan Donnellan both worked as research assistants responsible for day-to-day statistical analysis. We appreciate their contribution.

The word processor is a marvelous tool that facilitates and speeds up the writing. However, it takes a talented and capable person at the keyboard. We thank several typists who transcribed the tapes and began the process of creating a manuscript. The final manuscript in its many drafts though is the work of one person, Anita Waters. We were fortunate enough to have her help through the grinding months of writing and rewriting, and some of the early editing of the manuscript.

Our editor, Marianna Fitzpatrick, worked mightily to save us from the jargon of our professions. We consider ourselves most fortunate in having had her time for many months to help us rewrite the manuscript into what we hope is a readable book. We have also been blessed with support from Arnold Tovell, editorial director of M.E. Sharpe. He waited patiently through missed deadlines, never pressuring us and remaining encouraging and expectant. When he finally did receive the manuscript his response was swift and supportive.

Above all, we can never thank enough the men of the Vietnam Generation who gave freely of their time in long interviews to share with us the details of their personal lives, especially those who went to Vietnam. We cannot cite these men by name, for we promised them anonymity, but we want to acknowledge their contribution. These men strengthened our conviction that their generation's experience deserved to be studied in depth and brought into the public light. We hope we have helped them tell their story as they saw it.

Finally, whatever help and support we have received, the responsibility for the book and its findings is ours alone.

Ellen Frey-Wouters and Robert S. Laufer

INTRODUCTION

During this century the United States has fought four major wars—World Wars I and II, the Korean conflict, and the Vietnam War. The Vietnam War, by far the longest and most divisive of these actions, forced Americans to confront a series of national moral and political dilemmas. It challenged the role of the United States in the world and raised grave questions about how wars should be conducted. The issue of a citizen's obligation to his country during wartime became an acute moral problem for many Americans.

Direct American involvement in Vietnam came to an end more than a decade ago. But the discovery of the personal, social, and historical legacies of the conflict goes on. The Vietnam War will continue to take on new meaning as Americans seek to understand their present and chart their future by reexamining their past.

This study focuses on a central aspect of the Vietnam War: the way it was viewed by the generation that came of age during that conflict. It examines the attitudes of those who went to Vietnam to fight and those who experienced the war at home in the United States.

The issues raised by the Vietnam War were most pressing for the men whose ages made them potential or actual combatants in the war. How they resolved these issues and dealt with the consequences of their decisions is central to this work. In addition, we explore how the war experience influences attitudes toward war and future military intervention in the Third World. In the broadest sense, this study is a story about war, the things men do in war, and the ways that war affects them.

Understanding the war and assessing its impact on the Vietnam Generation are on-going processes into which we were able to tap through our research. At our request, a household probability sample of 1,259 men in ten locations in the United States[1] whose lives were touched directly or indirectly by the war joined with us in a mutual learning process, formulating their experience of the war years by means of a three- to six-hour interview. Their voices fill these pages, as veterans and their nonveteran peers recall the powerful experiences and feelings that shaped their lives during the Vietnam years.

In recent years, public awareness of the Vietnam War has changed dramatically. Today, the nation seems willing, often eager, to examine the meaning of the conflict. The war's consequences are still being felt in our foreign policy, in our economy, and, above all, in the daily lives of its veterans. The views of the Vietnam Generation, therefore, deserve our close attention. Their voices most closely chronicle the war's effects on our society, and their stories stand as vivid reminders of the past.

The War Experience: Stress and Its Aftermath

The first segment of this four-part study is designed to provide the reader with a sense of the war years, to specify key aspects of the war experience that play a systematic role in Vietnam veterans' postwar lives, and to examine social and psychological problems experienced by returnees in the aftermath of the conflict. The Vietnam veterans' story is considerably more complex than that of their peers. Thus, throughout the volume, this group of respondents is our prime focus, and the character and repercussions of their war experiences are of central concern.

The experiences of men at war leave a lasting impression. The question, beyond what happens in combat, is what type of stress it is that men undergo in war that most deeply affects their social and psychological adjustment in later life. To interpret the long-term effects of the war on its veterans, we carefully examine the role of war stress. Our model for estimating the results of wartime pressures focuses on three aspects of the war experience: combat, witnessing abusive violence, and participating in abusive violence.

Chapter 1 sets the scene for the analysis to come, providing an overview of the war as experienced by Vietnam veterans to give the reader a feeling for the nature of that conflict and the responses it evoked among its veterans. We also define those aspects of the war experience that will be used throughout this study to measure the psychological and political implications of the Vietnam years.

Regarding the effects of the war, the subject of chapter 2, we focus primarily on three issues: the problem of readjustment to civilian life during the reentry period, the psychological effects of the war experience, and the ways in which war disrupts the social life of its veterans.

A substantial literature, much of it written by veterans, suggests that veterans' homecoming difficulties were intensified when they were confronted with vocal challenges to the war's legitimacy. The unpopularity of the war and public awareness after 1968 that the United States could not win it created a serious problem for returning veterans. There were no victory parades, and men slipped back into civilian life unnoticed and alone. Chapter 2 closely examines the painful readjustment to civilian life, citing the trauma of reentry as noted by veterans.

Chapter 2 further reports the results of our general inquiry into the long-term effect of the Vietnam War experience. In the later years of the war and during its immediate aftermath, public attention began to focus on our fighting men. Initial reports by military officials and psychiatrists reassured the public that Vietnam veterans would have no special problems resulting from their service. But returning veterans, the mass media, and some scholars soon began to paint a different and disturbing picture of men who were having difficulty readjusting to civilian life. It appeared that the Vietnam War might leave a legacy of troubled veterans who felt ill-used and resentful. As Vietnam veterans' organizations began to press their view, veterans' difficulties became increasingly defined as an explosive social problem and a volatile political issue.

Finally, chapter 2 investigates the special difficulties Vietnam veterans may suffer due to the war. These include alienation, psychiatric symptoms, medical problems, drug and alcohol abuse, deviant behavior, and marital problems. In the course of this inquiry, we compare Vietnam veterans both with their soldier peers in the military who did not go to Vietnam and with men who did not enter the military. Two questions are posed: 1) do Vietnam veterans have more problems than their peers, and 2) if so, can these reasonably be attributed to their wartime experience?

Our concern here is twofold: 1) how do veterans subjectively assess the effects of their experience; and 2) regardless of how they feel the war has influenced their lives, what epidemiological evidence do we have that they continue to have more psychological, drug and alcohol, or social problems than their peers? Throughout, the emphasis is on the long-term social and psychological effects of the stress invoked by combat and witnessing and participating in abusive violence.

Views of the War

Part two of the study examines how our respondents feel about the Vietnam War. It is now commonplace to investigate how the war divided generations and affected the character of American political life. Yet much of the current debate pays little attention to the way the generation that fought the war on several fronts perceived it, and how that perception shaped political attitudes in America. In the final analysis, it was the voices of Vietnam veterans and antiwar activists that created a climate that affected decision making and public opinion. To understand the war fully, we need to see it through the eyes of the generation most directly affected by the war, whose views are examined in chapter 3.

The perceptions a nation has of its allies and foes are a major factor in any conflict. The cause around which a country asks its fighting men to rally must be politically and morally defensible. This was clearly the case in World War II, a conflict in which America's allies inspired trust and showed their willingness to share the burden of battle. The circumstances surrounding the Vietnam War, however, were much more complicated. In chapter 4, we look at how the Vietnam Generation viewed its ally, the South Vietnamese Army, and its foes, the North Vietnamese Army and the Vietcong.

Finally, chapter 5 explores the feelings of the Vietnam Generation toward the Vietnamese people as well as their perception of Vietnamese feelings toward the United States military presence. It also looks into the generation's views of the effect the war was having on the Vietnamese.

Perceptions of the Conduct of the War

Part three concentrates on the Vietnam Generation's views of the conduct of the war. Our discussion embraces four specific areas: the war against civilians and the environment, the use of unnecessarily cruel weapons, the treatment of prisoners of war, and perspectives on individual responsibility in war.

Every war causes large-scale death and suffering to its fighting men as well as to the civilian population on whose territory the battles are fought. But the moral outrages inherent in war are often minimized when the ethical justification of the conflict is seen as sufficiently strong. The Vietnam War, as noted, was not generally perceived as a clear-cut struggle between good and evil. Moreover, the nature of the fighting in this guerrilla war without fronts created a setting especially conducive to abusive violence, a scenario in which it was often difficult to distinguish between noncombatants and the enemy. One important question that is examined in part three is to what extent concern over the high incidence of American acts of abusive violence and revulsion at the fate of thousands of innocent civilians killed or maimed by the arms and strategies of a high technology army undercut the willingness of the Vietnam Generation to support American involvement in the war.

A second, equally important thread that runs through this section is the effects of the wartime commission of acts of abusive violence by *all* parties to the conflict. The low regard of human life and suffering that characterized the general mode of operation of the South Vietnamese Army, the Vietcong, and the North Vietnamese Army substantially contributed to the brutality of the war. We therefore also examine the Vietnam Generation's views of and responses to acts of abusive violence committed by both the enemy forces and our Vietnamese ally. In so doing, we will explore how these acts shaped a generation's response to each group of combatants and affected their general view of the war.

We embarked on an analysis of the Vietnam Generations's views of abusive violence because we had good reason to believe that this aspect of the war experience is central to understanding the long-term effects of the war. In addition to noting the importance this factor is accorded in clinical studies, our interest in abusive violence stems from the emphasis it is given in our transcript material. Respondents who served in Vietnam spoke of the impact of the brutal episodes they saw perpetrated by all combatants against civilians and prisoners of war, as well as the use of unnecessarily cruel weapons. Nonveterans, although their exposure to such events was secondhand, also expressed their reaction to such violence on the part of both enemy and allied forces.

Actions committed against innocent civilians have long been considered to be the least humane and most unjustifiable of wartime activities. Chapter 6 begins by discussing some of the laws of war that protect this population and the relevance of these rulings to the Vietnam War. It then examines how the Vietnam Generation views certain actions the North Vietnamese Army and Vietcong, the South Vietnamese Army, and the American forces committed against civilians and the environment. Finally it examines Vietnam veterans' personal involvement in and general responses to such acts.

A second form of recognition of the inhumanity in warfare can be found in the attempt to control the production and use of unnecessarily cruel weaponry. In chapter 7 an examination of how such weapons are regulated today and how they were employed in the Vietnam conflict is followed by an overview of the feelings of the Vietnam Generation concerning the cruelty of specific arms and the circumstances under which they might be employed. This segment ends with an exploration of Vietnam veterans' responses to the use of cruel weapons based on personal experience.

Regarding the treatment of prisoners of war, the subject of chapter 8, our analysis begins with a discussion of those rights POWs have gradually achieved. We then attempt to demonstrate how deeply disturbing the treatment of many captives was to Vietnam veterans during the course of the war. We next turn to three significant related issues: how Vietnam veterans view the fate of certain prisoners, to what extent they may basically break with their generation regarding the nature of POW rights, and, given the nature of the Vietnam conflict, whether they believe that the protection to which regular soldiers were entitled should be extended to guerrilla fighters as well.

The principle that individuals are criminally responsible for violations of the rules of war is an important aspect of individual responsibility in times of conflict. Chapter 9, which ends part three, offers an examination of how international liability for violations of such rulings has developed through history and how the Vietnam Generation perceived the question of individual responsibility. The extent to which the generation was aware of humanitarian law and its perception of why existing international regulations were violated in Vietnam receive special focus, along with an analysis of generational attitudes toward the extent to which governments, officers, and soldiers are responsible in time of war.

The Political Legacy of Vietnam

The question that concludes this study is how the wartime experiences and images of the Vietnam Generation influence their perceptions of the fundamental issue of military intervention by U.S. forces in situations similar to Vietnam. As part of this assessment, part four includes the issue of how our respondents view resistance past and future. We also examine whether or not men would wish their sons to serve in the military in a war like Vietnam. This approach allows us to address the question of future intervention in both general and specific terms.

Methodology and the Implications of the Findings

Our sample contains 1,259 men who were of draft-eligible age during the Vietnam War (see appendix for a more complete description of the sample). The sample includes Vietnam veterans, era veterans, and nonveterans. The sample was drawn from ten sites chosen to represent four sections of the country on matched economic and demographic characteristics and collected in two waves: the Northeast in 1977 (wave I, N=341) and the South, Midwest, and West in 1979 (wave II, N=918). Though not a national probability sample, it does represent several regions and city sizes in the continental United States and does, at minimum, adequately represent the population in those ten sites. Our sample consists of a group of Vietnam veterans (N=326), Vietam era veterans (N=341), and nonveterans (N=592). The sample contains 860 whites and 399 blacks. The men in the sample were born between 1940 and 1953.

Depending on the interviewees' preferences and circumstances, the interviews were conducted either in the homes of our respondents or at project offices. The interviewer used a life history format and took the respondent through his life prior to his entry into the military, his military service, the readjustment period after leaving the military, and his current situation. The interview covered a broad range of issues including psycho-social functioning, careers, marital history, military experience, political attitudes, and feelings about the war. For nonveterans we covered essentially the same ground except that we substituted the period of greatest concern with the Vietnam War for the military experience section of the interview. The interview was composed of a broad range of standard survey items that asked the respondent to choose one of a series of possible closed-ended responses to a question; it also provided the respondent with an opportunity to express in his own words what he saw and how he felt about his experience and himself. These open-ended questions were tape recorded and subsequently transcribed verbatim and are the data that made it possible to do the textual analysis. We content-analyzed a significant portion of the narrative material to make it usable in traditional statistical modes of analysis. Moreover, the thematic analysis of the narrative material supplied by our respondents identifies the underlying issues discussed. The interview with Vietnam veterans took between four and a half and six hours; it was somewhat shorter for the Vietnam era and nonveteran population, approximately two and a half to three hours.

Our range of respondents allows us to generalize beyond those men interviewed to the larger population, the Vietnam Generation. We have defined the Vietnam Generation as men who were between the ages of 18 and 26 during the years 1964–1972, who served in the military or were age-eligible for military service during those years. These criteria assure that we are dealing with the reactions of young men who attained social and political maturity during the Vietnam War and that our study covers the years of military eligibility in this population.

To defend our findings as statistically reliable, our approach to the analysis of the data has been guided by the statistical tools of social science research. At the same time, we have attempted to make the study as immediate and accessible as possible by providing a dynamic analysis of the Vietnam experience.

Every chapter begins with a statistical profile of the groups within the study population on the key issues examined. This is followed by an elaboration of the main themes underlying the statistical presentation. The balance between the statistical and narrative-thematic material varies in accordance with each chapter's focus. The importance of the statistical profiles lies in their ability to help us estimate more precisely the significantly different ways that the various study groups perceived the meaning and effects of the Vietnam War.

Our strategy throughout the volume is to present variations between generational groups—Vietnam veterans, Vietnam era veterans, and nonveterans—and within single groups, such as those articulated by Vietnam veterans as a consequence of their different military experiences. The between and within group differences are presented in proportionate form. The findings are generally presented in terms of percentage differences between groups; and occasionally we use average or mean scores to this end. Thus, our presentation is bivariate in terms of the relationships between two measures. However, as the methodology appendix demonstrates, we used quite a different analytic procedure, i.e., regression or multivariate techniques, to arrive at the findings.

The use of regression analysis allowed us to determine systematically whether or not the discrepancies we found in the course of this study were statistically significant when we took into account possible alternative explanations for these differences, i.e., controlled for other factors. For example, if we found a statistically significant relationship between combat and attitudes toward the war, we then tested to see whether that relationship would be nullified by such alternative characteristics of the population as preservice factors, draft status, or the branch of the military in which respondents served. The ability to examine simultaneously the association between several potentially competing predictors of attitudes toward or effects of the war experience substantially enhances our confidence in the significance of those relationships that remain. In the social sciences, this exercise is referred to as controlling for spuriousness or confounding effects. Throughout the study all the relationships we report as significant were tested in the type of statistical model described above.

The use of both sampling and statistical procedures, commonplace in the social sciences, is vital to interpretation of the findings of this study. These procedures permit us to move beyond the limitations inherent in much of the prior literature on the Vietnam Generation. Compared to case studies, studies of readily available populations, studies that rely solely on narrative material, or even those that do sample but compare groups in this population without controlling for other relevant factors to explain differences, the findings of our study form a more reliable basis for generalizations and our work stands as a social science survey of this population.

No study, of course, is devoid of limitations, and ours is no exception. To begin with, our sample is not a full national probability sample of the males in the Vietnam Generation, since the resources for such a study were not available at the time. Therefore, we basically replicated our study ten different times, and the analysis controls for the variability in the communities we examined. The types of communities that fell outside the scope of our sample, however, are not represented. Although such communities are relatively few, this characteristic of our study must be kept in mind.

Secondly, we concentrated our analysis on the commonalities found across the ten communities in our study. To keep the volume to a manageable length, we do not go into some of the interesting differences between the communities surveyed.

Thirdly, if we could repeat our interviews today, there are many additional issues we would attempt to study and many questions we would rephrase. At the same time, studies designed since our work began have drawn from our analysis and have devised their interviews with our help. Such is the nature of research.

There is a final limitation of our study that deserves mention here. We studied only males. Although females make up a very large part of the Vietnam Generation, they comprise a relatively small portion of the Vietnam veteran population. Indeed, current estimates place their number at about 5,000. At the time we prepared our study, there were no lists of female Vietnam veterans from which we could acquire a representative sample. Today such lists exist, and we hope that those studies now in the planning stage will pay this population's story close heed.

The renewal of interest in the legacy of Vietnam has fostered a growing literature that aims to help us understand how the war experience touched the lives of those who lived it and what the conflict meant to Americans as a whole. We hope that this volume will contribute to the on-going investigation into a complex and critical moment in our national past.

PART ONE

WAR STRESS AND ITS AFTERMATH

CHAPTER ONE

THE EXPERIENCE
OF WAR

This chapter is designed to provide the reader with a sense of the war years and a description of the key experiences through which we interpret the legacy of Vietnam.

As noted in the introduction, the Vietnam veterans' story is considerably more complex than that of their era veteran and nonveteran peers. Thus, throughout the volume this group of respondents is our prime focus. The character of their war experiences and an attempt to determine which of these experiences would prove decisive are the central concerns of this chapter.

First Impressions

Vietnam was a strange and dangerous place for American soldiers. Its strangeness attracted some and repelled others; but its dangers threatened all veterans exposed to the mayhem of war. The movement of young men from a modern world they knew and whose parameters they intuitively understood into an alien physical and social environment where words, feelings, and behaviors had to be consciously organized was profoundly unsettling. The young American soldier came to Vietnam empowered to make changes in a world he comprehended barely if at all. Most soldiers who went to Vietnam were under the impression that they were coming to the aid of a land whose people were beset by an enemy preying on their freedom. At the same time they knew that they had come to fight a war, so they entered Vietnam with profound trepidation. Their lives were now at risk, and intuitively they understood they would leave this land transformed.

First impressions of Vietnam were generally negative for most Vietnam veterans (56%). Only 9% reacted in a positive way upon arrival. Another 25%

felt ambivalence, often noting that the country was beautiful but that they were afraid of the war. A small group (10%) had no first impressions of Vietnam because they had no direct contact with the country. This was notably the case for navy men, stationed on ships.

Generally Negative Impressions

In the narrative, those who stressed that they had negative feelings on arrival in Vietnam generally talked about their first exposure to the war. A small group, however, could not believe there was a war in progress because everything seemed so peaceful. This latter reaction is demonstrated by a veteran who served in the army:

> When we off-floated from the navy vessel that we came over on we were in full battle gear, rifles, everything. We splashed through the water, walked up the beaches and crawled up the bank, and the first thing I saw is a school bus picking up kids to take them to school. So my impression was what am I doing here in battle gear. We were in the middle of a fishing village. It was very incongruous, I guess, and very confusing. It was not what I expected . . .

But for most respondents there was an immediate awareness of an on-going conflict around them. They realized that at any moment the enemy might attack. They observed that the war was different from what they had expected. At home they had seen many heroic John Wayne movies. They had heard a lot about the war and had witnessed battle scenes on television. Now, suddenly they were "where it was at" and they knew: "this is real, this is war, this is not John Wayne." Arrival was especially traumatic for those who witnessed the dead and injured being brought into their first base camp. A captain in the marines recalled:

> I guess my strongest impression was watching all the wounded coming in on the helicopters because the base camp had a medivac unit. . . . They were bringing them in by the hundreds, bellies blown out and legs hanging off. Arms missing, eyeballs missing. That's your first impression right there. You're only out of a Helio for five minutes and already you see all these guys laying out there with their guts hanging out.

Many were immediately thrown into the middle of the war and report different first reactions. Some were prepared to fight. An army infantry man remembered:

> We went in a C-141 in full combat gear as a troop movement. We landed right in Chu Lai and then, when we were getting our orientation, mortars started

coming in and everybody started running including the sergeants that were telling us to be calm. . . . I was ready.

But the plurality of Vietnam veterans reported a negative response to their first exposure to the war. Often they were anxious and confused, frightened about what might happen. Many thought, ''This is it. I don't think I'm going to make it.'' A marine reported the following first impression of combat:

I was scared because I did not know what to expect. My first night there we had the living hell mortared out of us by a couple of gooks. Next morning I saw the bodies they had caught. One American had been hit with a 50-caliber round and it had just blown him open. There was nothing left there. Another guy had been caught with an M-16 round, it blew half his head off. That being the first thing I saw over there, really it got me. The worst part of the Vietnam experience for me was that first day.

For many veterans, the fear of combat they experienced on arrival in Vietnam was accompanied by a sense of alienation. A veteran who was in the navy expressed these feelings as follows:

I arrived in the middle of the night. It was 98 degrees and it seemed like we bounced along in trucks forever to get from Danang airfield to camp. The next day I woke up and realized that I was living in a 15x32 tin-roof hut in the middle of what seemed like a monstrous sand dune. To one side I could see the South China Sea; to the other side I could see the terrain, the river valley. That morning within hours of my first awakening I saw more than I wanted to see. I felt a sense of homelessness, of being overwhelmed by the physical fact that a 17-year-old kid is really in Vietnam and that there are bullets being fired.

And an army man responded:

What did I first feel? Panic. The realization you are so far away from anything that you could even come close to calling your own. The mass of troops . . . massive equipment . . . it was all mind-boggling. The realization that you are not a little kid any more playing cowboys and indians, arguing who was shot and who was not. The reality was there. There was no turning back. It was definitely awe-inspiring.

A substantial number of veterans admitted that upon arrival in Vietnam they experienced doubts about why they were there. Questions arose in their mind about the meaning of the war. They felt that they were ''the liberators,'' but they had no clear picture of what ''the liberation'' was all about. Many wished they had not come.

Another important first impression reported by Vietnam veterans is their sharp awareness of the poverty of the Vietnamese people. Respondents stressed the poor living conditions, the "misery and disease," and considered the Vietnamese lifestyle "an insult to human beings." The following examples are typical of this response pattern. A veteran who was in the navy spoke this way:

> I was shocked. I had never seen anything like it in my life, how the people lived. You got to remember I was still a kid then and I didn't know any of these things—the homes that the people lived in, if they were lucky enough to have a home—the little boats they lived in.

And an army man commented:

> When I was flying over Vietnam I saw the land was scorched, burned right down to the core, and I said, "Wow, what kind of place is this?" Then we landed and when I stepped out at the airport I saw the people there messing around with the garbage and children running around half-naked and I knew I was in another world.

For some Vietnam veterans the first impression was the realization that they were not welcomed by the civilian population. A marine expressed this feeling as follows:

> I was wondering what I was doing there, because when I first got to Nam, we were riding on the back of a truck with no weapons . . . and the little kids were throwing things at us. I said, "Wow! what's this? We are over here helping them and they are throwing rocks at us." Then a Vietnamese yelled "Marines go home."

Other Vietnam veterans reported that their first impression of Vietnam was of a difficult physical environment characterized by heat, dust, and dirt. An army lieutenant recalled:

> It was hot enough so that when you stood in one place the sweat ran down your sleeves, . . . dripped onto the ground and you could watch the drops falling rapidly. I have never seen such heat anywhere even though I had been in hot places. I remember saying to myself, "My God why are they fighting a war here?"

And a marine captain noted:

> I didn't like where I was living. Grimy, scungy, looked very disease ridden, muggy. It looked like a little hell. It was something I never imagined that they would send us to.

Generally Positive Impressions

As noted above, only a small group of Vietnam veterans had a positive first impression of Vietnam. Their basic attitude was that they had come to Vietnam to fight a war and that was what they were going to do. An army man explained this view as follows:

> I thought it was great. . . . We were in a relay station waiting to be assigned to different divisions and companies. I thought I was going to Quang Tri, which is up north and that was where the fighting was . . . a lot of it . . . good fighting. But I was going to Quang Ngai and it was kind of quiet there. I know I was disappointed because I would have liked the action.

Those who had a positive first impression of Vietnam also stressed that they had come to assist the South Vietnamese Army (ARVN) and the Vietnamese people in their fight against Communist aggression and that it was clear to them upon arrival in Vietnam that these people required aid. An army infantry sergeant recalled:

> That's the first impression I got, that somebody needed to help these people and we were over there to help them; I thought, "Well these guys can't fight a war alone if they had to." . . . Even after I went to the field I thought, "Well, we're doing something to help the Vietnamese."

The War Experience of Vietnam Veterans

At the same time that they were trying to adjust to their new surroundings, Vietnam veterans were fighting a war. How they came to be in Vietnam, the circumstances of their presence, and how they endured the conflict would mark them forever.

In conceptualizing the effects of the war on our veteran respondents we considered three aspects of their military careers as potentially important contributors to the impact of the war experience on their lives: structural characteristics of veterans' military history; behavioral indicators of war stress; and subjective responses to the stress of war.

Structural Characteristics

The structural elements of veterans' military history include draft status or mode of entry in the military, branch of service, and rank. The length of the conflict, changing attitudes in the United States toward the war, and significant modifications in military strategy led us to include another measure as well: the period during which men served (pre-1968 or post-1967).[1]

A good deal of literature on the war emphasizes that draftees entered the military under duress and therefore were likely to respond quite differently from men who voluntarily enlisted. Furthermore, there has long been a general sense that the Vietnam War was fought by draftees. The core of the antiwar movement's militant opposition to the Vietnam War over the years invested heavily in draft resistance. Thus it was one of the "given" assumptions of the war that the draftee issue was important in understanding veterans' response to the war and its consequences.

Our data, as table 1.1 shows, pose a fundamental challenge to the notion that the Vietnam War was fought by draftees. Overall, only 35% of the Vietnam veterans and 34% of the Vietnam era veterans fall into this category. Thus, nearly two-thirds of all Vietnam veterans were enlistees. However, as table 1.2 demonstrates, there is considerable variation in the proportion of draftees and enlistees by branch of service. Nonetheless, even in the army, which has by far the highest ratio of draftees to enlistees, we found that only 50% of the Vietnam veterans were draftees. In the other branches between 75% and 95% of the Vietnam veterans were enlisted men.

Table 1.2, panel B, indicates that it is in the Vietnam era army that draftees (58%) outnumber enlistees (42%). This suggests that a disproportionate number of enlistees were sent to serve in Vietnam.

In table 1.3, we see that men who went into the army and marines were proportionately more likely to see Vietnam duty. Among Vietnam veterans the men who served in the army represented 61% of the troops and in the marines 11% while in the Vietnam era military, army veterans represented only 51% of the forces and marines 6%. Conversely, air force veterans composed 23% of the Vietnam era military but only 8% of the Vietnam veteran forces. The navy alone seems to have had roughly equal representation within the Vietnam (20%) and Vietnam era (18%) veteran populations.

Finally, if we examine the veterans' rank during military service we see in table 1.4 that there were a greater proportion of noncommissioned officers in Vietnam (36%) than in the Vietnam era (25%) military. This difference, as table 1.5, panels A and B, show, is largely a function of the much higher ratio of NCOs in the Vietnam than Vietnam era army (43% vs. 28%) and marines (29% vs. 13%). The explanation for this disparity may well lie in the rapid promotion of privates during the war. It is probable that many of the men who achieved NCO rank would not have done so in the peacetime military. As table 1.4 shows, 7% of the Vietnam and 6% of the Vietnam era veteran population were officers.

During the long years of fighting, the political climate surrounding the Vietnam War changed, as did the levels of American involvement and troop commitments. We therefore created a variable to analyze the effects of being in the military or exposed to the draft at varying stages of the conflict. In so doing, we divided the war into five major periods based on the number of American troops in Vietnam and the distinctive changes in the nature of the conflict. The periods chosen were 1) 1961–65; 2) 1966–67; 3) 1968–69; 4) 1970–71; and 5)

1972–75. As the succeeding chapters will show, there were distinctive differences between the men who served before 1968 and after 1967.

Behavioral Indicators of War Stress

The military characteristics soldiers carried with them to Vietnam tell us something about their relationship to the war. The experiences during their tour of duty, the stresses of war they encountered in Vietnam, decisively differentiate the meaning of the war in their lives. We focus here on three behavioral aspects of the war: combat; witnessing of and participation in abusive violence; and the issue of killing Vietnamese. As we describe these experiences below, the need to specify the nature of war stress in Vietnam becomes clear.

In casual conversation the meaning of terms such as combat seems evident. However, when we try to measure combat or other causes of war stress, conventional assumptions about the content of these experiences are inadequate. Instead, we require careful specification of what we mean by combat or abusive violence in Vietnam. The changing character of warfare, especially guerrilla war, over time, as well as advances in technology influence how we define these experiences. The problem of creating adequate measures has already been recognized in the literature on the effects of the Vietnam War, but our approach, developed in the late 1970s, differs in important ways from earlier efforts.[2] Current research continues to develop increasingly sophisticated approaches to the measurement of war-zone trauma. Increasingly it is apparent that specifying and differentiating the nature of this trauma are vital to understanding the effects of war. As emphasized below, we need to understand the distinct aspects of the war-zone trauma that are significant. In subsequent chapters we will see that specification of the key war stressors helps us identify the legacy of the war.

Combat

Combat is a generally recognized indicator of war stress. Our combat scale (Laufer et al., 1981) is essentially a measure of the extent to which the veteran's life was threatened, with the range of experiences included providing a latent measure of the frequency of exposure to life-threatening situations.[3]

Because of the moral and psychological implications of this act, the experience of killing is treated separately here.

Respondents frequently cited the life-threatening character of the combat experience. A helicopter pilot in the army reported:

> I started going crazy. I could not seem to handle the kinds of pressure I was under. I started getting hallucinations. I could not sleep . . . I was waking up all the time. We flew extraordinarily long missions every day. This problem I had got worse and worse. The flight surgeon there said, take these tranquilizers but

only at night because it is illegal to fly under the influence of a drug. They should calm you down. I did that and I still got worse. It was this thing in my brain. I continued flying. . . . I was aware that I was starting to disintegrate. My nerves were going and I could not sleep and I was losing weight. It was tearing me apart and I knew it.

An army sergeant talked about his combat experiences as follows:

The date we got shelled was the Tet offensive in 1968. I think it was January 30th. They were shooting at us constantly. . . the ammunition dump blew up. It was about two blocks away from our compound and blew us out of bed, it was like an atomic bomb believe me. Scared the hell out of me. Before then it was not too bad but after the Tet offensive we were scared to sleep. We were a total wreck because we did not know when the next attack was coming.

Witnessing of and participation in abusive violence

Witnessing of and participation in abusive violence are two additional measures of war stress we found to be important in assessing the effects of the war experience.[4] The stress of war in a guerrilla campaign differs markedly from that experienced in conventional conflicts. Our narratives show that many of the strains placed on conventional forces in guerrilla warfare stem from an inability to distinguish between noncombatants and the enemy. This problem is, for the most part, absent in a conventional conflict. Guerrilla warfare creates pressures that lead to and sanction acts of brutality against civilians and prisoners of war. The American experience in Vietnam saw a significant number of such episodes by the North Vietnamese, Vietcong, South Vietnamese, and American forces. Three general types of episodes are described in our transcripts: actions against civilians, actions against prisoners of war, and the use of cruel weaponry. Twenty-two percent of our Vietnam veteran respondents were exposed to abusive violence, and 9% participated in such actions.

Under the pressure of combat, Americans sometimes responded to captured enemy soldiers by abusing them and at other times took no captives at all. An army sergeant noted:

One day my unit came to the rescue of our sister company. I was in B Company. A Company was being attacked and they were overrun by hundreds of NVAs. And we were like a few miles away. I was in the mechanized infantry so we jumped in our tracks, armored personnel carriers, and in one day of combat we killed, by body count, 881 NVAs. We did not take one prisoner of war because anyone who was there was killed. [I see, if they surrendered, they were killed anyway?] Yes, we did not take any prisoners at all. And it was just hate because A Company was wiped out . . . there was only one survivor that particular day.

And this is the way we were. [What effect do you think this experience had on you?] Effect? None.

There were a variety of circumstances under which violence against civilians took place. In some instances civilians were found in free fire zones, sites defined as off limits to noncombatants. Anyone caught in these areas was presumed to be enemy and treated as such. A marine sergeant described the effect of this policy on the civilian population:

> I travelled past Montagnard villages. These villagers were felt by one officer to be supporting the North Vietnamese and Vietcong. The officer commanded us to attack the villagers, taking them hostage and moving them to a camp. We did attack them, killing five or six of them, although we never found any weapons among them. These tribesmen were in a zone that was designated free fire zone. The South Vietnamese government said they would be treated as North Vietnamese or Vietcong if they were caught in the area.

Other types of abusive violence in which Americans participated were physical abuse and killing of civilians, slaughter of livestock, and destruction of property. An army infantryman reflected on the effects of such incidents as follows:

> These acts make you think there is no God. It destroys a whole lot of young men . . . because when they come home they are not the same anymore. They cannot do the things that everybody might want to do . . . the simple things . . . play ball or go bowling . . . stuff like that. All of that is dead. You do not want nothing to do with that any more. It doesn't mean anything. The prisoners of war? They walked them off to the bushes and they killed them. Girls got raped. . . . The animals, buffalo, they need to farm their land. The GIs know they need them but they kill them just to give them a hard time. I could not understand that. They called it practice. Practice!

Clearly U.S. soldiers were not alone in abusing civilians and combatants. Indeed, American soldiers who witnessed abusive violence insisted that the enemy, Vietcong (VC) and North Vietnamese Army (NVA), as well as their South Vietnamese allies (ARVN), engaged in abusive actions routinely. Moreover, Americans often argue that their own abuses stemmed from the example set by the Vietnamese. A marine reported the following type of enemy action:

> I got friendly with two girls, two little orphans. They were killed in a bomb raid . . . on the village . . . they were in the orphanage. [How did you feel after that?] Downright disgusted and mad. . . . I could see bombing us but not an orphanage or the village. They actually knew the whole setup. Because where

we were set up was here and the village was over there and they just bombed mostly the village, before they even touched us.

Whatever their experiences with enemy and allied actions against civilians, there is a special sense of shame in the response of American soldiers who saw their countrymen participate in the abuse or killing of Vietnamese civilians. An army man expressed his feelings this way:

We'd go through villages and destroy homes. I usually never took part in these things. I alway found an excuse to walk away or be on the other side. And then there was the thing I was mentioning earlier, gathering guys in a pit and shooting them. . . . [You managed to stay out of that too?] Oh yeah definitely . . . if there were just people that were suspected by the soldier's own discretion . . . of being Vietcong, they were killed and their homes were destroyed. . . . [What effect did you think these kind of experiences had on you?] I guess for awhile I was ashamed to be an American and I guess I was as responsible as everybody else for these acts even though I wasn't directly responsible. To me it's all a very perverted way of thinking that you can just destroy somebody's life just because you want to.

Killing Vietnamese

Finally, we examined whether or not the veteran reported having killed in Vietnam. We treated this measure separately because the importance of killing someone may lie in who it was and under what conditions it happened.

Killing occurs in a wide variety of situations. Sometimes it is an unpremeditated reaction to a sudden and unforeseen situation, often it is part of a planned confrontation and at times it is calculated. Further, killing in war occurs at a distance where the victim is anonymous as well as close up where the victim has a face and even, as our discussion of abusive violence indicates, has a personality. This variation potentially differentiates the meaning of the act of killing for the soldier and affects his answer to the question "did you kill or think you killed Vietnamese?"

There are instances in wartime where soldiers must act so rapidly that they have no time to respond emotionally. A veteran who served in the navy describes the following experience:

It was just before dusk, I guess you would call it twilight. We just kind of stumbled on the Vietcong and fortunately for us they had their weapons laying on the ground. We had ours on our person. This one gook reached for his automatic weapon and I shot him. . . . The first instance that it happened it was like a flow of adrenalin or whatever, I felt great. It gradually sank in and made me sick. And then the next day I found out the kid was only 14 and that did not help.

And an army artillery man noted:

> We were outnumbered in an ambush and surrounded by Vietcong. I had to fight
> my way out and I do recall having hit several Vietcong by the way in which their
> shadows, their outlines fell to the ground. This was at night, not in the daytime.
> I first felt great. Later it hit me and the effect was one of depression, one of a
> nonfuture, discontent.

A more premeditated element of battle involves organized combat, where it
is the responsibility of the soldier to carry out a mission or protect his lines and
men. An army infantry officer who was in heavy combat reported:

> I personally shot several of them. I directed fire of the company that resulted in
> their deaths. Those were basically the circumstances. They were combat situa-
> tions and I was in charge of the combat force, so I naturally bore the responsi-
> bility for that. . . . I'm afraid I didn't have much reaction at all. . . . No, it was
> necessary. . . . I was concerned about American soldiers, and so I didn't have
> any recriminations at all.

A marine captain expressed a similar view:

> How did I feel? I saw dead bodies . . . and my instinct was it happened to them
> who might be around to injure us collectively. . . . So I looked at it as a military
> act . . . they were just soldiers and they were trying to penetrate our lines and
> we were trying to stop them. . . . I didn't worry about the act, it was something
> that you were trained for.

A third aspect of the killing of enemy soldiers involves revenge for what the
enemy has done to one's buddies or a reaction to discovering the mutilated
remains of American units. An example of the first type of situation is described
by a navy veteran:

> When we were out on the river, we were hit three times and they sunk our boat.
> There were twelve men aboard and only four of us made it back. It happened so
> suddenly, I heard a mortar round hit. I went up the stairs and there were dead
> people lying everywhere. I found the captain, his legs had been blown away. I
> found my buddy, he was lying over the 50 caliber, dead. I pushed him off and
> then I went crazy. I just started shooting at the beach, at the trees, at anything
> that moved. Then the ship started going down and we had to swim back to
> shore.

An example of premeditated revenge where killing becomes a source of
satisfaction is described by a marine who explained why he enjoyed killing
Vietnamese.

I got to the point where I started to get a kick out of killing. . . . It took a while, about six months there. After seeing what they do to someone you are on line with. We were on patrol one time and we were looking for another squad that was missing for two months. We found what was left of them. Their bodies were of course decayed, left out in the sun, their ID cards were nailed to their foreheads, to their skulls. That turned you very cold towards the people we were fighting against.

Finally, the killing of enemy troops in war is perceived as part of the ''job,'' the reason men are sent to war. Killing the enemy engenders desensitization to the human characteristics of the victims. Men shoot at each other and must move on and repeat that action over and over again. An army infantryman who was in heavy combat observed:

Initially, you know, you don't really think about killing Vietnamese. They are shooting at you, you are shooting back. Then sometimes you have to go out and search the bodies. And you see the personal effects on them, you see their pictures. But you can't really let it get into your head too deep. After the action, you just count up the bodies and see how many you got.

The guerrilla character of the Vietnam War led to the killing of civilians who were perceived to be collaborating with the enemy. Generally, veterans justified these measures as acts of self-defense. The following remarks by a marine typify this attitude:

[I] shot an old lady. She was not supposed to be out after six o'clock and we did not know if it was a Vietcong or not so we shot her with a grenade launcher. . . . The lady was giving away our position at night and then we would be overrun the next day, so she got killed. . . . A little boy came over with a case of pop and would not open them. There was a booby trap of hand grenades in it and so he got killed.

There were other occasions when killing occurred under duress and conflicted with the perceptions men brought with them about war and its limits. The following example illustrates how the conditions surrounding the act of killing could clash with a soldier's innate expectations:

I figured over there it was kill or be killed. But my first killing upset me. I was ordered to kill a 12-year-old kid and I did not want to shoot him. The kid had a gun and the lieutenant came up behind me and told me to kill him. I said: ''Sir, I cannot, he is just a kid'' and he said: ''I order you to, I will give you a court martial.'' And I said ''I do not care.'' I just started to turn away and the kid raised his rifle and I shot him. I did not eat or sleep for three days.

Finally, killing of Vietnamese civilians also occurred in situations where they were simply bystanders exposed to crossfire. An example from an army helicopter pilot illustrates the difficulty soldiers faced in situations where civilians found themselves in the line of fire:

> I spotted where the fire was coming from. . . . There were people all over on the ground watching these helicopters. . . . And out of this group I'd see a tracer coming up. I knew that they were around a machine gun and I saw the machine gun. So I told my right hand gunner to fire at the ground to give the people a chance to get away but they didn't move. I was screaming—you can't hear anything in helicopters—I was screaming, "Get out of the way, Get out of the way!" And they wouldn't get out of the way. And the gunner tried everything, he could not get to them. They would not move and I said, "Get them." And he got them. I felt good about knocking out the machine gun. I felt bad about killing the people. We killed five civilians and the machine gunner. . . . I'm trying to forget the entire incident. But I find that I don't think I can. I wish I had not killed those people. I had dreams about that. It was very surreal you know, I very clearly saw them die and I felt very responsible for it.

These illustrations of the different contexts in which American units killed in Vietnam indicate that for a veteran to say he killed someone there tells us relatively little about what happened, nor does it give us very much insight into the meaning of the event. The action of killing is caught up in other experiences already dicussed in the sections on combat and abusive violence, and the emotional response to the act is discussed in depth later in the chapter.

The above quotes suggest that there is a variable response to the killing of the enemy in Vietnam, which influences the extent to which the traumatic quality of the experience is acknowledged. Even more important, it is clear from the responses by veterans who were aware that they killed enemy combatants that the killing occurred in widely differing frameworks. Indeed it appears that the action derived its meaning from its association with other aspects of war stress, such as combat, witnessing of, or participation in abusive violence.

Subjective Indicators of War Stress

Along with eliciting descriptions of their war experiences from our respondents, we explored how veterans reacted to what they underwent. In the following discussion, we concentrate on several specific responses to the death and dying that accompany war. We asked our respondents to tell us what they thought were the most important aspects of their war experience, to describe their response to combat, to express their attitudes about being killed or wounded, and to explore their feelings about the death and dying of Americans and Vietnamese.[5] From the answers to these questions several dimensions of subjective responses to war trauma emerged.

Importance of survival

The dominant response to the war experience reported by Vietnam veterans was the need to survive (56%). Predictably, the greater the involvement in combat, the stronger the focus on staying alive. Indeed, 66% of heavy-combat veterans report that survival was their chief focus. The combat situation, with its threat to existence, clearly left a vivid impression on most of those involved.

The feeling of survival is especially strong for those who served during the later periods. A marine who was in Vietnam during the Tet offensive described his feelings as follows:

> Most important? To survive. I was always scared. Whenever you got pinned down. I was scared most before the operation when you got briefed. They told you you were going up there for a routine thing, but you always knew "boy look out." . . . The night before, I really could not sleep.

Many veterans realized that the only way they could survive was through a collective effort. Respondents often expressed a deep concern for the survival of their unit. Some noted that several men in their unit smoked pot or drank too much on duty and therefore could not be counted on. But the rest looked after each other.

Officers and NCOs often provide good examples of a rational coping with the dangers of combat. They admit that they had to come to grips with the prospect of being killed or injured and tell themselves, "well, that is a possibility but I won't dwell on it." They felt their most important task was to cope emotionally with the danger of combat and to respond to it rationally and calmly so that their unit as a whole could survive. A marine captain described his first priority this way:

> That I came out unscratched . . . that my men came out unscratched . . . that's what it was all about. . . . When so many people are counting on you, you had to maintain a philosophy that would maintain your stability and your sanity.

Survival became especially important for those veterans who had already been wounded. An army infantryman who was in heavy combat responded:

> Most important? The first time I was wounded I walked in a mine field. The whole platoon walked in it. So we had to probe our way out of there. It took us about an hour and a half to get out of the place. The second time I was wounded was when we got overrun. That was December 22, 1968. The night of the 22d we were dug in underground . . . and all hell broke loose. We were surrounded. There were about 350 of them and only 64 of us. The only thing that held them off was that we had the perimeter dug in so good and we had wire around it. By

the time we got air support, they were in on us, about 40 or 50 of them were in the perimeter. We had to fight that 40 or 50. . . . That was the night I got wounded. I lost a number of friends, 15 guys.

Despite their deep concern with personal survival, many combat veterans mastered their fear and showed great courage in battle. An army artillery corporal who was in heavy combat exemplifies these men:

[The most important thing?] I almost got killed there a couple of times. I think the most frightening thing that is always clear in my mind is the time a rocket hit ten feet away from me. It exploded. I ran to the gun and I fired back. I don't know why I did that. I was scared. I feel that it may have helped stop them from firing on us. Because after that they changed their directions. Once in a while if I talk about Vietnam I think about that incident. I could not imagine myself doing something like that.

Combat veterans also often explained that while their primary concern was staying alive, coping with the war experience heightened their perceptions in many ways. This is evident from the following remarks of an army airborne:

The single most important thing is I survived. . . . The second most important thing I would say . . . was the insights it gave me on life and living. . . . I really felt that I was learning lessons . . . I was seeing things that I would never see again . . . I should be open to it . . . so I could learn from what was happening around me.

Reactions to combat

Numbness. For many Vietnam veterans, as table 1.6, panel C, shows, the combat situation obliterated feelings. Blanking out, or being so involved in what was going on that there was no time to feel, was a fairly typical reaction (20%). Marines are more inclined than those who served in other branches to deny having feelings about combat exposure. They often argued that they acted out of pure instinct, following orders without question or fear. A marine who was in heavy combat gave the following account:

Combat is the most difficult thing to explain because it's something that never lasts a long time . . . even if it lasts two hours, it seems like a minute. The mind goes as fast as bullets and there is no time for feelings.

A substantial number of air force and navy personnel also admitted that they felt nothing during combat, due in part to the fact that they were too busy to think. At the same time, they stressed that often before and after battle they experienced anxiety and fear. An air force veteran noted:

> We always thought, before going up, what kind of mission we were going to have. . . . Then when we got down we thought, well that was not as bad as I thought it would be or boy that was worse. . . . During combat I was preoccupied, your mind was on your job. If you stopped to think you could be causing yourself to get hurt or somebody else in your crew. To me the job came first and then thinking afterwards and before, but no thinking during.

Fear. Seventeen percent of combat veterans responded to the combat experience with fear. Those who served in the army are less inclined to have had no feelings and more often admitted fright during the fighting. This was especially true of heavy-combat infantrymen. Members of that group described men who were sent into the bush on operations after less than forty days in service. Their inexperience heightened their fear and led them to seek ways to alleviate their panic. According to some of the reports in the narrative, narcotics were available, even from the medics. Those who wanted to stay up could get uppers; those who wanted to sleep could get downers. Often men stayed high to hide from the possibility of death. This feeling of fear is demonstrated by the following reply made by a heavy combat army infantryman:

> It was really frightening. Everybody just kept their head down and then shot at anything on the other side of the bushes that moved because that was all you had to go by. There were no lines or anything over there. Everybody was just scattered out. You just had to keep your eyes awake and watch and hope you were not shooting at your own men over there. I tell you it was really bad.

A veteran who was an army airborne described a fear-ridden month this way:

> The whole year . . . I was . . . operating only about eight to ten miles from the Cambodian border. And about the first of May we got the word that we were going into Cambodia and it was going to be . . . combat assault. They came with eighty helicopters and moved us out in one day. For the next thirty days it was just hell, because there's where they really were the strongest in Cambodia. That was their rear area. And we lost a lot of men and that was the worst time. . . . Helicopters, medevacs were always coming in and out with people fucked up. They oftentimes couldn't even get them out before they started to rot. It would be body bags lined up waiting for the big chopper to come and take them down to Saigon. I just knew we were getting the shit kicked out of us up there. The units that I was in had high casualties, like maybe 20–30% companies wiped out.

Self-preservation. Other veterans reported that their main response to combat was a strong commitment to their own survival (20%). They complained that they were sent into battle every day. Often the first feeling they had during the initial firefight was fear, "the pounding of the heart," "the cold feeling." After they dealt with these sensations, they concentrated on their personal safety. Every move they made was thought about and planned to enhance their chances of getting out alive. A veteran who was in the army infantry noted the effects of this self-absorption as follows:

> I only thought about my own survival. Every time somebody got killed I was just glad it was not me lying there. And I used to think, "What am I doing over here anyway?" Getting out safe was the only thing I had on my mind. I changed so much in Vietnam. I became selfish and hard and scared.

And a marine who was in heavy combat and had been wounded expressed the following feelings:

> All I thought about was survival and I knew I could survive. My main objective was to protect myself. . . . The first couple of times Americans got killed or wounded it bothered me. But those are things that are going to happen. . . . You have got to protect yourself. You go out and kill them before they get you. Better them than me.

Despite their fear or self-interest, some veterans found a larger meaning in the war experience. A pilot noted:

> Combat scared the hell out of me. The possibility of being killed was foremost in my mind. I thought about it a lot . . . I saw a lot of people die. A fellow was shot right next to me in an aircraft and that shakes you up. Thirteen of us graduated from flight school, went to the same company, and only three, two others and myself, came back from that group. On Christmas day, I watched a friend get shot down and crash and heard him go all the way to the ground until his aircraft exploded. . . . I was scared and sad, but I also knew that combat was a tremendous learning experience. I was forced to look at myself and other people and to see how easily life is taken. More than ever before, I experienced the value of life.

Feelings about being killed or wounded

Vietnam veterans were asked how they felt about the possibility of being killed or wounded. As is to be expected, those veterans whose exposure to physical threat was low (20%) did not present detailed answers in the narrative to this question, while moderate-combat veterans (58%) and heavy-combat veterans (72%)[6] more often expressed their feelings.

A large group of combat veterans (50%) admit that they were frightened and deeply concerned about the possibility of being killed or wounded. The patterns of the occurrence of fear differ. Some veterans insist that they were only afraid during their first few weeks in Vietnam. Thereafter, they claim to have adjusted to a new way of life. Others report that they were afraid both in the beginning and at the end of their stay in Vietnam. An army man spoke for this latter group:

> They had an old saying. The first thirty days and your last thirty days are the worst. After the first thirty days you do not care any more until you get down to your last thirty days and then you worry. Who the heck wants to catch it in the last thirty days.

In the case of some respondents, one specific incident triggered their fear. A veteran who served in the navy reported how he realized what had frightened him and how his fear finally dissipated:

> My first action involved the Vietcong doing some abominable shooting with 5-inch rockets. They managed to wreak havoc with the local villages surrounding the airfield—six hours of fighting fire. I found that I reacted pretty coolly. But, at least a week afterwards, there was a time when I was alone and I suddenly became deathly afraid. To the point where I did not know where my head was. I was shivering at the thought that I was going to be killed and that I could die in the next day. Then this passed and basically after that I was aware and I was cautious but not afraid. I have one image that I think is hooked into some of that fear, from the same incident. When the fire had basically died down, there was nothing left but smoldering ruins, we found an old man. He was down on his hands and knees, charred black and that, the picture of that man, I always see that. It will always come to me when I think of death by fire.

Our respondents were also asked: "Did you have any pictures or images in your mind concerning how you might die or be wounded?" It becomes clear from their responses that many veterans were more afraid of being seriously wounded and perhaps permanently maimed than of dying. If death had to come they wanted it to arrive as quickly as possible. A veteran who was an army airborne expressed his overwhelming fear this way:

> I was somewhat afraid of being killed. But I felt that . . . if I was killed, it would be very quick. . . . The overwhelming fear that I had—my major one—was like losing my legs or my arms, this was always in the back of my mind. We were on a little base camp with sand bag bunkers all the way around. And frequently we got incoming mortar and rocket fire. That was just like death dropping out of the sky . . . some of that shrapnel could cut your leg off.

Those who were actually wounded understandably present some of the most vivid pictures of their encounters with their feelings of mortality. A veteran who served in the army reported as follows:

A mortar shell went off in the roadway and I was hit with a piece of shrapnel. It cut me in the stomach. It was dark and the first thing I did was to check to see if I was still able to father children because that is about where the wound was and there was a feeling of relief when that worked all right. Then I did not really know how badly I was wounded. I lit a match and there was a whole bunch of blood. So we stuck a sulphur pack on it. . . . Once I found out that everything was still there and I was not going to die I was not too upset, but I was very shaken you know.

An army infantry sergeant who was in heavy combat added:

We were about to set down for the evening . . . and all of a sudden—boom— something went off. There'd been a trip wire that all of us had overlooked. I dived away from where I thought the explosion came from and landed on my face and couldn't move after that . . . I knew that my legs had been hit. I didn't know how bad. I was comforted there for I guess about ten minutes before medevac came out and it was not really until I was in the hospital that I realized that I'd lost a leg . . . and the other was pretty bad off too. . . . The second day I was there, the hospital was shelled. I felt quite helpless there . . . being strapped to the bed and everybody running and ducking. It was terrible.

Finally, the war in Vietnam had its share of mistakes causing "friendly fire" to kill Americans. For some combat veterans the most vivid and feared images of death were those of being killed by their own forces. An infantryman put it this way:

I figured I would burn up. [I] thought that I would probably get killed by my own men. That is the thing that bothered me. I knew this guy. It happened to him. A plane flew over. They dropped some napalm on him. Got him and about twenty other dudes and they were all burned up. But he lived and when I saw it, it scared me. I said to myself . . . what kind of a place is this. You are supposed to be fighting these people and your own men are killing you.

A substantial group of combat veterans (20%) recounted that they were not afraid of the danger around them and argued that they did not worry about being killed or injured. A marine officer stated:

I was injured when the vehicle I was riding in hit a mine and from that point on for a couple of months I had some fears but I never really felt I would get killed. It was not a primary problem. . . . Never thought about it really. We always used to say better you than me, you know. We did not have it all that bad.

Feelings about the death and dying of Americans

Vietnam veterans not only knew fellow Americans who were killed or wounded, they witnessed such events (table 1.6, panel A). Fifty-one percent of all Vietnam veterans saw Americans killed. The level of combat in which the veteran was engaged played a decisive role here: 85% of those in heavy combat saw Americans die as compared to 60% for moderate combat and 15% for low combat. Veterans who saw their fellow soldiers killed or wounded were eager to describe their feelings about it. Seventy-two percent of those who saw the death or wounding gave a response.

The reactions to American deaths were varied. The most common response was one of sadness and grief (42%). A sizeable minority felt shock at American losses (24%), while others responded with anger (21%) or denied they had any feelings about these deaths (14%). Black Vietnam veterans were less inclined to deny experiencing emotion (7%) than were white veterans (17%). The level of combat exposure also shaped the response pattern: 22% of high-combat veterans denied having feelings about American deaths as compared to 12% of the low-combat veterans. Clearly, for the high-combat veterans, denial of feelings served as a survival technique.

Sadness and grief. Grieving for the loss of buddies was more or less intense depending on how close the veteran was to the victim. Many veterans saw long-time friends die. This was especially traumatic. An army infantry man gave the following testimony:

> We were on patrol and ran into a firefight. And we were moving up one at a time and when my buddy started to move up he got his head blown off. . . . He was dead on the spot. . . . At first I was concerned with staying alive and couldn't do much about it but after everything died down and we'd picked him up and taken him to the rear—it all kind of hit me at once. . . . It was the most atrocious thing I'd ever seen. A friend of mine—somebody I had grown up with and here he is dead with half of his head missing. I started thinking about his parents, about the things we did when we grew up together . . . I was maybe ten feet from him. . . . I had some people that I wasn't as close to get killed. . . . But that was really the closest friend I had that got killed. . . . These other guys . . . it hurt—it didn't hurt as much as [name's] death. But any time you develop a comradeship with a group of men it really tears you up to see one of them get . . . killed.

Many respondents were unable to forget the loss they suffered. A black veteran spoke as follows:

It was a drain emotionally as well as physically. You talk and develop close contacts; he tells you about his family—it's just like you are part of that family, you're like brothers. . . . One white buddy who did not see the point of war got killed. I cried something fierce when he died—because I felt that he had more to live for than I did, he had his college behind him. Whereas I was a high school dropout. Me and him were real close.

For many, feelings of sadness were so deep that they created a permanent sense of loss. An army infantry squad leader reported that after he came home he was unable to forget how his friend had died. He described the incident as follows:

A friend of mine, my buddy John, was killed and I just saw myself die. He was almost a mirror image of me . . . it hurt, it really hurt. . . . When I sent my squad off the hill he was the last one to come out of the helicopter . . . and when he landed, he landed on a stump and he screamed and I was standing there just looking at him and I couldn't help him . . . nothing I could do. Just go over there . . . and lay him down until the helicopter had landed and take him back to the hospital.

A veteran who served in the army also talked about the long-time effects of the death of a buddy:

We had been ambushed. . . . We regrouped . . . I handed the machete . . . to Steve to take point and there was a look in his eyes that was just like . . . "Don, I'm going to die now." We hadn't gone more than 30 or 40 feet when fire opened up and Steve . . . was hit. He did die and he was left there in that area. We withdrew back and were not able to get him out. . . . Now, my nightmare started almost instantaneously. The next night I had a dream about it and it reoccurred for a few months. . . . Then after getting out of the service it reoccurred again . . . I did have flashbacks of it.

And a veteran who served as an army airborne reflected:

It was really very sad. How could this happen way over here? . . . They were so far away from home. I would always think what their parents were doing at that particular time while they were over here dying. What the people who loved them would feel when they found out. I have never been able to forget it.

Anger. Many respondents felt anger when they saw the death of Americans. An army artillery corporal expressed this feeling as follows:

Black, white, or whatever, they were Americans. You feel that is close and hitting home. I felt angry and powerless. It was a mixture of feelings. . . . It is very difficult to explain. If I was talking to another Vietnam veteran, you would get a better feeling, if more than just one person was trying to explain it to you.

Others wanted revenge or lashed out at what they perceived to be a useless waste of human life. A marine reported:

We were ambushed one time. . . . They had us pinned down for about four hours and we had a lot of dead and wounded. I lost a good friend then walking point . . . I was angry and mad—wanting revenge. . . . I guess it's a natural thing to want revenge when you see somebody you have liked a lot killed or hurt real bad.

And a veteran who was in the army explained his response to the deaths of Americans:

My reaction? It was a loss. I missed them and wished there was something I could have done to help. You hate to see them go and then you go on and you get quieter and sneakier. The more guys you know that you liked that got killed over there, the more vicious you became yourself inside. You get more quiet, more sneaky, and you became a real soldier.

Denial of feelings. As noted above, about 14% of Vietnam veterans denied reacting to the death or wounding of Americans. These veterans seem to be repressing the experience in order to concentrate on survival. A veteran who was in the navy and worked in a military hospital told us:

I have seen a lot of dead soldiers. A lot of marines. Stationed at the hospital, I used to take them off the helicopters on the stretchers. . . . I didn't have a reaction . . . I knew I had to do it . . . I did it. . . . I have seen a marine captain, young, 30 years old with both his legs blown off and he was still alive. He lived, too. . . . Things moving so fast . . . incidents like that. . . . I forgot about them . . . I never thought about them, until I came home and then it was in the past.

A heavy-combat veteran who was in the army explained that the death of Americans was something that he "just blotted out":

I had a complete coldness, a lack of reaction. I think it was the atmosphere at the time. Either we were conditioned that way, or I conditioned myself to be that way. I thought about that many times. That it was a possibility that you lived with and you just accepted it as that. It wasn't an individual being killed—it was just something that happened.

Other Vietnam veterans felt acceptance at American deaths (12%). This was especially the case for certain officers and NCOs. Since their primary obligation was to make sure that their men returned to their families alive, they had to believe that in wartime some men will inevitably die. A marine lieutenant explained:

> As a combat company commander I had a very strong reaction to losing any man to either wounds or death. My attitude, however, was that we were in a war and I had to expect it and just be the best possible decision maker I could be and do what I could for them to put them at their best attention. My reaction at that time was to facilitate their evacuation to medical facilities. It was an expected type thing. If you are in a war you are going to be among people who are wounded.

Responses to the death of Vietnamese

Reactions to the death of the Vietnamese, as table 1.6, panel B, shows, are somewhat different than responses to the death of Americans. Again, some veterans report experiencing sadness, but other common responses include a feeling that the killing of Vietnamese was justified and a general indifference to their fate.

Thirty-six percent of Vietnam veterans reported sadness when they saw Vietnamese get killed. At the same time, sizeable minorities felt that the deaths of the Vietnamese were justified (22%) or felt apathetic (28%). Seventy-four percent of those who saw Vietnamese killed talked about their reaction to this experience. Ninety-five percent of high-combat veterans saw Vietnamese die, as compared to 71% of moderate-combat and 13% of low-combat veterans. Black veterans were less inclined to feel apathy (19%) than white veterans (31%).

Death of enemy forces. A substantial number of veterans reacted to enemy losses with the same emotion they felt for the death of American units. This attitude is demonstrated by the following responses. An army lieutenant recalled:

> I was sad. It was a shame to be hurt, more so for them than for us. Medical treatment was usually not going to be as good and even if it were, if they suffered any disability they were not liable to be compensated for it. They did not care for their own wounded very well and so those people who were injured and wounded had to suffer a great deal.

An army sergeant expressed his reactions as follows:

> That's a hurting thing to see, all your friends get killed and there's nothing you can do. . . . The Vietcong—my enemies. . . . [How'd you feel about their deaths?] The same . . . I just couldn't see people killing people. . . . I never

was brought up that way or taught that way. This is basically what it is to me, man taking man's life. For what? Because somebody told us to do it? . . . I damn near broke down and cried.

Veterans working in military hospitals also reported feeling equally grieved at the sight of wounded American and Vietnamese soldiers. One noted:

Going to the hospital I saw wounded all the time. Helicopters would come in and they would need litter bearers. Once one of our choppers came in and I grabbed one end of a litter as it was dragged out of a helicopter. The gunner in the helicopter made me turn around and handed me a boot with the stump of a leg sticking out of it that belonged to the guy on the litter who was almost dead, an American soldier, a marine. I wheeled the litter in and went off in a corner and puked my guts out. That was the worst I really saw of American soldiers. I saw Vietnamese with bodies mutilated terribly . . . [What was your reaction?] . . . I would have to say a feeling of despair, sorrow, and again anger and frustration.

A group of Vietnam veterans argued that the enemy had to be destroyed. One respondent, a Marine Corps sergeant, expressed this feeling as follows:

I had to put myself into a state where it is not just a person. See it as an enemy. That enemy is a threat and it must be eliminated. Because of their intentions. How could a person be a person with the intention to bring Communism out like that. So I had to satisfy my own self. Otherwise hell, I would crack up. Any type of army which is against freedom, or democracy or restrict[s] people, I am against it.

The most common theme presented by those veterans who felt that the killing of enemy forces was justified was a combination of revenge for the deaths of Americans and the belief that the chances of their own survival were increased by the killing of Vietnamese—"when you kill them they are gone, they can not ambush you." A veteran who was a participant in abusive violence expressed his reactions this way:

Almost a feeling of vindication for the fact that any Americans had to be there at all and definitely retribution for the Vietnamese atrocities on United States servicemen and also a feeling of self-preservation. Okay, somebody shot at you, you shot back at them and the better shot won. The prevailing reaction was here is somebody who is aggressively trying to hurt me. The enemy was the enemy. Right, justification was not necessary. It was the simple fact of being in the war.

Another group of Vietnam veterans expressed indifference to the death of Vietnamese. For some, this denial of feeling was clearly a survival mechanism. Others argued that Vietnam proved to them that they were tough enough to do what they must, even when this meant shooting at others. They viewed killing as part of their job, a task to be done without emotion. Still, most of the group expressing apathy said that their first killings had left a strong impression. Their desensitization to enemy deaths came gradually, after exposure to battle. A heavy-combat veteran who was in the army infantry commented:

> It got to a point to where I did not mind seeing it at all. When I first went over, the first time it made me sick. I got initiated in that real quick within thirty days after being there. I got into a mortar platoon for a while and we worked with a unit and they had some sort of a radar scope. It would detect movement and we dropped mortars in on a group that night and then in the morning we went out with our infantry to pick them up. It did not bother me at all.

Death of civilians collaborating with enemy forces. Those veterans who were exposed to the shooting of civilians *suspected of being Vietcong* had varied reactions. Some felt that these actions were necessary, others responded in a conflicted or neutral way. A veteran who was in the navy presented a neutral response pattern:

> Our unit picked up five Vietnamese civilians who were supposedly giving information to the Vietcong. We took them into the helicopter. You hear people say it is not true, but it is true because I have seen them do it. First they talked to one old man and he was yelling and crying. They asked him a question and he kept shaking his head and they booted him right out of the door. They did this right down the line until all five were gone. I just stood there and watched.

But many veterans were upset when they witnessed the killing of civilians suspected of being Vietcong. An infantryman expressed his concern as follows:

> He was a real young kid. . . . I didn't know whether he was a Vietcong sympathizer or whether he was friendly or one of the village people. He was told to halt and didn't and he was shot. I felt kind of bad about that.

Death of Vietnamese civilians. The death and maiming of Vietnamese women and children who were clearly noncombatants made Americans recoil at the costs of war. Many Vietnam veterans knew children and cared for them. It was deeply upsetting when they found them dead or wounded. One veteran had the following reaction:

What really did hurt the most was the civilians being killed because they had nothing to do with it. The most important thing that I still recall was . . . there was this small boy and he had his right knee blown off from one of our bombs. They dropped a bomb right in the village. When we went through it, we found this boy. He was the only one alive. What really turned me off was that all they did for him was give him some morphine and left him there. They did not even try to get him to a hospital.

Finally, Vietnam veterans recall scenes of civilian carnage that traumatized them deeply and generated an urge to get away from the death and dying of the war. One respondent recalled:

It was a tragedy because people laid in the streets dead. They piled them up on the side. You would watch them as you went by. It was something that turns your gut. The reaction was that you were there but you do not know why you were there and you do not know why everybody was blown apart . . . blood . . . you want to get out, because there are too many innocent people killed.

A veteran who served in the army infantry added:

Well, when I saw the enemy get killed I felt shitty, but inside my mind I kept hearing over and over—it's the right thing to do, this is our job. And when I saw innocent people get killed, usually by our own unit killing them, that made me feel even worse, that I was a part of this whole unit. I was an American. I was supposedly fighting for peace and [was] killing innocent people, destroying their homes.

Yet at times there is a profound ambivalence associated with veterans' feelings for Vietnamese civilians, who, even if they were not actively engaged in the conflict, were often perceived to acquiesce passively in the killing of Americans. An army infantry sergeant reported the following episode:

I've seen some weird things, like a Vietnamese family came out of a village. One of our platoons [was] out in the middle of a rice paddy. . . . [They] gave them candy and food and the Vietnamese walked off and their children walked off, then another hundred feet or so [the platoon] gets the shit kicked out of them. They [the Vietnamese] knew it was gonna happen.

Predispositional Factors in War Stress

Exposure to stressful experiences is an important aspect of being sent to war, but not all men are exposed to the same degree of war stress, even if stationed in Vietnam. Factors affecting whether soldiers are exposed to war stress take two forms: 1) factors related to individual characteristics determined before entry into the service, and 2) factors related to type of military service. The former refer to resources and dispositions individuals bring into the service with them, and the latter to resources and characteristics men develop as a consequence of entering the military. Each of these factors was examined in terms of every type of stressful war experience to establish if they determined patterns of stress exposure.

The only preservice characteristic that slightly increased the likelihood of combat exposure was the individual's level of preservice education.[7] Those who failed to complete high school had a higher level of combat exposure, i.e., a higher mean value on the combat scale as a group, than those who completed high school or those who began college before entering the service. The mean for the group who did not finish high school was 7.2, that for the group who completed high school was 5.3, and that for the group that had at least one year of college prior to entering the military was 5.8.

Of the factors related to military service, only branch of service significantly contributed to levels of combat exposure. Ground forces in Vietnam saw considerably more combat than did the navy or air force personnel, and marines saw more combat than those who served in the army. The ranking of combat exposure by the average level in each branch is: navy (2.9), air force (3.1), army (6.9), and marines (7.8).

A number of preservice factors affected whether veterans reported having killed. Men who came from families with higher levels of education were more likely to report such action: 55% of those who came from families where the parents were college educated reported having killed, vs. 46% for those whose parents only finished high school, and 47% for those whose parents never obtained a high school diploma.[8] By contrast, veterans who did not finish high school before entering the military reported killing someone more often (70%) than did those who finished high school (44%) or than those who had begun a college education (49%).

Two service-related factors were also related to having killed. Men who served during or after the Tet offensive in 1968 were more likely to have killed someone (55%) than those who served in Vietnam in the earlier stages of the conflict (46%).[9] And once again branch of service was an important factor. The rank order of branch in relationship to having killed is identical to the ranking found on combat exposure. Naval veterans were the lowest (26%), followed by air force personnel (35%) and army units (57%), with marines reporting the highest killing rate (75%).

Exposure to abusive violence, in both its witnessing and participative forms, has little relationship to preservice characteristics of veterans. However, witnessing abusive violence shows the rank order by branch found on the other measures of war stress. Naval veterans were the least likely to witness abusive violence (8%), those in the air force slightly more likely (12%), and those who served in the army or the marines most likely of all (28%).

Veterans who participated in abusive violence, however, did have two distinctive preservice traits: first, they were more likely to come from families where the parents had a college education (12%) than from families where the parents had only a high school education (6%); and, second, they were more likely to have had histories of juvenile problems (18%) than other groups (7%).[10] In terms of the military-related characteristics only one was important, whether the veteran had enlisted or was drafted into the service. Draftees were less likely to have participated in abusive violence (4%) than were enlistees (12%). Of the four war-stress variables examined, only for participation in abusive violence is there rough parity in rates among veterans across the branches of service: 10% of naval veterans reported such participation along with 10% of air force units, 9% of army men, and 12% of marines.[11]

In sum, the findings show that killing someone and participating in abusive violence are more conditioned by preservice characteristics than are combat exposure and witnessing abusive violence. The weak effect of premilitary education on combat exposure is the only preservice effect on the latter two variables. On the other hand, both parents' education and premilitary education had an effect on the probability of killing someone; and parents' education and a history of juvenile problems contributed to the likelihood of participating in abusive violence. The combination of preservice effects and the low rates of participation in abusive violence among draftees, compared to enlistees, shows that certain types of individuals were more disposed to engage in this activity. The pronounced effects of branch of service on combat exposure and witnessing abusive violence, as well as killing someone, show that these experiences were largely conditioned by outside circumstances and became almost inescapable when men were placed in certain positions. Branch of service is not an unproblematic indicator of context, however, because it is likely some men choose to enter the navy or air force to decrease their involvement in the war. Still, the absence of preservice effect on combat and witnessing abusive violence suggests these were generic features of serving in the ground forces in Vietnam. The total absence of race effects on any measure of war trauma further reinforces this conclusion.

The transcript material suggests that there is great variability in coping with the stress of war. Yet despite the range of responses, we find no systematic pattern of predispositional effects in the analysis that predicts the emotional response patterns to war trauma. Although this finding parallels the results for the effects of the experience on measures of war stress, it is perplexing.

The extent of combat experience and the witnessing of abusive violence are largely outside the control of the soldier, but the response to the trauma these factors invoke is, at least in part, an individual response. Thus, we would expect that the characteristics the individual brings to the situation would play a significant role in determining his response to events.

Our data do not permit the conclusion that the relationship between individual characteristics and the response to war trauma is insignificant. They suggest, however, that the social determinants we usually expect significantly to affect individual behavior do not appear to be a major determinant of coping with war trauma. Since we have only retrospective data and have no prospective personality measures prior to exposure to war stress, personality indicators may be important in understanding the response patterns.

In the absence of a systematic relationship between background characteristics and responses to trauma, we are led to an interpretation that emphasizes the social context in Vietnam as the salient factor in understanding subjective responses to traumatic stress. It may well be that the world of war is so distant from the range of other social experiences in which adolescent and young adult coping mechanisms are developed, that situational factors related to the immediate social support system of the individual play the dominant role in socializing his emotional response.[12] Under these circumstances the development of coping styles would evolve through learning from significant others in this field, either buddies or those experienced in the dark environment called "war." We suspect these men become role models for novices.

Relationship Between Behavioral and Subjective Responses to War Stress

After developing both behavioral and subjective measures of war stress we asked whether these measures were interrelated.[13] We do find some relationships between behavioral and subjective indicators of traumatization. Combat, the measure most systematically related to emotional reaction, is associated with three distinct responses: fear, self-protection, and the denial of feelings. Combat is also associated with a concern with survival. This is evident from the previously discussed preeminent concern of combat veterans with personal survival while they were in Vietnam.

The relationship between combat and the numbing response to seeing Americans killed is one indicator of the importance of numbing responses to war stress. The prevalence of numbing responses among veterans is also apparent in the association between 1) witnessing abusive violence and the response of no feelings to combat; 2) participation in abusive violence and the response of shock to American deaths; and 3) participation in abusive violence and the concern with survival.

We also explored the association between emotional responses to death and dying and the combat experience. The key finding here is that there appear to be distinct patterns of emotional response to the traumas of war within the combat, exposed, and participant groups in our study.

The pattern of association we found in the combat group showed that men who denied experiencing traumatic stress at the death of Americans professed a similar indifference to the death of the Vietnamese. Combat veterans who allowed the shock of the death of buddies to penetrate, however, responded more openly to the death of the Vietnamese and acknowledged that the dying of the Vietnamese saddened them. When we examine how combat veterans responded to the experience of combat we find that those who acknowledged fear also admitted responding with sadness to the death of the Vietnamese. However, when we examine the association between the reaction to combat and response to the death and dying of the Vietnamese, we find that those who reported that their prime concern was survival were most likely to feel the death of the Vietnamese was justified. Hence, denial of the trauma of combat was associated with 1) denial that the dying of buddies and Vietnamese had an effect; and 2) anger at the death of Americans. In both instances the denial of the threat of combat is associated with responses that indicate emotional defenses against acknowledging other forms of trauma.

Among witnesses to abusive violence we find very much the same pattern as we did among the combat veterans. Fear of combat is accompanied by openness to the pain of Vietnamese dying (sadness); those whose prime focus was self-protection justify the fate of the Vietnamese; and the witnesses who said they had no feelings about combat state indifference to the fate of the Vietnamese.

Among participants in abusive violence we find only part of the pattern of associations evident in the other groups. Denial and rage are both present in the findings but there is no evidence that any portion of this group acknowledged sadness at the fate of the Vietnamese. Participants who denied responding to the death and dying of Americans felt that the killing of the Vietnamese was justified; and we find similar justification for the fate of the Vietnamese among those participants who said they had no emotional response to combat. However, among the participants who expressed fear of combat we found an extremely strong relationship with anger at the death of Americans. Thus it appears that among those involved in abusive violence, emotional responses to the trauma of war involved substantial numbing or denial of feeling or alternatively utilizing rage to respond to trauma. In each instance the response is to externalize emotions either by defending against the intrusion of feeling or by letting go and directing anger outward.

Indicators of War Stress Used in the Study

In our analysis of the legacy of Vietnam, we utilize six measures of the war experience: branch, rank, period of service, combat, witnessing abusive violence, and participation in abusive violence. Draft status and subjective responses to the war are also important aspects of the veterans' story, and indeed the knowledge of the latter issue is crucial to an understanding of the complexity of the Vietnam experience. However, neither the draft status of the veterans nor their subjective responses to the stress of Vietnam were systematically related to the broad range of social and political consequences of the war. Yet, if we are to present a coherent interpretation of the social-psychological and political aftereffects of the Vietnam experience we must focus on those aspects of the war experience fundamental to the meaning of the Vietnam War in the personal and political lives of the veterans. Thus the story of the impact of the Vietnam War that we present will unfold through the six key measures described above that differentiate Vietnam veterans.

Vietnam Era Veterans' Experience

In our study, Vietnam era veterans appear as an undifferentiated group compared to Vietnam veterans and nonveterans. Our analysis of this population showed that no particular aspect of their military experience created special subgroups with distinct attitudes toward political issues, nor, as the subsequent chapter indicates, were there any adverse psychological effects of being in the armed forces during the Vietnam War years. Thus, Vietnam era veterans are treated strictly as a comparison group. We do not explore their internal differences because they do not appear to add a special dimension to our understanding of the Vietnam War in American society.

Nonveterans' War Experience

The Vietnam War spawned an opposition that was active, vociferous, and influential. Although only a modest proportion of the nonveterans in the age group could actually be described as antiwar activists, that minority played a crucial role in the drama of Vietnam in American society. As our data will show, they form a distinct group whose views of the war differ substantially from those of their peers. At the same time, we found that the members of this generation who were not moderately or actively involved in the antiwar movement do not exhibit evident polarity with the antiwar activists. Rather, it is the nonveteran supporters of the war who provide this counterpoint. Thus, our analysis of the nonveterans is based on two distinct issues: an attitude (support for the war) and a behavior (active opposition to the war). This approach creates some methodological problems, whose solution we describe in appendix A on methodology. Conceptually, however, this approach is not paradoxical. Nonveterans who supported the war felt little call to action. Their beliefs were reinforced by leaders of the U.S. government and the military in Vietnam. Opponents of the war, however, were forced to strike out at the political leadership of the country if they hoped to alter official policy and its implementation. Their struggle, which was long and protracted, is not the issue here. Our aim, rather, is to clarify why we have utilized these two stances of the nonveteran population to examine the lasting images of the war. Below we will summarize the character of our sample in terms of involvement in the antiwar movement and the extent respondents expressed support for the war.

Antiwar Activism

Our approach to the measurement of antiwar activism was to ask nonveterans how many antiwar activities they engaged in during the course of the war. We focused on two periods in their lives: the years before they were eligible for the draft and the years they were most involved with the war (period of greatest concern). Antiwar activities were broadly defined. They included going to lectures; taking part in "teach-ins"; participating in local or national demonstrations; acting as an organization leader; picketing recruiters, military installations, or military bases; and any form of civil disobedience directed against the war.

Seventy-one percent of the sample engaged in one or no actions against the war, but less than 20% of our sample said they never participated in an antiwar act. This group represents the low antiwar activists group in the study. Of the remaining respondents, 17% said they engaged in two to four antiwar activities (moderate activists), while 12% reported that they were involved in more than five antiwar activities during the course of the war (high antiwar activists).

Antiwar Activism and Predispositional Factors

In the course of our study we found that the level of antiwar activism is associated with different aspects of socio-economic background and attitudes toward the military. As table 1.7 demonstrates, moderate or high levels of antiwar activism are higher among whites (32%) than among blacks (12%). Activists also come from higher socio-economic backgrounds.[14] Table 1.8 shows that 27% of the high antiwar activists come from families where at least one parent had had some postgraduate training, compared to 6% of the low activists. Finally, as table 1.9 indicates, heavy involvement in antiwar activism was more common among the under-thirty (17%) than among the over-thirty group (6%) in our study.

Levels of activism were also related to nonveterans' attitudes toward military service and their awareness of alternative ways of avoiding it. Among those who were active participants in the antiwar movement only 9% expressed positive feelings about the military, while 64% had negative perceptions of the armed services (tables 1.10 and 1.11). Comparable figures for the low activists were 31% and 39%. Furthermore, as table 1.12 indicates, the high activists were much more likely to believe there were no advantages to military service (39%) than the low activists (20%). Antiwar activists, moderate and high, were also much more likely to be aware of ways of avoiding military service. We asked our respondents about their knowledge of seven possible alternative solutions for avoiding military service. In table 1.13 we see that 51% of the high activists and 42% of the moderate activists were aware of all seven options compared to 21% of the low activists. Ignorance of more than three options was very common among the low activists, 57% compared to only 27% of the high activists.

There are two interesting absences from this list of significant relationships. First, other feelings about the military often mentioned by nonveterans, i.e., concern with death and injury and concern with career disruption, did not distinguish between those who were active aginst the war and those who were not. Roughly equal proportions of both groups cited these disadvantages. Second, those who were active were not more likely to have changed their draft status even though they were more aware of alternatives to military service. It can be inferred from these nonfindings that those who were active were under no greater threat of being drafted than those who were not. That there were not basic differences in specific priorities and concerns between activists and nonactivists emphasizes the importance of the basic differences in the general dispositions of these two groups as reflected in tables 1.10–1.13. The activists were more negative toward the service quite apart from its specific disadvantages. This difference in dispositions can be partially traced back to the different socio-economic backgrounds of these two groups.

Attitude Toward the War

We also asked all nonveterans about their views of the war during the "period of greatest concern." This question required respondents to reconstruct their attitudes during a particular period and differentiate it from their current position. The problem inherent in retrospective reconstruction is one that cannot be resolved. Surely, there was some confusion after the fact. However, despite its imperfections, this method seemed the best way to examine the effects of support for the war using a comparable time frame for activism against the war. Indeed, as our data show, nonactivism was not a good measure of support for the war, as 67% of the nonveterans say they opposed the war, while only 19% say they were for it. The 19% of the sample who acknowledge supporting the war, like the antiwar activists, potentially represent polarities in this generation. Clearly, the war was extremely unpopular in the study's age group, but whether we have accurately estimated the exact proportion who opposed the war during the "period of greatest concern" we cannot specify with the certainty we would like. We are confident, however, that it is highly likely that those who acknowledge support of the war during that period reflect a distinct part of the nonveteran population. As the analysis throughout the book demonstrates, this group is consistently different from the rest of the nonveterans. Indeed, our findings indicate that the prowar nonveterans' attitudes to a broad range of political issues are somewhat more distinct from the overall nonveteran group than are those of the antiwar activists.

Support for the War and Predispositional Factors

Supporters of the war in our population, like the antiwar activists, also had some predispositional characteristics that differentiated them from their nonveteran peers. We find in table 1.14 that supporters of the war are significantly more likely to be white (22%) than black (10%). Prowar respondents, as table 1.15 demonstrates, come from families where parental education was lower than among their peers who opposed the war. The parents of the war's supporters more often had less than a high school education (32%) or were high school graduates (36%), while parents of antiwar respondents were less likely to have less than a high school degree (25%) or only to have completed high school (32%). The difference between these groups is even more dramatic at the postgraduate level, where 13% of the parents of those opposed to the war had some postgraduate training compared to 6% of the prowar group.

Attitudes toward the military also differentiate the prowar group in our study. Only 32% of this group expressed negative feelings toward the military, compared to 55% of the respondents who opposed the war (table 1.16). Supporters of the war rarely commented that they saw no advantages to military service (13%), while 31% of those opposed to the war emphasized the absence of any advantages to military duty (table 1.17). Why, then, did these men remain outside the military? Part of the answer can be found in table 1.18, where we asked about the disruptive effects of military service on career development. Although we found that antiwar activists were not more concerned with career disruption than the low activists, in table 1.18 we see that supporters of the war expressed significant concern about the disruptive effects of military service on their careers. Fifty-six percent of the supporters of the war saw the military as a career disruption, compared to only 40% of the opposed group. Reflecting on these findings we surmise that the war supporters in the nonveteran population are more likely to be upwardly mobile than the antiwar activists. The time that the military takes out of the life of a veteran appears to be perceived as a barrier to desired mobility by the former population. As these men come from families that have fewer resources than the antiwar activists or those who opposed the war, they may have been unwilling to take additional career risks that they appear to associate with military service. This suggests that they have little opposition to military service in principle but exempt themselves from military service to secure their future.

Conclusion

This chapter has described the aspects of the Vietnam experience that we will use throughout this study to examine the psychosocial and political legacy of the Vietnam years. It also has provided an overview of the war experience of Vietnam veterans to give the reader a sense of the nature of that war and the feelings it generated among the veterans. As noted earlier, we will henceforth focus on the effects of only six aspects of the experience that consistently differentiate Vietnam veterans' response to their war experience: branch of service, rank, period of service, combat, and witnessing of or participation in abusive violence. We have not internally differentiated Vietnam era veterans and use them only as a comparison group with Vietnam veterans and nonveterans throughout the book. Differences among nonveterans will be examined in terms of involvement in the antiwar movement and support of the war.

The succeeding chapters will illustrate how the main subgroups, Vietnam veterans, Vietnam era veterans, and nonveterans, relate to the war. Throughout, we focus on the images of war evoked by Vietnam veterans and their nonveteran peers, as they recall the powerful experiences and feelings that shaped their lives during the Vietnam years. Our analysis turns largely around those in the generation for whom the Vietnam War is most likely to be an organizing experience, shaping the course of their personal and political lives. For it is their voices that define the effects of the war on American society, and their eyes that serve as critical lenses through which we can interpret the past and define the future.

CHAPTER TWO

THE EFFECTS
OF WAR

The experiences of men at war mark their lives indelibly. The question, beyond what happens in combat, is what is the type of stress men endure in war that most profoundly influences their subsequent lives.

To comprehend the political aftermath of the Vietnam War, it is essential to understand the costs of the war for those who fought it. After the demonstrations ended, the antiwar movement receded and its members went on with their lives and careers. Vietnam veterans were not so fortunate. For these men, picking up the pieces of their lives was enormously complicated by the stress of their war years. Indeed, the struggle of Vietnam veterans to come to terms with their demons became the central force in reawakening interest in the meaning of the Vietnam War for American society. Over the last ten years, the key to understanding the persistence of the Vietnam War as a political issue is to be found in the social and psychological travail of its veterans and in our society's efforts to come to terms with their needs.

Our objective in this section is to specify the key aspects of the war experience that play a systematic role in the postwar lives of Vietnam veterans. We largely rely on research findings previously published in a more statistical format in a variety of other publications.[1]

The chapter focuses primarily on three issues. First, it explores the problem of readjustment to civilian life during the reentry period. Second, it describes the psychological costs of the war experience. Finally, it examines how war disrupts the social lives of veterans, in terms of deviant behavior and marital patterns.

To interpret the effects of the war, we must estimate the role of war stress. Our model for this analysis focuses on three aspects of the war experience described in the previous chapter: combat, witnessing abusive violence, and participation in abusive violence. This chapter focuses on how these three factors contribute to postwar social and psychological adjustment.

Readjustment to Civilian Life

Going to war creates a gulf between the warrior and his fellow citizens who have not directly experienced warfare. After a war, most soldiers trade in their uniforms and guns for civilian jobs. Even in World War II, where returning soldiers were welcomed home, the transition from combatant to citizen-worker was thought to be difficult. World War II veterans, especially those who saw combat, were seen as losing something when they assumed mundane civilian roles.[2] The unpopularity of the Vietnam War and public awareness after 1968 that we would not win it created a new and serious problem for Vietnam veterans. Clearly there would be no victory parades. Men slipped back into civilian life anonymous and alone, often questioning the value of their sacrifice.

A substantial literature, much of it written by veterans, suggests that veterans' difficulties in readjusting to civilian life were exacerbated when they encountered even greater challenges to the war's legitimacy than they had anticipated. Furthermore, Vietnam veterans comprised a rather small minority of their age cohort—and a larger minority, but still a minority, within the military. The men who saw heavy combat were a smaller minority still. It therefore seems reasonable to suggest that Vietnam veterans were separated from their countrymen by a gulf larger than any experienced by World War II and Korean War veterans. As our data and the Harris Report (1980) suggest, the division within the age-cohort at prime risk during the war appears to be a chasm. The pronounced cultural differences between generations in the sixties and the fact that older veterans had won their wars may have made it especially difficult for Vietnam veterans to communicate with participants in previous conflicts.

Social Reintegration of the Returning Veteran

The Vietnam War's unpopularity resulted in a lack of public enthusiasm for its veterans.[3] Media presentations by Vietnam veterans themselves emphasized the negative aspects of the war; and those Vietnam veterans who chose to write about the war stressed its destructive side. The stigma associated with being a Vietnam veteran, combined with the veterans' minority status, eventually caused Vietnam veterans to be defined as a "social problem."

In general, Americans believe that veterans' service and sacrifice entitle them to special government help, and they support the expenditure of funds for veteran programs that they think are war-related.[4] However, the Harris Report also shows that the public and veterans tend to disagree about what specific problems are associated with postwar adjustment. For example, veterans in general are much more likely than their civilian counterparts to attribute problems such as "lack of direction in life" to the war, while the public is typically unwilling to help veterans deal with such problems. Therefore, although over time the public has come to feel more strongly that veterans of the Vietnam era have been treated less well than veterans of other wars, it is unsympathetic to many of the problems they cite.

The difficulty of readjustment

It appears that the Vietnam War did in fact create a gulf between its veterans and the civilian society. Readjustment appears to have been difficult because "people at home didn't understand what you had been through" and because the time spent at war left Vietnam veterans feeling "left out of everything that was going on at home." Era veterans also attest to having felt excluded and misunderstood when they came home. These conclusions are based on responses to the three items listed in panel A under Feelings of Alienation at Homecoming.

Panel A

Two Scales Concerning Social Reintegration*

*Feelings of Alienation
at Homecoming (3 items)*

1. People at home just didn't understand what you had been through in the armed forces.

2. Having been away for a while, you felt left out of everything that was going on at home.

3. Readjusting to civilian life was more difficult than most people imagine.

*Belief that People and
Government Support Veterans (4 items)*

1. Our presidents and their administrations have done and are doing all they can to help veterans return to civilian life.

2. The American people have done everything they can to make veterans feel at home again.

3. Most people at home respect you for having served your country in the armed forces.

4. People at home made you feel proud to have served your country in the armed forces.

*The items were originally used in the 1971 Harris Survey, "A Study of the Problems Facing Vietnam Era Veterans: Their Readjustment to Civilian Life."

Veterans as a group generally felt somewhat (51%) or very (34%) isolated when they returned home. As table 2.1 shows, there is a modest association between combat experience and feelings of isolation at homecoming. Among heavy-combat veterans 39% report feeling extremely isolated, while only 27% of the moderate-combat veterans share this sense of intense alienation. However, the table also indicates that very few moderate- (7%) or heavy-combat (5%) veterans felt no isolation compared to 16% of the low-combat group. Table 2.2 indicates that for combat veterans who served after 1967 there was a significantly greater sense of aloneness, evident among the moderate- (45%) and heavy-combat (49%) veterans. Thus, it appears that combatants coming home during the latter years of the war felt an even greater sense of distance from American society than did earlier returnees.

Vietnam veterans also typically believe that the American people have not respected and supported them, as indicated by their responses to the four items in panel A labeled Belief that People and Government Support Veterans. Table 2.3 demonstrates that there is substantial agreement that the U.S. government and people failed to support its veterans. Only 24% of all veterans feel they received high levels of support. The table additionally shows that Vietnam veterans (41%) were somewhat more likely to feel rejection rather than support from American society when compared to Vietnam era veterans (36%). Lack of support clearly was more hurtful to Vietnam veterans, because they returned nursing physical and psychological wounds of war. As table 2.4 shows, however, it is the veterans who witnessed abusive violence in the later years of the war, i.e., post-1967, (69%) who feel most strongly that they received little support from the government or the U.S. public.[5]

Table 2.5 provides evidence that the alienation from government persists among veterans. Nonveterans (37%) are significantly less alienated from governmental institutions than either Vietnam (27%) or Vietnam era (24%) veterans. In table 2.6 we see that among Vietnam veterans, those who did not witness abusive violence (30%) indicate that they are significantly less alienated than those who did (23%). The sense of alienation we find in the latter group is consistent with our earlier finding, in table 2.4, that veteran witnesses (69%) were the most convinced that the government and people failed to support them when they returned from the war. Table 2.6 demonstrates, however, that there are relatively high levels of alienation in both witness and nonwitness groups (41%). Thus, the sense of apartness we found during the homecoming period persists.

The sense of isolation expressed by Vietnam veterans is further illustrated by table 2.7. One way to deal with a traumatic experience like war is to discuss it. Yet, almost from the first, observers noticed that Vietnam veterans were reluctant to speak out. We also found Vietnam veterans less willing than Vietnam era veterans to discuss their experience. In a series of questions about what they did when they got home from the service, veterans were asked whether they had "talked a lot about what they had been through" and whether they had been "anxious to get involved in everything." Panel B shows the full wording of these questions and how they are scored.

Panel B

Two Questions about Social Reintegration

1. Would you say you talked a lot about what you had been through, talked about it some, or did you keep pretty much to yourself about it?

Scoring:	talked a lot	100
	talked some	50
	kept to self	0

2. When you got home were you anxious to get involved in everything or did you not want to participate in things with other people?

Scoring:	anxious to get involved	100
	did not want to participate	0

Table 2.7 indicates that Vietnam veterans say they talked less than era veterans about their experiences. Sixty percent of all Vietnam veterans report they kept to themselves, as opposed to only 29% of Vietnam era veterans. As tables 2.8 and 2.9 suggest, the more deeply involved in the violence of the war, the less likely veterans were to speak of their experiences. Although the differences in these tables are not statistically significant, they do underline the extent to which the violence of the war was kept locked inside those men who felt its destructiveness. Only 2% of the participants, 7% of the witnesses, and 7% of the men who saw heavy combat reported that they "talked a lot" about their time in Vietnam. Between 65 and 70% of our sample kept their experiences to themselves.

Turning to the extent to which Vietnam veterans were eager to pick up their lives and able to relate easily to others, we find evidence that the post-Tet period (post-1967) is associated with greater reluctance to reintegrate. Generally men who served in this latter period held back more. It was among these veterans who either witnessed or participated in abusive violence that we find the most evident reticence to get involved. As table 2.10 demonstrates, men who witnessed (62%) and participated in (59%) abusive violence were significantly more likely to withdraw from social relations after returning home than men who were not exposed (48%). Still, even in the not exposed group it is evident that a very substantial portion of the Vietnam veterans kept their distance from their peers.

The difficulties Vietnam veterans experienced during their reentry period are also reflected in the distance between their expectations and the reality they encountered upon return home. We asked the veterans how they felt things had worked out compared to their expectations. As tables 2.11 and 2.12 show, two groups of veterans who served after Tet (post-1967), combat veterans and veterans who witnessed abusive violence, felt that things had worked out far worse than they expected. Among the veterans who served after 1967, 41% of the moderate- and 57% of the heavy-combat veterans felt things had turned out worse than anticipated; and 62% of those who witnessed abusive violence felt that their plans had gone awry compared to only 31% of the veterans not exposed to abusive violence.

In summary, we can see that the readjustment period was generally difficult, but for veterans exposed to the more extreme forms of stressful experiences in Vietnam, combat and abusive violence, serving in the latter years of the war proved the greatest handicap to readjusting successfully to civilian life.

Veterans' descriptions of readjustment problems

The interview transcripts cast useful light on why some men found the readjustment period difficult. Many respondents complain that they came home to a country that ignored them and provided little support for their difficult readjustment process. Many feel that their cold reception made the return to civilian life more disappointing and troublesome than anticipated. The following testimonies dramatize their concern.

Lack of a hero's welcome. Some Vietnam veterans were deeply upset by the fact that they were not embraced by society as brave warriors. They were proud of having served in Vietnam and were convinced that their participation in the war had purpose and significance. One marine veteran, who was involved in heavy combat, described his homecoming as follows:

> When I came out of the military, I was very self-confident and strong, until I was out for a while and got exposed to society and found that the confidence was a false confidence based on what I did in the marines. I had to face the very cruel reality that none of it carried over. Even to this day people criticize what I did there. That is what led to my confusion, because I was under the impression that I was going to be looked on highly for doing my job for my country and I found the complete opposite to be the case. . . . My family didn't know what Vietnam was all about and what a man goes through in combat. . . . The VA should give more attention to the walking wounded, guys like myself that are psychologically distraught and uprooted by this type of experience, helping them determine what the hell they are going to do with the rest of their lives. I'm 32 going on 60, having trouble coping with the demands society dictates.

An army man expressed similar bitterness about the way he was viewed upon homecoming:

I think that the Vietnam veterans do not get enough recognition for what they did. A lot of people just forget about it altogether. Nobody seems to forget about the World War II veterans and there are still parades. Nothing is ever done to recognize us. We never really had a big homecoming like World War II when they won the war. We did go and serve our country and what have we got for it?

A marine officer talked about the lonely homecoming Vietnam veterans faced. He pointed out that after other wars most soldiers returned together, but this was not the case with Vietnam veterans:

This is one of the few wars where few would ever talk about what they had experienced because when you finally left Vietnam you were flown to the States and discharged with no bands. There was no fanfare. You almost felt coming back that you were guilty of something rather than that you had served your country due to the attitudes that were prevalent at the time and since. The Vietnam veterans should have been recognized for having done their best despite the outcome. I think that is where the failing has been.

Isolation from peers. Many Vietnam veterans expressed feelings of alienation from others in their generation. A veteran who served in the army and saw heavy combat in Vietnam illustrates this attitude. Homecoming was especially difficult for him, because he went back to college and suddenly had to face the antiwar movement:

In Vietnam, I didn't have a real understanding of the war. I just knew I had to do it and that was it. . . . After I got back to the States I realized that the Vietnam supporters were under fire, that people were very negative about the war. When I went in, there were no antiwar demonstrations. All that happened while I was over there. . . . When I returned to college I was maybe three–four years older than the students I was in class with, but their viewpoints were entirely different from mine. I found it hard to adjust because at that point there was a lot of criticism about the people who had served in Vietnam. . . . I did not verbalize my beliefs while in college, I stayed to myself. I felt like nobody, unwanted. As a matter of fact I felt very guilty. . . . I was totally confused in terms of right and wrong. I came back with less pride than when I went over there.

Many Vietnam veterans had a hard time readjusting because they felt disassociated from their friends. An army man who witnessed abusive violence explained his experience this way:

My plans were looking up people that I thought were friends, seeing everybody
that I missed so much while I was gone. But I soon realized that I could not
communicate with them any longer. They had spent their time while I was over
there in the war getting up in the morning and reading the paper and saying,
"My God, so many GIs got killed in Vietnam today. That is real bad." Then
they would finish their coffee and go to work. They do not think about it
anymore. There was no way I could relate to them how I really felt. That made
it very difficult for me to fit back into the system.

Alienation from society. Many Vietnam veterans felt isolated not only from
members of their own generation, but from Americans in general. A marine who
participated in abusive violence explained his pain at the way he was received
upon homecoming:

[How did you feel when you came back?] I worked for the phone company then
and Vietnam was big in people's minds and you would walk into somebody's
house and you talk with them and the first thing you know, "Oh were you in the
military?" Yeah. They would say, "Were you in the marines?" and they made
you feel like you were a killer. That you did wrong by serving your country. A
lot of people resented you. You could not talk about it. You were trying to hide
it. I mean that is how I felt. Because everybody was against it. You would talk
about it in a bar and you would be by yourself and twenty people would be
saying . . . "Well, they don't want you there. Why are you there? Why are you
fighting for the country?" It was just like you went for a lost cause. That is how
it made you feel.

Some veterans reported that on returning from Vietnam they felt like
strangers in their own hometowns. The following remarks by an army infantryman who was in heavy combat illustrate this attitude:

I was drunk for three months. I bought a motorcycle. That was the middle of the
winter and people knew I was home. Nobody knew me down here any longer.
That was the strange part. There was a new nut in town. In February I was
riding a god damned Honda in the snow . . . drunk. I felt demoralized. I was
pretty happy-go-lucky before then. By the time I came back I pretty much lost
all my earlier ambitions. I was really hyper when I came home. Afterwards I
just wanted to sit in a little safe corner of my own.

Political alienation. Many Vietnam veterans continue to suffer from political alienation, and they cite their lack of trust in government as one outcome of
their involvement in the war. A veteran who was drafted and served as a first
lieutenant in the army infantry explains his response to the war as follows:

What stands out most in my mind is the total waste of the whole thing in terms of certainly human life first, and the dollars that it cost this country to maintain that fiasco. It left a bad taste in my mouth as far as the political and military hierarchy was concerned. I have, based on the experience there, been turned off by our foreign policy in general.

Unwillingness to talk to others. Significant numbers of veterans admitted that they were not willing to talk about their wartime experiences. Vietnam was like a bad dream and they could not understand the things they had done there. An army man who witnessed abusive violence put it this way:

[What do you think changed you in the military?] Knowing that I probably killed somebody. That scared the hell out of me. When I start thinking, well I pray to God that I didn't kill somebody's husband or son and I still do today. I tried to forget the whole thing, I didn't want to remember it. . . . I just wanted to put it out of my mind. . . . It was three years before I'd even say that I was in Vietnam.

Overview

The process of readjustment was most likely to differentiate combat and theater veterans from their age peers who were not in the war. The disillusion we find among a substantial portion of Vietnam veterans can be attributed to several factors. In all wars some men exposed to combat feel revulsion against death and dying.[6] In the case of Vietnam, disillusionment also set in because of the final outcome of the war. The sacrifices veterans made appeared pointless. Finally, the divisions over the war in American society were an additional stress with which Vietnam veterans had to contend, making readjustment even more difficult.

Our findings also indicate that for Vietnam era veterans, readjustment to civilian life does not appear to be complicated by the war. We suspect that if we could compare Vietnam era veterans with men leaving the military during the peacetime years after the Korean War and before the Vietnam War, we would find the transition to civilian life to be quite similar in both veteran populations.

A reasonable interpretation of our findings might argue as follows: All wars involve human costs; the Vietnam War took a particularly heavy toll because the U.S. involvement in Vietnam remains controversial. The conflict surrounding the war also made readjustment substantially more difficult for veterans exposed to war stress, especially if they served after Tet (post-1967).

However, every war a nation enters costs lives and poses readjustment problems for veterans of the war; and many wars are controversial at some point in time. The question therefore is: Do Vietnam veterans have more social and psychological problems today, and can these in any way be attributed to their war experiences?

Veterans' Descriptions of Current Problems

Many veterans still have troubling thoughts about their war experiences and frightening dreams or nightmares. One of the most common desires expressed by our respondents is the urge to forget what happened. Back in Vietnam, it appeared that getting home would automatically end the nightmare. Upon their return, however, veterans have discovered that they have changed in profound and sometimes disturbing ways. Haunting memories recur in their thoughts and dreams. Many of those who acknowledged that the war had and continues to have a negative impact on them focus on the violence and brutality they encountered and admit that they remain troubled by remembrances of death and dying.

Vietnam veterans continue to be preoccupied with memories of the combat experience itself. They remember specific dangerous encounters and their minds keep drifting back to these situations. During the night they are suddenly back in combat and they have frightening dreams. An army man admitted that he is still troubled by his combat memories:

> I have a tendency to relate back, to have dreams. For example, when I went to see the movie *The Deerhunter*, it gave me a sleepless night. I was trying to forget some of the combat that I had . . . some of the close encounters. . . . Once, the platoon in front of us got completely wiped out. I think we suffered something like forty-nine Killed in Actions. That was a nightmare to me. A big ground attack . . . right at dusk. The only thing I can remember is me running. I fell into a river and I stayed there all night.

A veteran who was an army artillery cannoneer reported:

> I have reoccurring dreams of Vietnam. . . . I would be in a situation where I would have a gun and no bullets or I would have bullets and could not find a gun. I would be running and fall and there would be somebody in back of me. But it is always in a dense foliage type of place, very green. It is like running away from somebody chasing me.

Many veterans are bothered by mental images of how they might have died or been wounded. A helicopter pilot noted:

> For years after I left the army I underwent psychiatric care because it affected me very, very strongly, to the point that I just did not stop having hallucinations and felt that I was going to die any minute. I finally overcame a large part of that, but I still have dreams, wake-ups, fear, and anxiety. I have emotional problems based on incidents in Vietnam with me to this day. I suspect that it will always be there.

The memories of Americans killed or wounded, especially buddies, continue to trouble many veterans. An army man presented his most painful memories of Vietnam as follows:

> I would like to forget the screams I heard by the men that got shot. . . . Just something that you never forget. There is always a constant reminder that flashes you back right to them. Maybe the helicopters that go over . . . the police helicopters. It throws me right back into Vietnam. A noise, a big firecracker, a gun, a backfire . . . anything that resembles somebody being shot at.

For many, the loss of American lives is most salient because they were so isolated in Vietnam and they became very close with their buddies, as if they were family. A veteran who was in the army infantry reported:

> I took the death or wounding of Americans very hard. Hearing the horror of their voices. To this very day I still have frequent nightmares about some of my friends that were killed when I was nearby. It hurt very bad. Because you are isolated, away from your relatives and friends, you become very close in Nam, like family. . . . I was definitely changed by the war and affected. The death and dying in Vietnam is one of the hardest things for me to forget.

Veterans not only remember Americans killed or wounded, they often relive their own involvement in these events and wonder if they could have acted to change things. An army man expressed this feeling as follows:

> [What are you trying to forget?] The death that I saw. . . . At night I will just think about it. Sometimes you see the faces of some of the guys you knew, especially the people that were in your section that you lost and you wonder maybe if you did something different they would still be around.

In battle some men were torn between the realization that in order to survive it was necessary to kill and the awareness, even while killing, that the enemy was human like themselves. Upon homecoming, memories of death and killing persisted in spite of attempts to forget.

Other combat veterans were not bothered by the killing while they were in Vietnam, but after homecoming they too suffered from troublesome memories. A veteran noted:

> I did not feel anything at first because it was a natural thing to do. If you do not kill them they are going to kill you. But there were a lot of repercussions after I got out of the service. I had dreams. I still have dreams occasionally . . .

[about] all the people I killed. It was sickening. I began to realize that they were human beings. It is a terrible feeling.

And an air force sergeant commented:

I was flying on the B52s with bombs. . . . It didn't hit me too hard. I was thinking that we were killing the enemy. . . . [After homecoming] I got sick. Broke down. . . . I have a nervous condition. . . . I'm trying to forget the bombing. . . . I got . . . guilt feelings about that. . . . They do come to my mind at any given time.

Another veteran respondent, looking back at how the war affected his life, noted:

The first couple of years after I got out were hard. I could not admit to anybody what I had done. Nobody understood what the war had done to us. . . . At times, when I am sitting someplace alone or reading, something suddenly comes over me and I will just start thinking about Nam. I wished I would forget, but those things will be with me forever I guess.

Other veterans remain affected by memories of the suffering of Vietnamese civilians, especially children, that they witnessed during the war. An army infantryman offered the following assessment:

What really did hurt the most was the civilians being killed, because they had nothing to do with it. . . . I still think about it. I wish I could forget but I can't . . . I just start thinking about when I was in Vietnam and that comes into my mind.

Another army man reflected:

It was mainly the children of Vietnam. They always stick in my mind, I'm always seeing the children poorly dressed, underfed, several of them crippled or mutilated. . . . Just anytime Vietnam is mentioned or anything to do with Vietnam is mentioned, I always start thinking about the children again.

In the narrative material combat veterans often reported symptoms of hyperarousal, ranging from "feeling irritable" or "short tempered" to suffering "outbursts of sudden anger." They occasionally experience "feelings of losing control," are "jumpy" or "easily startled," or "have attacks of fear and panic." They admitted that often anger or fear builds up and then explodes "like a bomb inside of them." This frightens them and makes them anxious. Some recalled that they were tense for a number of years after reentry, but finally readjusted to civilian life and no longer suffer from hyperarousal. An army infantryman described his condition after leaving Vietnam this way:

> I will tell you it was really nerve wracking over there. After I came home I kept hearing mortars come in every night and I could hear them old whistling sounds. When I was home I would jump right out of bed some nights. Now I feel somewhat better.

Others acknowledged that their emotional and psychological well-being has not really improved since they came home. A marine suffered from severe hyperarousal for a number of years and occasionally he still feels jumpy and suffers attacks of panic. He talked about his problems as follows:

> [After homecoming] most of the time, I spent it at home. And by myself. And it took me about a month to get used to my bed. I was sleeping on the floor under my bed. Later on, when I was married, my wife used to wake me up and catch me off guard and I used to hit her. I told her that it was part of a reflex from the service, because everytime I was trying to get into a deep sleep, something would always happen and I would have to jump up. But after awhile, she learned not to bother me. All I had experienced was how to make a bomb, how to kill somebody, or how to shoot a rifle, and so I felt kind of lost. . . . A lot of people say I was changed. I was quiet when I went into the service and I got more violent. I did a lot of yelling and screaming when I was there. Now, I think my temper is kind of short.

Psychological Costs of the War Experience

The descriptions of the recurrent psychological problems Vietnam veterans experience as a result of exposure to war stress can be more systematically measured through the use of the standard psychiatric epidemiological instruments. The results of this exercise present a more technical picture of the effects of war stress on veterans, but one that is consistent with what they said in the narrative section of the study. Our concern about the long-term impacts of exposure to war stress on the Vietnam population and the effects on veterans' mental health led us to utilize such instruments in our study. Our approach to the mental health issue is threefold. First, we measured whether or not Vietnam veterans experience the need to forget things that happened. Second, we included an elaborate, well-established measure of general psychological well-being, the Psychiatric Epidemiological Research Interview (PERI). Third, we incorporated a measure of what is commonly referred to as Post-Traumatic Stress Disorder (PTSD) in the Diagnostic and Statistical Manual (DMS-III). In the pages that follow we examine the extent to which the mental health of Vietnam veterans or those exposed to specific aspects of war stress is systematically affected by their experiences.

In the mental health measures we find a consistent pattern of results that indicates that simply being in Vietnam does not generate serious mental health problems. Only those who were exposed to significant amounts of combat and/or witnessed or were participants in abusive violence demonstrate long-term problems of this kind. The pattern of findings also suggests that postwar sequelae, symptoms which are specifically related to stress of war, are especially common among men who saw combat as well as those exposed to abusive violence. More general, diffuse psychiatric symptoms, however, are most likely to be associated with witnessing of and participating in abusive violence, but are not especially evident among combat veterans. Furthermore, race differentiates response to the extreme stress of abusive violence. The implication of our findings is that general psychiatric symptoms are related to exposure to specific but extremely intense stress (abusive violence), while persistent stress (combat) over time has a more circumscribed effect on symptomatology.

The general symptomatology measured by the PERI scales exhibits no relationship to combat, but a strong relationship to witnessing of and participation in abusive violence. These effects vary by race. The first point to be noted here is that the five scales listed in table 2.13 are associated with war stress (demoralization, perceived and active hostility, angry feelings, guilt). With the exception of the Demoralization Scale, abusive violence is related primarily to hostility and guilt. The pattern of findings is consistent: whites who witness abusive violence and blacks who participate in abusive violence have significantly more symptoms, while white participants report significantly fewer symptoms. Table 2.13 presents the mean (average) scores of each group on these scales.

On five measures of generalized (PERI) symptoms we find that the witnessing of and participation in abusive violence have a significant effect on the extent to which veteran respondents continue to be psychologically troubled. The most comprehensive of these measures is the Demoralization Scale, which taps a general sense of depression and anxiety. As table 2.13 shows, we find distinct patterns for whites and blacks. Among whites not exposed to abusive violence the average score on the scale is 17.97, while the overall black score is similar (18.99). Whites who witnessed abusive violence (21.13) show significant increases in their score, however, indicating more psychological disturbance, while participation (15.52) significantly reduces the score, indicating less trauma. Among blacks there is a steady increase in the score from witnessing abusive violence (20.89) to participation (27.25). The most dramatic difference, as table 2.13 indicates, is between the elevated score of black versus white participants.

The pattern as described above, as table 2.13 demonstrates, persists across the scales that measure guilt, angry feelings, and perceived and active expression of hostility. The measure of guilt shows that the unexposed whites score 19.11 compared to 22.65 among the exposed and 14.89 for the participants. Again there is a steady increase in the scores of blacks from 17.67 for those not exposed to 28.42 among participants. On all three measures of anger and hostility, we see that black participants score highest of all groups, while white participants score lowest among those who were exposed to abusive violence, and whites who witnessed abusive violence consistently score higher than the other groups. Thus the second point to be stressed is that among whites we find clear evidence that we cannot expect all war stress cumulatively to increase postwar psychological symptomatology.

The above findings raise two sets of questions. Do our sample's responses indicate that white participants have better mental health, i.e., do not experience psychological distress as a consequence of their experience? Second, how can we explain these rather dramatic differences in postwar symptomatology? The prior question needs to be addressed first. Once we have concluded our examination of the psychological response to the trauma through an analysis of Post-Traumatic Stress Symptomatology, we can better explain the differences we have just described.

Post-Traumatic Stress Disorder and Symptomatology

The literature on Vietnam veterans has focused on Post-Traumatic Stress Disorder (PTSD). Therefore, we have investigated how war stress is related to stress symptoms and the PTSD. Our approach to this issue is somewhat unconventional, but the conceptualization and measurement of PTSD is in dispute. The justification for our approach is carefully delineated below. We provide a general overview of the findings and prevalence estimates of PTSD in our study as well as supporting tables for those more comfortable with multivariate statistical models.

A number of models of traumatic neurosis or stress disorder emphasize two dimensions of the response to trauma: 1) a repetition of images, thoughts, and effects from the traumatic event and 2) defenses against these repetitions.[7] Horowitz has developed this framework into the most elaborated model of stress disorder. He focuses on the two mental states of "intrusion," including intrusive-repetitive thoughts, nightmares, hypervigilance, and pangs of strong emotion, and "denial," including inattention, amnesia, constriction of the thought process, and emotional numbing.[8] These two states alternate until the traumatic event is integrated into the individual's world view.

The DSM III criteria for PTSD include three symptom criteria: 1) Criterion B, "Reexperiencing of the trauma," which corresponds to Horowitz's intrusion state; 2) Criterion C, "Numbing of responsiveness to the world," which approximates Horowitz's avoidance state, although more severely defensive; and 3) Criterion D, which is a miscellany of symptoms. A close examination of the symptoms in Criterion D reveals that they can be differentiated into symptom clusters that are either subsets of reexperiencing phenomena or defensive maneuvers to avoid the trauma. Thus all three criteria can be organized

Panel C

The Stress Symptom Inventory

(1) feelings of dizziness
(2) feeling anxious or tense
(3) headaches
(4) stomach troubles
(5) trouble remembering things
(6) feeling numb
(7) losing interest in usual activities
(8) feeling irritable or short tempered
(9) trouble sleeping, staying asleep or oversleeping
(10) frightening dreams or nightmares
(11) feeling sad, depressed, or blue
(12) feeling the impulse to lash out
(13) feeling easily tired
(14) occasional feeling of losing control
(15) feeling jumpy or easily startled
(16) attacks of sudden fear or panic
(17) thoughts of how you might die
(18) feeling confused or having trouble thinking
(19) trouble trusting others
(20) feeling that life isn't meaningful
(21) troubling thoughts about military experience
(22) feeling that what other people care about doesn't make sense

Hyperarousal Scale

(1) feeling irritable or short-tempered
(2) feeling the impulse to lash out
(3) occasional feeling of losing control
(4) feeling jumpy or easily startled
(5) attacks of sudden fear or panic
(6) trouble sleeping, staying asleep or oversleeping

Intrusive Imagery Scale

(1) troubling thoughts about military experience
(2) frightening dreams or nightmares
(3) thoughts of how you might die

Numbing Scale

(1) losing interest in usual activities
(2) feeling that life isn't meaningful
(3) feeling that what other people care about doesn't make sense
(4) feeling numb

Cognitive Disruption Scale

(1) feeling confused or having trouble thinking
(2) trouble remembering things

DSM III

Diagnostic criteria for Post-Traumatic Stress Disorder

A. Existence of a recognizable stressor that would invoke significant symptoms of distress in almost everyone.

Dual Stress Disorders

A. The experience of war trauma
   1) combat experiences
   2) witnessing of acts of abusive violence
   3) participation in acts of abusive violence

B. Reexperiencing of the trauma as evidenced by at least one of the following:

1) recurrent and intrusive recollections of the event
2) recurrent dreams of the event
3) sudden acting or feeling as if the traumatic event were re-occurring, because of an asso-ciation with an environmental or ideational stimulus

C. Numbing of responsiveness to or reduced involvement with the external world, beginning some time after the trauma, as shown by at least one of the following:
1) markedly diminished interest in one or more significant activities
2) feeling of detachment or es-trangement from others
3) constricted affect

D. At least two of the following symptoms that were not present before the trauma:
1) hyperalertness or exaggerated startle response
2) sleep disturbance
3) guilt about surviving when others have not, or about behavior required for survival
4) memory impairment or trouble concentrating
5) avoidance of activities that arouse recollection of the traumatic event
6) intensification of symptoms by exposure to events that symbolize or resemble the traumatic event

I. Disorder Based on Reexperiencing

A. Intrusion
1) troubling thoughts about your experiences in the military
2) frightening dreams or nightmares
3) thoughts of how you might die

B. Hyperarousal
1) feeling irritable or short-tempered
2) feeling the impulse to lash out
3) occasional feeling of losing control
4) feeling jumpy or easily startled
5) attacks of sudden fear or panic
6) trouble sleeping, staying asleep or oversleeping

II. Disorder Based on Denial

A. Numbing
1) losing interest in usual activities
2) feeling that your life wasn't
3) feeling that what other people care about doesn't make sense
4) feeling numb

B. Cognitive Difficulties
1) feeling confused or having trouble thinking
2) trouble remembering things

around the two dimensions of reexperiencing and defensive phenomena.

In severe forms of traumatic neurosis or stress disorder clinicians have noted that one or the other of the two dimensions may be dominant,[9] i.e., an individual is likely to be overwhelmed with memories, nightmares, and emotions associated with the traumatic event or is likely to be highly defended against such reminders. There is evidence from empirical investigation that one dimension may be dominant at a particular time.[10] Further, evidence suggests that certain responses to trauma tend to be established early and persist over time in one or the other mode.[11]

The four columns in panel C show the four stages in which we tested the effects of war stress on symptomatology. The initial test concerned whether exposure to war stress increased rates of symptomatology at the time of the interview, well removed from the times at which the men had been exposed to the stressful experiences. Stress symptomatology was measured as an additive scale of the number of symptoms the respondent reported experiencing in the year before the interview. The items in the symptom inventory, listed in column 1 of panel C, were chosen from the literature on traumatic events and early drafts on the specification of PTSD in DSM-III.[12] Only general combat exposure was found to lead to higher symptom rates among stress-exposed groups.[13]

A more refined test was made by disaggregating the general symptom inventory into four scales based on distinct symptom clusters as shown in column 2 of panel C. The pattern of effects found in this test was more complex.[14] Combat exposure contributed to hyperarousal and intrusive imagery symptomatology, witnessing abusive violence to intrusive imagery symptoms, and participation in abusive violence to hyperarousal, numbing, and cognitive disruption symptomatology.

The variation in symptom responses to stress and traumatic experiences shown by the pattern established above suggested that Post-Traumatic Stress Disorder may not be the comprehensive phenomenon specified in the DSM-III. In the current DSM-III formulation of PTSD, in order to be diagnosed PTSD positive, symptoms from each criterion category must be present (at least one each from criteria B and C, and at least two from criterion D).[15]

The different linkages between stress exposure and symptom response clusters led to the expectation that PTSD may be a disorder in which one of the two dimensions may dominate the symptom picture. We hypothesized that it may occur as either of two types of response to stress, a reexperiencing or denial-based form of the disorder.

The elements used to construct the measures of reexperiencing and denial-based disorders and their comparability with the DSM-III specification are shown in columns 3 and 4 of panel C. The symptom clusters, though not perfectly corresponding to those in the outline of PTSD, were sufficiently comparable to allow a valid test to be made. The limited number of specific symptoms in each cluster, in fact, made the test a conservative one because individuals were less likely to be judged PTSD positive than if the number of symptoms were larger.

In examining the relationship between war stress and the reexperiencing and denial disorders separately, there was a significant relationship between combat exposure and the reexperiencing-based disorder, and witnessing abusive violence and the reexperiencing-based disorder. However, neither of these types of stress exposure were related to the denial-based disorder. Rather, it was participation in abusive violence that proved to be significantly related to the denial-based disorder, while having no relationship to the reexperiencing-based disorder.

The prevalence rates presented in table 2.14 show a clear linear relationship between combat exposure and exhibiting reexperiencing-based disorder.[16] Only 22% of low-combat veterans were positive on reexperiencing-based disorder while 32% of high-combat veterans were positive on this long-term response. Correspondingly, only 19% of men not exposed to abusive violence were positive on reexperiencing-based disorder while 40% of men who witnessed abusive violence were positive on this disorder. The prevalence rates and regression estimates in table 2.14 for the denial-based disorder show a similar strong pattern but only when comparing those who did and did not participate in abusive violence. Only 15% of veterans who did not participate in abusive violence were positive on denial-based disorder compared to 41% of veteran participants.

Finally we turn to the issue of how much energy veterans invest in trying to blot out their memories of Vietnam. In table 2.15 we see a linear effect of combat on investment in forgetting the war experience. Nearly 56% of the heavy-combat veterans and 49% of the moderate-combat veterans report that they try to forget what transpired as compared to only 34% of the low-combat veterans. Thus, as the PTSD measure suggests, the war continues to intrude on the thoughts of the war-stressed veterans, and they continue to battle their memories.

Veterans Who Participated in Abusive Violence

The narrative material indicates that white veterans who participated in acts of abusive violence are generally unwilling to talk about the effect the war had on their lives. Moreover, those involved in the most serious forms of abusive violence are often the most likely to deny the significance of their acts. The following two examples illustrate this response pattern. A veteran who served in the navy reported that after coming back from Vietnam all he wanted was to "relax, have fun, not confront anything that would cause me worry or care." When asked how the Vietnam War affected his life, he responded:

> I think it was a very great influence on my life. I really think that I am a better, more rounded individual because it was an education and an experience. . . . The military can provide an individual with a basic strength and fortitude, if you call it guts, to rely on himself and to rely on others in a given situation.

Yet it seems clear from this respondent's transcript that the war marked him indelibly. He uses drugs and admits that his experiences "left me somewhat hardened and jaded, so to speak, not really caring about a human individual, as much as I may have before."

When asked whether his experiences changed him, a marine observed:

> No, being in the service, you just do what they tell you to do and you just go along. . . . I do not think I have changed. I suppose I am about the same, just going along. [Effect of war?] You realize life and death situations . . . matured me.

But again, in terms of true impact, this veteran seems seriously troubled. He uses drugs, fights with his friends, and has been convicted on drunk and disorderly charges. While he denies any wartime effect other than maturing, he gives the impression in the narrative material that he is disturbed.

A minority of the white participants were willing to talk about the effect the war had on their lives. A veteran who was in the army as a squad leader suffered seriously from numbing:

> I am trying to forget . . . the whole deal in Vietnam, it was like a bad dream. Once every three or four months—I'd be depressed or somehow it will come up and it gets me down real bad. Then I just go and get drunk. . . . [I was] a lot different than before I went in. All my friends when I got out said that I was not right—"there is something wrong with you, man." . . . It is just like three years of a big void—a black spot in my life. I just cannot remember, or don't care to, what happened. It is like I was dead for three years there.

One interpretation of the above is that white participants in abusive violence literally have developed a reduced ability to experience their inner states or, in the Freudian sense, can more actively repress inner turmoil or memories. Indeed, the absence of significant intrusive imagery in this population argues for just such an interpretation, especially when compared to white combat veterans, witnesses to abusive violence, and black participants, all of whom show evidence of significantly higher levels of intrusive imagery.

Judging from what they report in the transcripts, most black respondents were shaken by their participation in abusive violence while they were in Vietnam and admitted a variety of negative symptoms after homecoming. An army sergeant who had a very difficult time after homecoming and still has symptoms of intrusive imagery, hyperarousal, and cognitive difficulties presented the following picture of his life after Vietnam:

> I still have nightmares. . . . It is not always best to go talking about . . . some of the sneaky dirty things one did during that time period. . . . You feel kind of

sorry for yourself if you think back about that, you might even cry sometimes. It would be hard going to sleep. It just gets on your mind. I won't talk about it to anybody . . . I have emotions, feelings that are kind of good and bad and confused. . . . I really try to forget about it.

The readjustment of another army man after returning from Vietnam reflects similar difficulties. He expressed his sense of unease as follows:

[I am trying to forget] . . . the killing . . . mangled bodies . . . everything like that. Usually when I see the rain . . . when it is bad weather out . . . and there is a lot of noise around me . . . I cannot stand too much noise. Socially, I cannot be motivated. Motivation . . . it is not there. The desire . . . it is just not there. My head is not there. Today, I am still struggling and I am going to the best of my ability to struggle on. I am just trying to survive. [How would you describe yourself today?] Disabled.

Veterans Who Witnessed Acts of Abusive Violence

The narrative material indicates that for white veterans, witnessing abusive violence was a specially upsetting experience that left a permanent imprint on their lives.[17] They often reported persistent and troubling memories that they probably will never be able to forget. At the same time, many feel that their war experience has taught them greater humanity. The following examples illustrate the attitudes and response patterns of these veterans.

After his reentry in the United States, a navy seabee remained anxious, had nightmares, and was haunted by the mistreatment of Vietnamese children:

[So you have noticed a big difference from the person you were before you went in the military until now. You are more nervous?] Right. I have attacked my wife. She came up behind me and scared me one time and I just went at her. I did not see her. She started screaming. She got scared. I got scared more than she did. [Scared of yourself?] Right . . . [Trying to forget?] Yes. Anything to do with kids and seeing the way these kids grew up maimed and butchered. That is a bad scene. . . . When I see my own two kids, I am glad that they are not involved in anything like that. The war gave me an appreciation for human life.

A veteran who served in the army continues to have bad memories and suffers from demoralization. He commented:

I would like to forget the killing and the slaughter. The children, I still remember them. I would like to forget a lot of things but they still come back in my mind. . . . [Are there times when these thoughts occur more frequently?] During depressing times. I think I have changed a lot. Today I would describe myself as not trusting . . . in the basic value of human life. But I also have more compassion for people.

Attitudinal and Contextual Factors and Psychiatric Symptoms

Before we examine marital and deviant behavior patterns in the Vietnam veteran population, we need to ask whether attitudinal or contextual factors can help us understand the differential response of the white and black participants to the stress of war, as measured by the PERI scales. For the answers to these anomalies, we turn to our attitudinal data on cultural tolerance, views of the war, and views of the use of abusive violence, as well as to our transcripts in which veterans explain their reactions to their experiences in Vietnam.[18]

Three explanations for the differential response of the white and black participants are possible. The simplest of these is that white participants in abusive violence are more likely to have sociopathic tendencies, have a history of delinquent behavior, enter the military, and be predisposed to engage in abusive violence. Second, situational/contextual factors may determine the likelihood of men becoming engaged in abusive violence and determine how the experience is psychologically incorporated at a later time. Finally, it could be that racism among white participants contributes to their acting out and limits their psychological and moral sensitivity to this behavior.

It should be noted that both blacks (29%) and whites (32%) in our sample were equally exposed to abusive violence in Vietnam, and that 14% of blacks and 8% of whites in our sample participated in these acts. In neither case is the difference significant. There were, however, some general differences in the background characteristics of the participating groups. Participants in abusive violence, both white and black, reported more involvement in preservice delinquent behavior (37% vs. 18% among those who did not participate), and they were less likely to complete high school before entering the service (41% vs. 19%). Our data also show that participants in abusive violence were more likely to be enlistees (84%) than draftees (64%). Though predispositional factors and selection preferences do play a small part in predicting participation in abusive violence, they do not indicate how or why psychological responses to these actions should differ by race.

Responses of white participants

Our findings show that white participants differ systematically from the white exposed group on a range of attitudes. Participants were less likely to criticize the violence of war; more negative toward the Vietnamese; more likely to believe the Vietnamese were hostile to U.S. servicemen; more willing to accept the unrestricted use of weapons such as napalm, dum-dum bullets, and booby traps; and less willing to afford captured guerrillas protection under rules covering prisoners of war.

While white participants were more thoroughly aware of the destruction the war brought to Vietnamese society and its people, they felt little empathy for the victims. In addition, white participants generally believed that all groups of combatants used a broader range of abusive violence against the civilian population than was believed by those who were merely exposed to abusive violence.

Our transcript material also shows striking differences between these groups in their reaction to Vietnamese society and the victims of the violence. Whites who were only exposed generally acknowledged and empathized with the suffering of the victims. Furthermore, veterans in the exposed-only group were more likely to acknowledge that their experiences were traumatizing and to articulate the revulsion they experienced at the time.

Whites who participated in abusive violence articulated a distinctly different view of their encounter with abusive violence than did their peers who were only exposed. The former group felt distant from the condition of the Vietnamese population, alienated by their poverty and passivity, and disturbed by the parasitic atitude of those they met. They often reported open hostility toward the Vietnamese, in some cases stating their feelings in explicitly racial terms. Even when not directly expressing hostility to and alienation from the Vietnamese, they generally evidenced a well-advanced indifference to the value of life, especially Vietnamese life.

The capacity of white veteran participants to neutralize their feelings about the abusive acts they committed suggests the presence of what has been commonly called the "gook syndrome."[19] Indeed, although only five of the nineteen white veterans in our sample who participated explicitly used racial stereotyping in discussing their impressions of the Vietnamese, the transcript material shows that whites in this group were in most cases alienated from the Vietnamese population and did not feel that noncombatants had the right to be protected from harm. Furthermore, the respondents who participated in abusive violence actively denied the traumatic quality of their experience, having managed to numb themselves to the human misery they encountered.

Responses of black participants

An examination of the orientation of black participants shows they generally held attitudes similar to those of whites who were only exposed to abusive violence. The scores of black participants on the PERI scales were also higher than those of the white exposed group. In addition, black participants generally felt positive and sympathetic toward the Vietnamese and were less supportive of the war and of unrestrained warfare than white participants.

In the transcript material, we find that black participants were often severely traumatized by their experiences. These men tended to perceive the Vietnamese as victims of circumstance, as people trying to get by in a difficult situation. Consequently, when they took part in episodes of brutality, they felt severe internal conflicts and developed a deep sense of guilt for their behavior. Several reported that in brutalizing others, they were dehumanizing themselves; they feared they were becoming animals.

The capacity of white participants to dehumanize civilians and other non-combatants was not matched among the blacks. Where whites who were involved in abusive violence developed a number of mechanisms for estranging themselves from the true nature of their acts, blacks found themselves confronted with a basic contradiction between their actions and their sympathy for the victims.

Factors influencing veterans' response, by race

The different ways that these two veteran groups managed their experiences suggest that the whites who participated in abusive violence can generally be distinguished from other veterans by their disregard for the consequences of their actions and their inability to experience the suffering of their victims.

White participants and whites who witnessed abusive acts exhibited a consistency between attitudes and behavior. In the participant group, we find indifference to the fate of civilians, combined with a total war orientation. Among the white exposed veterans, we find a reversal of attitudes toward civilians and toward the scope of acceptable behavior. Only among the black participants do we find evidence of conflict between attitudes and behavior.

Why is the contrast between behavior and attitude that is evident among black participants absent in white respondents? Due to the differences in attitudes and psychological responses between the exposed and participant groups, we cannot claim that the cause is attributable to race. White veterans as a whole were not negatively disposed, unsympathetic, and hostile to the Vietnamese; only the white participants exhibited this orientation. Thus, it cannot be argued that value systems and attitudinal sets that distinguish whites and blacks are the operative force. An explanation that is consistent with the data is that a racist or dehumanizing orientation to the enemy and civilians emerged among white participants through a process of social conditioning.

Our transcripts suggest there are several factors contributing to this dehumanizing orientation. First, we find that cases of abusive violence generally did not occur as isolated actions by individual soldiers. Rather, they involved the action of combat units or subgroups within the unit. Thus, individuals may have had relatively little room for maneuver in trying to avoid participation in these episodes.

Second, subsequent to their actions, these groups apparently became cognitive minorities, providing mutual support and justification for their acts. This support, however, appears to be most effective for whites. Our data and transcripts indicate that blacks were oriented not only to their unit, but also to the community of blacks in Vietnam. In combat, blacks and whites worked closely together, but at most other times, units and companies polarized into racially separated groups.[20] Indeed, 60% of our sample said race relations were better in combat than in noncombat situations.[21] In the community of black veterans, attitudes sympathetic toward the Vietnamese were pronounced. Black participants were also more likely than their white counterparts to have social relationships with Vietnamese civilians. The contrast between values/attitudes and actions can plausibly be attributed to the two distinct spheres of experience, i.e., the combat unit and the social community of black veterans. The tensions arising from these contradictions are consistent with the high levels of demoralization, guilt, and angry feelings we find among black participants.

The pattern of the onset of stress symptoms adds further support to the above interpretation. The higher rate of symptom development at the time of service among black participants relative to other groups, including white participants, indicates that this group of men was less psychologically insulated from the stressful experiences to which it was exposed. The absence of this insulation, our data suggest, stemmed from the lack of peer support for these men's actions.

The contrast between the exposed and participant whites can be understood in a similar fashion. Exposure to abusive violence primarily occurred in situations that did not involve the individual and his immediate group. Witnesses generally reported actions of the VC/NVA, the ARVN, or other American units, rather than action of their own forces. Since these respondents were not socially invested in the groups committing the acts, there was no immediate social force to bring these acts into the realm of acceptable behavior. The shock of witnessing the inhumanity of which men were capable could be acknowledged because of the social distance between the observers and the actors.

A final feature of the observed pattern should be noted. While the exposed white and black participants look remarkably similar in their responses, it is likely that their reactions have quite different meanings. As individuals, whites exposed to abusive violence were not directly implicated in particular actions. Given the character of their experiences, the high levels of psychological demoralization and guilt they felt probably represent a generalized response to the character of the Vietnam War. The higher absolute scores of black participants on the Demoralization and Guilt Scales suggests that black participants are more likely to be responding to deeply embedded feelings of individual responsibility for personal acts.

In dealing with the characteristics of white participants, it must be kept in mind that we are dealing with a small proportion (9%) of the white Vietnam veteran population. Also, our findings show that white Vietnam veterans who were exposed to abusive violence react quite differently from participants in abusive violence. Racism, in our study, appears in a social context where attitudes condoning abusive violence are prominent. The interpretation of the role of social support in this process is speculative at present, but this interpretation enhances our understanding of how psychological mechanisms rooted in the social environment are implicated in the experience of stress.

Effects of the War on Veterans' Social Behavior

The third major issue we address in this chapter is the extent to which Vietnam veterans or those exposed to war stress exhibit deviant behavior and/or show disruptive marital patterns.[22]

Incidence of Deviant Behavior

In terms of our study, we categorize deviant behavior as alcohol and/or drug abuse and being arrested after leaving the military. Our findings indicate that combat veterans were significantly more likely to have problems with alcohol, while participants in abusive violence more often resorted to the use of marijuana or heroin.

Drinking or drug use

We asked our respondents how many months in the last two years they drank "at least a six-pack of beer, or a bottle of wine, or several drinks of liquor *at least one evening a week*." This was our measure of weekly drinking. We then asked how many months in the last two years they drank that much "almost every day." This was our measure of daily drinking. The major finding from these two measures was that combat veterans on the average drank more heavily than their peers. We found that among combat veterans there was an increase of a fifth of a month of daily drinking for each point on the combat scale. As the mean score for all Vietnam veterans is only 1.8 months for the entire two-year period, the effect of combat on daily drinking is quite strong. For example, the average increase for the high-combat veterans in the number of months they drank daily would be between 2 and 2.6 months of daily drinking, i.e., 3.8 to 4.4 months of daily drinking in the last two years or about one-sixth (17%) of the entire two-year period, compared to one-twelfth (8%) of the time for the entire Vietnam veteran population.

Again, drug use is related to participation in abusive violence but not to combat. Of a broad range of drugs only marijuana and heroin were used significantly more often by the participants. The finding on marijuana use is the more reliable of the two findings. Nearly two-thirds of the participants (65%) compared to a third (34%) of the nonparticipants reported using marijuana since leaving the military. Heroin use was very rare in this population. Only .5% of the nonparticipants reported using it, while 8% of the participants reported its use. However, given the very small number of respondents this finding is not as strong as it appears.

Arrest

The most powerful finding in this area of the study is the relationship between combat and postservice arrest. Twenty-six percent of the heavy-combat veterans and 20% of the moderate-combat veterans were arrested after leaving the military compared to only 6% of the veterans who saw little or no combat. Turning to conviction rates we see that proportionately heavy-combat veterans (17%) were substantially more likely than either moderate-combat (11%) or low-combat (6%) to be convicted of the crimes for which they were arrested. One explanation for the higher rate of convictions among heavy-combat veterans is that they engaged in violent crimes (5%) ten times more often than low-combat groups (.6%) and more than twice as often as moderate-combat veterans (2%). However, it is important to emphasize that the preponderant majority of crimes committed by even the high-combat veterans were for nonviolent offenses (20%).

We also found evidence that participants in abusive violence were more frequently arrested than their peers who did not participate in abusive violence. Participants in abusive violence (27%) were arrested at virtually the same rate as the combat group, while among the veterans who were not exposed to abusive violence only 12% were ever arrested. It is also interesting to note that the participants had by far the highest rate of multiple arrests: 9.4% compared to 4.5% of the witnesses, 2% of the veterans not exposed to abusive violence, and 4.8% of the heavy-combat veterans. Again, it must be remembered that although the differential rates of arrest among participants appears very substantial, the number of men represented in these statistics is quite small. Thus, we present what we consider a noteworthy finding with the caveat that it must, given the size of our sample, be considered tentative.

Finally, it should be noted that among those who witnessed abusive violence we found no evidence that there was a significantly greater tendency toward deviant behavior on any of the dimensions we have discussed.

Disruptive Marital Patterns

The pattern of findings discussed above suggests that a substantial number of war-stressed Vietnam veterans have serious problems coping with their military experience long after they return to civilian life. We next turn to the question of whether these psychological and behavioral problems spill over into relations with spouses or partners. Our findings indicate that, indeed, combat and witnessing of and participation in abusive violence are related to the formation and breakdown of intimate interpersonal relationships.

The general effect of military service can be seen in the need of Vietnam veterans to establish marital ties. Vietnam veterans (84.2%) were significantly more likely to marry than either era veterans (81.5%) or nonveterans (70%).[23] Marital patterns, moreover, are strongly related to the years men served in the military. Our data indicate that there is relatively little difference in marriage or divorce among Vietnam veterans who served in the early years of the war, i.e., prior to 1968. Indeed, the data show significantly lower rates of divorce for that period among Vietnam veterans (19%) than their era veteran (28%) or non-veteran peers (31%). However, among Vietnam veterans who served in the later years of the war (after 1967) we find alarmingly higher rates of divorce and an earlier age of entry into marriage. At the time of the interview, only 19% of the age-matched nonveterans who were eligible for service during the post-1967 period and 26% of the era veterans who served during these years were divorced. The low-combat group (2%) were the least likely to have been divorced, while only 17% of the moderate-combat group were divorced. However, 49% of the high-combat veterans and witnesses to abusive violence who served after 1968 had been divorced. Interestingly, only 19% of the participants in abusive violence from the post-1967 period were divorced. This finding, however, is offset by the very high rate of marital dissatisfaction (56%) expressed by the participants.

A Conceptual Interpretation of War Trauma

In light of our findings on the problems war-stressed veterans encountered on their return home and the long-term effects of the war experience on their psychological and social well-being, we need to delve into the dynamics of coping with the experience of war.[24]

The problem that confronts us is conceptualizing the relationship between war stress and the developmental tasks of the early adult years and then develop-ing a model of how the interaction between war stress and early adult develop-ment influences the rest of the life course. The model of human development proposed is primarily concerned with the process of adaptation to life through the interaction of psychosocial maturation and social history.[25]

We generally send young men (18–24) to fight our wars. Obviously, some portion of the officer corps and a group of the noncommissioned career soldiers who lead armies are older. The brunt of battle, however, is carried by young people who would be busy building their lives were it not for the call to arms. Many of these soldiers deemed old enough to die for their country would be too young to buy a drink in a bar. If they were civilians they would be going to school, probably dependent on their families for financial support, living at home or at the university subject to parental or in-loco parentis regulation of their lives, or starting their occupational careers. Our armies rely on young men only recently adolescents, who in most circumstances would be labelled pre-adults or youth.

The appropriate task for people at this age is to develop a stable identity, complete their education, enter the world of work, and, within the norms of their communities, find spouses, i.e., establish early adult life structures. There is an abundant literature that indicates this process is complex, time consuming, and fraught with peril even under the best of circumstances.[26] To paraphrase Keniston, this period involves the process of establishing a sense of self and a relationship between the self and society.[27]

Even under the right social conditions, this is a confusing, often tumultuous period in the development of the individual. It can also be a period of social as well as personal rebellion.[28] It is a time when young men explore their options and exhibit a sense of immortality, recklessness, and commitment. It is, most of all, a time for experimentation, of slowly crystallizing beliefs and ideologies.

The dominant characteristic of the men we send to war is that they are only partly formed—they are in the process of becoming. The ego-defenses are maturing, ideas about the world are being developed, and social identity is at a formative stage. The young soldier, prior to his entry into war, can be described as a cauldron full of emotions, ideas, and themes waiting to be forged. War is a force that turns the emotional-moral world men grew up in on its head. For example, the archetypical foundation of civil society, the injunction "thou shalt not kill," is waived in war.

Vaillant's work on ego development offers us a productive point of departure for interpreting the consequences of immersion in warfare on the development of the young adult because he so explicitly focuses on the contribution of specific types of ego mechanisms to "healthy" adult functioning. Vaillant elaborates a hierarchy of ego-mechanisms that, he argues, contribute to effective social functioning. He uses labels such as mature, neurotic, and immature to characterize specific ego-mechanisms to emphasize that mental health (self-actualization) is enhanced by developing mature ego-mechanisms, and that the ego styles also contribute to more satisfying social relations and careers.[29]

The moral order of warfare represents a radically altered social order, which requires individuals significantly to restructure their ego-mechanisms. In a wartime scenario, "mature" ego-mechanisms of everyday life for the management of interpersonal relations and intrapsychic stress are likely to prove ineffective. In general the skills necessary for survival in war are largely uncorrelated with those learned in civil society.

A white veteran who served as an officer reflected on the pressures and tensions that work on soldiers in combat and their consequences over time:

> The kind of tactics that the Vietcong and NVA used to kill Americans, maim Americans, with the mines, the pungee sticks, and the booby traps, when men would see their friends injured and killed and maimed, see their arms blown off and their legs blown off, it was the kind of thing that I think worked on their minds and made their killing of the enemy, when they had the chance and the opportunity, much easier and less personal. I think where troops did mutilate the dead or where they shot and killed the enemy soldiers when they didn't have to, when they were defenseless, or when they burned the villages, I don't really feel, knowing the troops—and knowing how they were thinking at the time—that they found anything but gratification in it and no conscience.

The mature defense mechanisms of civil society, suppression, altruism, humor, or sublimation, may not necessarily be as effective in the warfare society. Indeed, a reasonable argument can be made that if preoccupation with survival so characteristic of soldiers is one of the dominant values of men at war, then such neurotic or immature defenses as repression, displacement, dissociation, reaction formation, acting out, and projection may well prove effective, i.e., mature, mechanisms because they enhance the chances of survival.

If survival is the prime concern of the soldier, the solidarity of the unit in which the soldier fights comes a close second because the functioning of the group is instrumental to each of its members.[30] Protection of the group and its solidarity in the environment of war involves aggression and violence against all those who threaten it.

In civil society group protection is also important, but within strictly defined boundaries. In war, although there are supposed to be some boundaries, they are not necessarily observed. Certainly there is ample evidence that, forced to choose between the safety of the unit and civilians' rights or those of POWs, soldiers are prone to protect themselves first; more importantly, their behavior is likely to be supported by their peers and superiors.

Warfare by definition involves projection and displacement of aggressive impulses outward against the "enemy." The dehumanization of the enemy is characteristic of warfare. A marine commented:

> I mean killing a gook was nothing. . . . It didn't bother me at all. Could have butchered them like nothing. I really had no feelings. . . . You got a wounded gook and he is wounded bad and you put him out of his misery. As far as just shooting them, to me it was just like shooting a deer or something like that . . . I really had no feeling about the job.

Release of aggression through what we normally label immature or neurotic defenses is often accompanied by anxiety reduction in the soldier. The connection that appears to develop is that acting out against the "enemy" provides a psychic release from fear. The soldier learns to connect anxiety reduction with acting out and is encouraged to feel this is a "mature" response because the sources of tension can be categorized in terms that make acting out acceptable.

There is also a tendency among soldiers in Vietnam to adopt an attitude that legitimates random violence and impulse release to enhance their stature and exercise power over civilians.

The above examples of how the hierarchy of ego mechanisms of civil society are inverted in the normative order of warfare raise important questions about the transition to civilian life for soldiers. The problems are especially acute for young men in the process of identity formation. If we assume that the process of maturational development proceeds in all societies, then we must ask how identity formation is affected by entry in a society of war during late adolescence and youth. And we must further question how the serial transitions from civil society to war and back to civil society in a period of three to four years are experienced in terms of perception of the self.

In Vietnam, the tour of duty for most soldiers was only twelve months. Thus, the individual barely settled into his violent soldier's identity before he was pulled back out of battle. It is often argued that the limited duration of the war experience makes the subsequent transition easier. An alternative explanation may be more plausible. The rapid transition to civilian life leaves the individual *traumatized* because the moral order into which he entered during the war continues to exert tremendous power over his values.

A veteran poignantly explains the difficulty of reentry into society after being in an environment that breaks the boundaries of civilian society:

I think a rehabilitation program where they teach a person how to live around civilian people again . . . is a good one. Teach them how to be a human being with human rights, even though he probably knows, but, people do forget when their mind is in an uproar. Kind of analyze him to see if he is capable of handling civilian life, instead of just letting him go on his own.

The transition to civilian life is likely in its early stages to lead to generalized anxiety accompanied by intense feelings of confusion. Indeed, our data suggest that the sense of disorientation often described in the early postservice period is likely to result from the feeling that there is a concentrated attack by others on the most strongly valued elements of an identity constructed in the crucible of war. The transition from war to no war involves unlearning a whole host of reactions and patterns of behavior that are essential for survival in war but frightening and disturbing, or perceived as peculiar by civilians.

As two veterans vividly illustrate, the war continued to play a role in their lives after homecoming, leading to bizarre behavior and exaggerated fears about the hostility of the environment.

I would not come out of the house—not unless it was night and I was going to see my fiancee. [How long did this last?] Oh about a couple of months. Then, finally, I went looking for jobs. . . .

[When you came out, what kind of person were you?] Oh, a little shaky. See like the cars come by and they could blow their horn and it would frighten me. . . . You could speak to somebody and they would not speak, like they did not know you. I would get mad. [What was important to you?] I don't even know. [You said that you had psychological problems. What kind of problems?] I got a nervous problem, a communication problem, I cannot explain things.

For a significant proportion of soldiers the homecoming was accompanied by identity diffusion. The problem the soldier faces after the experience of war is to *resocialize himself*, and to cope with the experience in which his self-image must be reworked if he is to survive in civil society.

One veteran emphasized the problem of accepting the norms of society after being in war this way:

> [I was] totally confused in terms of right and wrong. I don't think my ambitions were as strong. And I had a lot of hate feelings which I really can't explain. It was just hate and mistrust.

And another veteran emphasizes the loss of direction and identity diffusion that resulted from his wartime experiences.

> I had no ambition, no outlook on life. I did not care. I did not want to work. I did not want to do anything. . . . Hanging out and doing nothing. Sleeping all day and staying out at night . . . we smoked and we drank. This went on for five years now.

Veterans must also discover or rediscover the capacity for empathy and intimacy, which too often dissipates under the stress of war. Two veteran respondents explained how the war toughened them in a way that made it difficult to respond to the needs of significant others in their environment.

> I was more hardened. Much more hardened. [What do you think was responsible for the change?] Being in a place where you have the constant knowledge that you can be killed at any time, I suppose.

> I was a much more changed person. . . . I had a completely different outlook on life. I had seen how people take advantage of other people and . . . I would say I had a more violent temper. . . . I . . . just couldn't handle things.

Furthermore, as John Wilson points out, the premature encounter with mortality contributes to psychologically accelerated aging, which interferes with the need to build a life structure in early adulthood.[31] The consequences of the traumatic encounter with death and dying are evident in the response of a veteran to a question about what he did when he returned home.

> Bumming around—collected unemployment. Started drinking pretty heavy. . . . [Had you changed?] Oh yes, I just did not care anymore. I thought I was dead you know. For quite a while I could not believe I came back. . . . But then I started to make a go . . . like I had a second life—a second chance—so I said I wanted to do better now.

The Effects of Trauma on Growth

From the preceding discussion we hypothesize that at the stage of life of most soldiers in Vietnam, exposure to war constituted a major interference with the maturational process. The interference may be conceptualized as a trauma that involves the general inversion of the young adult's moral order, the freezing of his social development (interpersonal and career), and the stunting of his emotional development (empathy), all of which occur because they are necessary for fulfilling the soldier's role, and the premature encounter with mortality.

We need to see the effects of war stress on the developmental process in terms of a decisive trauma that requires the development of extraordinary adaptations which are singularly useful in a uniquely limited setting. These limited adaptive styles become profoundly ineffective in "normal" human settings. The transition from warrior to civilian veteran encompasses the psychological problems of reorganizing ego defenses and identity.

The veteran of war faces one problem all veterans encounter—catching up on the early adult tasks of career development. However, there is also the added burden of readaptation to the civil society and the incorporation of the war experience into an integrated identity morally connnecting the early stages of development to the "warrior" and postwar self. The problem can be seen as the difficulty in answering the question "who am I?" after learning more than one wants to about "what am I capable of?" To put the issue somewhat differently, the image of the self the adolescent grew into is irrevocably shattered by the experience of war. The problem is to find a postwar self-image that can tolerate the capacities of the self learned in war.

The developmental transition described requires an extended moratorium after leaving the military. There is, as described below by a veteran, a need to be alone.

> [I] kept pretty much to myself. Unless there was another guy that was there, then you could always talk about it. I was reluctant to get involved, I guess.

The ability to cope with the life course tasks of early adulthood for veterans exposed to war stress depends, then, on the capacity to undertake a major reorganization of adaptive ego-mechanisms. The process of adaptation to the second pre-adult stage for Vietnam veterans becomes a life-long factor in their development. In projecting the effects of war stress through the life course, we need to account for the direct effects of war experience on mental health, quality of life, and physical well-being; but there is also the indirect effect through the life course structure built out of and during the period of adaptation to civilian life. We should expect to find that decisions about school, job, marriage, and children made during the period of adaptation will reflect tensions and unresolved conflicts associated with war stress.

As this veteran shows, the war could also profoundly change the direction of men's lives:

> I was psychologically wounded, not mentally disturbed to any great degree, at least I did not realize the degree that I had. [You had given up on the plans to become a surgeon?] To go into medicine, yes . . . it takes many years before you can get yourself in a position to go back to school, I just could not adjust to the lies and deceptions in school, so I just put it aside.

The basis for subsequent disruptive expressions of war stress are thus laid down during the period of adaptation and early adult life course development. To the extent that important components of war trauma are repressed, unresolved, or ignored they become key candidates for later eruptions. Unfortunately, late-appearing symptoms or deviant behavior may not be intuitively identified as war-related. Thus, identifying the etiology of later adult crises among war veterans involves a complicated analysis of the effects of war stress on the different stages of the life cycle.

Conclusion

The Vietnam War continues to shape the direction of the lives of its veterans. The Vietnam veterans most adversely affected by the war are those who experienced high levels of war stress. Readjustment and marital problems weigh most heavily on those who served after Tet (post-1967). Psychiatric symptoms provide evidence that blacks who participated in and whites who witnessed abusive violence report more symptomatology. However, the general findings on the denial dimension of PTSD and the higher drug use and arrest rates among participants generally indicate that the white participants do not emerge unscathed from their war experiences. Our data also show a persistent mistrust of governmental institutions among veterans, with veterans who witnessed abusive violence seemingly less trusting of these institutions than other veterans.

The persistence of social and psychological problems among Vietnam veterans should not, however, overshadow two basic points. First, the problems in this population are not strongly intertwined. Thus, it appears that there is not a large group of Vietnam veterans that is severely disturbed and unable to carry on the tasks of adulthood. Second, although war experiences have disrupted the lives of these men and continue to do so, a majority of Vietnam veterans are able to deal with their war experiences. Indeed, many of these men cope ably with their wartime past. In highlighting the continuing disruptive effects of the Vietnam War for its veterans, it is important to keep in mind that the majority have gone on to productive lives in spite or even because of their encounter with the stress of war.

PART TWO

VIEWS OF THE WAR

CHAPTER THREE

ATTITUDES TOWARD
THE WAR

This chapter presents a short discussion of some of the conflicting factual claims, legal arguments, and opposed conclusions dominating the analysis of the nature of the Vietnam War as well as the question of American involvement in the conflict. Against this background, it then presents in detail the views of the Vietnam Generation regarding the war.

The Nature of the War

The character of the struggle for control of South Vietnam has been the subject of prolonged debate, directed toward the ultimate question of whether or not U.S. military involvement there was lawful. Various major positions have been taken by those who have written about the nature of the conflict, showing the wide disagreement on matters of both fact and law pertaining to the Vietnam War. A wide range of opposed conclusions on the principal issues have been reached, and there is much that may always remain disputable with regard to a political and legal appraisal of the United States' involvement in the war.[1] Since many of the conflicting arguments are presented in these pages by members of the Vietnam Generation, it seems useful to clarify the points that are in dispute.

1. Disagreements regarding questions of fact. For example, what is the actual date of the beginning of American involvement in Vietnam? What is the origin of the National Liberation Front? Was the Vietcong rooted in the South or was its formation instigated and controlled by North Vietnam? At what period of time and in what numbers did North Vietnam begin sending regular North Vietnamese troops into the South?

2. Disagreements regarding specific legal issues. Was South Vietnam "a state"? Was the war in Vietnam "a civil war"? At what point, if ever, would it have been justified to regard the involvement of North Vietnam in the conflict as "an armed attack"? Which forms of military intervention in foreign societies are legally permissible and which are not?

The Vietnam War was a special type of international war. The outcome of the conflict depended not only upon the will of the internal participants but upon the major role played by actors outside the territory involved. As the Civil War Panel of the American Society of International Law has observed, many of the disagreements surrounding the conflict are caused by the complex character of the Vietnam War:

> . . . in which it is difficult to identify clearly the timing and significance of external involvement and, consequently, in which it is impossible to gain broad agreement as to the relative weighting of internal and external factors in considering the causal sequence leading to the armed struggle for control of the society.[2]

Arguments of the Prowar Faction

Many of those supporting U.S. involvement in the war insisted that American intervention was an attempt to enforce the principles of the United Nations Charter in Asia. The argument was as follows: North Vietnam had attacked South Vietnam in violation of Article 2 of the Charter and the United States had every right to join South Vietnam in "collective defense" under Article 51 of the Charter. The United States had also undertaken commitments to assist South Vietnam in defending itself against Communist aggression from the North; thus the introduction of United States military personnel and equipment was justified. This assistance had been promised at the end of the Geneva Conference in 1954 along with additional later assurances to the government of South Vietnam. In addition, the argument continued, the United States had undertaken an international obligation to defend South Vietnam in the Southeast Asia Collective Defense Treaty, signed on September 8, 1954. A separate protocol to that treaty made its provisions applicable to Cambodia, Laos, and "the free territory under the jurisdiction of the state of Vietnam." Since North Vietnam violated the Geneva Accords of 1954 from the beginning, South Vietnam was justified in refusing to implement the election provisions of the accords and in establishing a separate state.[3] While he was secretary of state, Dean Rusk described the organization of a durable peace as "the great central question of our day" and declared that checking Communist aggression in Southeast Asia was essential to that aim.

These supporters accepted the U.S. contention that the Geneva Accords of 1954 established a demarcation line between North Vietnam and South Vietnam. The accords, they argued, provided for withdrawals of military forces into the respective zones north and south of this line and prohibited the use of either zone for the resumption of hostilities or to "further an aggressive policy." They further contended that, during the five years following the Geneva Conference, the Hanoi regime developed a covert political-military organization in South Vietnam based around Communist cadres it had ordered to stay in the South. During the period from 1959 to 1965, their argument continued, North Vietnam had also moved thousands of armed and unarmed guerrillas into South Vietnam. Beginning in 1964, the Communists had exhausted their reservoir of southerners who had gone North. Since then the greater number of men infiltrated into the South were native-born North Vietnamese. By 1966, many regiments of regular North Vietnamese forces were fighting in the South. The war's supporters contend that the "external" aggression from the North was the critical military element and constituted an armed attack.

But among the many Americans who were opposed to U.S. policy in Vietnam, the United Nations Charter was also frequently cited. The American government, they contended, had engaged in an illegal war in Vietnam in violation of international law and morality.[4] They argued further that both South Vietnam and the United States had violated the Geneva Declaration of 1954 by hostile acts against the North, unlawful rearmament, and refusal to carry out the 1956 national election provided for in the declaration. In addition, the United States, in their view, had violated the United Nations Charter by its military intervention in the civil war.

Arguments of the Antiwar Faction

Those who opposed the war made the following points:[5]

South Vietnam was never a separate state

A separate state or nation of "South Vietnam" had never existed. A convention signed in 1946 between the French commissioner and President Ho Chi Minh recognized the Vietnam Republic as a free state. Mutual hostility between the French and the Viet Minh resulted in the prolonged French-Indochina War (1946–1954). This war of independence generated heavy French casualties and about one million deaths among the Viet Minh. Peace was finally negotiated, and on July 21, 1954, the Geneva Conference ended with the adoption of a "Final Declaration," which reconfirmed the independence of a single, united Vietnam. An agreement was reached for the temporary division of Vietnam into two zones for a two-year period.

A few days before the conference ended, France, in cooperation with the United States, installed Ngo Dinh Diem as premier of the "State of Vietnam," that is, the Saigon regime that had been established by France with Bao Dai as president in 1949. The French gradually pulled back their troops from Vietnam, and the United States took over their functions, supporting the Diem regime and that president's successors. The reunification of the two zones of North and South Vietnam, which was promised for July 1956, did not materialize. Instead, the United States maintained the Saigon regime, despite increasing disaffection and insurgency in South Vietnam. From the beginning, the main purpose of the United States was to make the temporary division permanent and create a separate "country" of South Vietnam.

South Vietnam was not subjected to armed attack by North Vietnam

Many opponents of the war argued that the American intervention was not justified by the right of collective self-defense. The Charter of the United Nations permits collective self-defense only in case of an armed attack, and no such armed attack existed in the case of Vietnam. A military build-up by the United States in South Vietnam started almost immediately after agreement was reached at Geneva in 1954 and provoked the infiltration of Vietnamese into South Vietnam over the eleven-year period between 1954 and 1965. From the antiwar critics' perspective, a civil war was going on in Vietnam, and the only proper course for states that were not themselves placed in the necessity of self-defense was to abstain from intervention.

The United States was engaged in a struggle for power

Opponents of American intervention felt strongly that the United States pursued its military course in Vietnam because it was determined to defeat a Communist-led insurgency that had sprung up years before in South Vietnam as a consequence of many domestic and international factors, only one of which was encouragement and support by North Vietnam. Most Vietnamese were concerned with obtaining their nationhood unencumbered by foreign domination. The United States was perceived to be fighting on behalf of a native regime dominated by a reactionary military elite which practiced the politics of military dictatorship.

The anti-interventionists believed that Communist leadership under Ho Chi Minh had for several decades represented almost all of the forces of anticolonialism and nationalism in Vietnam. Unaided, the reactionary forces, they contested, would have had no prospect of resisting a popularly based nationalist movement. According to many opponents of the war, the Communist victory and subsequent reunification of Vietnam have merely confirmed the process of self-determination internal to Vietnam that evolved from the early efforts against the French.

Aftermath of the War

After the Paris Peace Accords were signed in January 1973, the war went on for another two years until Saigon's collapse in April 1975. The Vietnam War was such a traumatic and divisive experience that once the last American combat forces were withdrawn from Vietnam many Americans tried to forget the conflict. But it soon became clear that this was not an easy task. Most Americans agreed that the war in Vietnam was markedly different from any other experienced by the American nation. It was the first war rejected during its fighting by a substantial part of the American people, and, in retrospect, many Americans continue to have serious doubts about the wisdom of having entered that conflict. Independent survey studies carried out in the postwar period show that several years after the end of the war, a majority of the American public agreed that we should have stayed out of the fighting in Vietnam. In addition, respondents perceived the war's lasting effects on the United States as almost entirely harmful.[6]

Today, over a decade after the war's end, scholars, journalists, and military specialists are starting to look afresh at the conflict. The many important unresolved questions that they are trying to answer include: How did we get involved in Vietnam? Why did we lose the war? What are the lessons of the war?

It is now commonplace to look back on the Vietnam War and examine how it divided generations and affected the face of the American political landscape. It has once again become credible to argue that we could have won the war or were on the verge of winning it when we gave up the fight. Yet much of the debate that continues and undoubtedly will rage on for decades prefers to ignore how the generation that fought the war on several fronts perceived it, and how that perception influenced the political consciousness of America. In the final analysis, it was the voices of soldiers, activists, and the politically disenchanted that created an environment that influenced decision making and public opinion. To understand the war fully, we need to see it through the eyes of the generation that lived the war at the ''front(s).''

Variables Affecting Pro- and Antiwar Stances

In the following pages we examine the factors that affected whether or not a member of the Vietnam Generation opposed the war, introducing several variables, including military status, race, the time period during which men served or were eligible to serve, branch of service, and the level of involvement in the antiwar movement. We then focus on the issue of abusive violence and its effects on views of the war.

Our findings on attitudes toward U.S. involvement at the time of the war suggest that there were significant intragenerational differences surrounding the value of the American involvement in Vietnam. A more profound finding is that among those who took a position on the war, opposition was more characteristic than support for U.S. involvement. As table 3.1 shows, support for and opposition to U.S. involvement in Vietnam among the Vietnam Generation were, not suprisingly, affected by whether or not one was in the military. Vietnam veterans

(46%) and era veterans (32%) were significantly more likely to report support for the war than nonveterans (19%). Vietnam veterans were also least likely to express opposition to the intervention (45%) compared to nonveterans (67%) and Vietnam era veterans (49%). Although the differences among levels of support and opposition within the generation are substantial, it is worth emphasizing that even among Vietnam veterans fewer than half voiced support for the war.

A second important factor that had an impact on level of support within the generation was race. There is an extraordinarily low level of support expressed by blacks for the war, as evidenced in table 3.2. Blacks were five times more likely to oppose the war than to support it (73% vs. 13%). Thus, while only 29% of the whites supported the war compared to 57% who opposed it, whites were significantly less likely to oppose the war than blacks.

Third, we see in table 3.3 that the time period during which men served in the military or were most likely to be threatened by the draft also affected attitudes toward the war. Among respondents who served or were eligible for service in the years after the Tet offensive (post-1967), support for the war is markedly lower, 20% compared to 34%, and there is a corresponding increase in opposition to the war, 64% vs. 55%. Although our sample indicates more opposition to the war in this age group than was characteristic of the general population, the trend toward increasing opposition is consistent with the public opinion polls that showed increasing opposition by the American public after the Tet offensive. The change in attitude toward the war among Vietnam veterans highlights the general shift in feelings about the war. A majority of the Vietnam veterans (55%) who served in the early years of the war supported the war effort; only 36% opposed it. As table 3.4 shows, in the later years of the war there was a complete reversal in the levels of support (36%) and opposition (54%) to the Vietnam War in this population.

A veteran's view of the war was also affected by the branch in which he served. Marines, for example, were much more supportive of U.S. military involvement than men who served in other branches of the military. Indeed, as seen in table 3.5, marines are the only group of Vietnam veterans where support for American military involvement reached two-thirds of the population, while only about 43% of veterans of the other services reported that they backed U.S. participation. Moreover, in both army (49%) and navy/air force (44%) a plurality opposed the war, while only 23% of marines expressed opposition to the Vietnam War. Thus, we can see that the Vietnam veteran population was far from homogenous in its appraisal of the American war effort. Interestingly, we find no significant relationship between degree of exposure to combat and attitude toward the war.

The heart of the antiwar movement lay among the nonveterans of this generation, especially on college campuses. As table 3.6 shows, opposition to the Vietnam War varied substantially between those who were heavily engaged in antiwar activities and those with little antiwar involvement (93% vs. 60%).

Abusive Violence and Perceptions of the War

Attitudes in the United States toward the war reflected more than political-strategic differences. The guerrilla nature of the fighting raised questions about the conduct of the hostilities. Therefore, when we began our study we considered it vital to find the significance of the Justice in War question in the political perception of the war. To this end, we carefully investigated a range of Justice in War issues, which will be discussed in subsequent chapters. In this chapter we open up only the question of whether the conduct of the war affected personal and political postures vis-a-vis U.S. involvement in Vietnam. In our analysis of the effects of the Vietnam War on the lives of Vietnam veterans we discovered that exposure to what we call abusive violence plays a vital role in determining the postwar adjustment of Vietnam veterans. In light of our findings we now examine the impact of abusive violence on views of the war within the generation.

The findings presented in tables 3.7 and 3.8 show that a majority of respondents reported that awareness of abusive violence affected their general view of the war. Vietnam veterans' perceptions of the conflict are only slightly less affected by the "dirty" side of war than era veterans and nonveterans.

The most interesting finding in this respect is that whites are significantly more likely than blacks (65% vs. 40%) to report that their view of the war is affected by an awareness of abusive violence. This finding appears to be a function of the fact that black support for the war was very low, hence an awareness of the "dirty" side of war did not noticeably alter their views.

As table 3.9 indicates, the most important factor affecting personal responses to abusive violence among Vietnam veterans was direct exposure to this type of action. Among Vietnam veterans who witnessed abusive violence, 67% reported that their personal views of the war were influenced by their exposure, while 83% of participants in violently abusive acts reported that their views were affected by the events. Among veterans who did not see this aspect of the war in Vietnam, only 47% said their personal view of the war was influenced by this issue. Many veterans undoubtedly heard of incidents of abusive violence. Our findings argue that indirect exposure to the abuses accompanying the war had relatively little influence on perceptions of the war.

The relationship between awareness of abusive violence and political opposition to the war demonstrates how important this issue was for the Vietnam Generation. Indeed, awareness of the "dirty" side of war substantially contributed to increasing opposition to the Vietnam War, with over 40% of Vietnam veterans, Vietnam era veterans, and nonveterans reporting that such violence contributed to their antiwar stance. In table 3.11 we see that awareness of the "dirty" side of war again contributed significantly more to white than to black opposition to American involvement in Vietnam (46% vs. 22%). Our interpretation of these findings is that there was a greater reservoir of potential support for the war among whites in the generation. Thus, the process that led whites to oppose the war was significantly affected by their awareness of the "dirty" side of the Vietnam War, because evidence of abusive violence was more disturbing to their image of the United States.

Although there are relatively few differences among main subgroups in the generation over their response to abusive violence, there are important differences elsewhere, notably among Vietnam veterans as a result of their differential exposure to the stress of war, and between nonveterans based on their involvement in the antiwar movement.

The most powerful impact of abusive violence, as table 3.12 demonstrates, is on those Vietnam veterans who personally witnessed this facet of the war. Of those who directly witnessed abusive violence, 57% turned against the war as compared to 32% of those who did not, and 44% of the participants in abusive violence. Comparing the finding on whether or not abusive violence affected veterans' personal views of the war or led them to turn against the war demonstrates that witnessing abusive violence was substantially more important than participation in affecting opposition to the war among Vietnam veterans. Only slightly more than half of the participants who say they were affected by abusive violence turned against the war. However, 85% of the witnesses whose personal view of the war was influenced by abusive violence report that the experience led them to turn against the war.

Combat experience, however, had no systematic effect on the likelihood of soldiers turning against the war. Our data suggest that exposure to violence and life-threatening situations per se does not lead to higher rates of rejection of the war; but direct exposure to abusive violence against other human beings turned substantial numbers of American soldiers against the war.

As tables 3.10 and 3.13 show, however, among nonveterans participation in antiwar activism does substantially influence the extent to which personal views and opposition to the war were affected by abusive violence. Low activists (54%) are significantly less apt to have their views of the war influenced by the question of abusive violence than moderate (82%) or high activists (85%). The difference between activists and their less active peers is clearer when we examine whether or not abusive violence contributed to opposing the war. Only a third of low activists turned against the war because of their awareness of abusive violence compared to nearly two-thirds of the moderate activists (64%) and 56% of the high activists. The small difference between moderate and high activists who say awareness of abusive violence contributed to their turning against the war suggests again that the effects of abusive violence were greater for those who were less rather than more actively opposed to the war.

If abusive violence played an important role in increasing opposition to U.S. involvement in Vietnam it was far from the only issue that diminished American enthusiasm for the war. The question that our statistical findings raise is why there was generally so little support for the war. Our narrative material helps us understand the logic behind the statistics in the preceding pages. The transcripts also show ways in which the Vietnam veterans' views about the war are different from those of Vietnam era veterans and nonveterans. The following sections detail the similarities and differences in attitudes toward the war among Vietnam veterans and their peers.

Vietnam Veterans' Views of the War

Support for American Involvement in the War

Among the supporters of U.S. intervention in Vietnam, only a minority presented a nonideological collective security argument. These respondents noted that in response to a request from the government of South Vietnam, the United States had assisted that country in defending itself against an armed attack from North Vietnam. Thus, the United States was engaged in collective self-defense consistent with its international obligations. This attitude is demonstrated by the following remarks made by a white marine:

> We were fulfilling our international obligations. . . . The North Vietnamese were the aggressors against South Vietnam, a separate country. And seeing them as aggressors I just felt generally negative about their presence and their actions in South Vietnam.

Another small group of supporters felt that vital American economic, political, and strategic interests justified U.S. involvement in the war. A Chicano who supported the war observed:

> We were in Vietnam because our leaders felt that South Vietnam had the potential to be the largest rice-producing country in the world. By controlling Vietnam, we would have a political leverage over China by controlling her food supply. Others wanted the country as a military base. And, of course, Vietnam is very rich in natural resources, not excluding oil.

But most supporters of American policy in Vietnam spoke as defenders of what they perceived to be a "right order of humanity" and a "free world" against the onslaught of Communism. Even if there had been no North Vietnamese aggression, they argued, it was legitimate for the United States to destroy an indigenous Communist revolutionary threat within a country. Their view centered upon the belief that all forms of Communism are evil and it is always adverse to U.S. interests to allow a society to become Communist. This image justified the destruction of the enemy, the Communist forces, and vindicated the death and suffering inflicted upon Vietnam. A white sergeant in the marines expressed this ideological view as follows:

I felt the United States was doing good and necessary things in Vietnam . . . to check the spread of Communism. . . . The Vietcong were nothing but animals. Their entire political ideology reflected brutality and contempt for freedom. They would kill anybody who got in their way or opposed their way of thinking. What we were doing for the people of Vietnam was bringing them out of their old ice age into the modern world and into democracy.

Many supporters believed in the domino principle, which maintained that the fall of South Vietnam would only be the beginning of a Communist conquest of all Southeast Asia. A white marine captain expressed this view as follows:

I guess I subscribed to the domino theory at that time in that we were trying to protect our allies, not so much in Vietnam but if Vietnam fell then maybe Laos and Cambodia and maybe Thailand.

Supporters also expressed their fear that if Communism was not stopped in Vietnam it would soon be on their "back doorstep." A white sergeant in the airborne infantry observed:

Well, I wanted to fight there. Hell you have to stop Communism somewhere. It was like a disease, a malignant disease, Communism. I do not want my son to grow up and somebody tell him do this and do that. I felt we were really doing something over there. People could be free and we would stop Communism.

Among the group of Vietnam veterans who felt positively about American involvement in the war, many felt that the war should have been escalated, to ensure quick destruction of the enemy. As one respondent said, "If you are going to fight a war, let the aircraft go in there (North Vietnam) and wipe everything to the ground and then put your own infantry in." A "limited police action" controlled by "the politicians" was doomed to fail. Officers in particular seemed convinced that the United States lost the war through a failure of political will, rather than a failure of arms.

A white air force officer expressed this feeling as follows:

I believe that 90% of the problems were due to the politicians being involved and their wishy-washy attitudes and they could not make a decision. . . . I believe that in a matter of a year or two years if we had been allowed to use military tactics we could have ended it at considerable savings in lives and dollars.

The same sentiment is expressed by a white marine officer:

I feel that we were let down. I do not think the military really could be responsible because they had to listen to the Congress and the president as to what to do. With no intention of winning the war by conventional methods, the whole war became a very sick operation. I do not think we should ever fight a static war. If we are going to commit our bodies to a war then we better be ready to win.

And a white army lieutenant voiced his frustrations as follows:

I believed that we were there because we were asked to be there and that a commitment took place between government heads. Unfortunately we were not really there to win the war. . . . The ridiculous thing was that the generals were sent out to fight a war and then they were told how to fight it by political people back home who had no knowledge of the situation. So the generals were exceedingly frustrated and that frustration got passed all the way down. As a result we ended up pulling out with our tail between our legs.

Another group of prowar veterans did not blame the politicians for America's defeat. Instead, they argued that the military command structure was inefficient and the strategies used ineffective, resulting in many mistakes and eventual defeat. According to this view, the army lacked a strategy and concentrated on fighting an antiguerrilla war in the South while North Vietnam was the real battlefield. Most of the criticism of this group is directed at the generals, the chiefs of staff, the "upper brass," the commanders. A white captain in the marines pointed out:

I just couldn't see some of these shots that some of the generals and, of course, the chiefs of staff were calling. I mean, if we were over there to win that war, we could have won it. . . . We could have wiped that country (North Vietnam) off the map . . . it was a big game is what it was. You know, let's play the game, put a little more guys in, and we'll never put quite enough in to win, we'll just put enough in to screw things up for a while. And that was my whole impression.

Another white marine officer felt equally resentful toward the military authority in Vietnam:

The biggest resentment I had for military authority was its failure to take the offensive into North Vietnam with intentions of ending the war. I felt that the only place where the war could be ended or decided would be in the major cities in North Vietnam rather than in the defensive position in South Vietnam. Because we were in such bad positions we had problems.

Because of their ideological commitment to fight Communism, many supporters expressed regret that the United States had pulled out of the war. A white army captain noted:

I was all for it . . . all for the involvement. . . . I felt that what we were doing was right and I still feel that we should have finished our commitment considering the investment. . . . There were some wasted lives but I saw nothing really wrong with what we were doing. Christ—that's what the army is for.

These supporters also often pointed out that the outcome of the war proves the justice of the American involvement. They argued that current socio-economic and political conditions in Vietnam are extremely poor and that the civilians were better off when American troops were there. A white air force lieutenant presented this argument as follows:

Right now [1979] I react to the great numbers of Vietnamese who are leaving the country. Apparently because they do not find the living conditions suitable. Whereas when the United States forces were there, there was no mass exodus of the people in spite of the fact that there was a war. Why didn't they leave in 1968? . . . My conclusion is that they found it then an environment that they could exist in and prosper in, but they don't now.

A minority of supporters never developed an insight into the meaning of the war and supported American involvement because of a "flag and country patriotism." A white marine explained this attitude as follows:

I joined the Marine Corps, they were the toughest. . . . The Vietnam War had started and I wanted to be part of it . . . to fight for my country . . . to do a job. . . . I did not question the reasons for our involvement.

And a black air force sergeant argued:

I'm for whatever Congress is for . . . whatever our leaders say—I'm a follower. If they said we had a purpose over there, we had a purpose over there.

Confused or Conflicted Response Patterns

About 10% of our respondents found it difficult to take a clear stand for or against the war. Some veterans faced a conflict within themselves: while basically in support of the war they were upset by some of its consequences. They wanted to go to Vietnam and felt patriotic in so doing, but after they arrived there they became aware of what the war meant to the civilian population. As a result, they developed confused or conflicted feelings about the war. A white veteran who enlisted in the air force had the following to say:

[What concerned you most about the war?] The local poverty standards, and the people—how poorly off they were—and the kids, especially the kids. A lot of them were orphans and they were on their own. I was glad to be there, with the people. But I wasn't glad to be there because people were getting killed. That was a conflict. I think we should have been there, probably, overall. Were we really there to free the people? Were we there to save name, or whatever? I still have a problem. I still find myself justifying why we were there, defending the country, without really a good argument.

These veterans often admit that they did not understand the war. One of the biggest problems they faced in Vietnam was that they did not know why American troops were fighting there. They were told that it was to stop the insurgent Communist forces, but the Vietnamese people did not seem to welcome the American presence. In addition, they heard of demonstrations at home, like the Kent State University protest, and this gave them mixed feelings. Moreover, we were not winning the war and this increased their sense of bewilderment. As one white veteran who served in the army infantry put it:

I went into the infantry . . . to prove that I was a good citizen, a patriot. . . . In Nam, when I arrived, I thought that we were fighting for a good cause. Then later on, I got the impression that the people did not want us there. Before Vietnam I was very naive. After I was there, I did not understand the reason for all these deaths and killings.

And a white veteran who was in the air force reported:

During the war I was confused, hearing so much propaganda from one side or the other, not knowing for certain what was going on. I do not like the way the war ended. Why should a country send so many of their men and women over there where a large percentage of them were wounded, many mentally and physically, and killed and then turn around and say, hey we are done. To me everyone who was wounded, maimed, or killed over there was lost for nothing.

Opposition to American Involvement in the War

As noted earlier, although Vietnam veterans are more likely than their peers to have backed the war, supporters were not in the majority. In essence, this means that while they were in Vietnam, a plurality of veterans were participating in a war they clearly opposed or to which they had a variety of confused responses that amounted to less than full support for the American involvement. Upon return home, opposition to the American role in the war often intensified. At the time of our interviews, a majority of Vietnam veterans agreed that we should have stayed out of the conflict.[7]

The narrative material indicates that a plurality of Vietnam veterans supported the war during their military training and upon arrival in Vietnam. Only a small group of veterans arived in Vietnam with an antiwar attitude. This negative attitude is especially prominent among those who were drafted during the later phases of the war. A white army engineer who was in Vietnam before the Tet offensive explained:

> During the earlier part of the war the predominant attitude among the GIs in Vietnam was—"hey, what is everybody doing in the United States. Here we are fighting a war and you have all these hippies that are against us. I don't understand. Why don't people appreciate us?" It was later on, in 1968 and 1969, that the attitude among the GIs fighting shifted and coincided with the American people. Then they were opposed to the war.

A plurality of veterans favored the American involvement at first, but after being in Vietnam for a certain length of time, they changed their view. This turnabout is clearly expressed by a white veteran who served in the navy:

> [At home] we never had much of an antiwar movement because it is a small community. I actually thought the war was right when I joined. You know, I was sort of brainwashed that it would be an honor to go fight for the country. . . . My mind changed after that, in Vietnam. I found out that we were not fighting for our country. We were fighting in a civil war in another country. . . . We were the aggressors.

A substantial number of veterans explained that they increasingly turned against the war because they identified with the antiwar movement at home. For some, this identification began in Vietnam and intensified after homecoming. A white army infantryman talked about his feelings about the war as follows:

> I think most of my feelings came after I left Vietnam. Most of the guys who were stationed where I was (back in the States) were Vietnam veterans. . . . One of the main functions of the unit . . . was riot control . . . for the immediate area since we were near Washington, D.C. One time we did go into Washington, D.C . . . it was during one of these demonstrations when they marched against the war and they had us in the Commerce Building in full gear and guns and ready to go out there, you know. And that . . . was the only function . . . I didn't want to be a part of because I felt that the people wanted a demonstration. I didn't think the war was right anyway so I wanted it to end just as soon as anybody else. And as far as doing that, every guy that was there really didn't want to be there. I don't think I could have fired my weapon in that case . . . even if people are throwing rocks or something, I don't think I could have.

Some Vietnam veterans argued that they did not really understand that the war was "senseless" until after they got out of Vietnam. Upon his return to the States, a white air force captain explained that he felt that he had been "conned" and that he decided not "to make the service a career."

And a white veteran who served in the army reported why he turned against the war after homecoming:

> Going to Vietnam was something adventurous. I had never been in a foreign country before. I never thought about the meaning of the war as long as I was there. I was simply doing my job. It did not really sink in until maybe six months to a year after I left Nam. I sat home a lot and watched the T.V. programs. It is only then that I started thinking and realized what the war was all about. It is kind of hard to explain why we were even there.

Major factors inducing antiwar feeling

Using the narrative material, we were able to examine the attitudes and experiences that affected the likelihood of veterans' turning against the war. These include the following main themes:

> *The political character of the war.* According to one group of critics, the Vietnam War was a civil war, being waged in a complex postcolonial setting. The United States was engaged in an ideological struggle for power against revolutionary nationalism. This constituted aggression, and the only proper course for the United States was to abstain from military intervention in a civil war abroad. This criticism of the nature and goals of the American involvement in the war is expressed most often by those veterans who identified with the antiwar movement as well as by many black veterans. A black veteran who served in the army infantry noted:

> The people of North and South Vietnam wanted to unite their country. Why should somebody tell them that they can't? . . . We had no business being there because it was a civil war.

Another black army infantry veteran observed:

> I thought of it as similar to when the United States had its fight between the states, the North and the South. Nobody outside got involved in that war and the United States should not have let itself get involved in a North and South civil war. Let them work it out between themselves.

Many veterans changed their view of the war while being in Vietnam because they increasingly viewed the South Vietnamese government as an undemocratic and dictatorial body, undeserving of United States support. A white veteran who was in the army infantry expressed his disillusionment as follows:

> Before I went I was under the illusion that the South Vietnamese government
> and the South Vietnamese people wanted us there, that they did not want to
> become Communist. After I was there I saw the way the people reacted to us.
> We had no support from them. I began to feel that the South Vietnamese
> government was corrupt. I saw no need in our being there.

Often this critical attitude toward the South Vietnamese government was
combined with a growing understanding of the cause that the Vietcong was
fighting for and a deeper sympathy for the Vietnamese people. A black marine
who had enlisted because he supported the war and who had received advanced
training in counter-guerrilla warfare explained why he became critical of American involvement:

> When I first began to hear about Vietnam, I thought: "The United States is right
> . . . they've always been right, so they're right this time." . . . But then you
> get over there and you see some of the stuff that's happening and you figure
> these people—they're fighting for a cause . . . they really believe in this. So
> what the hell are we doing over here?

Another group of critics stressed their conviction that no vital American
political or strategic interests were involved in the Vietnam War. Since the
conflict did not seem to present any real threat to the United States, they argued,
the cost of participation in the war was much too high for the country. Indeed,
they often concluded, United States involvement in Vietnam could be construed
as a form of imperialism. A black veteran who was drafted out of college and
served in the army airborne was already against the war when he arrived in
Vietnam. He expressed his feelings as follows:

> I was completely against it . . . because it was wrong. . . . We invaded this little
> country and we just didn't have any business at all sending the army and the air
> force in there to bomb the hell out of them. It just seemed like a classic example
> of bullying, you know . . . for ideological reasons . . . and it seemed like so
> many people were dying because of ideological bullshit.

And a black veteran who served in the army infantry explained why he
opposed the war:

> I felt that the United States was trying to take over this country—to rule it . . .
> make them their possession, like their slaves. . . . The Vietnamese, you know,
> are nothing like American people. They are living in huts and they are out in the
> rice paddies. . . . They are working all day long, eating very poorly, sometimes

they do not eat at all. And then all of a sudden they come up against somebody outside of their world: the American government telling them "You cannot do what you are accustomed to do."

Many critics also felt that private economic interests were benefiting from the war. They pointed out that the war economy provided people in various companies with jobs "because as long as you can blow things up and have things remade money flows." That was one of the main reasons the war lasted as long as it did. As one respondent noted: "While we were being killed, Shell Oil Company was happily drilling right off the coast." A white army cannoneer had the following to say:

> Somebody was getting rich on it . . . Boeing, McDonnell/Douglas, Chrysler, Colt, and any of the big-powered companies. Whoever made the fatigues, whoever made the boots. Braniff Airlines because they were the only airline that took us home. You know there was a ton of money being made.

The nature of the war experience. While for some, opposition to the war was primarily shaped by political arguments, others stressed the war experience itself as the main reason they turned against American involvement in the conflict. The suffering of the American troops and the maiming and dying of so many young men had a particularly powerful impact on the attitudes of veterans. This response is especially important among veterans who were exposed to heavy-combat situations, in which a significant number of Americans were killed or wounded. They noted that at first they were "just following orders," but then they "started to wise up to a lot of things" and decided that we did not belong in Vietnam because "men were being killed needlessly" and "this terrible war was draining America of some of its best manpower." A white marine expressed this feeling as follows:

> Thirty years ago the Japanese bombed Pearl Harbor. We had to fight. But this time nobody bombed the United States. We didn't have to go to Vietnam to fight but we ended up there anyway. Americans died for something that we knew we were going to lose. . . . Look at all the people that got killed. . . . If they weren't killed possibly together they would have produced technological advances which would have far outborn the profits of the war.

A black marine saw it this way:

> I felt horrified about it . . . I felt that it was rotten. I was a full-grown man and it made me cry. . . . Seeing fellow Americans—white and black—no matter what color they were—just seeing them dying. I hated the war.

And a white paratrooper noted:

> We got hit, the mortars were coming in, machine gun fire everywhere. My buddy was a squad leader and two of his men got hit. He went to pull them out and he brought the first one back to safety. He went after the second one and a mortar round came in and got him. He died four hours later. He was close to me. It all seemed so pointless, all of this dying. I thought more and more about the war and I turned against it. I turned against the government and the military. I really wanted to rebel.

Another common theme in the transcripts of Vietnam veterans, especially those who witnessed acts of abusive violence, is a growing opposition to the war because of the military strategies used by the combatants against Vietnamese civilians. This group of veterans watched the escalation of the war with increasing anxiety and felt that the intensification of violence threatened the survival of the Vietnamese people. They argued that the plight of the Vietnamese should have been the first and not the last consideration of all concerned, concluding that the fate of the people of Vietnam was the real issue and that the conflict should have been resolved without intervention by outside powers, preferably through peaceful settlement.

A white army infantryman who witnessed American acts of abusive violence against civilians told us about his response:

> I was ashamed to be an American and I guess I was as responsible as everybody else for these acts even though I wasn't directly responsible. To me it's all a very perverted way of thinking that you can just destroy somebody's life just because you want to. . . . I grew to detest the war and the government's actions and everything else that was in the name of peace and righteousness and America.

A white veteran who was in heavy combat gave us his reaction to the "dirty" side of war:

> I have just seen too many people killed . . . too many young children killed. I have seen too much of the evil way in war. It's fatherless, it's motherless. . . . If there is ever another war that comes up, I have had thoughts on just leaving. . . . I would like to forget the slaughter. I would like to forget a lot of things but they still come back in my mind.

Other Vietnam veterans who were not exposed to the "dirty" side of war in Vietnam often turned against the conflict once they were back home and received reports about cruel actions against civilians. A white veteran who was isolated on a navy ship while he was in Vietnam explained his later change of view:

When the information about My Lai came out, I believed that we were doing this in Vietnam and I found that unacceptable. Worse, in the succeeding few days, I found that quite a number of Americans were accepting it as permissible. Our psychology with regard to the Vietnamese was such that it did permit the occurrence of these incidents. I believed that quite a number of people that I had known in Vietnam were capable of committing these acts. This was not permissible in itself and, worse, it was not acceptable to me that the American people would accept this as right. Insofar as we were accepting it as right, we had destroyed ourselves. We were doing something which was worse than the cost of losing the war. When the My Lai incident became public I was asked to speak to a group about the war. I had been friends with a number of people who were active against the war. I had not participated in many of their activities. When this happened I changed my mind basically and did speak with them against the war.

The prosecution of the war. Other respondents presented strategic arguments. Their thinking was in harmony with the general public disenchantment springing from the failure of our substantial military investments to yield victory. Like the general public, this group of respondents was strongly affected by the Tet offensive in January 1968 and the consequent widely advertised American defeat. One group of antiwar veterans agreed with their prowar peers that the war was lost because the nation's political leadership would not let our troops win that conflict. Yet for them this became the reason they turned against the American involvement.[8] They explained that toward the beginning of their stay in Vietnam they had been "very hawkish." If they had been allowed to "unleash our military power," they noted, they could have "ended the war quickly." Instead, they had found themselves victims of "a big political mess at the expense of a lot of limbs, and all the rest of it, a lot of lives." This led them finally to turn against the war. They felt that "never again should our American boys be asked to go into a war that we do not expect to win."

A white veteran who served in the army infantry arrived at the same conclusion:

I'd say during the last two or three months when I was there, when we discovered that we weren't fighting to win, . . . that's when I decided this is a fucked up war. This is not a war—this is a game to the politicians.

Another group of respondents argued in favor of a more limited commitment. While they favored American participation in training programs as well as various forms of U.S. military assistance, they took a strong stand against the employment of American troops in Vietnam. These views are marked especially among those who were in Vietnam after 1968. A white veteran put it this way:

The United States did have a treaty signed with the Southeast Asian countries . . . so I guess they could not get out of it one way or the other. But I felt they should have done like the Russians or the Chinese and just supply the people with arms and supplies and let them fight their own war. If they are capable of doing it fine . . . if they are not, that is up to them. That's their country.

A plurality of antiwar veterans felt strongly that we could never have won the war. They pointed out that the North Vietnamese would have continued to fight for as long as necessary to win. Moreover, the Communists had a nationalistic appeal that prevented the South Vietnamese from accepting the Saigon government. In the eyes of the nationalist Vietnamese, the Saigon regimes were consistently dependent for their survival on the United States, and they were weakened by poor leadership and corruption. This attitude is expressed by a white veteran who saw heavy combat:

We couldn't win that war, because these were people who were fighting for the land and their very lives and everything that they held dear to them. . . . The French had been there, and they left, because they couldn't beat these people. They wouldn't give up.

The impact of the conflict on American society. While Vietnam veterans who supported the war generally do not talk about the impact of the fighting on American society, veterans who believe our involvement in that conflict was mistaken or who actively resisted or demonstrated against the war are more likely to see the war as the cause of a whole range of negative international or domestic effects. They stress the deterioration of the nation's confidence in its institutions, especially the government. But while the negative impact of the war on America became one of the main reasons for nonveteran opposition to American involvement in the conflict, for antiwar veterans this issue generally seems to be of secondary importance. The political, strategic, and humanitarian factors discussed earlier in this section are predominant in the narrative material. The following remarks by a white Marine Corps lieutenant illustrate the concern with the negative effect of the war on America:

The problem with the Vietnam War was that it was a complete betrayal of everyone who thought he was doing what his country asked of him and found that he was contributing not at all to this country's welfare or to the welfare of South Vietnam. We were made a party to deception. The American people were lied to by a succession of presidents and senators and congressmen, heads of departments and cabinet members, and by military leaders. Everyone that had any experience at all with the Vietnam War is bitter about it. The conscientious objectors, the resisters . . . those who served in combat roles were lied to in a concerted action of the entire government. When leadership is that corrupt, that dishonest, then it bodes ill for the country.

Nonveterans' Views of the War

Support for American Involvement in the War

Political reasoning

As was to be expected, the arguments presented by the prowar nonveterans are quite similar to those of the Vietnam veterans who supported the war. A minority of nonveterans argued that the United States was justified in helping South Vietnam in collective defense against the armed attack by North Vietnam. They pointed out that during the Second World War we accepted the obligation to help the victims of aggression and in the postwar period we continued this policy. Our involvement in the Vietnam War was similar to the action undertaken in Korea. A white nonveteran explained this position as follows:

> It was a collective self-defense action under the SEATO Pact against an armed attack by North Vietnam. The South Vietnamese asked for our help and it seemed legitimate. We didn't want someone overrunning their country if they wanted to have our type of political democracy. Therefore, we were going to help an ally. It's like helping England in World War II.

Most nonveterans who supported American involvement in the war were strongly anti-Communist and pointed out that Communism presents such a danger to the "free world" that it must be stopped everywhere. As one respondent argued, "We had a free state there and we were backing a free government at their request" with the purpose of preventing "the infestation of a Communist takeover." Another white nonveteran noted:

> I believed that we needed to stop Communism at certain points. . . . I figured democracy provided me with being able to do what I wanted to do. . . . I wanted it safe in my lifetime and for my children to be able to enjoy the same benefits that I have, carefree and able to choose what I wanted.

Strategic considerations

Like many of their Vietnam veteran counterparts, prowar advocates also generally assumed that the United States could easily have won the war. They argued that American presidents, from John Kennedy to Richard Nixon, never had "a real moral commitment to win in Vietnam and to stop Communism there." How could they expect to win a limited war against an enemy, North Vietnam, whose commitment was total? One of our respondents expressed this feeling as follows:

> The major thing that concerned me about the war was that the Americans weren't going all out to win. I felt we should have gone further definitely. If

. . . this war was necessary to stop the Communist movement from coming, possibly to our shores, then certainly it was important enough to go beyond that. For instance, at the time of Nixon's bombing of the harbor, I felt that it was necessary. I felt if the commitment was there, why not press it further? We were over there to defend a moral commitment to that other entity, South Vietnam; a commitment that we would defend them.

These advocates stressed that because of this lack of commitment, successive political leaders never developed a coherent strategic plan, and they did only the minimum necessary to avoid losing Vietnam during their own tenure in the White House. They were afraid both to risk losing Vietnam to the Communists and to accept the decisive recommendations of their military advisers, which could lead to war with China or a domestic backlash. So they chose a middle road, doing only what was necessary to prevent a Communist takeover at the time. The result was that the army was caught up in a static guerrilla war, futile search and destroy operations, and a strategy of advance and retreat.

Many prowar advocates also argued that the United States should have concentrated on attacking the real source of Communist strength—North Vietnam—cutting it off from the South and gradually destroying its power. A white respondent expressed this attitude as follows:

> I felt that our involvement there was just, it was to protect the freedom of the Vietnamese people. But the war was being run politically, not militarily and so there was an unnecessary prolonging of the agony. . . . We should have done everything in our power militarily to cripple North Vietnam and stop the war.

Some resentment was also expressed that the United States was fighting the war according to the rules of warfare. One white nonveteran noted:

> I felt we ought go in and rout them. Get it over with. I know that being the world power we are, and with everyone looking up to us, we have to do things that other countries wouldn't have to do, like fight the war according to the rules. But it still bugged me. We should have just proved our superiority, which we could have done.

Most prowar advocates agreed that under the restrictions imposed by the presidents, through civilian leadership and management of the military on the combat level and without permission to cut off Hanoi's use of Laos and Cambodia, the critical strategic initiative remained in Hanoi's hands. Under those conditions the war could only be lost. These respondents share a common bitterness with many prowar veterans that "a just war" was not fought correctly and they blamed the political leaders. Most of the prowar nonveterans also strongly disapproved of the antiwar movement and were upset that the people at home were not supporting the war.

Many prowar nonveterans also felt that the United States should not have pulled out of the war until after Communism had been defeated. This attitude is expressed in the following quotation:

> The government of the United States and the American people should have realized then that Communism would get bigger if we don't stop it. . . . They didn't stop it so it got bigger. I do not agree with that . . . I did not like the way the war wound up. I think we did the right thing but we just backed out. If we're going to stop Communism, as the world stands today there is no way we can get to the front door. It looks like it is coming out the back door, side doors, whatever. If we're going to stop it we got to plug the holes, otherwise they'd bury us.

Humanitarian concerns

Though prowar nonveteran respondents generally were deeply concerned about saving the Vietnamese people from Communism, they expressed little distress in the transcripts about their fate and did not have much regard for Vietnamese lives. Nor did they have as strong a reaction to the death or wounding of Americans in Vietnam as other groups. One small group of prowar respondents expressed concern and did not want to see the war end because by pulling out, many Americans' lives were lost for nothing. A white nonveteran observed:

> I don't think we should have ever pulled out. . . . I think it was awful rotten of this country to send men over there and get them butchered and shot up, legs cut off, a lot of men killed, then pull out and accomplish nothing.

Antiwar Activism

Activist nonveterans generally reported that they were deeply concerned about the American involvement in the war both politically and morally. They did not discount the obvious fact that they were candidates for military service. When draft calls started to escalate and the war picked up, their own participation in the conflict became a possibility, and this obviously had an impact on their attitude toward the war. But most did not believe that they would have to go to Vietnam, and they felt that their concern about the war remained general rather than becoming strictly personal. The transcript material makes it clear that many factors influenced their views of the war. However, certain arguments are stressed more than others. The following main themes appear in the narrative material:

The political-moral character of the war

The arguments presented by the activists are generally similar to those of the

Vietnam veterans who opposed American involvement in the war for political-moral reasons. They most often defined the conflict as a civil war and did not feel that it was our war to fight. They pointed out that Vietnam had been one country historically and was artificially divided by the French and Americans. A white high activist observed:

> The North Vietnamese and Vietcong had a cause. These were the people who were indigenous to that country. It was a civil war, something that we had no business being involved in. They were taking the initiative, trying to mend their country and adopt a political system that was more fitting to their country and culture. . . . I felt that . . . we had no right to be there. We weren't defending an American territory. . . . We were continuing the colonial war of the French after they had been defeated . . . and before that we were already involved and gave them military assistance for their war in Indochina.

Both Vietnam veterans and nonveterans who opposed American involvement in the war stressed very strongly that we were supporting a corrupt, dictatorial regime. The awareness of the "tyranny within the South Vietnamese government" for some activists indeed became the main reason they became strongly opposed to the war. One moderate activist noted:

> I thought our involvement in the war was immoral because we supported people who were corrupt and were not in touch with and did not care about the general plight of their own people.

Others stressed that the United States was using "the political machines" in South Vietnam in order to impose its own standards on the people, thus denying them the right of self-determination. A high activist made the following comments:

> I was moralistically very opposed to the fact that we were involved in Vietnam. I didn't believe that we should be over there imposing our standards on another group of people. I certainly didn't believe in killing them for those standards. I didn't think that the political machines that we were supporting over there were for the good of the people and I felt we were withholding the right of free choice from those people at that time.

As will be discussed in the next chapter, a majority of the antiwar activists, while rejecting the legitimacy of the South Vietnamese government, did not feel positive about the enemy. This view is expressed by a white high activist:

> The South Vietnamese were trying to make a living with a corrupt government on one hand and a bunch of marauding people's army soldiers on the other hand, and they were just caught in the middle.

Antiwar activists pointed out that we were not only illegally interfering in a civil war, we were also destroying both North and South Vietnam and were foreign aggressors. The American intervention, they said, was against the principles of this country. It was also often argued that if we were really concerned about world peace we should have encouraged a peaceful settlement of the conflict. A white moderate activist remarked:

> They should have handled the war themselves. I think that our involvement in there, if we were concerned about world peace, should have been in initiating peace, peace conferences or whatever, rather than going in and taking one side in a civil war.

A majority of activists seemed to downplay the Communist dimension of the Vietnam War and felt that we had become involved in Vietnam because of a misplaced "Communist conspiracy hysteria." They rejected the domino theory that was expressed by Washington as a justification for being in Vietnam. They did not think the United States should enter militarily into battles in order "to safeguard the world from Communism."

Others argued that "halting the tide of Communism" is in harmony with American interests. But they felt that if we entered into internal conflicts by siding with one party only, we would encourage the other side to rely more on Communist countries. Concern was also expressed that the Soviet Union and China could use the American involvement in the war as an excuse for further escalation of the arms race.

Generally activists concluded that since there were no vital American interests involved, we had no reason to be in Vietnam. They also pointed out that the main reason we did not end our involvement in the war sooner was that various presidents were unwilling to admit defeat and the conflict provided the military with power, careers, useful experience in fighting a guerrilla war, and an opportunity to test out all kinds of new weapons. The wartime economy also enriched important economic interests. A black high activist noted:

> America made a big mistake. . . . America feels that the only way to have a prosperous economy is during a wartime period. . . . I didn't think they were really concerned about the Vietnamese being taken control over by the Communists because it was inevitable that was going to happen. . . . I felt that it was a war created by the corporate structure.

Finally, a small group of antiwar activists pointed out that what concerned them most was that the Vietnam War was an undeclared war, that our rationale for participating in the conflict was built around the "flimsy Gulf of Tonkin resolution." They would have responded differently to American involvement if Congress had passed a formal declaration of war. In the words of one white high activist:

We had no reason to be there unless it was official. . . . I probably would have felt a lot different if Congress had said, we are now at war. As opposed to, we are going to send some military advisers. See when I first heard the term military advisers, I actually believed that what we did was send . . . high-quality planning type of military officers over there to map out strategy—explain to them about weaponry, deal with tactics. But soon thousands of American troops were fighting an undeclared war.

The harm done to Vietnam veterans

The suffering inflicted on Vietnam veterans is often mentioned as one of the main reasons nonveterans turned against the war. The price paid by the combatants, especially the 60,000 fatalities, is much more salient to activists than to prowar nonveterans, and there is a high level of concern for the impact of the war on veterans' lives. Black antiwar activists are more likely than whites to cite the problems caused for veterans and their families (especially in terms of loss of lives of black veterans) as the main reason they turned against the war. Still, in the view of the majority of activists, Vietnam veterans have had a large share of the burden of a meaningless war.

Activists often cited relatives and friends who went to Vietnam and died, came back wounded, or became psychological casualties. Many were introduced to drugs during the war and returned addicted. What sense was there for young Americans to go to Asia to get killed, they asked. A white high activist explained this kind of opposition:

> Some relatives had gone and I didn't like the effect it had on them. . . . I had three cousins that went. . . . I had a cousin that was a medic . . . who took care of guys returning from Vietnam, and his letters reflected an opposition to the war, that any war would do this to young men—I guess he saw some real horror stories come back and he would work in the hospital that fitted them with arms and limbs. . . . I felt that the military was using Vietnam to test their hardware. It could have been Chile . . . or anywhere.

As noted, black activists were especially concerned about the fate of black veterans. They felt that too many blacks were fighting in Vietnam against their will and at great expense, often dying in a war they did not believe in. A black moderate activist expressed this attitude as follows:

> I was concerned for my brothers that had to go into the military service whether they would make it home alive or not. . . . Many people were getting killed and I don't think that they really understood why they were there. Just seeing how it affected different people's lives. Some of my friends who didn't drink before came back drinking. Some of them that didn't smoke were getting high. Some

of them were really messed up and some of them were nearly alcoholics. And it just did something to me on the inside.

Along with a personal response to the fate of relatives and friends, a general concern for Vietnam veterans was expressed. A white moderate activist explained why he turned against the war:

It outraged me every Thursday evening, when I used to listen to the evening news and hear the count of people who had died in the previous week. I just couldn't understand why the government pursued the course it was pursuing.

And a white high activist had this to say about the killing:

I first became really opposed to the war in high school. There was a National Honor Society trip to Washington and they were giving us a tour through Arlington and the guy pointed to these two hillsides covered with crosses and he said that a year ago those hillsides were empty. And it was at that point that I realized we weren't getting a whole lot out of this particular venture and it was costing an awful lot more than it was worth.

Abusive violence against the Vietnamese people

The acts of abusive violence committed by all parties to the conflict against Vietnamese civilians were another important reason why many activists turned against American involvement in the war. Generally, nonveteran activists agreed that all sides were violating the rules of warfare. A black moderate activist observed:

The insurgents fought with whatever weapons they had and whatever way they knew. The same way that they fought against the French. . . . I think we adopted the same type of behavior. We were fighting a brutal war and the civilians were the innocent victims.

Many felt that American forces engaged in unnecessary killing of the civilian population, especially as it became increasingly evident that we could not win the war. The war was having a terrible effect on the Vietnamese, the country was being destroyed, we were laying waste to the land and people to the point of genocide.

Activists stressed their unwillingness to be involved in a war against innocent people, a war they found ''so cruel that the federal government could not create any cohesion in the country in support of its involvement.'' Moreover, a substantial number of them cited the way the war was conducted as the *main* reason they turned against it. This attitude is expressed in the following quotation by a white high activist:

> It seemed to be a very brutal war. Like, for example, the mass defoliation of Southeast Asia by all kinds of strange chemicals and very heavy usage of bombs. I remember the Christmas bombing of Hanoi, that just struck me as a really brutal thing to do. It seemed to be completely senseless and unnecessary. And that was my general impression about the whole war. It was something I was very ashamed of.

Activists often made the point that our abusive violence against civilians had caused us to lose the war. The Vietnamese people had increasingly turned against the American forces and denied them the support they needed. A white high activist expressed this feeling as follows:

> We committed acts of cruelty against the people. . . . Under those conditions the war became a losing proposition. I felt there was no way we could win, to use that phrase, the hearts and minds of the Vietnamese people.

The impact of the war in Vietnam on America and American society

Activists are much more concerned about the domestic repercussions of the war than other members of their generation. They perceived the impact of the war on the United States both during the hostilities and in the postwar period as overwhelmingly negative. While they do not all agree on what effects of the war are most important, they share a general concern for what they perceive to be Vietnam's destructive impact. The war was not only a mistake, they submit, but a costly one. A white high activist explained why the effect of the war on the United States was his main concern:

> The political implications, what was happening in this country, I think concerned me more than the actual fighting itself. . . . The effect that I felt the war was having on the American political system—on the American people in general. I guess what it sort of foretold for our country.

While activists are likely to see the war as a major cause of a whole range of domestic problems, in the narrative material they often stress what they perceive to be the most significant impact of the war on American society. The following main themes appear in activists' responses:

Loss of confidence in American institutions. This seems to be the most important theme since it is presented by so many activists. The deterioration of confidence in American institutions is perceived as being caused, or heavily influenced, by the American involvement in the war. It resulted in a lack of trust in government to do what is right and often caused an alienation from the American political system. This loss of confidence is expressed in the following statements. A white moderate activist explained why the Vietnam War made him lose respect for the United States:

> You felt you couldn't trust [the leadership] . . . claiming they were close to a settlement and people kept on getting killed . . . war can kill a country, in more than one way. And this is what has happened. I think the moral fiber of America today is not what it was during the Kennedy-Camelot years . . . I think it was a sad time for all of us.

Attitudes toward the military also changed and often resulted in a loss of confidence in the army. A white high activist expressed his shift in attitude toward the armed forces as follows:

> It changed from Hollywood stereotypes, of an organization far away from me, to one that was very present, one that was no longer filled with John Waynes, but filled with madmen, who were doing severe harm to the society I grew up with.

Concern was also expressed about a "callous disregard" on the part of political and military leaders for how the country felt about American involvement in the war.

Finally, some nonveterans turned against the war because they were upset about the government's handling of the antiwar movement. They felt that strategies were used that from their perspective were unworthy of this nation. A high activist recollected:

> One of the first things that concerned me about the war was the way that citizens protesting it were literally exposed to gestapo, Nazi-like tactics— which doesn't seem right in a democracy.

Social divisiveness created by the war. Other activists stressed the social schisms created by the war, rifts that split the nation into factions and polarized the people. A high activist presented his view of the situation as follows:

> It just struck me as incredible at times. I think that there was a real difficulty on both sides of opinion about the war, a gap in terms of the way in which the arguments were perceived. I think people probably spend a certain amount of effort simply avoiding bringing it up in situations where they thought that there might be someone present who was on the other side of the fence, simply because it was a very difficult thing to discuss.

Negative economic and social effects. Activists also pointed out that the war was too costly, that the money should have been used elsewhere. The cost of the war, they felt, was draining the nation, tying up resources that could have been used to solve domestic problems. Moreover, the preoccupation with the military effort distracted from the needed concentration on the social and economic needs of the people. A high activist spoke of the futility of our investment in Vietnam as follows:

> Over fifty thousand guys had been lost, billions of dollars spent, and none of us saw any return on the investment, assuming that it was the right thing to do to begin with, which it wasn't.

Mixed effects. One group of activists argued that there were limited positive aspects to the Vietnam experience, that the American public had become more aware due to the mistakes made during the war. A high activist expressed this attitude:

> We were involved in things that we really had no business being involved in right from the start. We had made a grave error. . . . It certainly affected our economy, it affected our emotional climate, it affected the growth of the country. And in some ways those things were positive. America did some painful growing during that time. And I think in that process individuals grew too. So did I. Tough times make you reflect.

Conclusion

The transcripts show that those Vietnam veterans and nonveterans who supported American involvement in the war argued that it was the duty of the American government to check the efforts of the international Communist movement to take control of South Vietnam. As the leader of the "free world," the United States is seen to have special responsibilities for dealing with Communist aggression which the nation must accept. These respondents do not deny that fighting the war in Vietnam was difficult and impinged directly on the lives of thousands of American young men. But they feel that this sacrifice had to be made in order to build a stable world order free from Communist interference.

The narrative material further makes it clear that the antiwar activists, more than any other group in our sample, were primarily motivated by the moral nature of the American involvement in the war rather than by disillusionment over our failure to win the conflict.[9] For them, the main issue was not whether the United States could win the war but rather the devastation that such a victory would entail. While the general public, as well as many Vietnam veterans, became "doves" in response to American defeat, concluding that the war was not to be won by being "stepped up," and that hence the only alternative was to step down, the antiwar activists' disenchantment with the war seems to reflect responses to offensive actions and not reactions to news of military defeats and frustrations. These activists were strongly affected by the extension of the war in 1965 by sending bombers to attack the countryside of North Vietnam and by the Cambodian incursion in May 1970. This does not mean that the antiwar activists are a uniform group, and one will find both types of opposition patterns, the political-moral and strategic, among antiwar activists. But it seems true that a substantial majority of the activists were motivated by deeply held ethical principles, and they turned their concern into a critical examination of the many different facets of the American involvement.

Overall, the American involvement in the war as seen through the eyes of the majority of the Vietnam Generation was a grievous mistake. While there are some differences in perspective between the Vietnam veterans who opposed the war and the antiwar activists, they generally agree that the conflict was a civil war in which the United States ought not to have entered militarily. They do not feel that it was a war in which the Americans had substantial interests to defend, nor do they subscribe to the domino theory. They believe that basically American efforts were to bolster a regime in South Vietnam that did not merit our support. They contend that the South Vietnam government did not represent the best interests of the Vietnamese people and was not worth saving. Nor do they feel that the United States had a sufficient stake in the area to merit our level of sacrifice in terms of dead and wounded Americans, the loss of Vietnamese lives, or the enormous sums of money we were spending in a struggle that we could not win. win.

Finally, and this argument was especially important to the activists, the domestic impact of the war was negative, fragmenting the population and creating animosities among the people. The war was also a tremendous drain on the financial resources of the country, diverting needed funds from many social programs and activities—notably the war on poverty.

CHAPTER FOUR

FEELINGS ABOUT
OUR ALLIES
AND THE ENEMY

One crucial factor in any war is the view that a nation has of its allies and enemies. A great deal of government effort usually goes into depicting the foe as villainous and the ally as heroic. Anyone who has seen movies of World War II remembers the heroism of the English as they stood bloodied but unbowed against the Nazi onslaught and the courageous French, Dutch, Norwegian, and Danish Resistance members who often were forced to submit to indescribable tortures or death to speed the day when the "allies" could vanquish Nazism. Clearly neither our allies nor ourselves always measured up to the images of heroism displayed on the screen. Yet, there was enough similarity between the image and the reality to give credence to the not-so-subtle propaganda that pitted good against evil.

If a nation asks its men to sacrifice their lives or risk their limbs, it is reasonable that the cause in which they fight be defensible in moral and ethical terms. The ally should be willing to make the same sacrifices and endure the human costs of the war as those who fight on his land. These conditions were clearly fulfilled in World War II, and this helped build a national consensus on the war as well as define national feelings about our allies and enemies.

During the Vietnam War the situation was far more complicated. In this chapter we examine the Vietnam Generation's feelings about the American ally, the South Vietnamese Army (ARVN), and the enemy, the North Vietnamese Army (NVA) and the Vietcong (VC).

The Vietnam Generation's Views of the Combatants

When respondents were asked to characterize their attitudes toward the ally and enemy, feelings of mutuality with the allies were dramatically absent. Indeed, despite an evident hostility toward the enemy, sentiments expressed toward them in the narrative show more respect than is accorded to the allies.

Tables 4.1 and 4.2 show what may be one of the most startling findings in our study. No group in this generation has a more positive view of the ally (ARVN) than of the enemy (VC/NVA). The most telling part of these findings is that Vietnam veterans were three times as likely to report that they felt positive toward the enemy (24%) as the ally (8%). Furthermore, Vietnam veterans are also the most likely of any group to report that they felt negative toward their ally (50%). These findings suggest that American soldiers were constantly exposed to a situation where they unambiguously felt less respect for their ally than for the foe. The magnitude of their enmity for their supposed ally raises significant questions of how men coped with fighting a war under these circumstances.

The issues of opposition or support for the war pale in the face of the attitudes of this generation, especially Vietnam veterans, toward the combatants. How must it feel to risk life and limb for an ally one despises while facing an enemy one may fear but respects as a soldier? Among Vietnam veterans we find further disturbing evidence that those who were forced to share the burden of the conflict with the ARVN were the most likely to harbor hostile feelings about their allies. As table 4.3 shows, not a single marine reported having positive feelings toward the ARVN, and 56% reported they had negative feelings; comparable percentages for the army were 8% and 59%. On the other hand, only 28% of those in the navy and air force reported negative feelings for the ARVN. Thus, it is clear that Americans who were not generally in situations where their lives were likely to be jeopardized by their allies were much less hostile to them than their compatriots who worked with ARVN units in the field.

Race, as tables 4.4 and 4.5 show, has an interesting effect on attitudes toward the combatants. If we look at the entire sample of veterans and nonveterans, blacks are less hostile to the ARVN than whites (30% vs. 41% felt negative). They are also less negative about the VC/NVA (17% vs. 40%). However, among Vietnam veterans, blacks are no more sympathetic to the ARVN than are white Vietnam veterans. Yet, they do report substantially more positive views of the VC/NVA than whites (38% vs. 20%) and are less apt to report negative feelings toward the enemy (28% vs. 40%). This suggests some degree of identification among nonveteran blacks with the Vietnamese as nonwhites, which carries over to the ally as well as the enemy. In Vietnam, however, contact with the ARVN dissipated the reserves of good will that blacks brought with them.

The effect of period of service on support for the ally is mirrored in table 4.6, which presents our findings on Vietnam veterans' attitudes toward the

ARVN. Hostilily expressed by Vietnam veterans toward the ARVN jumps by a third (60% vs. 39%) in the later, post-Tet, years. Moreover, the proportion of Vietnam veterans who hold a positive view of the ARVN shrinks to a mere 5%. We do not attempt to determine the causal pattern between hostility to the ARVN and opposition to the war in this study. However, it seems fair to suggest that the negative views American soldiers held of their allies were not conducive to maintaining enthusiasm for the war effort.

The relationship between combat experience and relative views of the ARVN and the North Vietnamese and Vietcong (VC/NVA) is another noteworthy finding. Veterans exposed to heavy combat were twice as likely to have positive views of their enemy as of their ally (30% vs. 14%). Indeed, as table 4.7 demonstrates, moderate- and heavy-combat veterans hold significantly more "positive" views of the VC and NVA (32% and 30%) than is found among those who saw little combat (12%).

As we see in table 4.8, nonveterans' perceptions of the ARVN were also negative or ambivalent. Positive attitudes toward the ARVN were rare regardless of the degree of political activism. Among the low activists only 9% indicated that they had a positive view of the ARVN compared to only 1% of the high activists. The larger differences, as table 4.8 indicates, are among the proportions in the three activist groups who felt mixed/conflicted and negative. The moderate and high activists report negative views of the ARVN more than 50% of the time compared to 30% of the low activists who express similar views.

Among supporters of the war, in table 4.9 we find the first group in our study in which a substantial proportion of respondents view the ARVN positively (21%). Even in this group, however, 38% hold a negative view of the ARVN.

Comparing the views of the VC/NVA among nonveterans, in table 4.10, we see that the high activists have a distinctly more positive view of the enemy than either the low activists or the moderate activists. Fully 56% of the high activists indicate pro-VC/NVA sentiments, compared to 26% of the moderate activists and only 12% of the low activists. Equally interesting is the low proportion of all nonveterans who hold a negative view of the VC/NVA. Although the high activists are least likely to have a negative view of the enemy (20%), only 36% of either the moderate or low activists respond they had a negative view of the insurgents.

In table 4.11 we find that the prowar nonveterans are the only group in the study in which a substantial majority (61%) hold the negative view of the enemy common to nations at war. The small proportion of prowar nonveterans in the study underlines the distinctiveness of the Vietnam War. The distinction between the evil enemy and good ally simply did not take hold for this generation.

The narrative material provides us with an insight into the reasons why the Vietnam Generation views the ARVN in a generally negative or ambivalent fashion. The transcripts also show why the generation's responses to the enemy are not overwhelmingly hostile.

Vietnam Veterans' Attitudes Toward the South Vietnamese Army

Positive Views

The small minority of Vietnam veterans (8%) who had a positive view of the ARVN generally served in the navy or air force and were in Vietnam during the early pre-1968 period. They had relatively little contact with the ARVN and were not dependent on them during combat. The following remarks by a veteran who served in the air force and was in Vietnam from 1965 to 1967 are typical of this population:

> They were just doing their job. It is their country, their fight. But we got along. I have never seen any hassles between them and the Americans. Half of the time they stayed in town. They weren't on base or anything because we had no need for them due to the fact that we had our own MPs. I'd see them on the roads going and coming from combat zones, different combat zones. Friendly, they would wave to you.

Negative Views

The three most common themes presented by Vietnam veterans who had a negative view of their ally (50%) are the following:

The ARVN were not good soldiers

Many Vietnam veterans who had a negative view of the ARVN felt that the South Vietnamese troops had all the easier jobs and were not dedicated to the war effort. Most considered the ARVN cowardly. This attitude is demonstrated by the following two replies. A veteran who served in the army noted:

> Well, they were organized and equipped with the help of the United States and supposed to be the best Vietnam had to offer, and yet when it came down to having to get the job done most of them would rather run than fight. They were a real enigma. You know, these elite corps would strut around in their special hats or special decorations or shoulder patches but then when the going got tough they were nowhere to be found.

A marine lieutenant observed:

> In any battles in which we participated with the ARVN, the ARVN always seemed to fire late. They would always turn and run and the marines would wind up fighting the whole battle. This was not all of the time, but in the ones

that really got hot it seemed like reports always came back that they had high-tailed it.

Others commented that the ARVN were not only poorly trained but also lazy and untrustworthy. A veteran who served in the army explained this attitude as follows:

I felt that they were lazy; they did not seem to pitch in. When Nixon was in office, he started a Vietnamization program, and that is when we were starting to bring the Vietnamese Army more into our operations so that they could learn to handle it on their own. In that respect I found that they were very untrained. They did not give a damn about anything. We ended up doing all the work. You know, it was like "Why should we do it—the GIs will take care of it." They were highly unorganized. Their leaders were very incompetent.

A veteran who was in the army infantry observed:

We worked with the fifth ARVN division for approximately four months. We would go out on patrol together. We knew that it was a fairly hot area and at noontime crash bang down go the pots and pans and they start building fires and here you had been afraid to step on a twig. They would steal anything they could get a hold of so we did not dare leave anything laying around.

The ARVN could not be politically trusted

Those criticizing the ARVN pointed out that this was not a conventional but a guerrilla war. Moreover, they stressed the fact that to the Western eye the natives looked alike, be they ARVN, Vietcong, or North Vietnamese. Thus the enemy could infiltrate U.S. camps with relative ease. In addition, the average ARVN soldier came from the country. Therefore he tended to support the Vietcong more often than the Americans and did not want to fight. For these reasons the ARVN could never be really trusted. An army helicopter pilot reflected:

I carried some Vietnamese troops in helicopters and they did not want to get out of the helicopters. And that happened on more than one occasion. So if they did not want to fight, what the hell was I doing there? I felt that we all had been tricked. . . . The Vietnamese officers I knew said that, yes, the Vietnamese were behind us in terms of knocking out the Vietcong, but the Vietnamese officers were in the elite of their society and so they were caught up in the same political structure from Saigon as Ky and all those other guys. The average soldier came from the country and they had no knowledge of anybody except the Vietcong and the Americans. They tended to support the Vietcong more often than they supported the Americans. I felt that they strongly wanted to keep their country Vietnamese. They must have had a hell of a conflict, the guys getting caught up in the ARVN, you know.

An additional reason why the ARVN could not be trusted was that they had no political loyalty: many worked part time for the enemy. A marine sergeant observed:

Many times we proved there is no doubt at all that many of the ARVNs were working for the South Vietnamese during the day and for the North Vietnamese at night. We provided them with military armament and in one particular instance a highly specialized land mine blew up one of our trucks. They had placed it there the night before themselves.

Corruption among the ARVN was also cited as a reason for distrust. An army man told the following story:

Well, we did not trust them because we never knew exactly what side they were on. Out in the valley there was a basic training area for ARVNs and the story was, supposedly from good sources, that one entire company once it received its weapons just disappeared and defected. There was a lot of graft with their officers.

The ARVN committed atrocities

Many critics reported that they witnessed cruel acts committed by the ARVN, especially against civilians and prisoners of war. For some veterans, like the navy seabee quoted below, this became the main reason that they turned against the ARVN.

Well there was a VC prison camp not far from us. The way these people were treated, they were put in cages. They were given a bowl of rice to eat. That was their meal for the day. They were badly mistreated. The Vietnamese personnel took charge of the prisoners. They were the worst. It was not the Americans who were cruel to the prisoners. It was the Vietnamese themselves who were cruel. I just became disgusted with the whole thing.

It is interesting to note that some navy and air force personnel who had no joint combat experience with the ARVN and initially felt friendly toward them, became hostile after they saw them engage in inhumane actions.

For those who were dependent on the ARVN during combat and already had a negative attitude, the witnessing of acts of abusive violence committed by their ally often only intensified their hostile feelings. A veteran who served in the army infantry described his reaction as follows:

I had a couple of experiences where I saw ARVN troops really mistreating villagers and suspected Vietcong prisoners. These guys were terrible. They would beat up on suspected prisoners. They were just nasty people.

Mixed/Conflicted Views

Among Vietnam veterans, a substantial number (42%) had a mixed or conflicted view of the ARVN. There are many reasons for this ambivalent attitude. Some respondents who were never in combat with the ARVN pointed out that they had heard good as well as negative stories about the ARVN. A navy officer who had no direct exposure to the ARVN noted:

I suppose my opinions or attitudes were in conflict because I heard conflicting things about them. I would hear they had taken some military action that was successful. They were adopting whatever tactics we were trying to teach them and using them successfully and adapting what we told them to their own environment. They were using it to defend themselves and so I would feel pretty good about that. But I would hear just as many things that were negative; poor discipline among the military on and off the battle field, and a reluctance to fight. There was a lot of corruption and bribery, and buying of favors among not only the military but political people that were somehow involved with the military.

It was also pointed out that while the ARVN were generally poor fighters, some units performed with great efficiency. Many respondents cited dedicated soldiers, while adding that others were untrained, cowardly, and lazy. This type of conflicted attitude is generally weighted toward the negative rather than the positive view. A veteran who served in the army noted:

First of all there were too many people in uniform. Everyone was on the payroll. They were very poorly trained and definitely could not handle the modern technology of our armed forces. There was only one unit that was held in high esteem by the Americans and that was the ARVN Ranger Battalion.

A marine added:

There were many cases where there were very dedicated soldiers really doing a good job. However, there were a lot of soldiers who were very complacent and untrained, and a lot of the soldiers could not care less either way. Basically, it was an untrained, unorganized army.

A veteran who served in the navy concluded:

I hated them because they would run away and leave our marines to die. They could sit along the side of a road with a transistor radio and run the antenna and tie a handkerchief on it and that was a signal to the Vietcong that they did not want to fight. So they did leave them alone. You know, a lot of them were South Vietnamese soldiers by day and then during the nighttime they were Vietcong. A lot of them were dedicated soldiers trying to save their homeland. A lot of them were bums.

Some veterans, while being critical of the ARVN, expressed a certain amount of sympathy for them and felt that they were victims of the war and of the South Vietnamese government. An example of this attitude is provided in the following description by an army lieutenant:

Many of them were not as effective fighters as they ought to have been because they were weary of the war and sometimes their loyalties were divided. And, of course, sometimes they were afraid to fight because they saw no sense in losing their life. If they became disabled, their family would receive a pittance even for them. So they had much more to be afraid of by being hurt or even by being killed in relation to their family. They had no insurance, that sort of thing, which made it a lot harder for them.

Finally, a number of Vietnam veterans, while admitting that the ARVN could not be trusted, blamed the Vietcong for the ARVN's wavering attitude. A black army veteran explained:

You could not trust them. You never could tell whether or not they were on your side or the enemy's side. They were allowed to mingle off in the villages and stay downtown. When the Vietcong raided the village and attacked at night and if they did not obey the rules and regulations of the Vietcong and they decided to come back they were punished by the Vietcong. . . . You saw them hanging on a tree somewhere.

Veterans' Attitudes Toward the Vietcong and the North Vietnamese Army

As noted earlier, Vietnam veterans had many different responses to the enemy. The following narrative material provides an insight into their thinking.

Positive Views

The VC and NVA were nationalists fighting a war of independence

Veterans who presented this argument were generally against the American intervention in the conflict. They often argued that the VC and NVA had mobilized Vietnamese nationalism in order to fight a war of liberation against colonial overlords. The enemy forces were authentically Vietnamese and were helped by their own countrymen, while the Saigon government accepted massive help from white foreigners. They also stressed the Vietcong's and North Vietnamese record of military success against enormous obstacles and concluded that such success could not have been achieved without widespread popular support. The following two illustrations are typical of this view. A black army infantryman stated:

> I respected the Vietcong. . . . The French tried to take over Vietnam. They have been in a constant turmoil since the beginning of time almost. Other countries coming in trying to take them over. I always thought of them really as mighty warriors, having fought against some of the best equipped armies in the world and they did not even have boots. They were in sandals or tennis shoes and had very meager rations. They lived off the land. It was their kind of war.

A white infantryman noted:

> The Vietcong are nationalists. They are you and me saying: "We do not want you people coming here and telling us how we have to live." Those people had been defending their country for so long that I think for an American to understand them is a very, very rare thing. . . . [What stands out most in your mind?] The awesome, meticulous, sheer quantity of organization that can be assembled toward one end in terms of people's freedom. It reshaped my thinking and I turned against our involvement in the war.

It was also argued that from the standpoint of many peasants the war was a battle against starvation. Land reform by the Saigon government had failed and there was a tradition of exploitation and cheating of the peasants by corrupt landlords. The policy contrasted with the Vietcong's concern with the welfare of the peasants. A black veteran who was in the army airborne concluded:

> I thought that what the North was trying to do would be good for the country. Take it over. [But the South Vietnamese government you felt was corrupt?] I know they were corrupt. . . . They also exploited the peasants. I felt . . . they [the North] were taking on a country twenty times as large as they were and despite the odds, they were never giving up and they were fighting to reunify their country. And to free the peasants.

Vietnam veterans noted that meeting Vietcong and North Vietnamese soldiers sometimes altered their political view of the enemy. A white army lieutenant who had a very negative view of the North Vietnamese as "the aggressors" explained his change in attitude this way:

> Most of the prisoners that I have talked to honestly believed that they were
> repelling invaders from their native land. They felt that it was white men in a
> yellow war and they just felt that we did not belong there. They felt their land
> was their own and they were fighting for a just cause.

While some veterans developed a positive political view of the enemy in
Vietnam as a result of discussions about the war with fellow Americans, others
derived new insights through contacts with Vietnamese civilians. A black veteran
explained how he came to an understanding of "what a Vietcong was, what a
Communist was":

> The lady who washed the clothing for the men in the barracks had a son in
> prison. And I asked, "Why is her son in prison?" They said, "Well, he's a
> Vietcong." Then it dawned on me, well he's a Vietcong, they're Communists,
> and he's just like me. If I don't believe in what my brother believes in do I
> become the enemy? And should I fight him because of that? I somehow came to
> an understanding what a Vietcong was, what a Communist was . . . I felt them
> as being people who wanted their land. The North wanted to keep their Asian
> political thought for themselves. I felt that Asians should not try to be Ameri-
> cans but they should be Asians. I felt that we were wrong in trying to turn them
> into Americans. . . . Stop trying to be big brother of the world.

Many veterans who already held a positive view of the enemy while in
Vietnam found their perception of the VC and NVA as nationalists strengthened
after homecoming. A white veteran explained his experience as follows:

> One of my goals when I started going to school [after the war] was to find out
> what . . . the Vietcong were like and the North Vietnamese. They had been
> fighting for many years before we were there. They fought the first Indochina
> war with France and they got France out of there in 1954. They had many years
> of experience in fighting that type of war. Revolutionary war they call it. That is
> one thing I believe the Americans did not understand . . . that type of warfare.

The VC and NVA were loyal and dedicated soldiers

The loyalty and dedication of the VC and NVA are a prominent theme among
those veterans who had a positive view of the enemy forces. It is presented by
both veterans who opposed and who supported the American involvement. It was
pointed out that the Vietcong and North Vietnamese Army had to compensate
through organization, loyalty, and dedication for the American and Saigon governments' great advantage in military equipment. Many of these respondents

also commented that it would have been extremely difficult for the Americans to win the war. No matter how many VC/NVA units were killed, more would be sent to replace them. The enemy would not give up. The following remarks illustrate this strongly held view. A black veteran who served in the army observed:

> The Vietcong? . . . When you consider the equipment, the conditions that they were living under, having to train under and the job that they were doing with it. It made you think, what if he could get real training and have some real good equipment—we wouldn't have a chance—The NVA? . . . Well . . . when you think about how they had to get that equipment in there . . . truck or backpack it all the way down the Ho Chi Minh Trail under cover at night and they were still able to infiltrate enough supplies and personnel into the South and give you all the battle you want. So if he was that determined it's enough to make you respect him, plus the fact he was a good fighting man.

A black Marine made a similar point:

> I felt positive because they [the Vietcong] were very strong fighters and very strong willed. Even stronger than Americans and under extremely adverse conditions, many of them just died out there in the field from lack of supplies and food. See—they had no planes, no trucks . . . everything they did was on foot. I thought they were extremely strong to stand up to us. We had to have all the conveniences just to fight them. They had none. The North Vietnamese also fought a hell of a war. They did not give up. Nothing would stop them.

Generally, those respondents who had a positive view of the enemy spoke with equal respect about both the Vietcong and North Vietnamese Army. There was not much difference in their view of the VC as compared to the NVA, although it was noted that the Vietcong faced much greater hardships, while the North Vietnamese Army was better equipped and fought in a more traditional way. But some veterans expressed a greater feeling of admiration for the VC than for the NVA. A black veteran who served in the army did not have much to say about the NVA but spoke at great length about the Vietcong. He made the following points:

> The Vietcong . . . had no air force, hardly any artillery. They had no machinery, no engineers to build with, they used what we left and they beat us. They had a great many plans in effecting guerrilla warfare. They had good intelligence units and they most of all had the determination that they were right.

These respondents also often argued that even without the support of the NVA, the Vietcong would have continued their guerrilla war against us for a very long time. A white army cannoneer observed:

The Vietcong, they lived on very little. They were dedicated. I felt that it was going to take a long time to end the war. You did not have to be in the country too long to realize that. . . . They captured all kinds of American military paraphernalia, jeeps, tanks, artillery pieces, helicopters. . . .

But others expressed greater respect for the NVA. The period served seems to affect this attitude. Those who served before the Tet offensive of 1968 reported that the Vietcong bore the brunt of the fighting and suffered serious losses. Those serving after 1968 pointed out that the Vietcong increasingly had to be replaced by North Vietnamese regulars, turning the struggle into a more traditional type of war between the NVA and American units. A white air force officer who served during the later stages of the war did not perceive the Vietcong as a dangerous enemy but explained why he respected the NVA:

[I felt] positive as far as their abilities to do the things that they were doing against the odds they were fighting against. I had a very deep respect for their discipline, the tenacity and just the wherewithal to move the large number of troops and equipment they were moving and get that much through 300 miles. You have to stand in awe of people and leadership because of that.

A small minority had different views of the VC and NVA as soldiers. A white marine captain hated the VC but made the following positive remarks about the NVA:

Positive from the standpoint that he was a good soldier. He wasn't a rice-blowing, spear-chucking little slant-eyed native. He was a well-trained, well-equipped, well-armed and apparently very purposeful or very well-motivated soldier who was dying for what he believed in. [How did he stack up to American soldiers?] Probably better.

Negative Views

Among those Vietnam veterans who had a negative view of the Vietcong and North Vietnamese Army (37%), the majority supported United States involvement in the war. But this is not always the case, and a group of Vietnam veterans who were against American involvement responded in a very hostile way to the enemy forces. A white artilleryman expressed this view as follows:

I hated them because of their mad ideologies, their inhumane treatment of captives. They believed in a total Communist takeover and I did not believe in what they preached. At the same time I did not think we should have been over there. I think the United States should have provided the South Vietnamese with additional military weapons and with good military advisers to make sure the

Vietnamese forces were properly trained. I think that they should have defended themselves without the United States getting themselves directly involved in the struggle.

The following main themes are found among those who held a negative view of the enemy forces:

The VC and NVA represented Communist ideology

Violently anti-Communist arguments were often presented. The enemy held a hated ideology and must be destroyed. The following two remarks illustrate this point of view. A white marine explained:

> We were there to kill them. We were there to flush them out and rid South Vietnam of their harrassment and killing. We were trying to keep the Communists from being in power. They were against everything I believed in. I have been taught freedom of speech, democracy.

A white army infantryman agreed:

> [The Vietcong?] . . . Why did you hate them so much? . . . I don't like Communism—they're part of Communism . . . in a way—they're an affiliate of Russia and I don't like Russia—it's just the idea, that people who are forcefully taking over unarmed people—old people—that I couldn't stand.

The VC and NVA were the enemy of the South Vietnamese people

Respondents pointed out that the activities of the Vietcong were directed toward acts of terrorism and assassination. According to this view, the use of intimidation and force by the Vietcong accounted for much of the peasant cooperation that occurred. Units would go into a village and kill the chief or the local official to get village support by showing that they meant business. The Vietcong's methods of recruitment and taxation among the peasants reflected their dictatorial attitude and their willingness to sacrifice the welfare of civilians to the progress of the war. They in no way represented the people. A white veteran expressed this view as follows:

> I did not care for the way they went about trying to inflict their beliefs and their ways on their own people. I mean it was just like Nazi Germany. They would torture and force people to beckon to their call. Anybody who associated with the Americans would be killed. I definitely do not approve of that type of strategy, which is probably the reason we were there.

A black veteran who was in the army saw the Vietcong as follows:

They were always leaving examples of their presence to let you know that they had been there . . . leaving somebody dead. When the Vietcong went through the villages and programmed these people they would turn around. The next time when they come to work for the United States government, like a lot of people who worked on the base, you would not know whether they had been programmed or not because of the fact that the Vietcong would treat them so bad and torture them. That was the hardest point of the war because of the fact that you did not know whether that person was a Vietcong now or whether he was still a Vietnamese.

These respondents often argued that the Vietcong ignored the rules protecting civilians in wartime and did anything they wished. They attacked villages and nonmilitary objects and tortured and killed innocent civilians. A white veteran presented this view of the Vietcong:

The Vietcong would stop at nothing to kill, maim. More often they would rather maim than kill anybody who stood in their way. They would use any method to do what they wanted and I realized there were very few rules in war they accepted. Some of the things they did with children, old men are not to be believed. They were the worst sort of animals. They had no respect or reverence for anything.

A similar negative view is expressed about the NVA. Respondents pointed out that they rejected North Vietnamese aggression, dictatorship, and mass control and argued that everybody has the right to have an elected government and their own way of life. A black veteran noted:

The North Vietnamese wanted to impress upon the South Vietnamese their ways and not let the South Vietnamese people live as they would want to live. They were bringing in Communism and taking over, and when they take over you lose all your rights, all that you have, you have to give to the government and start all over. What the South Vietnamese had was capitalism. And then when North Vietnam came in that was destroyed.

The VC and NVA engaged in inhumane treatment of American troops

The two acts most commonly mentioned here are mistreatment of American prisoners of war and the mutilation of bodies of dead Americans. A black veteran talked about POW mistreatment by the Vietcong and North Vietnamese this way:

I have seen some of the prisoners who have escaped from the North Vietnamese and the Vietcong. They were really treated shoddily. The Americans treated their Vietcong prisoners pretty good. Almost to the point that after the Vietcong got in there, they did not want to leave. The Vietcong very rarely followed any of the conventions . . . or rules of war for the prisoners.

A white army infantryman explained his hatred for the enemy as follows:

Well I saw . . . mutilation of bodies—our bodies—I mean United States men. . . . After they were already dead there was no real sense in punching their eyes out or delimbing them. . . . Well, there wasn't really anything I could do but I think it just kind of built a hatred in me for them at the time.

The VC and NVA were the enemy

Some Vietnam veterans pointed out that they felt negative about the VC and NVA only because they were *the enemy*. A white marine officer expressed this view as follows:

The Vietcong were one of our enemies there and it is hard to feel positive about an enemy. I did not have much contact with Vietcong where I was. The NVA was the people we were fighting and they, like the Vietcong, were our enemy. I was there as a fighting man to kill the enemy.

Guerrilla warfare breeds mistrust

While the negative responses to the VC and NVA are not always the same, most Vietnam veterans did not really keep them separate in the narrative material. A minority had a substantially more negative response to the VC than to the NVA. They explained that they had strong hostile feelings about the Vietcong because they were guerrilla fighters. You never knew where they were and you could walk right into them. A black army infantryman told us about his experiences:

[Why did you feel negative about the Vietcong?] Because you really didn't know where they were. Like, you might be going through what they would call a friendly village and all of a sudden all hell breaks loose on you. You never did know who the Vietcong were. You had to always be on the alert.

The following remarks by a white veteran who was in a tank regiment also illustrate this attitude:

I think they [the VC] were worse than the North Vietnamese. The North Vietnamese stood right out and said we are the North Vietnamese and they were trying to win a battle. The Vietcong would sneak around and ambush whenever they could or use sniper fire.

Another reason for the negative feelings expressed about the Vietcong is that they had "dual identities." During the night they were the enemy but during the day they might hide among civilians and be unrecognizable. A white air force officer explained:

> From what I understood, living on an air force base and army installations in Vietnam and going through villages right near by those bases, I got the impression that the Vietcong were right in our midst. We were attacked on several occasions. We were mortared, grenades were tossed into the quarters. Apparently the Vietcong were right nearby. That was at night. In the daytime there was never a problem. I do not know if the Vietcong were hiding or that they had dual identities working, who knows, on the military installations in the daytime. Nobody knew and nobody was sure if they did. [You could not recognize them?] That's right.

Mixed/Conflicted Views

A substantial number of Vietnam veterans (38%) had a mixed or conflicted response to the Vietcong and the North Vietnamese Army. The most important theme expressed by veterans who responded this way seems to be a mixture of fear and respect. They felt that the Vietcong and the North Vietnamese Army were good fighters, even if as an enemy they were dangerous and unpredictable. A white army veteran expressed this feeling as follows:

> I respected the Vietcong a lot more than the ARVN. He was good, he knew what he was doing. He was fighting I guess for what he believed in. While the ARVN were fighting for nothing, most of them would run. I respected the Vietcong, but I was also afraid of them. They were trying to kill me.

A white army pilot explained why he felt conflicted:

> I had to feel negative, because they [the Vietcong] were trying to shoot us, they were out to get us. But I also . . . respected them . . . as far as disciplined military people they were superior. They would sneak in behind you through mine fields and barbwire fences. During the Tet offensive in 1968, some snuck into our air base and blew up fourteen helicopters. . . . You have to be dedicated to build something like the Ho Chi Minh trail. It is all physical labor like the pyramids. The tunnels, the underground network that they have is just being discovered. . . . Although maybe it was not motivation but the outcome of a modern form of dictatorship.

Others had conflicted feelings because while they sympathized with the political cause for which the enemy was fighting, at the same time they held them responsible for much of the destruction that was taking place in Vietnam. A white veteran responded this way:

> They were ripping the country apart. . . . They did not like the French. They sure as hell did not like us. But I can also honestly believe that if somebody was fighting over my country and they were siding with what I would consider a civil war faction, I would probably get just as bent out of shape towards us as they did. Rationally speaking, I suppose it is just protecting your own back yard.

Some veterans felt that many members of the Vietcong and NVA had been forced to join the Communists. A white infantryman expressed the following view:

> Of course, I hated the North Vietnamese and the leaders of the Vietcong. They were the enemy, they were Communists. However, through talking to my friend who at one time was a Vietcong, I found out that the majority of the Vietcong had no intentions of being a Vietcong: they were forced into it. The aggressors would come into their village and kill some of their people and force the young men to join the Vietcong, saying: ''If you do not join us, we are going to kill your family.'' . . . That is why I had compassion for them. The only thing I had against them was that they were the enemy.

Another white army infantryman noted:

> The North Vietnamese government were just nasty people. They have a dictator. . . like it was back in Hitler's days. Ho Chi Minh, he was no good. And the North Vietnamese Army had to listen to him. But basically they were human and they had feelings too . . . I am sure they had to go. The North Vietnamese ran a dictatorship.

Those Vietnam veterans who made several trips to Vietnam often changed their view of the VC and NVA. This is well illustrated by the following description given by a white veteran who served in the navy and made three trips to Vietnam both before and after the Tet offensive:

> Well, at first I thought the NVA were bad guys and that they were trying to overrun South Vietnam and take it. Then later I found out that there was a North and South Vietnam because of the French and the Americans, that really it was probably theirs to begin with and they were not trying to overrun the South Vietnamese. Toward the end they were trying to overrun us. They were good fighters.

Nonveterans' Attitudes Toward the South Vietnamese Army

While only a small minority (5%) of all nonveterans had a positive view of the ARVN, some difference of opinion remains between the antiwar activists and those who supported American involvement in Vietnam.

Prowar Nonveterans

Even among those who supported the war, a positive view of the ARVN is not often encountered (21%). However, a minority felt that the ARVN represented the South Vietnamese people in their fight against Communism. One nonveteran noted:

> I felt that if they were there helping to represent the South Vietnamese people, that God help them and give them all the authority they need to stand up to the Communist invasion.

More often a negative (38%) or mixed or conflicted (41%) view is expressed. Many prowar veterans agreed with their Vietnam veteran peers that while the ARVN were our allies, they had not wanted to fight, causing additional Americans to lose their lives. A nonveteran had the following to say:

> What did I think about the ARVN? . . . We are talking about our allies . . . but they did not want to fight. Even though I believe in a fight for democracy—here we were having our friends, relatives sent over there to solve *their* problems. . . . I think most of our soldiers were saying if it wasn't for you we wouldn't be in these mudholes and having to live like this over here. We could be home in warm beds, with our families and our children.

Antiwar Activists

As noted earlier, among high antiwar activists only 1% had positive feelings for the ARVN, and only 7% of moderate activists had a positive view.

Many of those who had a *negative view* pointed out that already during the days of the French colonial occupation Vietnamese troops had been used to suppress their own people and that the ARVN had continued that suppression. A high activist put it as follows:

> I had studied the history of the war and felt that these people were basically traitors to their own country. That they were the remnants of the French colonial forces . . . and were basically fighting to protect their material acquisitions. They were plain mercenary. They wouldn't even pay their way.

It was also noted that the ARVN were not an army of the people of South Vietnam. They were "sort of a private warlord's army," supporting a dictatorship that had been created by the United States. Since this dictatorship would collapse without American support, many looked at the ARVN as an extension of the United States Army in Vietnam. Activists stated that their main objection to the ARVN was that it was on the wrong side of a civil war, supporting a faction that was not representative of the population of Vietnam and was not interested in protecting the national well-being. A high activist expressed this attitude as follows:

> My largest objection to the ARVN was political. My perception of the politics of South Vietnam made the Saigon regime the bad guys. So ARVN was the bad guys. . . . I thought the United States armed forces were the military arm of a political group that I opposed.

Many also felt that the ARVN was enormously corrupt, and they did not understand how we could look upon them as allies. Not only were they poor soldiers, but the "top brass" were profiting handsomely from the war. A high activist provided the following description of the ARVN:

> I believed that they could not have begun to resist the Vietcong without American assistance. So in a military sense I did not have a very high opinion of them. . . . As far as the generals and some of the top brass in that army, I thought a lot of them were just making a lot of money on war, diverting supplies, selling them for themselves.

Activists also often turned against the ARVN because of their opposition to acts of abusive violence committed by the South Vietnamese Army. A high activist asked our interviewer:

> Do you remember the picture of the general—with the pistol up against a guerrilla's head . . . that sort of turned me off about the ARVN. I couldn't see the barbarism, the cruelty.

Often those who held a *mixed or conflicted view* of the ARVN felt strongly that American troops should not have become involved in the war, but their view of the combatants was not clear enough to take a side. They pointed out that they knew little about the ARVN and could not determine whether they had had qualified people to train them so that they could have fought the war alone. Nor did they have an understanding of the real motivation of the Vietcong. Which faction, they wondered, was the real representative of the Vietnamese people?

Nonveterans' Attitudes Toward the Vietcong and North Vietnamese Army

While overall only 19% of all nonveterans had a positive attitude toward the VC and NVA, substantial differences appear in the narrative material between prowar nonveterans and antiwar activists. Those nonveterans who supported the war generally had a negative attitude toward the enemy. But among activists more positive feelings are expressed, and the majority of high antiwar activists (56%) and a substantial minority of moderate activists (26%) felt positive about the VC and NVA.

Prowar Nonveterans

As might be expected, the majority of nonveterans who supported the American involvement in the war expressed strong feelings of ideological hostility toward the enemy. The NVA was seen not as a nationalistic movement, but as Communist aggressors and tools of the Soviet Union. This hostile attitude toward the enemy is demonstrated by the following two replies. One nonveteran stated:

> The government that they represented, the Communist government, was invading the South Vietnamese country. That was what I felt negative about. . . . They were the aggressors invading another country, they were basically doing the dirty work for Russia.

In the same vein, a nonveteran described the Vietcong this way:

> The Vietcong were the enemy. You ask yourself: "Why are they doing this, why are they killing innocent people?" They are all Communists and I am opposed to Communism. My attitude was stop them over there rather them have them somewhere off our coast . . . let us put a stop to Communism. . . . We do not want another Cuba.

A small group of prowar respondents based their animosity against the NVA and VC primarily upon the acts of abusive violence committed by the enemy against American forces. They had heard, through the media, about "the atrocities that took place toward the American troops over there." The NVA and VC were considered sadistic and devoid of scruples. This view is evident from the following remarks made by a nonveteran:

> It was primarily their tactics of fighting that upset me . . . their boobytrapping and hearing about a lot of their other tactics. They bring little kids with bombs up to a bunch of GIs and blow them up. Some of the things that you heard about seemed almost inhuman. It was just like they had no soul or no conscience.

Respondents also noted that atrocities were being committed against Vietnamese civilians. But this does not seem to be an important theme for those who supported American involvement in Vietnam. A small, concerned minority, however, was equally upset about "the terrible things they were doing to young American boys" and the violence directed against the civilians.

Finally, one group of respondents expressed hostility for the Vietcong as part of a general hostility toward *any* form of guerrilla warfare, which they viewed as illegal, unacceptable activity. The Vietcong were terrorists that should not be permitted to operate in Vietnam. The following example illustrates this response pattern:

> I think anyone would have felt negatively toward guerrilla warfare; it's a terrorist type activity; it's not what would normally be considered noble in war—to hide behind trees, set booby traps and stuff like that rather than confront the enemy.

Antiwar Activists

The thematic material indicates that the antiwar activists did not tend to whitewash the Vietcong and North Vietnamese Army or turn them into paragons of virtue. While recognizing that the Communists were dedicated to their cause, many activists viewed them with mixed or conflicted or even negative feelings. At the same time, they indicated that their feelings about the war were *primarily* directed against American involvement in the conflict, as opposed to support for the North Vietnamese or Vietcong.

Those activists who had a positive view of the VC and NVA, while not denying either group's Communist character, looked upon them primarily as legitimate forces for independence, revolutionary factions trying to liberate Vietnam from both internal and external enemies. Both groups were thought to be much more representative of the actual desires of the Vietnamese people than the ARVN and South Vietnamese government. Since it was their country and they represented the majority of the people, they had a right to decide the future of their nation. Because peaceful settlement had failed, an armed conflict was the only solution for Vietnam.

Activists also argued that during the war, the Vietcong was not merely a puppet of North Vietnam, as many American officials insisted, but had a life of its own. Indeed, they were South Vietnamese, not "Communist infiltrators from the North." The following remark by a high activist illustrates this point:

> I first thought that the Vietcong were the bad guys. But then after looking into it deeper and seeing their struggles I realized that the Vietcong were actually not North Vietnamese but South Vietnamese who were trying to get a just government. I looked on them as revolutionaries, just as we had our own revolutionaries in this country.

Activists who have a *positive view* of the Vietcong felt that they were fighting for freedom, a laudable act. This feeling was strongly conveyed by the high activists, as the following quotation illustrates:

> I felt that if I were Vietnamese I would quit the ARVN and join the Vietcong. I tended to think that those who stayed in the ARVN were misguided. . . . I thought that they [the Vietcong] were fighting for the freedom of their country. And I admired them for that.

These respondents also respected the NVA and pointed out that they had been fighting for their country's independence for many years and were totally dedicated to the liberation of Vietnam. One high activist noted:

> I think they had a right to do what they were doing. They were fighting to reunify their own country, to keep foreign elements out of their own country. . . . I feel that Ho Chi Minh was the legitimate leader. . . . I had admiration for General Giap, he was pretty brilliant in some of the things that he did.

As noted earlier, a substantial number of activists had a *negative attitude* toward the VC and NVA. Some interesting reasons for this stance are presented in the narrative material. Certain respondents argued that the Vietnamese had been aggressive for centuries, always using whatever means they could to overtake neighboring territories. A high activist noted:

> I felt negative about the NVA—if you go back into their history, some 400 years they've been warring. . . . I agree that they had a legitimate grievance in Vietnam and that the partition was forced upon them, but I just had the feeling that if it wasn't that, they would have embarked on a war of aggression against their neighbors, because it's in their history.

Other activists, while opposing the American involvement in Vietnam, took a strong stand against Communism. They felt that the type of action we took in Vietnam only weakens our struggle against Communism.

Respondents were also against enemy forces because these units were killing Americans and using brutal methods of warfare. For these activists, opposition to the American involvement in the war was most often based upon their concern for the fate of the American fighting men. This sentiment is expressed by a moderate activist:

> Being at one army hospital, I saw a lot of firsthand experiences because the top floor of the hospital was for Vietnam returnees, and some of the guys who came back you just look at them and it would be enough to turn your stomach. That definitely had an effect on my attitude towards the enemy because they were the ones that did this to them.

Finally, activists, like their Vietnam veteran peers, expressed serious concern about the acts of abusive violence committed by the NVA and VC. The following observation by a high activist is typical of this attitude:

> I think that they have matched our American brutality blow for blow, except perhaps with less fire power. They didn't have huge planes to defoliate the countryside, and they didn't have napalm and a lot of other agents of terror the United States had. But I do think it's a mistake to forget the kinds of brutality they were capable of. Even in defense of their own country.

It must be pointed out again that many antiwar activists had a *mixed or conflicted* view of the VC and NVA. The transcript material enables us to understand this attitude. While some activists pointed out that they knew little about the VC and NVA, most respondents in this group are in general agreement that the VC and NVA were fighting for a just cause. The three main explanations given for the mixed or conflicted attitude are the following:

The VC and NVA were the enemy of the United States

Some activists were torn between their loyalty to the United States and their support for the cause for which the VC and NVA were fighting. This attitude is demonstrated by the following reply by a moderate activist:

> I felt conflicted, because you can't back them, because they're fighting against your country, but then you also respect them.

The VC and NVA were killing Americans

Some respondents, while basically agreeing with the cause the VC and NVA were fighting for, realized that these groups were shooting United States units. The resulting conflicted feelings are clearly expressed in the words of a high activist:

> I felt a lot of ambivalence. I mean here were people who were killing American soldiers. I felt that there was more justice in their cause than in the cause of the ARVN or the South Vietnamese government. I felt that the Vietcong were fighting for ideological principles for which I felt basic agreement. . . . I felt for the American servicemen who were going to Vietnam, these were the people who were killing them, or sending them back without legs. I felt ambivalence.

The VC and NVA engaged in abusive violence against their own people

The issue of the mistreatment of the civilian population by the VC and NVA is troublesome for many activists who had great sympathy for the enemy's political objectives. Although some respondents managed to ignore this issue, other activists strongly condemned abusive violence, citing it as the main reason they felt negative about the VC and NVA. But respect for the cause of the VC and NVA combined with antipathy toward their type of warfare also led to an ambivalent view of the enemy forces. A high activist explained it this way:

> I felt that they had a justifiable legal, political position. However, they were ultimately warriors who . . . were engaged in—at least—as inhumane methods as anybody else was. . . . They were using very nonconventional warfare, they were using these booby traps. These things maliciously just kill people and trap people. I didn't agree with their type of warfare.

Conclusion

In light of our findings it seems reasonably clear that one of the major factors influencing this generation's view of the Vietnam War, regardless of an individual's relationship to the war, is antagonism toward the military forces that were our presumed allies. In trying to assess the meaning of the American intervention in Vietnam it would be well to keep in mind the generation's view of the combatants involved in that struggle. It is imperative to try to see the conflict through the eyes of American soldiers who risked their lives in Vietnam. American soldiers who had direct contact with the ARVN in the field, and who often were involved in battles against the enemy with the ARVN, evidence little regard for their supposed allies. Indeed, the response of the marines to the ARVN is a powerful reminder of the antagonism between the allies. Nowhere else in this study do we find such a large group responding so homogenously on any issue.

CHAPTER FIVE

PERCEPTIONS OF VIETNAMESE CIVILIANS

Because so much fighting has occurred since the Second World War and may well continue in the future, it is clearly important to secure regard for the noncombatant immunity of the civilian population during armed conflicts. This chapter first examines the current status of civilians in wartime. Subsequently, it explores the feelings of the Vietnam Generation toward the Vietnamese people as well as their perception of Vietnamese feelings toward the United States military presence. It also looks into their views of how the war affected the Vietnamese.

The Immunity of Civilians During Armed Conflicts

According to current international law, a civilian is any person who does not take a direct part in the hostilities as an active member of the organized conventional or guerrilla armed forces. In order to enjoy complete protection, such persons must refrain from committing hostile acts.

Concerned observers have noted that in an armed conflict it is inevitable that at times some members of the armed forces will mix with the civilian population. Unless the definition of the civilian population were to lose all meaning and the protection to which that group is entitled were to be destroyed, it has, therefore, been accepted that such a limited presence does not deprive the locality of its civilian character. On the other hand, if whole contingents of troops are located among the civilian population, the site becomes a legitimate military target, but the combatants must use the prescribed precautionary measures in attack laid down in conventional and customary international law.

The civilian status of a person is meant to guarantee that that person will be kept out of hostilities and safe from attack. To ensure such protection, however, it is necessary that in case of doubt as to a person's status, that person must be treated as a civilian and must not be considered as a military target. The assumption is valid only insofar as the appearance and actions of the civilians are such as might be generally expected of a person claiming civilian status.[1]

The immunity of civilians is subject to the condition that they must not take a "direct part in hostilities." What should be understood by these last four words? The expression covers acts of war intended to strike at the personnel and matériél of enemy armed forces. The *direct* part that civilians might take in fighting should be differentiated from an "indirect" contribution to the war effort which they might be called upon to carry out at various levels, for, in modern warfare, all a nation's activities contribute in some way or other to the pursuit of hostilities.

Military Necessity and the Civilian Population

The systematic terrorizing of whole populations is a strategy of both conventional and guerrilla war, a game plan used by established governments as well as revolutionary movements. Its objective is to destroy the morale of an entire nation or a part of its population. Its method is the indiscriminate killing of innocent civilians. It violates humanitarian law as well as principles of morality. Despite this, terrorism has been defended. The defenses represent one version or another of the military necessity argument. The argument as stated sets the interests of innocent people at a lesser value than the victory to be achieved. Any act of force that contributes in a significant way to winning the war is likely to be called permissible. It is also argued that in modern war the combatant status has been extended beyond the class of soldiers. The development of military technology has turned war today into as much an economic as a military activity. Therefore, the argument continues, many civilians have lost their noncombatant immunity because their work directly contributes to the business of war as suppliers of the means of fighting. Under those circumstances, workers are stripped of their civilian status and "noncombatant immunity" becomes a meaningless principle.

The humanitarian view rejects this approach and argues that the rules of war are grounded in a theory of individual rights under wartime conditions. As Michael Walzer has pointed out:

> The war convention invites soldiers to calculate costs and benefits only up to a point, and at that point it establishes a series of clearcut rules—moral fortifications, so to speak, that can be stormed only at great moral cost. . . . Belligerent armies are entitled to try to win their wars, but they are not entitled to do anything that is or seems to them necessary to win. They are subject to a set of

restrictions that rest in part on the agreements of states but that also have an independent foundation in moral principle. . . . The rules of "fighting well" are simply a series of recognitions of men and women who have a moral standing independent of and resistant to the exigencies of war. A legitimate act of war is one that does not violate the rights of the people against whom it is directed.[2]

As defined above, a civilian is any person who does not take a direct part in the hostilities as an active member of the organized armed forces. Those civilians who make what soldiers need to fight should not be attacked if their activities can be stopped in some other way. Civilians have a right to "due care," and the task of saving civilian lives must be accepted.[3]

The Problem of Guerrilla War

An important problem of guerrilla war is the rights of civilian supporters. Have these civilians lost their immunity? Or do they still have rights vis-a-vis the antiguerrilla forces? It is undeniable that the political ideology of the guerrillas weakens the separation between combatants and noncombatants. Guerrilla war is a "people's war," authorized from below. "The war of liberation," according to a pamphlet of the Vietnamese National Liberation Front, "is fought by the people themselves; the entire people . . . are the driving force."[4]

In fact, while guerrillas do engage in terrorist attacks against government "collaborators," they often will attempt to differentiate between combatants and noncombatants if only to show that they are not enemies of the people. But the distinction for the opposition is more difficult to make. The day-to-day existence of guerrillas is closely connected with the daily existence of the people around them. They often fight where they live; their military strongholds are not bases, posts, or camps, but villages. Still, it is generally agreed, this closeness does not deprive the civilian population of its war rights.[5]

The frequency of internal conflicts in certain parts of the world prompted one extremely important insertion into the Geneva Conventions of 1949: common Article 3. This article, applicable to all wars which are not of an international character, lays down the essential humanitarian rules that ensure basic human treatment to civilian victims of these conflicts.[6] Protocol II Additional to the Geneva Conventions of 1949, adopted in 1977, develops and supplements Article 3 and provides for fundamental guarantees for all persons who do not take a *direct* part in the hostilities as active members of the organized armed guerrilla forces although its high threshold of applicability demands a full-fledged civil war rather than sporadic hit and run tactics favored by guerrilla forces. In regard to the treatment of civilians, these rights are similar to those found in Protocol I and will be discussed later in these pages.

But what if the guerrillas cannot be distinguished from the people and a "people's war" is a reality? Michael Walzer has concluded:

There is . . . a moral argument to be made if this point is reached: the anti-guerrilla war can then no longer be fought—and not just because, from a strategic point of view, it can no longer be won. It cannot be fought because it is no longer an anti-guerrilla but an anti-social war, a war against an entire people.[7]

As critics of the Vietnam War have pointed out, one of the most important problems of the war was the absence of conventional military fronts. Combat could occur anywhere. American troops formed territorial units enclosed within hostile territory, units incapable of establishing control by winning the support of the majority of the people. But legally the existing closeness between the guerrilla forces and the people did not deprive the Vietnamese civilians of their war rights and their immunity. Toward the end of the war, it became increasingly difficult to isolate the guerrillas from the people. At that point, the American effort was doomed because, from a strategic point of view, the war could no longer be won. The whole nation had become the target, and the only remaining strategy involved a war against civilians.

One of the issues often lost sight of during the national debate over the merits of the Vietnam War was its human consequences for the Vietnamese people. In an attempt to bring this important question into focus, we will examine in the following pages how the Vietnamese were perceived by the Vietnam Generation. The importance of this issue derives from a fundamental dilemma not often acknowledged in the literature on the Vietnam War. Political imperatives spring from definitions of the national interest as interpreted by governmental and ancillary elites. These elites then attempt to persuade the general public to endorse their definitions. The language of persuasion since World War II has revolved around the phrase "fighting Communism," an abstraction which tends to block out the meaning of the struggle for existence in the daily lives of the people whose nation our leaders perceive to be "threatened." In other words, the coded language required to build support within the United States obscures the everyday life of a people while emphasizing the global political consequences of the "war." In that process, the American people often receive little more than simplistic stereotypes of those they are preparing to "assist." When, as in Vietnam, the consensus on the political objectives breaks down, the ensuing debate usually centers on political-military logic, execution of policy, and their consequences for Americans. Thus even the opposition too often neglects the human meaning of the intervention. On those occasions when the human tragedy of war does break through the political debate, it is too often due to a special horror carried out by one of the parties to the conflict. Such extreme situations do not convey much about everyday life, and what remains absent is a sense of who the people are we purport to be "helping."

Regardless of why we were in Vietnam, the judgment of the war cannot ignore the costs of the intervention to the people we were ostensibly trying to help, the Vietnamese. The issue became part of the national debate over the validity of American involvement in the conflict. It is, therefore, important to examine this attitude toward that population of the generation most directly involved in the war.

The Vietnam Generation's View of the Vietnamese

How does the Vietnam Generation view the Vietnamese civilians? Our findings suggest two general trends. First, there is relatively little hostility toward the Vietnamese. Vietnam veterans (31%) are the most likely to harbor negative feelings toward the Vietnamese compared to either Vietnam era veterans (25%) or nonveterans (12%); but even among Vietnam veterans only three in ten focus exclusively on hostility to the Vietnamese.

The second important trend we find is that Vietnam veterans are much more likely to express diverse views of the Vietnamese. As table 5.1 shows, Vietnam veterans (31%) much more often than either era veterans (21%) or nonveterans (16%) respond that they have ambivalent feelings about the Vietnamese. The predominant response of the nonveterans is to describe the Vietnamese in sympathetic terms (72%). The range of responses to the Vietnamese by Vietnam veterans is obviously related to the personal contact Vietnam veterans had with Vietnamese. While nonveterans and era veterans depend upon impressions of the Vietnamese people through media sources, Vietnam veterans draw on life experiences. Since most nonveterans believed the war was destructive to the Vietnamese, it is not surprising to find they are more likely to say they felt *sympathetic* toward the people. The expression of sympathy from nonveterans is based on a *general* feeling of compassion. Many Vietnam veterans, on the other hand, due to firsthand contact with civilians, express a range of stronger and *more personal* feelings of either a positive or negative character.

Among nonveterans, the usual impact of activism on perceptions of war-related attitudes is not evident. There is a small difference between the high activists' (6%) and the low activists' (14%) tendency to characterize the Vietnamese negatively, but this difference does not achieve statistical significance (table 5.2). However, the character of the descriptions of the Vietnamese and the logic behind the perceptions of that population do differ significantly, as the transcript material shows. Our statistical findings capture several distinct perceptions of the Vietnamese, all of them positive but reflecting quite different ways of relating to the Vietnamese from a distance.

The question to which we now turn is how the war experiences of the Vietnam veterans influenced their feelings toward the Vietnamese. Veterans' views of the Vietnamese are affected by four factors: race; personal contact with the Vietnamese; combat; and exposure to abusive violence. In the general sample, we found no significant effect of race on feelings about the Vietnamese. Among

Vietnam veterans, however, as table 5.3 shows, we find a very substantial difference between black and white Vietnam veterans. Black Vietnam veterans (49%) more often say they had positive feelings for the Vietnamese than white veterans (35%); and they infrequently express hostile feelings about the Vietnamese compared to whites (10% vs. 36%). Although white Vietnam veterans are generally less sympathetic to the Vietnamese, interaction with the people alters their perceptions. In table 5.4, we see that Vietnam veterans who report personal contact with the Vietnamese also describe the Vietnamese in much more positive terms than those veterans who indicate they had no such interaction (46% vs. 29%). Thus, we can see that hostility to the Vietnamese in the Vietnam-veteran population seems limited largely to those white veterans who had little personal contact with the people.

There are, of course, distinctly different types of contact with the populace in war. Men who experienced heavy combat, or who were exposed to or participated in abusive violence, are likely to have strong reactions to their experience that color their views of the Vietnamese. As tables 5.5 and 5.6 demonstrate, war stress in Vietnam had a significant impact on feelings about the Vietnamese. In table 5.5, we see that heavy-combat veterans (54%) express far greater ambivalence about the Vietnamese than either the low- or moderate-combat veterans (28%), and that they are very much less likely than the other groups to hold either positive or negative views of the Vietnamese. The most notable difference is the low proportion who hold unequivocally sympathetic views of the Vietnamese (18%). In Vietnam, soldiers too often felt threatened by civilians who were potentially hostile to Americans or sympathetic to the enemy, even though they were attracted to them as people. Those Vietnam veterans who saw the most combat seem to reflect in their feelings about the Vietnamese that pervasive sense of ambivalence so commonly associated with Vietnam.

Table 5.6 shows that witnessing of and participation in abusive violence fundamentally alters perceptions and feelings about the Vietnamese. The clearest pattern of effects is found in the witnessed group. This sample is much less hostile to the Vietnamese (21%) compared to either the not exposed (34%) or the participant group (41%). However, when we examine the positive and ambivalent columns in table 5.6 we see that the not exposed group (33%) has a less positive perception of the Vietnamese than the veterans who witnessed (46%) or participated in (41%) abusive violence. The participants in abusive violence (18%) seem much less ambivalent about their response to the Vietnamese than either of the other groups (32%). The bimodal response to the Vietnamese of the participants in abusive violence suggests that their actions forced them to take a definite posture. The witnessed group, on the other hand, appears to be deeply affected by their experience in a way that elicits sympathy for the Vietnamese, and they tend to see them primarily as victims.

The distinctive effects of combat and witnessing of abusive violence indicate that the suffering that accompanies war is experienced differently depending on whether or not the observer perceives himself or the other as the victim. Combat veterans who were not exposed to abusive violence may relate more to their own vulnerability, causing them to project some of their anger onto the Vietnamese as a source of their pain. The more plausible victim, in the eyes of the veterans exposed to abusive violence against civilians and POWs, is the Vietnamese. Again, on-the-spot experience contributes to sympathy for and a more positive view of the Vietnamese.

Vietnam Veterans' Perceptions

The narrative material underscores the fact that for Vietnam veterans, the country and its population were very real indeed. As a group, they tend to respond in more personal terms to the people, and the range of feelings expressed is greater than among era veterans and nonveterans. There is much dissension and disagreement among this sample on issues related to Vietnamese civilians. Respondents are almost as likely to have disliked the Vietnamese as to have felt sympathy and compassion for their fate, and Vietnam veterans are more likely than other groups to have strong positive feelings. A third group of veterans had an ambivalent attitude.

Positive attitudes

Those Vietnam veterans who had a positive response to the Vietnamese (37%) can be divided into two main groups: a minority who expressed a generally detached feeling of sympathy and compassion for the civilians and a majority who had a much stronger personal response.

Many of those respondents who expressed a general feeling of sympathy for the Vietnamese pointed out that they knew little about them. But they felt sorry for them and were aware of the destruction inflicted on Vietnamese society. Others tried to develop an insight into the Vietnamese culture, value system, and social structure and expressed some understanding as well as compassion for the civilian population. This attitude is reflected in the following statement made by a white Army lieutenant who saw heavy combat:

> I thought that they were industrious people. I think that you've got to understand that they come from a completely different social background and their value system is different from yours and that doesn't make it wrong. A lot of people tried to perceive them in the mold of their own value system, and that caused more problems with the Vietnamese people than anything else. I think, in their own way, they were as scrupulous, as honorable a people as ours. . . . I observed them and I realized the situation they were in.

Those respondents who had a strong positive perception of the Vietnamese often pointed out that they liked their culture, found them physically beautiful, considered them warm and friendly people, or admired their strength and courage. This group also stressed that the Vietnamese people were not the enemy and that they deserved special protection. They argued that the guerrilla-war nature of the Vietnam conflict did not justify disregard for the rights and the dignity of the civilians, especially innocent children. Often their concern for the civilians is expressed in an increasingly hostile attitude toward American involvement in the war and personal feelings of anger or guilt.

The impact of race. The narrative material makes it clear that generally black veterans not only felt more positive toward the Vietnamese than their white peers but also developed a deeper understanding of the people. While many white veterans expressed respect for the Vietnamese, they were inclined to note that a cultural wall remained between the Vietnamese and the Americans. Still, their positive feelings toward the people often became one of the main reasons they turned against American involvement in the war. A white Army infantryman explained:

> I liked the Vietnamese . . . I think there was a cultural or built-in blankness. You could get close to them but at the same time you could go one wall in and then you ran into other walls. . . . Meanwhile you live amongst them as best you can. . . . I think for an American to understand a Vietnamese emotionally or closely is a very rare thing. I admired and respected them. . . . It reshaped my thinking process. I became very antiwar. I got more radical while I was in Nam.

Black veterans often expressed a sense of racial identification. They noted that they were not against the war in the beginning. But after they arrived in Vietnam, they felt close to the Vietnamese. Regardless of the war in progress, these people were not their enemy. They were "just brown-skinned people," "my type of people," "brothers." Many black soldiers developed close friendships with Vietnamese civilians. In addition, many concluded that in some ways Vietnam was like the place they had grown up in. It had not been as hard for them in America because there was no war going on, but life had been difficult nevertheless, fighting for survival in a white society. As a result of their positive feelings for the Vietnamese, many black veterans gradually turned against American involvement in the war.

This strong positive attitude toward the Vietnamese people is well illustrated by the remarks made by the following two black respondents. A corporal in the marines who was in heavy combat expressed his feelings this way:

> [Vietnam] is one of the most beautiful places I had ever seen in my life. I used to like to take walks through the country. I was excited the whole time I was there.

The country, the people, I was seeing water buffalos and it made me feel that much bigger. I really liked the Vietnamese. I respected how hard they worked. I respected the family unit. . . . The way they had to survive there for themselves, you had to respect it. Sometimes 240-rockets—that is the big rockets—they would be coming in and the people would just duck down in the paddy; then when the shelling is over they went right back to work.

A veteran who served in the army explained why Vietnam reminded him of Panama, the country where he was born:

I found the people very interesting. . . . They were more or less like us . . . I am talking about black people. . . . They were getting ripped off in their own land. That's the way I looked at it. The country reminded me a lot of Panama. The heat . . . some of the lifestyles are similar. . . . I was able to relate right off.

The impact of personal contacts. As noted earlier, those Vietnam veterans who had personal contacts with the Vietnamese generally responded in a more positive way to that population than those who did not get to know the civilians personally. Many positive relationships with the Vietnamese developed, including special ties with girlfriends, civilians working on the base, people living in the villages, and, most important, children. At the same time, veterans reported bad experiences especially with profiteers and certain prostitutes. Such contacts shaped feelings in a more negative direction.

While many veterans spent their leisure hours on base, writing letters, going to service clubs, playing pool, seeing movies, others used their free time for contact with the Vietnamese. Some learned Vietnamese, and this made it easier for them to communicate with the civilians. Respondents noted that many men really enjoyed being with the people. They also felt that the Vietnamese had more respect for the GIs who spoke their language. They pointed out that while many Americans in Vietnam ran wild, got drunk, and caused fights, others worked to establish good relations with the civilian population.

Those who had personal relationships with the Vietnamese stressed that it was necessary to sit down and talk to them to get to know them. They pointed out that many soldiers had contempt for the Vietnamese because they did not realize that, even though the Vietnamese are different, they are human, with warm hearts and a deep respect for life. True, some of them were selfish and materialistic, but most of the population was generous and had a real love for family and country. A white veteran who served in the navy explained why he felt sympathy for the Vietnamese and how his friend, who had closer contact with Vietnamese families, developed a much stronger personal feeling for them:

I felt curiosity more than anything else; and sympathy after that. I tried to talk with them and sound them out about what they thought was going on and what they thought about us. It was difficult because I sensed a certain reluctance to say anything really negative to an American about what we were doing there in the country. It was difficult to get a clear impression. My friend McDonald did get into close contact with one or another Vietnamese family and he had a different impression altogether because of that kind of contact. He got to know them and liked them very much.

Veterans reported visiting the people in the villages and spending time with them. A black veteran who served as a platoon sergeant in the army had the following memories:

I stayed at some little huts. . . . If I had a week stand-out, I intended on spending my whole week or most of it in the village. I would go down there. I would see mama san, or maybe the village honcho, chief of the village. We'd sit down and we'd rap. I had been caught in the village when the Vietcong was there. They would hide me in a cellar. . . . I had some good, friendly relationships with a lot of mama sans, boy sans, poppa sans. Then I had sexual relationships with a lot of mama sans or girl sans.

A white army infantry sergeant reported:

I liked them. . . . I've gone into some of their hooches and they ask you—"You want something to eat?" They gave you chopsticks and you eat, you don't want to hurt their feelings. . . . If I come up on a village or a hooch and somebody's wounded I'd call a medevac. . . . You talk to them—try to get them some of your C-rations, especially the children.

Others reported that they developed friendships with the civilians working for the American forces. A white noncombat veteran who was stationed as a supply clerk in Saigon stated:

Well, the only contact I had was with the girls we worked with in Saigon. . . . They liked us . . . and thought we were helping the country. . . . They were just like everybody else. Normal people. They had feelings—some were Buddhist, some were Catholic—they cried—they got upset. They were secretaries, clerks. . . . I would say that working with the Vietnamese people was probably the nicest thing that I carried away from it. . . . They were super nice people—they were like sisters to us—we'd laugh with them—joke with them. . . . They cried when we left and we did the same.

Vietnam veterans also established ties with the "mama san" who took care of them. A black air force security police noted:

My mama san—she came in every day and cleaned up our hootch and stuff. And she was pretty nice. More or less, she was like an aunt and she took care of the guys and we met her family. We got a close relationship going.

A substantial number established close relations with Vietnamese girls. Some fell in love and married them. A white helicopter pilot described how the reality of war destroyed his friendship with a young Vietnamese woman:

I had a girl friend in Pleiku. . . . I fell in love with her, it was important that that girl became a friend of mine. I was thinking it was almost like Humphrey Bogart in Casablanca. . . . One night we were walking down the street and a grenade went off in a bar and killed some Americans. And I turned to protect her and she was gone. I never saw her again. I experienced the reality of the kind of tenuous friendship that you could build up in a war.

The relations with Vietnamese girls were not always physical, often the young women remained "just good friends." A black army infantryman put it this way:

I liked them. I had a lot of Vietnamese that I really came close to. . . . I got to know two young ladies. I knew their mother and father. I saw their father get killed on the highway one evening. He was coming from work because he was working for the American government. . . . Nothing physical, you know, we were just good friends. They taught me to speak a little Vietnamese. I taught them to speak a little bit of English. I know when I left there were quite a number of Vietnamese out there at the airstrip saying "Why you got to go?"

Their warm feelings for the children caused many Vietnam veterans to have a positive feeling for the Vietnamese. They explained that they got close to some of them, gave them food, and took care of them when they were ill. They shopped for them and bought them clothes or shoes. A black army man reported:

I can speak about the kids. Most of the time I was there I would bring them C-rations. I would take them something to eat rather than see them go digging around in garbage dumps. Most guys over there had a couple of families that they liked and looked out for . . . gave them C-rations and things like that . . . cigarettes and stuff, even money. We were good with money. I was making 120 dollars a month. What could I do with that in Vietnam?

The impact of abusive violence. As noted earlier, a plurality of Vietnam veterans who witnessed abusive violence (46%) developed positive feelings toward the Vietnamese people. Many reported feelings of compassion and a desire to help the local population. A white army captain noted:

I knew they needed help. I wanted to help them. The country was in pitiful condition . . . for the most part the people just lived in squalid conditions— terrible conditions.

Furthermore, our transcripts show that veterans who witnessed abusive violence were more likely to admit that their experiences were traumatizing and to express the repugnance they felt at the time. A white veteran expressed the following feelings:

I felt guilty being there. . . . We were there for the purpose of destruction. We were not there for the purpose of helping the people. We were purposefully reducing them to subhuman conditions.

As will be discussed later in this chapter, whites who *participated* in abusive violence expressed a distinctly different view of the Vietnamese than their peers who were only exposed to cruel and hostile acts. A minority of white participants expressed feelings of sympathy for the Vietnamese, pointing out that they really did not understand the Vietnamese although they felt sorry for them. One white infantryman explained:

They weren't too friendly. I didn't get around them enough to associate with them except for some of the females for sexual purposes. . . . They were weird to me so I just stayed away from them. . . . I felt sorry for them after being there for a while.

White participants more often reported an open hostility to the Vietnamese. But black veterans in the participant group were often seriously troubled by their experiences. These men generally reported strong positive feelings for the Vietnamese. Consequently when they took part in episodes of brutality they developed a deep sense of guilt for their behavior.

A black veteran's reflections on his experiences in Vietnam illustrate the conflict these men reported between their affinity for the country and the people and the violent acts they committed.

[I had] a difficult homecoming caused by my participation in killing and my feelings for the Vietnamese. I would go out on the weekends . . . and stay in the village with a mama san and just relax. I felt that they were part of me. I could see the suffering that they were going through. Sickness, illnesses, and things like that. Poor country! Killing the Vietnamese . . . had a tremendous impact on me. A lot of things were going on that I could not have any say over, but I was involved. I could not get used to the killing and I would have nightmares and dreams. The killing . . . mangled bodies . . . everything like that.

Negative attitudes

A substantial number of Vietnam veterans (31%) expressed negative feelings toward the Vietnamese people. Interpreting the findings, we discover that the following four *main* negative themes are expressed by Vietnam veterans in the narrative in response to the question: "What were your feelings toward the Vietnamese people in general? Why did you feel this way?"

They were the enemy. Respondents argued that the Vietnamese civilians could not be trusted because they were either supporting the war or were Vietcong sympathizers. This argument is often presented by heavy-combat veterans. It was noted that children, women, and the aged were often participants in the war. It was not necessary to be a guerrilla fighter to make a booby trap, plant a mine, or toss a hand grenade a few yards. American soldiers were often the losers in battles waged by those who appeared helpless and inoffensive. It was noted that these actions were not occasional aberrations; rather, they were basic features of Vietcong strategy. As a result, civilians were the enemy. They had forfeited their rights as noncombatants. One did not have to have any feelings about killing them. It was them against us. Respondents complained that Vietnamese civilians worked for the Americans inside the bases, that one could see them walking around, measuring all of the installations, and that shortly thereafter there would be an attack of rocket fire. You could not tell who were the Vietcong and who were the Vietnamese civilians. They told stories about children as young as nine who walked in and out of the American camps every day; at night they would go home and tell the Vietcong where the installations were. The following remarks by two heavy-combat veterans illustrate this attitude.

A black army infantryman commented:

> When I was in military training in the States, we used to spend hours at a time just listening to them telling us that it was our job to kill. They even had a song that said that you wanted to go to Vietnam and kill the Cong. Once you got to Vietnam there was not too much feeling about killing the Vietnamese left in you. . . . They always told us in training that even the kids are trying to kill you. So do not even trust the kids. So, although you smile and joke, you always had in the back of your mind that this woman, or girl or child might be the person that tries to do you in. As a result you never had any sympathy or use for them.

A white army infantryman expressed a similar attitude:

> It was all very confusing. During the day we did get our laundry done in some of the forward LZs. Charlie was there during the day pretending to be a civilian, all friendly to us. He might sell you a soda pop or beer during the day.

And at night he was shooting you at your perimeter. So you never really knew who were the civilians and who were the Vietcong in the villages.

They were exploitive. Veterans often complained that the Vietnamese people exploited the American forces. Some argued that the population viewed them as a meal ticket. "We were there, so we should feed them and clothe them." Others felt that the people were always trying to show soldiers a good time for money, "when they saw GIs they saw dollar signs." In addition, they often were thieves and "ripped us off." This argument is presented by heavy-combat as well as moderate- and low-combat veterans. Black veterans are less inclined than white veterans to stress such exploitation. A white navy seabee put it as follows:

> Most of them seemed to be living off the Americans. . . . Plenty of wood and junk and candy and cigarettes. . . . I didn't really care what the hell happened to them. . . . They tried to rip off my watch or my shirt, or give me this, give me that . . . and they were just bothersome . . . mostly the kids. . . . Sometimes you try and help them out . . . most of the time you'd like to kick them in the head.

They lacked appreciation. Respondents pointed out that Vietnamese civilians took it for granted that Americans would do the fighting. A white veteran who was an army gunner expressed his bitterness as follows:

> It was all right if we did the fighting and the dying, but they wanted no involvement. . . . I became very callous and had a tremendous amount of hate toward the Vietnamese.

Respondents also commented that the Vietnamese did not respect the American forces or try to help them in any way. The Americans were over there trying to save the civilians, but the people never told them where the enemy was or tried to give any real assistance. A white veteran who served in the Green Berets made this point:

> I did not care for them . . . they treated us like we were trash. There was no comraderie between the civilians and American troops and, after all, we were only there to help them. But they did not give any sign of respect to a GI. They only wanted to be left alone.

It was also observed that the Americans were giving the Vietnamese a better life but were receiving no appreciation for their efforts. The vast majority of the population, these respondents noted, did not even know the difference between capitalism or Communist rule. A white marine who was in heavy combat explained:

I felt I was helping . . . because with us came the seabees, with the seabees came wood, aluminum, houses, things that these people didn't have . . . they live in dirt. . . . I was driving through the village once with a captain and a group of kids picked up rocks and threw them at us. And I stopped the jeep and got up with my goddamn greasegun and I was gonna mow them down and the captain stopped me. He says, "No, don't do that." I said, "What are these sons of a bitches doing? What the hell did we do to them? We gave them food, man. We gave them toothpaste" . . . I couldn't understand it. That's why I got to dislike them so much.

Their lifestyle was contemptible. Some veterans expressed negative feelings about the Vietnamese culture and way of life. They considered the Vietnamese backward, primitive, and uncivilized. It was noted that "they lived like animals, uneducated, in dirty little villages, fighting for pieces of old bread." Some respondents called them lazy and unpleasant. They were also felt to be "really strange people, wearing black pajamas during the day." Contempt was often expressed along racial lines: they were "gooks" and "slopeheads." Black Vietnam veterans were much less inclined than their white peers to express this form of negative attitude. An army infantry man explained his view of the Vietnamese lifestyle this way:

Their way of living seemed so barbaric. . . . You could not relate to them because they lived in such primitive conditions. Their attitude toward Americans was a servitude type attitude. They really catered to you. They did not speak English and so you did see our guys swearing at them and calling them all kinds of weird names and they'd just sit there and smile and shake their head.

Abusive violence and views of civilians. As discussed previously, a majority of white participants felt either negative or ambivalent toward the Vietnamese. They generally felt aloof from the Vietnamese population and alienated by their passivity. One white veteran who had taken part in physically harassing civilians reported the following feelings:

They didn't seem to care. They were the sorriest race of people I ever run upon in my life. . . . They just didn't fight . . . we were doing all their fighting. . . . When they were around us they were happy and liked us and when they were around the Vietcong they were the same way with them, I'm sure.

Even when the white veterans did not express such marked hostility to the Vietnamese, they generally noted a well-advanced personal indifference to the value of Vietnamese life. A veteran who said he had taken part in destroying a village stated:

I started to lose my respect for life . . . you could be eating dinner and get up and walk out and wipe out sixty or eighty or ninety people and go right back and sit down and eat.

Moreover, respondents who participated in abusive violence somehow numbed themselves to human misery, as the following quote demonstrates:

I mean killing a gook was nothing really. It didn't bother me at all. I could have butchered them like nothing really. I really had no feelings.

Ambivalent attitudes toward the Vietnamese

Thirty-one percent of Vietnam veterans do not express clear positive or negative feelings for the Vietnamese people. Some of these respondents noted feelings of sympathy for the Vietnamese but also felt resentment that Americans were dying in a war that should have been fought by the local population. The following statement by a white navy veteran typifies this view:

Thanksgiving we anchored offshore and they brought the orphan kids on the ship and we gave them ice cream. That was nice because you always feel something for the kids. But then you look at them and say, well, your mother and father were killed because supposedly you're fighting the Communists and we're helping you—but should we be here? Is this right? If it was aggression against the United States fine, I wouldn't mind going to protect my family . . . but what were we protecting in Nam?

Other respondents mentioned that they truly liked the Vietnamese, but they agreed with those who had a negative view that you had to stay at a distance ''because you did not know who to trust.'' This view is articulated by a black heavy-combat veteran:

I liked them, but . . . little kids would come up to you and the Vietcong would booby trap them with bombs and he'll blow himself up and you. . . .So you know, you could not afford to get close. You had to be very careful.

It was also noted that while the Vietnamese were nice people they were very poor allies who gave minimal assistance to the American forces. The following statement by a white army infantryman who was in heavy combat illustrates this attitude:

How did I feel about them in relationship to the war, or how did I feel about them as a people and as a culture? I think as a people and as a culture they were magnificent, and I enjoyed living with them. . . . It's just fascinating to learn of another culture, their ways of life. As to their attitude toward the war and toward our being there, I was depressed about that. You were there fighting for their country. . . . They did not make it evident to me that I was there helping them or that they in turn would help me in any way.

A common theme found in the narrative is positive feelings for some Vietnamese mixed with a resentment for others who were exploiting the United States. Women and children especially were viewed with sympathy. A white veteran noted:

> I had very little feeling for the people. But the children, that was different. We would go out on these medical missions where we did go into the villages and take medical supplies and treat the children. It really bothered me to see the different diseases that the children would have at birth. Adults can take care of themselves, children cannot.

Others liked the rural peasants, while despising the city dwellers, prostitutes, and black marketeers. A white veteran who was in the army infantry expressed the following feelings:

> I think the villagers were having a pretty bad time of it, because we would go through the villages in the daytime. Then in the nighttime the Vietcong or North Vietnamese Army would come around to their houses doing the same thing we did, looking for information, harassing them. I felt really bad for the people in the countryside, for the farmers. . . . But I had no use for the others, the ones in the cities. The ones I met were after nothing but your money and trying to get what they could out of you. They are having a good time, I'm 10,000 miles away trying to keep from getting my ass shot off and it does not work for good relations.

A white infantryman explained his attitude:

> I found that they were a very greedy people, very selfish . . . I realized that it was not their fault. We had infected their culture, we gave these people a way of living they had never had before. When I got into isolated areas, I met people that had not been infected so much by our material wealth. They were very basic human beings. . . . They were very good to me, they were friendly and they did not ask for payment. These people, I guess, I considered the real true Vietnamese and I respected them very much.

Nonveterans' Perceptions

One of the interesting aspects of this study's findings is that whatever posture nonveterans adopted toward the war, we find little evidence of hostility to Vietnamese civilians. Among the two groups most often at odds, those who supported the war and those most active in opposing it, approximately 72% expressed positive feelings for the Vietnamese civilians; and only 16% of the prowar nonveterans compared to 6% of the antiwar activists expressed negative feelings. There is, however, a difference in feeling between antiwar activists and those who supported American involvement in the war. Antiwar activists are more likely to identify with the fate of the Vietnamese, while prowar nonveterans expressed their feelings less strongly. Nonveterans who supported the war are also more likely to harbor hostile feelings toward the Vietnamese than are the activists.

Prowar nonveterans

As noted in the previous chapter, nonveterans who supported American involvement in the war are generally strongly anti-Communist. Those respondents who had a *positive view* of the Vietnamese civilians most often pointed out that they pitied the people because they were under Communist control. One white respondent noted:

> I felt sorry for them. The Vietcong were butchers that were sent in to devastate the area and there were just so many innocent people getting killed, especially women and children. . . . I think we were making them really want to be independent from oppressive forces.

Those who felt *ambivalent* often complained that the people of Vietnam were not helping the Americans sufficiently in their battle against "the evils of Communism." A white respondent expressed this view as follows:

> I felt kind of mixed . . . the one thing that I *didn't* feel sorry for them about was that I thought that this country was giving them the opportunity to have their own freedom and they just did not seem to want to avail themselves of it. . . . I really believe that we were trying to give South Vietnam a chance to have a free and democratic government. . . . Let's face it, if it's not this country who is going to uphold democracy, it's not going to be anybody, because we're the only one with the money and the power to do it.

A minority of the prowar nonveterans expressed strong *negative feelings.* Some pointed out that the Vietnamese could not be trusted. They played a dual role: they would befriend the American forces during the day and stab them in the back at night. Other respondents commented that while they supported American involvement in the war as a necessary battle against Communism, they found the Vietnamese to be illiterate, uncivilized, and lazy, in short, "not worth getting killed for." A white respondent summarized this view as follows:

My view? I felt at that time they were uncultured, savage if you want to call it that. Just had a very bad attitude towards them.

Antiwar activists

Activists pointed out that they felt sorry for the Vietnamese people because they had been involved in warfare for a very long time, in conflicts that were devastating their lives and their country. A high activist noted:

> Basically, like all people, I have a humanitarian concept that they have a right to exist. My feelings in that were pretty much molded by Frances Fitzgerald's *Fire in the Lake*, which was a chronicle of the history of the Vietnamese people from their tribal existence to the conquest by the Chinese. I feel sorry for them, they lived with war for a long time.

Another high activist expressed these feelings:

> I felt a great deal of sorrow. I knew enough by then to know that they had been involved in war really since the early 1940s. We're talking at this time of twenty-five, almost thirty years of continuous war, which struck me as an unbelievable ordeal.

Activists felt sorry for *all* Vietnamese civilians because they were the innocent victims in a civil war. Men, women, and children, they noted, faced death at the hands of the combatants and by starvation. A high activist expressed this concern as follows:

> I thought the people themselves, North and South, were really going through hell. Their country was being decimated. They were losing family, friends, the land was being torn apart, all this fancy technology really decimated their country. I had a lot of sympathy for the people in general.

Many activists underlined the responsibility of the South Vietnamese government for the suffering of the civilian population. One high activist expressed this feeling as follows:

> I felt sorry for them. . . . They were victimized by their own leaders. With no say whatsoever as to what they should do. I think they were just pawns in this war. You could see their hurt, they were living in squalor because of this war. You could physically see that on newsreels or in reading.

These respondents also expressed great concern for the abusive violence committed by allied as well as enemy forces against the Vietnamese civilians.

This attitude is demonstrated by the following reply by a high activist:

> I pitied the South Vietnamese, because on the whole, when you excluded the ARVN and the Vietcong, the masses of men, women, and children simply wanted to be left alone and to live their own lives. Innocents were chopped up by both sides, and I recognized that too. It's not as if atrocities were committed by one side only.

For a substantial number of activists, the suffering inflicted on the Vietnamese became the *main* reason that they strongly turned against the American involvement in the conflict. A high activist explained why he opposed the war:

> I felt sorry for the Vietnamese people and the Cambodians and the people from Laos, because we were bombing the hell out of all of them and if we had stayed out of it, I don't think the war would have progressed to the dimensions it reached. It would have been a civil war. I don't think that so many people would have been uprooted, so many homes, so much good fertile land destroyed. It would have been another civil war, but something they could have resolved themselves.

While some respondents argued that their antiwar activism freed them from any involvement in the actual operation of the war, others felt "somewhat responsible" as American citizens for what was happening in Vietnam.

Despite the substantial majority of the activists (75%) who felt positive about the Vietnamese, a small group expressed an ambivalent attitude. Those respondents felt unsure that the Vietnamese "really wanted us there" and admitted ignorance of the people and their culture.

Perceptions of How the Vietnamese Viewed U.S. Military Personnel

The responses to the question of the way that Americans were perceived by their "hosts" mirror to a significant degree the findings on how this generation viewed the Vietnamese.

Vietnam veterans, as shown in table 5.7, are significantly more likely to feel that the Vietnamese held positive views of Americans (41% compared to 30% for era veterans and 25% for nonveterans); and they are less likely to believe that the Vietnamese were hostile to Americans (34% vs. 48% vs. 52%). There were also a rather substantial number of respondents in this group who thought the Vietnamese were ambivalent about the Americans: about 28% of Vietnam veterans fall into this category, as compared to 22% of the era veterans and 23% of the nonveterans.

The most significant finding here is the small percentage of the Vietnam

Generation that perceived the Vietnamese people as holding a positive view of the Americans there to ''help them save their country.'' Since only 41% of Vietnam veterans felt that the Vietnamese viewed them favorably, trying to fight in that people's behalf must have been a heavy burden.

Table 5.8 shows that those nonveterans who opposed the war were substantially more likely to believe that the Vietnamese held negative views of Americans (61%) than the prowar nonveterans (31%). These responses allow us to see that for those nonveterans who opposed the war, sympathy for the Vietnamese and the perception that the Vietnamese were unenthusiastic about the presence of U.S. forces were intertwined.

Views of Vietnam Veterans

The transcript material helps us understand the various ways American soldiers perceived Vietnamese feelings about their presence. It is noteworthy that those who served during the post-Tet period of the war generally had a more negative or ambivalent impression about their welcome than did veterans who served prior to Tet.

Positive attitude

Only a minority of the men directly involved in the war felt that they had the support and appreciation of the people for whom they thought they were fighting. The reasons for this positive view are clearly expressed in the narrative material. The most common theme is the perceived awareness of the Vietnamese people that the American forces were helping them in their fight against communism. Indeed, respondents noted that Americans were appreciated for being good allies and for protecting the people against the Vietcong and NVA. A marine who was in heavy combat noted:

> The longer I was there, the more I believed that what we were doing was right. Because the kids that I knew had lost brothers, fathers, uncles . . . had lost close relatives to the North Vietnamese . . . and there was resentment and a pleading for your help.

Some respondents pointed out that every Vietnamese villager they were close to seemed to be grateful for the American protection against enemy forces. They never had any trouble around their base camp. The smaller kids would come and help fill sand bags and the older people would also help in other ways. There were no incidents, like glass in bottles or poison or grenades thrown into a crowd of men. The Vietnamese were helpful allies. In addition, it was pointed out that the civilians had been in a pretty bad shape until the Americans got there. Then their lifestyle began to improve.

These respondents also often pointed out that the Communist forces were committing atrocities against the civilian population, while the American troops treated them humanely. A veteran who served in the army and witnessed abusive violence committed by enemy forces against Vietnamese civilians expressed this attitude as follows:

> I felt we were appreciated for being there and trying to help out. They enjoyed our company. We met and talked with them. . . . Most of them were refugees driven from their own sections of Vietnam and forced to live in a smaller area. Some of them were escapees from North Vietnam. . . . They told us of some of the atrocities performed by the Vietcong. These were primarily business people, farmers, and what you would consider an educated class of the Vietnamese.

Another army man who was also exposed to enemy acts of abusive violence told us of a gruesome personal experience:

> I was with a sergeant and we had gone into Saigon. This woman came running up and she was saying something in Vietnamese which I did not understand. But the sergeant I was with had married a Vietnamese woman and he understood what she was saying. She was thanking us for being in their country helping them. At that point she unwrapped her little baby and showed it to us. Little baby . . . could not have been more than a year and half old. No arms and no legs. The VC had come through her village where they had owned a small rice farm and because they did not have enough rice for them, this was the punishment that they endowed on them. They cut the baby's arms and legs off and raped her repeatedly and killed her husband.

Negative attitude

Some of those who held a negative view about Vietnamese attitudes toward the American forces pointed out that the Vietnamese civilians were hostile toward U.S. military personnel because they feared reprisals by the Vietcong. A captain in the marines noted:

> The adults had almost nothing to do with you . . . primarily because they were afraid of the VC. The VC visited all these villages all the time. . . . It was sort of like the reign of Hitler almost—you move out of line, we'll kill you. The VC, I'm sure, killed more of their people than they did ours. I'd bet on that.

But most of those who felt that the Vietnamese attitude was negative noted that the Americans were looked upon as hostile, destructive foreigners. The Vietnamese people did not want the Americans to fight there. Many Vietnamese considered the Americans alien and strange. A marine observed:

They hated us . . . even Vietnamese officers in Pleiku—there were some educated Vietnamese over there—said "basically we do not like you. . . . The kids that come up and grab you on the arm think that you are odd." I did not realize in the beginning that they hated us. See, I was under the impression that they probably were thinking of us as liberators.

And an army man had the following to say:

They did not want us there. We were destroying their country, their people. It was a tragic thing. We were hostile foreigners in their land. Having been occupied by the French, also a Caucasian race, we were just Frenchmen with a different last name.

Ambivalent attitude

Another group of respondents pointed out that the response patterns of the Vietnamese were quite complex. Their attitude toward the Americans was shaped by many different factors, including their political views, the type of contact they had with U.S. military personnel, the area they lived in, and their social class. Respondents noted that some Vietnamese were receptive to the Americans for purely selfish reasons: the U.S. military presence allowed them to make money, procure supplies, and exploit the military personnel. Others were dedicated to fighting the Vietcong and NVA and truly appreciated the Americans. Many were Vietcong sympathizers and hated the Americans, holding them responsible for what was happening to them, their family, and their country. These sympathizers "just kind of blanked you out," "would not talk to you," or "would give you a hostile stare."

This group of respondents considered the nature of the contact that linked Americans and Vietnamese as one of the most important factors shaping civilian response. A veteran explained his own experience:

The problem is that there were two different ways I got into contact with them. One was with these medical teams and those people accepted us with open arms. We were helping them. The other contact with the people was when we were in combat missions, then they would be very negative.

It was also stressed that the response of the Vietnamese civilians to the Americans varied from site to site: it was different in villages, in cities, and in and out of the battle zone. A veteran explained this difference as follows:

In the villages the Americans had to be looked up to because they knew you were there to push away their foe and to protect their farms and their animals. But in the cities where the people were more affluent, they were making the bucks off the Americans and in a way they despised us.

Effect of the period served in Vietnam

Contact with the Vietnamese led Vietnam veterans to conclude there was more ambivalence or even open hostility to the American presence in the post-Tet period than prior to Tet. Those veterans who were in Vietnam during the early stages of the war primarily reported anti-American demonstrations they saw in the cities. An army man who was in Vietnam before 1968 described the attitude of the Vietnamese as follows:

> I knew those who were very friendly and yet I had seen demonstrations. They marched through the streets yelling ''Americans go home.'' Burned a couple of jeeps downtown. It was some kind of power struggle going on between the Buddhists and the Catholics and they had organized demonstrations and marches through the cities. We were told to stay off the streets during these things.

The majority of those who served during the post-Tet period reported that while many Vietnamese had been grateful in the beginning of the war for American aid or had felt ambivalent about the U.S. presence, they were growing increasingly negative toward the American forces. A veteran who was in the navy expressed this view as follows:

> Well at first, for the most part, they thought we were trying to help them. But at the same time there was about an equal amount of fear of the Americans. . . . We were there with all our guns and weapons . . . running everything. They no longer had control of their own civil war. And as the war sort of wound down it was more negative. People began to lose support for the United States.

Those who were there during the final days of the American involvement generally agreed that only a small minority in the cities wanted the American troops to stay, and that most of the people in the villages had turned completely against the American presence. The people hated the war, they reported, and wanted it ended. A veteran described the Vietnamese response during this later period (1972–1973) when the war was winding down:

> The war was up north. The war was out in the jungles. People in the villages wanted us out. In the cities there was bitterness towards the Americans. There was talk about us pulling out. The nationals there, they knew what would happen to them if the Communists came in and we knew it. . . . It just kept getting worse and you could feel it. It was a defeatist attitude. The girls wanted to marry any American just to get out of the country. We knew that the American position was declining. It was visible. It is hard to really imagine. It was a country in chaos.

Views of Nonveterans

Thus far in our study, we have generally described the differing perspectives of the two groups most emphatic about their perceptions of the war, supporters of the war and antiwar activists. In examining the nonveterans' perceptions of how the Vietnamese viewed U.S. military personnel, however, we found that the degree of activism does not differentiate how nonveterans felt the U.S. forces were perceived. Rather, general feelings of support for or opposition to the war emerge as a prime factor. As indicated below, the greater a respondent's opposition to the war, the more he assumed that the Vietnamese had negative views of U.S. personnel. Fully 61% of the antiwar group thought the Vietnamese held negative views of the United States, while only 31% of the prowar group shared this assessment. Conversely, only 17% of the antiwar compared to 42% of the prowar group thought the Vietnamese held positive views of the United States. Interestingly, the group in our sample that was ambivalent about the war was nearly evenly split between those who believed the Vietnamese held positive views of the United States (42%) and those who feld that there was a negative reaction to U.S. personnel (44%).

Prowar nonveterans

A plurality of prowar nonveterans felt that the Americans were a welcome presence. The Vietnamese people, they contended, viewed United States military personnel as people coming to liberate them from the Vietcong and North Vietnamese in order to preserve their freedom. A respondent expressed this attitude:

> I felt that most of the Vietnamese people in the South wanted us there, to protect their rights. They did not want to be Communist. And because of that, I definitely thought they wanted to keep us there to help them so that they would not be overrun.

It was also noted that the Vietnamese were in favor of the American presence because it was an aid to their development and brought in lots of money. As a respondent observed:

> Their attitudes towards GIs were probably mercurial, you know, they see dollar signs in their eyes, something to do with money or goods or something that could be sold to them on the black market.

Other prowar nonveterans pointed out that the attitude of the Vietnamese was ambivalent or negative. They argued that it basically depended on the individual's ideology. A respondent commented:

> I think their attitude towards the United States was mixed. They needed our

help if they really wanted their freedom, if they didn't want their freedom, they objected to the U.S. military.

Nonveterans Opposed to the War

As noted above, the majority of nonveteran respondents opposed to the war felt that the general attitude of the Vietnamese toward the American forces was negative. A moderate activist noted:

> The South Vietnamese people—the ones we were supposed to be helping? You hear stories from your friends that have been over there and they come back. They were saying "Yankee go home . . . ." I think that they hated the United States military.

According to some respondents, while many Vietnamese openly hated the Americans, others expressed dislike but accepted the U.S. presence because there was not much else they could do. A high activist explained:

> I felt that they probably hated us, that is, the South hated us but were afraid of us, and the North hated us but weren't afraid of us. . . . I would say that the war probably decimated the spirit of the South Vietnamese but strengthened the spirit of the North Vietnamese.

Another high activist summed up the views of those who saw the Vietnamese response as varying among the population:

> I think [attitudes varied] depending on which Vietnamese we [are] talking about. I think there were probably elements in upper echelons in the military and government there who looked at the Americans as rich fools who were supplying them with things that they could peddle on the black market. I think from the standpoint of villagers, of the peasant population, some of them probably viewed the Americans as liberators, and some of them probably viewed us as the devil, and some of them probably were indifferent, because maybe by that time anything that was wearing a uniform and carrying a gun was classified in the same general sense, and they probably reacted to the South, the North Vietnamese armies, the Vietcong, or us in the same way.

Perceptions of the Effects of the War on the Vietnamese

The question of what American intervention meant for South Vietnam lies at the core of the debate over the Vietnam War. The official rhetoric concentrated on the need to protect South Vietnam from a Communist takeover by North Vietnam and generally downplayed the effects of the war on the local population. Frances Fitzgerald in *Fire in the Lake* argues, as do other critics, that the success of the revolution and the failure of the American intervention are attributable to the attention the revolutionaries paid to the reconstruction of Vietnamese village life destroyed by colonialism. Another argument used by critics of American intervention in Vietnam is that Vietnam was not in fact two countries and that we involved ourselves in a civil war. However one views the conflict, from the perspective of the majority of our respondents, the consequences of the American intervention in the conflict, in terms of the destruction of Vietnamese society, make the debate over the objectives of the involvement inconsequential.

As our tables show, the predominant view of the generation is that the war had a generally *negative* effect on the Vietnamese people. Indeed, an overwhelming proportion of Vietnam era veterans (68%) and nonveterans (77%) believe this to be the case (table 5.9). Vietnam veterans are more divided about the war's impact. Only 34% of the Vietnam veterans feel the conflict was a relentlessly negative force, while 26% see it as having both positive and negative consequences and a plurality, 41%, feel the Vietnamese benefited from the war.

Our data indicate that more than three-quarters of the nonveteran population see the war as destructive. As table 5.10 shows, there are some significant differences between those who were and were not active in the antiwar movement. Among those heavily and moderately engaged in the antiwar movement, nearly nine out of ten emphasize the destructive effect of the war for the people of Vietnam.

Vietnam Veterans' Views

Perceptions of the effects of the war on the Vietnamese among Vietnam veterans differ substantially as a consequence of race, combat, and participation in abusive violence. In table 5.11 we see that a majority of black heavy-combat veterans (51%) see the war as destructive of Vietnamese society, while only 29% argue that the Vietnamese benefited from the war. Whites who saw heavy combat, on the other hand, are more likely to see the Vietnamese as benefiting from the war (40%) and much less apt to see the negative effects of the war on the Vietnamese (32%).

In table 5.12, we find that witnessing of and participation in abusive violence also influence perceptions of the war's consequences for the Vietnamese. The most illuminating aspect of the findings is the proportion of those who witnessed or participated in abusive violence who emphasize the negative effects of the war compared to those veterans who were not exposed. Only 29% of the veterans who were not exposed to abusive violence focus primarily on the destructive elements of the war, while 43% of the witnesses and 53% of the participants emphasize the negative influence of the war on the Vietnamese. Although participants in abusive violence are the most likely to see the negative effects of the war, they are as likely to report that the Vietnamese benefited from the war as the not exposed veterans (40%). Only 7% of the participants fail to provide an emphatic response to the war, while 23% of the witnessed and 32% of the not exposed veterans occupy the middle ground.

If we compare the responses of the distinct Vietnam veteran groups in our sample, we can appreciate the magnitude of the differences in their perceptions of the war's influence on the Vietnamese. Only among black heavy-combat veterans (51%) and participants in abusive violence (53%) do we find a majority who emphasize the destructive aspects of the war. If we include the veterans who witnessed abusive violence, we have an additional group where a plurality (43%) perceive the results of the war more often in terms of destruction than of the benefits. These findings strongly argue that those veterans who saw the "dirty" side of the war are likely to interpret the meaning of the war for the Vietnamese in terms of the destruction created by the conflict. The significance of the interaction between race and combat lies in the fact that neither race nor combat alone was sufficient to lead veterans to respond to the costs of the war for the Vietnamese. The identification with the Vietnamese among black Vietnam veterans noted earlier does not in itself lead these veterans to emphasize the destructive side of the war; that response occurs only when blacks were exposed to heavy combat.

The above findings suggest that, although a substantial number of Vietnam veterans evince concern for the fate of the Vietnamese, the interactions between Vietnam veterans and the Vietnamese were fraught with tension and conflict. As much of the literature indicates, Vietnam veterans were often resentful, distraught, or confused by what many saw as a lack of support for the United States forces who were supposedly helping to save the local population from aggression. Added to this was the complaint, cited above, that certain elements of society used the military presence as an opportunity to exploit soldiers for pecuniary gain. Our data suggest that these factors play an important part in the reaction of Vietnam veterans to the Vietnamese people, a response Vietnam veterans discussed at length in the narrative material.

Positive effect

A minority of those respondents who felt that the war had a positive effect on the Vietnamese pointed out that the presence of American troops provided security to the people. Knowing how the Vietcong and North Vietnamese Army treated the civilian population, it was felt that they were better off with the Americans there.

The majority of those respondents viewing the war as positive for the Vietnamese people have a different argument. To their mind, the *main* positive effect of the American presence was the boost it gave the economy. The Vietnamese—rich and poor, villagers and people living in the cities—profited commercially from the war. The Americans brought money and business and were also the main employers. Civilians washed clothes, shined shoes, and swept rooms for gratuities. A black veteran noted:

The war had a positive effect on them, it provided a stimulus for capital. Vietnam is not an industrialized country and the war brought buildings and supplies. Prostitution was one of the major capital stimuli in Vietnam and this was due to the Americans being there. Most of these establishments were run by French and upper class Chinese, but they employed Vietnamese people. United States goods were sold all over the black market. In that context, the war to them was productive.

Respondents also mentioned that the American military presence helped to move the Vietnamese from a traditional to a modern stage of development. A veteran described this change as follows:

They were a bicycle era civilization and here we were putting them into a jetstream atmosphere. Our presence was leading them out of starvation. You see a lot of beggars but at least they were being taken care of.

Negative effect

Compared to those veterans who felt that the war had a beneficial effect on the Vietnamese, respondents who expressed a negative view were much more inclined to expand in detail on their misgivings. As seen below, they presented salient imagery of the suffering and destruction of a people, of the collapse of cultural and social structures, and of the devastation of the land and the economy.

The majority of respondents stressing the negative effect of the war came gradually to this awareness. When they first arrived in Vietnam, they were under the impression that the presence of the American troops had a generally positive influence on the civilian population. This changing perspective is especially evident among veterans who participated in or witnessed abusive violence against civilians. One white veteran who witnessed abusive violence against civilians made the following remarks:

When I first arrived in Vietnam, I wanted to believe that we Americans were God . . . that we were their saviors and that we could help them. But then I saw what happened to them as a result of the war. I had a lot of compassion for them, for the people in both the North and the South. At first, I felt that they were below us, that was the brainwashing and the propaganda. Later I began to feel that we had no business there and that we were hurting those people more than helping them.

While some veterans seem to be equally aware of the human cost of the war to both the North and the South Vietnamese, most referred primarily to the situation in South Vietnam. This is understandable, since American units were firsthand witnesses to the devastation created by the war in the South. One of the respondents, an army infantryman who was a participant in abusive violence, expressed his feelings as follows:

Their livestock had been destroyed. The people were being destroyed. Their homes were being destroyed. It just seemed that the whole country was going to be wiped out, especially South Vietnam.

Most veterans blamed all combatants, including United States forces, for the destruction of Vietnam. Others stressed that the United States was trying to protect the people and the environment as best as it could and attributed primary responsibility to the South Vietnamese government or the enemy forces. A white army man explained why he was against the South Vietnamese government:

I saw so much graft going on. There was a province chief's palace right next door to our compound and we used to see trucks going in and unloading USA rice and other supplies. But the people were starving. The corruption in the Vietnamese political system was obvious to us right there.

Once they became aware of the negative impact of the war on the Vietnamese, most Vietnam veterans developed feelings of compassion for the people. But a number of veterans combined this awareness with a contempt for the civilian population. This seems to be especially the case for some white veterans who participated in acts of abusive violence against civilians. While 53% of the participants felt that the effect of the war was negative, only 41% expressed positive feelings toward the Vietnamese. A white participant who was in the marines had the following to say:

Effect on the Vietnamese? Negative. I would have to include the figurative bastardizing of the populace, the moral decay, the degeneracy of the little kids that were clamoring around you and one of them has a razor blade and is slitting your back pocket to get your wallet out. Mercenary, valueless thinking, the way they acted. Give me candy, buy me coca cola, buy filthy pictures. It was almost pathetic and yet they were only gooks. I had a dislike for most of them. It was a prejudice in many respects. They were so backward, they were so far removed from any civilization.

Those veterans who were aware of the devastation of Vietnam are generally inclined to argue that it was not justified. A black veteran who served in the air force presented the following picture:

Effect? Devastating. You see the huts that they live in, the land that's barren and full of craters from the bombs falling, and children begging and mothers fighting for oranges and fruit and milk for their children. Anytime I had some food I would give it to them. . . . I felt it was totally an unjust thing. . . . Although I come from a poverty-stricken area, it gave me a feeling . . . that no matter how bad off I was, there was someone in the world much, much worse off than myself.

But others maintained that the killing of civilians and the destruction were unavoidable in a guerrilla war situation. A white captain in the marines who witnessed abusive violence argued:

> Every action we took in the war terrorized those people. I'm speaking of Vietnamese civilians . . . total pandemonium. That's what it was . . . the candle was being burned at both ends and they were in the middle and they had no place to go. . . . The Americans weren't exactly clean over their service there—there was an awful lot of napalm shook in places where it shouldn't have been shook and an awful lot of shells fell where they shouldn't have been falling and there were an awful lot of people killed that shouldn't have been killed. I also agree we had no damn choice in the matter. . . . In taking civilians at the same time we were wiping out the VC or the NVA . . . they figured if they intermingled amongst the civilians it would make it harder for you to get them. . . . They knew how to make you shoot children in order to save your own ass . . . they played a good game.

Many veterans presented a picture of a society-wide devastation, a scenario of total human, social, and material destruction. A white helicopter pilot who witnessed abusive violence talked about his experiences as follows:

> I had a chance to go in quite a few villages: they were beautiful. I remember I walked into a hut and saw a tool chest. I opened it up and there were all these strange tools for woodworking. Of course there was nobody there. I saw water wheels that they had some places that pump the water out. I realized they had a very beautiful culture and we were just burning it all down.

A white army lieutenant who also witnessed acts of abusive violence expressed this view:

> It was terrible. . . . Destroying families, which are the Asians' most precious heritage . . . the economy, everything from what manufacturing there was to agriculture, and creating a spirit of distrust among everyone toward each other. It also intensified the conflict between classes of people.

Other Vietnam veterans talked primarily about the destruction of people, the human suffering, the uprooting of families, starvation, and disease. Again, the fate of the children of Vietnam especially touched many veterans. A black veteran, who was an army airborne, witnessed abusive violence against civilians. He remembered:

> I think it was like hell for them. . . . They were hungry, they were starving . . . the kids were so skinny and then there was always the threat of death. They were caught in the middle between two opposing sides and I admired those who

survived and felt sorry for the ones who died. . . . Their society had been reduced to the bare essentials. . . . Those people were eating out of our trash dumps. . . . I really felt sorry for the kids . . . and I didn't feel they were emotionally capable of handling it. They shouldn't have had to handle that kind of an environment.

Most veterans are inclined to blame a whole range of military actions against civilians as the main cause of the destruction of the people of Vietnam. While those who witnessed abusive violence are generally more inclined to criticize these actions than those who participated in them, this is not always the case. For example, a white army infantryman who was involved in the mistreatment of cilivians observed:

We would evacuate villages that really shouldn't have to be evacuated . . . they had no place to stay. The people didn't want to leave the villages. They were born there. . . . They had the attitude—I was born here—I'm going to die here. You almost had to take them by force—pick them up and throw them in the truck. So you say to yourself, what the hell, if the people don't want to go, let them stay here.

Veterans also tend to argue that the war encouraged racial discrimination against civilians. They feel that racist attitudes in the United States Army were manifested in a variety of ways, ranging from inhumane treatment to a general lack of regard for civilians. The designations for the people of Vietnam, friend or enemy—"gook" or "slope" or "dink"—they contended violated the people's pride and identity. This feeling is especially strong among black veterans. A black veteran who served in the air force commented:

Effect on the people themselves? Looking forward to the day that it ends. It took away the South Vietnamese's pride in one another or self-respect because of foreign troops on their homeland and they did not receive much respect from the American GIs. I found the term "gook" very offensive . . . I tried to treat them as human beings, the way I wanted to be treated. I tried to give them all the respect I could.

Veterans also noted that the destruction of the Vietnamese way of life and culture had a negative effect on the country. The people were violently uprooted from their traditional lives and thrust into modern times. This upheaval shattered lives, broke up families, and created a culture shock. A white army infantry officer who witnessed abusive violence had the following to say:

You do not take a country like that and force it into the twentieth century overnight. Their young generation is lost somewhere between a very ancient Buddhist culture and a kind of modernized, screwed up Western culture.

Mixed effect

Consistent with our earlier findings, a group of veterans pointed out that not all Vietnamese were affected similarly by the war. While the general impact was negative, many Vietnamese were making very large profits out of the conflict, especially those in the cities who were pro-American and Westernized. A white marine captain observed:

> Certain elements of the Vietnamese were definitely profiteering from the war. . . . [Others] were very poor—they were starving . . . you take a young girl and you would think she was pregnant because she'd have a swollen belly but it would be . . . malnutrition instead.

A white veteran who served in the army presented a similar point of view:

> Well, the majority of the Vietnamese were farmers and I felt at the time that [the war] was disrupting their lives. But as far as the 1% of the population, they were more or less Westernized and looked at it from an economic standpoint, what they could get out of the war. That small percent was enjoying the war. I call them the money grubbers because that is exactly what they were. They all hated to see us go. They knew they were going to miss the revenue.

Nonveterans' Views

Our data show that nonveterans generally agreed that the war had a definitely negative effect on the Vietnamese and Vietnamese society. On the whole, we find little difference between the supporters of the war and antiwar activists on the consequences of the war. There is, however, one small difference. While 80% of the prowar respondents said that the war had a negative effect, this figure rises to 90% among the activists, and only 2% of the activists compared to 10% of the prowar group said that the war had a positive effect on the Vietnamese. Looked at conversely, the figures emphasize the general consensus about the consequences of the war. The narrative material shows that prowar respondents, while they were generally aware of the negative effects of the war, felt little human concern for the impact the war was having on the Vietnamese. They pointed out that the Vietnamese were used to war because they had been fighting for many years, thus the latest conflict was just a continuation of what had been going on before. Those who showed concern for the destruction inflicted by the war often felt such ends were justified in a war against Communism. A white respondent summarized this view as follows: "I felt that it was ravaging their country, but necessary to preserve their freedom."

Antiwar activists generally agreed that the war had a strong negative impact on the people of Vietnam. They talked about the killing, the defoliation, and all the other adverse effects that a highly advanced army brings with it when it becomes involved in a civil war in a foreign country. As one respondent said, "The people of Vietnam became the victims while politicians were squabbling over their dead bodies." Large numbers of refugees were fleeing the countryside and their lives were completely disrupted. Antiwar activists further observed that the Vietnam War was the most destructive kind of war one could possible imagine, "tearing families apart, uprooting them, creating a lot of orphans, prostituting their women, some of them." Basically, it was the innocent who suffered.

Activists seem more concerned about the *long-term* consequences of the Vietnam War than their veteran peers. They pointed out that the Vietnamese will feel the effects of the war for years to come. Successive foreign occupations caused social disruptions and the American presence seriously damaged the cultural fabric of Vietnamese society. A high activist concluded:

> Well, basically it totally changed their way of life. I mean the French had been there before, before that the Japanese, before that the Chinese. When the Western influence came in it definitely changed their way of life. The French imposed their language and their forms of government and their architecture and then when the Americans got there it really upset everything.

Activists remain interested in the current situation in Vietnam and reported that they are reading books, articles, and news stories covering developments in that country. The war seems to have left an imprint on their lives, expressed in a concern for the fate of Vietnam. One high activist talked about the hardship the Vietnamese still face:

> Just yesterday I saw a news report of the people getting a hillside ready for planting rice. They have to walk with these long bamboo poles and dig up the land mines . . . every five hundred square yards there's supposed to be an unexploded bomb or land mine.

A minority of activists seemed to have concluded that the Vietnamese people have lost control over their future. The war has left them weary and frightened. This attitude is expressed by a high activist:

> Talking about the masses—the people themselves—I felt pity. I had the feeling that—the expressions on their faces were always lost and sort of swept up in what was going on with no control over their future. . . . I guess they felt vulnerable and afraid. I guess that has sort of left its mark on them . . . they can be easily led now. A show of force would cause them to move in a direction that the show of force wants them to move in. I don't think there'd be any active resistance right now. I think they're just tired.

But a majority of activists agreed that despite all of the suffering of the past and the problems of the present and future, Vietnam has finally reemerged as a strong and united country. This positive conclusion is expressed in the following statement by a high activist:

> Well it certainly wasn't good for them. War rarely is when it is fought in your own country. I think that in a sense it made them a stronger people. Now that they're united they certainly have a very strong sense of identity and desire to be strong and maintain their own borders. I think it's the best that you could say about what happened to them.

Conclusion

As this chapter shows, there are fundamental differences in the way Vietnam veterans and their peers view Vietnamese civilians, how they feel the Vietnamese perceived our forces, and how they estimate the effects of the war on the Vietnamese. Among nonveterans, the political orientation toward the war seems to be the dominant factor, influencing their perceptions of Vietnamese civilians and the way they interpret the effects of the war. Vietnam veterans' views, however, seem on the whole to be shaped by their wartime experiences. Consequently, we find a more complex and varied set of reactions to the Vietnamese and the effects of the war among this latter group than are evidenced by their nonveteran peers.

Among nonveterans, antiwar activists focus on the suffering of the Vietnamese. In their eyes, the civilian population are victims whose immediate suffering outweighs all other considerations. However, for those nonveterans who supported the war, stressing the significance of the struggle against Communism, the Vietnamese tend to fade into the background and their fate, whatever the short-term costs, is balanced against the long-range benefits of defeating a Communist thrust. In neither case do the Vietnamese come into sharp focus as individuals.

Although Vietnam veterans also express these two viewpoints, their responses to the Vietnamese bring to life the people of Vietnam and humanize their fate. Several positive characteristics of the Vietnamese people observed by veterans during the war captured their attention. There is as well a special sensitivity to the fate of children caught up in violence from which they cannot escape. The poignancy with which veterans describe the suffering of the innocent young and their attempts to alleviate children's pain reflect intense personal responses to war. The contrast between veterans who sought to learn Vietnamese or communicate with the Vietnamese and those who reacted to the Vietnamese by distancing themselves from the people represent opposite poles of response to the pressures of the war. There is also a disparity between those who became deeply attached to Vietnam and the Vietnamese and those who, while using the local population to serve their needs, grew to hate those Vietnamese who benefited from the American presence. Finally, there is the ever-present duality of feelings toward civilians who were at once friendly and potentially threatening because of their allegiance to the enemy. Self-protection and selflessness warred, often within the individual soldier, in a land where the suffering of the civilians was acknowledged but their loyalty as fighters against the ''Communist'' enemy remained suspect. The range of responses to civilians among Vietnam veterans reflects their sense that the mission they came to carry out was more complex than they had originally thought.

Most Vietnam veterans entered the war with idealistic feelings. Our findings suggest that their sense of purpose was often eroded by their experiences in Vietnam. Vietnamese civilians often became the target of the frustration and rage that built up in soldiers faced with the realities of a guerrilla war. Indeed, many veterans developed strong feelings of hostility toward the local population. Contrarily, we also find considerable evidence that soldiers faced with the realities of what the war did to civilians often sought to ameliorate its effects. Our transcripts indicate that often instances of mistrust and hatred were counterbalanced by moments of friendship and respect.

The division that finally emerges among Vietnam veterans is between men who continued to differentiate between Vietnamese civilians in spite of the threatening environment of the guerrilla war and those who ceased to distinguish Vietnamese as friend or foe, civilian or combatant. The latter developed an implacable hostility to all Vietnamese and a total indifference to their fate. The former empathized with civilians, made efforts to bridge the cultural gap, and attempted to protect noncombatants caught in what these veterans came to see as a crossfire of contending forces whose devastation many Vietnamese sought to escape.

PART
III

PERCEPTIONS OF
THE CONDUCT
OF THE WAR

CHAPTER SIX

WAR AGAINST CIVILIANS AND THE ENVIRONMENT

Man's revulsion at the wartime treatment of his fellow man is nothing new. Indeed, if one turns to literature—the historical writings of the ancient Greeks, the "enlightened" works of eighteenth-century philosophers, the somber poems of Victorian Englishmen, and, most recently, the novels of Vietnam veterans—a common theme pervades: abhorrence of the inhumanity implicit in warfare. And of all warring actions, those perpetrated against noncombatants are uniformly viewed as the least justifiable and most inhumane.

Despite this deep concern for the general population during warfare, international law has been slow to come to the aid of the civilian. Yet, however gradual the evolution of international legal provisions fashioned to protect civilians during war, growth has occurred and continues today. In our violent world, it is imperative to pay careful attention to the laws of war protecting such persons.

This chapter begins by discussing some of these rules and their relevance to the Vietnam War. It then examines the Vietnam Generation's perception of the lawfulness of certain acts committed against civilians and the environment by the combatants (the NVA and VC, the ARVN and the American forces) and explores that generation's responses to such acts.

General Principles of Humanitarian Law

The predominant view prior to the General Treaty for the Renunciation of War of 1928 stressed the legality of warfare. Armed conflict was perceived as a form of politics, a means of diplomacy. Still, though war seemed unavoidable, it was felt that an effort should be made to spare the civilian population or at least minimize its suffering.

Generally cited as the first treaty to afford protection to civilians, the Declaration of St. Petersburg of 1868 stated that "The only legitimate object which States should endeavor to accomplish during war is to weaken the military forces of the enemy." The Hague Convention on Land Warfare of 1907 broke further ground by providing that "The attack or bombardment, by whatever means, of towns, villages, dwellings, or buildings which are undefended is prohibited." In other words, to ensure respect for the civilian population, the parties to a military conflict were enjoined to confine their operations to the destruction or undermining of enemy resources and military objectives, sparing civilians and their holdings. This rule constitutes one of the foundations of international humanitarian law applicable in armed conflicts.

Clearly, the way of warfare practiced in World War II violated the Hague provisions. Indeed, that war was conducted with the idea of making the civilian population suffer so cruelly that its government would capitulate. The German attacks on London, the use of the V1s and the V2s, the bombing of the German cities by the Allies, and the dropping of the atomic bombs on Hiroshima and Nagasaki were all attempts to tax civilians beyond endurance.

The Geneva Convention relative to the Protection of Civilian Persons in Time of War, of August 12, 1949, emphasized primarily the protection of the civilian population against an occupying power. But despite the many articles aimed at providing more effective protection for noncombatants during warfare the war in Vietnam followed the pattern of the Second World War. The general populace became prime targets in a conflict waged largely against civilians.

The Protocols Additional to the Geneva Conventions, adopted in 1977 and entered into force in 1978, illustrate the growing concern for the fate of civilians in conflicts such as Vietnam, Biafra, Bangladesh, Afghanistan, Lebanon, Namibia, Ireland, and El Salvador. While many articles of the protocols simply reaffirm the provisions of the 1949 Geneva Conventions, the ruling as a whole greatly extends the protection offered to civilians.[1] One author has commented: "It must be remarked that this amplitude of civilian protection can be read as no more than proportionate to the need and demand that historically has developed. It comes as a cloudburst after a long drought."[2] A short discussion of some of the main rules found in the most recent treaties relating to the protection of civilian victims of armed conflicts follows.

Protection of Civilians against Armed Attacks

As noted above, acts or threats of violence primarily conceived to spread terror among the civilian population are prohibited. Such acts, which are also prohibited under customary international law, are usually committed to compel the population to support or to abstain from supporting any party to the conflict. Any strategy by which the civilian population is made the main target of an attack in order to spread terror or to achieve an early capitulation has been outlawed.[3]

In addition, indiscriminate attacks, striking military objectives and civilians or civilian objects without distinction, are prohibited. In particular it is forbidden to attack, as one single objective, a zone containing several military objectives that are situated in populated areas and are at some distance from each other. The intention here is to prohibit target-area bombing, also called "carpet bombing." This method of waging total warfare causes very heavy losses among the population. Equally, belligerents are required to refrain from attacks "which may be expected to cause incidental loss of civilian life, injury to civilians, [or] damage to civilian objects . . . which would be excessive in relation to the concrete and direct military advantage anticipated."[4] This rule is intended to urge the attacker to consider soberly the consequences of his actions on the general population.

Localities under Special Protection

Present rulings accord nondefended localities and demilitarized zones special protection. The purpose here is twofold: to provide immunity for the population in the place where it lives and to preserve such sites along with the economic, cultural, scientific, and other values they represent.

Eligible localities must fulfill the following conditions: all combatants, mobile weapons, and mobile military equipment must have been removed, and no acts of hostility may be committed by the authorities or by the population. However, the presence in these sites of military medical personnel, civil defense personnel, civilian police forces, and wounded and sick military personnel is not contrary to the conditions stipulated.[5]

Protection of Civilian Objects

General protection of so-called civilian objects—places of worship, farms, schools, homes, etc.—has been provided for in several international conventions.[6] Moreover, two categories of civilian objects have received special protection, adding a new dimension to humanitarian law.

Objects indispensable to the survival of the civilian population

Starvation of civilians as a method of warfare is prohibited. It is illegal to attack or destroy foodstuffs, food-producing areas, crops, livestock, drinking water supplies, and irrigation works, whether to starve out civilians or to cause them to move away or for any other reason.[7]

Objects containing dangerous forces

In view of such dangers as flooding, which the destruction of certain works would entail for the civilian population, "Works or installations containing dangerous forces, namely dams, dykes and nuclear electrical generating stations, shall not be made the object of attack, even where these objects are military objectives, if such attack may cause the release of dangerous forces. . . ."[8] However, special protection shall cease for a dam, a dyke, or nuclear electrical generating station if it is used for other than its normal function and for regular, significant, and direct support of military operation.[9]

Protection of the Natural Environment

Largely because of the extensive and long-term damage suffered by the Vietnamese environment during the prolonged war, numerous measures have been taken to prohibit action hostile to the environment and climate, hence incompatible with human well-being and health. To this end, the use of meteorological, geophysical, or any other scientific or technological means of influencing the environment for military purposes is banned. Among the activities deemed prejudicial to the survival of the population are the defoliation of large parts of the countryside leading to a disturbance of the ecology and the use of chemicals to create rain destructive to the natural environment.[10]

Use of Precautionary Measures

It is generally accepted that those who plan or decide upon an attack must do everything feasible to verify that the objectives in question are military. But during military operations, even attacks on clearly determined military objectives are liable to have accidental effects on civilians and their property. With respect to these attacks, all feasible precautions in the choice of means and methods of attack must be taken with a view to avoiding, or at least minimizing, injury to civilians and damage to civilian objects. In addition, effective advance warning must be given of attacks that may affect the civilian population, unless circumstances do not permit.[11]

Treatment of Civilians in the Power of a Party to the Conflict

The international rules in this area are designed to protect persons against arbitrary authority of a party to the conflict in whose power they happen to be. The fundamental guarantees provided include humane treatment in all circumstances without any adverse distinction based upon race, color, sex, religion, political or other opinion, or on any other similar criteria. Any form of violence to the life, health, or physical or mental well-being of civilians and outrages upon personal dignity are forbidden.[12] The following examples demonstrate the progress made in this area since World War II.

The taking of hostages

As Gerhard von Glahn has noted, hostages have been taken throughout the history of war. The widespread reasons and purposes for this practice include "the securing of compliance with requisition demands and the prevention of espionage and sabotage."[13] Up until World War II, the safety of hostages depended to a large extent on customary international law. The International Military Tribunal at Nuremberg acknowledged the execution of hostages during the Second World War by enemy forces and classified the practice as a war crime. In 1949, the Fourth Geneva Convention concluded Article 34 with its statement that "the taking of hostages is prohibited." The mere taking of hostages now constitutes a serious violation of international law.[14]

Forcible transfer of civilians

The traditional lack of conventional international law to provide clear rules for the transfer of civilians has been corrected by the incorporation of a series of provisions in Article 49 of the Fourth Geneva Convention of 1949: individual or mass forcible transfers as well as deportations of protected persons from occupied territory to the territory of the occupying power are prohibited. The forceful displacement of the civilian population shall not be ordered unless the security of the civilians involved or imperative military reasons so demand. Should the parties to the conflict undertake such displacements, they shall take all possible measures in order that the civilian population be received under satisfactory conditions of hygiene, health, safety, and nutrition, and that members of the same family are not separated. Persons thus evacuated shall be transferred back to their homes as soon as hostilities in the area in question have ceased.

Reprisals against civilians

There have also been advancements in the law regarding reprisals. During the Second World War, underground movement activities were punished through reprisals against civilians. Article 33 of the Fourth Geneva Convention contains a prohibition against such reprisals aimed at civilians and their property, from belligerents in whose power they might be—an important curtailment of a right traditionally claimed by an occupant against an enemy population.[15] Protocol I extends this rule to the civilian population and civilian objects as a whole.[16]

Measures Regarding Women and Children

Protocol I reaffirms and extends the Geneva measures in favor of women and children. Article 76 provides that "women shall be the object of special respect and shall be protected in particular against rape, forced prostitution and any other form of indecent assault. Pregnant women and mothers having dependent infants who are arrested, detained or interned for reasons related to the armed conflict, shall have their cases considered with the utmost priority. . . . The death penalty for such offenses shall not be executed on such women."[17]

Regarding children, the protocol underlines the need for privileged treatment, which is justified by their physical and mental condition. This treatment involves, in particular, the provision of all necessary care and assistance so that children should not suffer any physical or moral aftereffects as a result of the conflict and that they may develop in as normal a manner as possible. In view of the general nature of this provision, age is not mentioned.

The protocol also provides that the parties to the conflict "shall take all feasible measures in order that children who have not attained the age of fifteen years do not take part in hostilities and, in particular, they shall refrain from recruiting them into their armed forces."[18] Not only has direct participation in the hostilities been prohibited, but also any other act involving transmission of military information, transport of arms, ammunition, and war matériél, sabotage, etc.

If, despite these provisions, children who have not attained the age of fifteen years take a direct part in hostilities and fall into power of an adverse party, "they shall continue to benefit from the special protection . . . whether or not they are prisoners of war. If arrested, detained or interned for reasons related to the armed conflict, children shall be held in quarters separate from the quarters of adults, except where families are accommodated as family units. . . . The death penalty for an offense related to the armed conflict shall not be executed on persons who had not attained the age of eighteen years at the time the offense was committed."[19]

Protection of the Wounded and the Sick

Even before the days of Florence Nightingale and the Crimean War, customary international law accorded special status to the sick and wounded. Most recently, the 1949 Geneva Conventions and other legal instruments provide immunity for these groups and declare that in all circumstances they shall be treated humanely and shall receive, to the fullest extent practicable, the medical care and attention required by their condition.

According to the 1949 Conventions and the Additional Protocols, the parties to the conflict are committed, without delay, to take all possible measures to search for and collect the wounded and the sick and ensure their adequate care. They have the duty to provide and maintain medical establishments and services. Medical personnel of all categories shall be allowed to carry out their duties and shall be protected. This protection extends to any establishment or unit, whether military or civilian, organized for medical purposes.[20]

Protection during Civil War

Protocol II Additional to the Geneva Conventions contributes significantly to the protection of civilian rights in noninternational conflicts. Provisions of international law may now govern the conduct of civil wars, whereas prior to the Protocol, the main reference to internal armed conflicts was common Article 3 of the Geneva Conventions.

Acts or threats of violence primarily undertaken to terrorize the population are forbidden, as are direct attacks on civilians. Starvation of civilians is illegal; therefore, it is prohibited to attack or destroy objects on which the civilian population depends for its survival. The taking of hostages and the forced movement of civilians are furthermore disallowed.

Efficacy of Humanitarian Law

The humanitarian law of armed conflict suffers from the same "weakness" of all international law: there is no effective supranational organization to enforce it. The fact that the parties to the conflict remain, in essence, the enforcers of the Conventions and Protocols necessarily calls into question whether there really has been a development in the growth of such legislation.

But is the potential for enforcement the only yardstick against which to measure the success of the protocols? Isn't there something more important? As the historian Geoffrey Best concluded in his book, *Humanity in Warfare:*

> The Additional Protocols, I confess, seem to me worth backing; not because they are likely to be more effective than previous conventions have been, and certainly not because our world shows any signs of quickly becoming the sort of world in which observance of such conventions is natural or easy, but because they do offer to States and the peoples inhabiting them something humane, civilized and decent: a manageable code by which their armed conflict may be limited and restrained. . . . they testify to the survival, even through experiences as discouraging as some through which we have recently lived, of the ideas that, after all, internecine strife is not the highest ideal of humanity; that men and women are not citizens of their nations alone; and that although men still find it necessary sometimes to fight each other, they can still understand the importance of discriminating carefully between the different means and styles of doing it.[21]

Treatment of the Civilian Population in Vietnam

During the fighting in Vietnam, certain war atrocities (i.e., acts committed in defiance of declared official policy) were committed by individual combatants from all parties to the conflict. In addition, the official tactical policies developed by the four main parties, the North Vietnamese, the National Liberation Front (NLF), the South Vietnamese, and the Americans, for the pursuit of their wartime objectives appear to have violated provisions in the Geneva Conventions of 1949 and other legal instruments. This caused great suffering to the civilian population.

With the exception of the NLF, all participants in the conflict were parties to the four Geneva Conventions of 1949. The South Vietnamese, American, and allied forces accepted the applicability of the Conventions, while the North Vietnamese and the NLF rejected their relevance. It must be remembered that the main international legal instruments of this century have a clear provision that in cases not covered by conventional or customary international law, civilian populations and combatants remain under the protection of the principles of humanity and the dictates of the public conscience.[22]

Protection of Civilians: The North Vietnamese and Vietcong

In June 1965, when the International Committee of the Red Cross sent a communique to the four principal belligerents stating that they were all bound by the 1949 Geneva Conventions, North Vietnam and the NLF were unwilling to admit that they were bound by the rulings. And indeed neither of the two fully obeyed the provisions.

The Vietcong declared not only that they were not bound by the Geneva Conventions, on the grounds that they were not signatories, but also that the Conventions contained provisions unsuited to the action and organization of their guerrilla forces. Vietcong units commonly ignored the requirements that combatants shall carry arms openly and "have a fixed distinctive sign recognizable at a distance," insisting that a revolutionary movement cannot possibly make a distinction between the civilian population and combatants.[23]

Furthermore, in Vietnam, children, women, and the aged were not only victims, but often participants. As General Vo Nguyen Giap, the leading military strategist of North Vietnam, has put it:

> The protracted popular war in Vietnam demanded . . . appropriate forms of combat: appropriate for the revolutionary nature of the war in relation to the balance of forces then showing a clear enemy superiority. . . . The form of combat adopted was guerrilla warfare . . . each inhabitant a soldier; each village a fortress. . . . The entire population participates in the armed struggle. . . . This is the fundamental content of the war of people.[24]

From the North Vietnamese perspective, the legal situation was further complicated by the fact that they considered the conflict a "civil" and not an "international" war. Telford Taylor has argued:

However that may be, there is no room whatsoever for a North Vietnamese contention that they are not bound at least by Article 3 and, since their regular troops are engaged with those of South Vietnam and its allies in South Vietnamese territory, there appears to be little force in their effort to escape responsibility under the Conventions in their entirety. The NLF, as a nonsignatory, is in a much stronger position with respect to the particular provisions of the Conventions but, of course, is bound, as is every organized military force claiming or aspiring to sovereignty, by the customary laws of war.[25]

Although many Vietnamese remained civilians in the true sense of the word, the North Vietnamese Army and the Vietcong often ignored their traditional rights as noncombatants. Indeed, beginning at some point in the late 1950s, the NLF waged an assassination campaign aimed at destroying the governmental structure of the South Vietnamese countryside. It has been reported that between 1960 and 1965, some 7,500 village and district officials were assassinated by Vietcong militants. The Front tended to include among "officials" anyone who was paid by the government (including teachers, doctors, nurses), even if the work in question had nothing to do with the oppressive policies the NLF opposed.[26]

Protection of Civilians: The Practice of the United States

The United States Military Assistance Command for Vietnam states in an introductory comment that its various directives "show a consistent national policy of concern for humanity, and for the institutions of the people of Indochina during the many years of war." The directives refer to such instructions as avoiding "indiscriminate effects of fire power on the civilian population," and taking "due precaution against the possibility of bombing noncombatants." Thus, taken at face value, there is considerable evidence in the directives for an underlying norm intended to minimize civilian casualties.[27]

It has been pointed out that in practice a number of United States wartime strategies violated one or more rules of war.[28]

Bombing of North Vietnam

From February 1965, when the bombing campaign commenced, until the end of the war, continuous air attacks took place. Towns and villages that appeared to have little or no military significance were devastated. Serious bomb damage took place in rural areas apparently remote from any worthwhile targets. Bombing campaigns included attacks on the dyke system that controlled irrigation for agriculture.

Blanket bombing of zones in South Vietnam by B-52's

This tactic forced civilians out of areas thought to be under control of the Vietcong. Since such strategic bombardment cannot by its nature permit discrimination between defended and undefended communities, it violates customary and conventional law.

Scorched earth and relocation operations conducted by ground forces

Large areas thought to be Vietcong-dominated were denuded. Homes, food, gardens, livestock—everything that could be of use to the Communists was destroyed. Refugees were forcibly resettled in isolated places, and family members were often separated. From 1967 on, the "pacification" camps were so crowded that army units were ordered not to "generate" any more refugees. Search and destroy missions continued. But now the peasants were often killed in their villages.[29]

Acts against the natural environment

By the end of 1966, more than half of the C-123 missions were admittedly targeted for crop destruction. Indeed, a 1967 Japanese study of United States anticrop and defoliation methods, prepared by Yoichi Fukushima, head of the Agronomy Section of the Japanese Science Council, reported that United States anticrop attacks ruined more than 3.8 million acres (half the arable land in South Vietnam) and resulted in the deaths of nearly 1,000 peasants and more than 13,000 livestock.[30]

Protection of Civilians: The Practice of the South Vietnamese

The South Vietnamese also engaged in many illegal acts against the civilian population and killed a great number of innocent civilians. Their totalitarian program of arbitrary arrest and political surveillance was responsible for the death or capture of about 200,000 people. Among the civilians being tortured and murdered, in violation of all norms of customary and conventional law, were people who served the National Liberation Front as clerks, postmen, low-level propagandists, and supply agents. It is impossible to tell how many of those arrested in fact had NLF connections and how many (often women and children) were merely relatives of political suspects, or persons who were simply opposed to the South Vietnamese government; the police seemed to make little distinction. There was an additional category of prisoners as well: people who were apparently seized at random simply for being in the wrong place.

In reviewing the actions of all parties to the Vietnam conflict, one must conclude that translated into human terms, the war and the military strategies used turned an entire nation into a target and shattered a whole society. In the end, the conflict became a battle against the civilian population.

The Vietnam Generation's Views of War against Civilians

The way the war was conducted played an important role in how the Vietnam Generation related to the conflict. In questioning our respondents, we investigated their views of the legitimacy of ten types of wartime action stemming from military policy by one or more parties to the fighting. For each act we asked first whether the subject considered it lawful or unlawful and next how commonly this act was committed by one of the three major military forces engaged in the Vietnam War (VC/NVA; ARVN; and American forces). The actions covered are grouped by category below:

> Violence against the Vietnamese: Abuse of Persons (ABPERS)
> Terrorizing, assassinating, or torturing civilians for political or religious beliefs
> Attacking hospitals and similar places
> Not giving medical treatment to wounded civilians in the battle area
> Killing hostages
> Mutilating bodies
> Raping civilian women
>
> Bombing and Shelling of Cities to Terrorize the Population (TERBOMB)
>
> Environmental Warfare (ENVWAR)
> Defoliating large parts of the countryside of South Vietnam
> Using chemicals to create rain to destroy the natural environment of the civilian population
> Destroying dykes (dams) to create widespread flooding in civilian areas

Classification of the query items into three modes of behavior—abuse of persons, terror bombing and shelling, and environmental warfare—is based on a factor analysis of the response patterns to these questions. Our analysis shows that the nine items in ABPERS and ENVWAR are perceived by our respondents as a cluster of issues which conceptually constitute a single dimension. The item TERBOMB did not fall into either of the other dimensions; we therefore treat it as a separate dimension of warfare and the tenth type of action.

Unlawfulness of Conduct against Civilians and the Environment

Our concern here is with an ethical-moral rather than a legal-judicial appraisal of the legality of the ten actions queried. We asked our respondents about their view of the *propriety* of these acts in terms of what they perceive to be acceptable or unacceptable conduct. In that context the findings reveal a most instructive insight into the Vietnam Generation's conception of warfare.

The most important finding in the analysis of the ethical-moral perspectives on warfare is that in only two cases are there substantial differences between test groups on any issue. First, veterans, especially Vietnam veterans, are somewhat more likely than nonveterans to accept the legitimacy of environmental warfare (57% vs. 51% vs. 43%). Second, blacks are substantially less likely than whites to sanction environmental warfare (70% vs. 50%).

Given this general consensus, the important factor becomes the rank order of those actions which the majority consider unlawful but which a substantial minority are willing to accept as justified.

Actions against individuals, including terrorizing civilians, attacking hospitals, withholding medical treatment from wounded civilians, killing hostages, mutilation of the dead, and rape, are opposed by 90% of the sample. Somewhat less strongly, the generation rejects the idea of bombing or shelling of cities to terrorize the civilian population by 75%. Finally, only about 52% of the sample condemn environmental warfare as unlawful.

In questioning our respondents we found that the more precisely an action was cited in terms of the consequences for individuals, the more likely it was to be rejected as immoral and illegal. Apparently, the better respondents could imagine the effects of these actions in graphic terms, the more repugnant the acts appeared. We also suspect that the responses reflect the moral codes of our peacetime society. Those actions most strongly rejected as illegitimate in wartime derive from the civil codes that make murder, rape, and torture illegal in everyday life.

Indeed, the legitimation of environmental warfare by nearly half the sample very likely reflects the extent to which the results of such actions are beyond the imagination of many of the respondents. We would guess that only a minority of Vietnam veterans actually experienced this aspect of war; and those who did may well have found that environmental warfare provided some protection from the "too often elusive enemy."

Conduct of the War by the Combatants

The general consensus on the ethics of warfare noted above dissipates when we turn to the question of which of the armies was more or less likely to engage in the ten activities cited. The judgments made by the different subgroups of the Vietnam Generation reflect the variety of the experiences entertained during the war years, as well as the various positions advanced by particular groups as justifications for and against United States involvement in the Vietnam War. Those fully cognizant of the behavior of the contending forces will find a blend of fact and fiction in the following assessments by the Vietnam Generation of the conduct of the VC/NVA, ARVN, and American forces.

For better or worse, the "truth" about the Vietnam War is likely to remain elusive no matter how well researched. As in all human events, perspectives, points of view, and attitudes will continue to color the evidence. Indeed, it is worth emphasizing in analyzing the Vietnam experience, as elsewhere, that what we believe to be true, and our interpretation of the meaning of the evidence, decisively influences our judgments. The historical legacy of Vietnam stems not only from what happened there but from what different groups within our society perceived to have transpired. Thus, ten years after the war has ended, what the Vietnam Generation thinks occurred during the conflict will, for most of them, remain the "true story" of the war.

Abuse of Civilians

As tables 6.1 and 6.2 show, all subgroups queried consistently attribute more frequent violations to the enemy forces than to the allies. This is most evident on the issue of abuse of persons. In addition, the South Vietnamese (ARVN) are perceived to abuse civilians substantially more often than the United States forces. There is relatively little difference between perceptions of the frequency with which the ARVN and United States forces resorted to the use of terror bombing against the civilian population. Throughout this section, as table 6.2 demonstrates, we will find that Vietnam veterans consistently report that *all* types of action against civilians and the environment were less commonly committed by all the parties to the conflict than do either their era veteran or nonveteran counterparts. There is only one exception to this rule. Vietnam veterans' assessments of the frequency with which the VC/NVA committed acts against persons are virtually identical with the estimates of all but the nonveteran activists: the antiwar activists feel that the VC/NVA actions against civilians were significantly less common than do other members of the generation. The general consensus on the behavior of the VC/NVA toward civilians is a function of the comparatively high proportion of all groups within the generation who ascribe actions against civilians as a very common feature of VC/NVA behavior.

Actions against Civilians

Turning from our general discussion to specific issues, we see more clearly how exposure to the war influences perceptions of its conduct. In table 6.3, we note that *all* groups overwhelmingly agree that the VC/NVA frequently mistreated civilians. Among the Vietnam veterans, 97% feel that the VC/NVA sometimes or frequently mistreated civilians, a view shared by identical proportions of the era veterans and nonveterans.

As tables 6.4 and 6.5 show, nearly 40% of the nonveterans and 33% of

Vietnam era veterans believe that the ARVN frequently abused civilians, while only 17% and 11% believe this was true of American forces. Comparative figures for Vietnam veterans indicate that only about 23% believe that the ARVN and 6% that the American forces *frequently* engaged in the mistreatment of civilians. The differences between Vietnam veterans and nonveterans are even more striking, highlighted by differences in the "seldom" category. Vietnam veterans are almost twice as likely as nonveterans to say that Vietnamese civilians were seldom abused by Americans (55% vs. 31%). The differences between these groups on the conduct of the ARVN vis-a-vis civilians, though still substantial, are much smaller: 21% of the Vietnam veterans say that the ARVN seldom mistreated civilians compared to 10% of the era veterans and nonveterans.

Bombing and Shelling of Cities to Terrorize the Population

Estimates of how often each army used bombing and shelling of cities to terrorize the civilian population are presented in table 6.6. The pattern of findings is similar to the previous section on the mistreatment of civilians. Vietnam veterans are significantly more likely to characterize this type of warfare as uncommon (seldom) when assessing the behavior of the ARVN and American forces (42% and 41%), while only 15% say the VC/NVA seldom engaged in this type of warfare. Vietnam veterans generally also argue that the VC/NVA more frequently used this tactic compared to the ARVN or American forces (31% vs. 8% vs. 17%).

Vietnam era veterans and nonveterans reach somewhat different conclusions on this issue. Each of these subgroups concurs that American forces (22% and 26%) and the ARVN (15% and 17%) were less disposed to use this tactic frequently than were the VC/NVA (36%). As table 6.6 indicates, however, only about 20% or less of the era veterans and nonveterans estimate that this tactic was seldom used by any of the armies in Vietnam.

Environmental Warfare

Finally, we explored the views of the generation on the practice of environmental warfare, including use of the defoliant Agent Orange, attempts to use new-found abilities to manipulate weather, and attacks on the dykes essential to the agriculture and village life of the Vietnamese. As only the United States had access to the weaponry involved, we concentrated on the extent to which this new technology was employed by American forces. The findings on this issue differ in one important aspect from the rest of the analysis presented in this section. Although Vietnam veterans perceived American use of environmental warfare as relatively less frequent than did their peers (table 6.7), fully 65% of the Vietnam veterans say this type of warfare was sometimes or frequently employed by the United States. Moreover, although only 26% of the Vietnam veterans assert that the

United States frequently relied on environmental warfare, 44% of the era veterans and 46% of the nonveterans hold to this view. Overall, more than 80% of the era veterans and nonveterans believe environmental warfare was sometimes used. Only 18% think its use was infrequent as compared to 36% of the Vietnam veterans.

Perspectives on the Conduct of War among Vietnam Veterans

In the pages that follow, we examine the Vietnam veterans' views of the combatants' conduct. The diversity in the ways our respondents experienced the war is reflected in their perceptions of the behavior of those party to the conflict.

The Conduct of the Vietcong and North Vietnamese Army

There are few differences among Vietnam veterans' perceptions of the conduct of the VC/NVA. There are, however, certain divergent views worth noting, especially as regards VC/NVA conduct against civilians and their use of bombing and shelling tactics. Four factors—combat, participation in abusive violence, race, and period of service—are associated with perceptions of VC/NVA conduct.

As table 6.8 demonstrates, combat exposure interacts with period of service to influence perceptions of the extent of NVA/VC abuse of civilians. Heavy-combat veterans who served after Tet were substantially more likely to perceive VC/NVA misconduct as common than those who served earlier. Fully 73% of the heavy-combat veterans who served after Tet compared to 57% of the pre-Tet veterans felt that the VC/NVA frequently violated the persons of Vietnamese civilians.

We find, in table 6.9, a similar effect of period of service on views of NVA/VC use of bombing and shelling (NVA/VCTERBOMB), albeit less overwhelmingly, than we found above. Men who served later are more likely to say that the VC/NVA frequently resorted to the bombing or shelling of cities to terrorize the civilian population (42% vs. 30%).

Black participants in abusive violence, as table 6.10 shows, are much less likely than their white counterparts to hold the view that the VC/NVA frequently employed this type of warfare (43% vs. 67%). The general pattern of findings in our study suggests that the very different feelings about the nature of the war and its conduct between black and white participants is being reflected in their differential assessment of the frequency of VC/NVA use of terror bombing.

The Conduct of the War by the South Vietnamese Army

In the analysis of Vietnam veterans' views of the conduct of the war by the South Vietnamese Army (ARVN) against civilians, we find that period of service is the best indicator of perceptions of ARVN behavior. Branch of service and rank also play a role, and again the effect of combat experience varies by race.

As table 6.11 shows, men who served in the military after 1967 report the ARVN more frequently acted in a manner harmful to civilians than do those who served in the earlier stages of the Vietnam War. The direct abuse of civilians by the ARVN was judged very common by 27% of the veterans who served after 1967 compared to only 19% of the pre-1968 group.

Branch of service generally led to different estimates of the ARVN actions against civilians. Men who served in the marines and army, as seen in table 6.12, were substantially less inclined than navy/air force personnel to report that the ARVN abused the persons of the Vietnamese or engaged in bombing or shelling to terrorize civilians. Only 19% of army and 13% of marine veterans report that the ARVN frequently engaged in the direct mistreatment of civilians, compared to 31% of those who served in the navy/air force. These differences should not, however, obscure the fact that a substantial majority in *all* branches of the service see the ARVN as persistently engaging in the kinds of abuse of their civilian countrymen that is rejected as unlawful by nearly 90% of the veterans.

Combat experience also interacts with race to affect the perceptions of ARVN conduct. Blacks who experienced low and moderate combat are notably less likely to say the ARVN acted out against civilians than are white combat veterans. In table 6.13 we see that only 16% of the white low- and moderate-combat veterans think the ARVN seldom abused Vietnamese civilians, compared to 41% of the low- and 50% of the moderate-combat blacks. The views of ARVN conduct against the Vietnamese civilian population of white and black heavy-combat veterans in table 6.13, however, show considerable agreement on the frequency with which they attribute abusive behavior to the ARVN.

The use of bombing and shelling to terrorize civilians (SVTERBOMB) by the ARVN is perceived as a function of period of service, combat experience among white Vietnam veterans, and whether or not the veteran was exposed to abusive violence. Vietnam veterans who served after 1967 are twice as likely to think that the ARVN frequently used bombing and shelling as those who served before 1968 (10% vs. 5%). A substantially greater proportion of white heavy-combat veterans (table 6.14) are persuaded that the ARVN seldom used bombing and shelling to terrorize civilians than is true of low- and moderate-combat veterans (51% vs. 38% for the two latter groups). Witnessing abusive violence, as we have consistently found, increases estimated use of all types of violence. As table 6.15 demonstrates, Vietnam veterans who witnessed abusive violence are substantially less likely to believe the ARVN seldom used terror bombing than the veterans not exposed to such behavior (34% vs. 46%); and participants in abusive violence are the group most likely to believe that the ARVN frequently employed this tactic (17%).

Conduct of the War by the American Forces

The perspectives of Vietnam veterans on the conduct of the war vis-a-vis civilians by American forces are the most illuminating. Combat experience and witnessing of and participation in abusive violence significantly affect the perceptions of the frequency with which American soldiers abused civilians, used bombing for the purposes of terror, and employed environmental warfare. Combat experience leads veterans to *lower* their estimates of the frequency of these actions, exposure to and participation in abusive violence contribute to *raising* the estimates of the frequency of such actions.

The period during which men served in the military also had a significant impact on the perception of the conduct of American soldiers toward Vietnamese civilians. As table 6.16 shows, those who served in the early stages of the war (1961–1967) are convinced significantly more often than those who served between 1968 and 1972 that Americans seldom abused the Vietnamese people (67% vs. 42%). Service in the later years, however, led to estimates almost twice as high as those of the veterans who served in the earlier period of the war that American soldiers sometimes or frequently committed these acts (58% vs. 33%).

Table 6.17 indicates that heavy-combat veterans are much more likely to report that American forces seldom abused Vietnamese people than those who saw little combat (65% vs. 51%). Heavy-combat veterans, however, tend to believe American soldiers more frequently abused Vietnamese civilians than do those who saw little combat (10% vs. 4%). Table 6.18 indicates that participation in abusive violence dramatically increases estimates of the U.S. forces' abuse of civilians: 64% of the participants compared to 35% of the witnessed and 38% of the not exposed groups believe that U.S. troops sometimes acted out against civilians. Furthermore, both the witnessed and participant groups (12%) are more likely to believe that such behavior by American forces was frequent than do veterans not exposed to abusive violence (3%).

Race and period of service both interact with witnessing of and participation in abusive violence and help to give us a better understanding of how the trauma of war influences perceptions of the conduct of war. As we indicated above, the participants in abusive violence appear most likely to attribute misconduct frequently to U.S. forces. Black participants view the behavior of American troops quite differently from their white counterparts. As tables 6.19 and 6.20 demonstrate, only 4% of the black participants say American soldiers seldom abused civilians, compared to 34% of their white counterparts; and 31% of the blacks say U.S. troops frequently abused civilians, a view shared by only 3% of the white participants. Combining the categories of "sometimes" and "frequently," we see that 96% of the black participants assert substantial U.S. abuse of Vietnamese civilians compared to 66% of the white participants. Table 6.19 also demonstrates that among whites, perceptions of U.S. soldiers as frequently abusing Vietnamese civilians are largely limited to those who witnessed abusive violence (13%): only 3% of the white participants and 4% of the not exposed whites share this view of American troop behavior. These findings, however, should not obscure the fact that regardless of race, the assertion that U.S. forces, at least sometimes, abused Vietnamese civilians is the predominant response of all participants.

Period of war service, as seen in table 6.21, has a less dramatic though substantial effect on the perceptions of those who witnessed abusive violence. Among witnesses in the pre-Tet period (1961–1967), only 40% believe that U.S. troops sometimes or frequently abused civilians, while 60% say that American soldiers seldom engaged in this type of behavior. Veterans who served after Tet virtually reverse the above figures. Fully 57% of the veterans who witnessed abusive violence after Tet believe American soldiers sometimes or frequently abused civilians while 43% believe such behavior was rare.

The response to the use of bombing and shelling of cities to terrorize the civilian population shows a different relationship between combat, witnessing of and participation in abusive violence, and perceptions of the use of this strategy by U.S. forces. In the total sample, combat has only a slight effect on estimates of USTERBOMB. In table 6.22, however, we see that white heavy-combat veterans (21%) are significantly more likely to attribute frequent use of terror bombing to the United States forces than either moderate- (12%) or low-combat veterans (17%). The most important finding in table 6.22 is that the greater difference is between the moderate- and heavy-combat veterans on perception of the frequency with which the United States resorted to this type of warfare, i.e., combat does not have a consistent (linear) relationship to estimates of bombing rates.

Among those who witnessed abusive violence, as table 6.23 indicates, 67% argue that the United States sometimes or frequently employed bombing and shelling tactics as compared to only 53% of those who were not exposed. Equally important is that the differences between the witnessed and the nonexposed are at the extremes. About equal proportions of each group say that there sometimes was bombing and shelling, but 47% of those not exposed respond that this type of warfare seldom occurred, compared to only 33% of the witnessed group. The differences are further magnified among the participants. Only 19% indicate that USTERBOMB seldom took place, compared to 81% who think it happened sometimes or frequently.

Finally, when we turn to the issues of environmental warfare we find that branch of military service has a decided impact on perceptions. In table 6.24 we see the marines (48%) and army veterans (42%) report that in their view the U.S. seldom used environmental weaponry compared to the air force/navy veterans (17%); and the differences between the estimates of the use of environmental warfare are accounted for at the extremes. Air force/navy respondents are twice as likely to say that environmental warfare was frequently employed by the United States military in Vietnam (40% vs. 20%).

Combat, as we have seen throughout the analysis, contributes to lower estimates of the frequency with which U.S. forces are perceived to abuse civilians (USABPERS) or bomb and shell civilians (USTERBOMB). In table 6.25 we find the same pattern of effects on the use of environmental warfare. Veterans who experienced heavy combat (16%) are less prone to say the United States frequently resorted to environmental warfare than are men who saw little combat (30%).

Combat, among whites, affects the perceptions of the frequency with which the American military used environmental weapons. As table 6.26 demonstrates, white veterans who saw little combat believe by more than two to one that the United States frequently utilized such weaponry compared to their heavy-combat peers (36% vs. 16%).

Environmental warfare does not appear to be differentially perceived by men who witnessed or participated in abusive violence. As table 6.27 shows, 28% of the witnessed group believe the United States frequently used environmental weapons, compared to 26% of the not exposed and 22% of the participants in violence.

In summary, the findings indicate that the perception of the conduct of American forces is most strongly affected by the degree of combat men experienced, whether or not they witnessed or participated in instances of abusive violence, and the period during which they served in the military. In the case of environmental warfare, the military branch served in also affected perceptions of the way in which Americans conducted the war. Witnessing of abusive violence and the period served both contribute to higher estimates of various types of conduct that caused harm to Vietnamese civilians. Combat, on the other hand, systematically reduces estimates of all types of actions against Vietnamese civilians by American forces.

The narrative material clarifies the ways in which Vietnam veterans responded differently than their peers. Obviously, the veteran group is most aware of the realities of Vietnam; and they often responded to the consequences of abusive violence more poignantly. A plurality were not only aware of but also sensitive to the suffering of civilians in the war. From the narrative material, it is evident that many veterans are troubled by acts committed against civilians by the Vietcong and North Vietnamese Army, as well as the ARVN, the Koreans, and the American forces. The legitimation of cruelty and glorification of killing traditional to war makes the sensitivity of many Vietnam veterans all the more remarkable.

Acts Committed by the Vietcong and North Vietnamese Army

In the narrative material veterans stressed that the Vietcong and NVA often did not respect the rights of the civilian population as noncombatants. One act commonly reported is the destruction of villages. A white veteran who was in the Green Berets witnessed the devastation wrought by the Vietcong. He reported:

> I have seen Vietcong come into villages and completely take over by force. They would shoot most of them that would not cooperate. I have seen little kids killed.

The widespread killing or terrorizing of civilians friendly to the South

Vietnamese government or the Americans was also reported. A white army infantry sergeant noted:

> Two five-year-old boys were killed because they had associated with our units when we were guarding a bridge. They could both speak Vietnamese and English and while we were there they gave us a lot of information and then one night a Vietcong or NVA woman came into the village and killed both of them. Imagine seeing children killed, it just makes you realize how cruel the war was.

Veterans also recalled that enemy forces attacked towns and villages indiscriminately, sparing nothing. A white combatant who was stationed in Saigon explained why a Vietcong attack on a hospital there became his most important wartime experience:

> It was November of 1966. They had a large military parade in downtown Saigon and I went to watch. The Vietcong . . . threw mortars in. Basically I think they were going for the military parade but they ended up hitting a French hospital. I could hear them coming in and steadily getting louder. The leaves in the tree above me were shaking and I was hugging the ground. . . . I felt sorry for the hospital and the kids that were there because there was also an orphanage in the hospital.

It was also noted that the Vietcong tortured civilians in order to obtain information. A white marine recalled:

> The biggest problem we had trying to get information from the people was that they were so frightened of the Vietcong. They knew we might threaten them but we really would not do anything to them in most cases, 95% of the time. They figured they were better off by not telling us on the Vietcong because if they told us they would probably come back and they would get tortured . . . like the village chief whose wife was eight months pregnant. They cut her stomach open and killed her and killed the chief and killed a couple of his kids in front of the rest of the village; those people knew that they meant business.

Acts Committed by the ARVN

In the narrative material veterans reported that the South Vietnamese forces terrorized and killed a great number of innocent civilians. The event most often described is the torture of civilians. While many veterans were shocked by what they considered to be the brutality of ARVN behavior, others justified such actions as an effective way of getting information. This attitude is typified by a white marine, quoted below, who strongly supported American involvement in the war and hated the Vietcong. He described what he saw as follows:

I want to make it very, very clear that the United States troops in my battalion were not allowed to interrogate any Vietnamese civilians. The ARVN did the interrogating. They once brought in a woman whose husband was a Vietcong. . . . They wanted to get information out of her. They stripped her to her waist and took a . . . generator . . . and they took one wire and put it to her left breast, the other wire and put it to her right breast and they started to crank it which could produce an electrical charge. And that was the torture I saw. . . . It was their prisoner and I had nothing to do with it. I just walked away. . . . It didn't have any affect on me to the extent that it changed me because I felt they [the Vietcong] were wrong. I still feel the exact same way.

Another white marine who witnessed the mistreatment of an old man and a young girl also felt that the torture of civilians was effective in terms of gaining information:

One time we were crossing a village to get information; we had a couple of Vietnamese marines with us and they were questioning this old man and young girl. They said they did not know anything. One marine was bending this girl's arm and the old man came over and stopped it and the guy kicked the old man in the teeth. He questioned the girl some more and still did not get any information, she would not talk. He broke her arm with an iron rod that he was carrying and then he got the information. What troops had been in there, and where they were going. I thought it was real effective as far as gaining information.

A white veteran who was in the army was fully aware of the brutality involved in the act he witnessed and was more hesitant to provide a justification. He had the following remembrance:

The infantry command post caught this guy and it was just an old man sowing his field. They put a bag over his head and the Vietnamese interrogated him. Every time the guy did not give the correct answer they punched him in the mouth. You could see the blood dripping down his neck. I was glad I did not have my head inside the bag. I mean you can't see . . . you don't know when you are going to get hit. You have to be tense and all of a sudden feel the crunching blow. It is a good way to get what you want out of somebody, I guess.

Other veterans were openly critical of the ARVN's mistreatment of civilians. They concluded that many of the South Vietnamese actions against civilians were inhuman and had no military justification. Veterans also reported hostility between different ARVN units, occasionally resulting in actual fights. Often Vietnamese civilians became the victims. A white navy seabee reported the following event:

[The ARVNs] were rivals. The story went that the commander of their regular foot soldiers had an involvement in town, he was the owner of a brothel. The commander of the tanks, he also had a brothel in town and they were competing. So they went down with the tanks and blew the brothel away. We saw a woman dead. She must have been eight months pregnant. The baby . . . her belly was on the bed. She was torn apart. I just wanted to get the hell out of there. I don't know what we were doing there. My reaction was just leave these people alone, let them solve their own problems.

Incidents Involving American Troops

As noted earlier, Vietnam veterans are less likely than others to attribute acts against civilians to U.S. forces in Vietnam. However, in the narrative material respondents most often talked about cases in which U.S. forces were involved and presented only sparse reports of NVA/VC and ARVN abusive behavior. This is especially true among veterans who either participated in acts of abusive violence or witnessed the event and its consequences.

Among the incidents most commonly reported are the destruction of villages as part of search and destroy missions; and bombing and shelling of friendly villages; killing civilians moving across a free-fire zone; taking villagers hostage and forcefully moving them to camps; forcing civilians to provide intelligence information; withholding medical assistance from wounded or starving civilians; blowing up river boats carrying civilians; killing children, women, and old men; and war against the environment.

Destruction of villages as part of search and destroy missions

Veterans who were personally involved in search and destroy missions against civilians, especially white participants, generally argued that the actions were necessary in order for the American forces to survive and win the war. A white veteran who was on navy patrol up and down a river reported:

We went into a village and there were no North Vietnamese around. The point opened up the village gate and it exploded and he got killed and it wounded two other people . . . and then two sniper rounds rang out and two more men dropped. So we backed out of the village and called in an air strike. Then we swept back through the village and we wiped out everything—people, animals, trees, birds, plants, flowers, grass—anything that was alive we just leveled. . . . I don't believe in the Geneva Conventions because if you're fighting a war and I got something that's illegal but it's going to help me win, I'm going to do it. I mean you just can't make rules in a war—how can they possibly say this is inhumane, you're fighting a war.

These veterans also maintained that the search and destroy missions were an important part of American military policy. They were sometimes assigned to interrogate civilians and admitted that those who withheld information would "get knocked around." After the interrogations were completed the area had to be cleared out and secured. A white army infantryman reported:

> I got more and more involved . . . in the mass killings. Some orders were written and some you had to kind of weed them out. They wouldn't come out and point blank tell you to go in and take this village and totally destroy it. They would tell you "to police it." . . . We knew what that meant. They would say "you understand policing" . . . and they'd just smile. . . .What are you going to do when they tell you "police this village" and they hand you about three hundred rounds of ammunition, when you normally take a hundred. . . . And your men got more plastic explosives, more dynamite than normal. . . . When we got through with that village, you would never know there was a village there.

A black army infantry man added:

> A lot of soldiers are briefed but they're not briefed properly. They're told to do one thing but the way it comes out of the person giving the order is to do a whole lot of other things. Like, kill all the animals, kill everything that lives. In other words, when I'm in this village, there's nothing to be left alive.

Others, especially those veterans who were not personally involved in these missions but witnessed their consequences, often condemned them and noted that the cruelty involved had a negative effect on them. A black army infantryman illustrates this attitude:

> When we got there they had found some VC in the village. They fired on everybody and burned the village out. . . . I got there a few minutes later. . . it had a terrible side effect on my thinking of the military. . . . I didn't want to continue because of that.

Bombing or shelling of friendly villages

Again, veterans who were personally involved in bombing or shelling friendly villages often attempted to justify their actions. A white marine noted:

> I participated in the shelling of friendly villages. . . . It is the price you pay for having a war. Civilians die.

Other veterans felt more conflicted. A white marine who witnessed the destruction of a village explained:

> When I was first in Vietnam we were bombed one night, mortared from a friendly village right outside the base and the general said we could not fire back and we lost twenty people. Halfway through Vietnam, they changed generals and the next time we got mortared from the village, we just destroyed it. They could not find the town on the map. . . . We also shed out some napalm in the wrong places . . . burning villages. . . . I saw napalm accidents where they burn people alive. I don't think this should have happened.

Killing Montagnards moving across free-fire zones

While some veterans reported that killing civilians moving across a free-fire zone was a necessary part of war, others responded in a negative way. A black veteran who was in the army recalled the following incident:

> I was working in the radio room and a report came in from a helicopter. They caught some people moving across . . . and the pilot was asking for clearance to fire at them because they were in a free-fire zone. . . . They were nomads called Montagnard. . . . This pilot called in for clearance, which he got. He identified them as women and children, a few old men. There were about forty of them. I took the call. I wrote the message down. This is where I really started feeling guilt. . . . I'd been there about two months . . . I thought that they [acts against civilians] were increasing my respect for human life. . . . I hadn't been confronted with it before, I had never made that conscious commitment not to do these kinds of things. But because I saw it, that's when I made a commitment. I certainly would never participate in abusing people like that.

Taking villagers and forcibly moving them to camps

Forcibly relocating villagers was sometimes considered necessary in order to safeguard the lives of the Vietnamese civilians. A white army infantryman who was a participant in abusive violence against civilians reported:

> I have seen them pulled out of their homes—loaded on the trucks—taken away to a safe camp, as they say. And the only reason we would do it is to save their lives. Could be because we know they're going to be overrun by VC or we have to annihilate that village—get rid of it so the VC can't use it. But they weren't maltreated. They were able to take anything they wanted—take an entire household—whatever they got.

Others who participated in this type of action were more critical and felt that often the evacuations were not necessary and violated the rights of the civilians. A white marine sergeant talked about one event in which he participated:

> The officer commanded us to attack the villagers, and move them to a camp. We did attack them, killing some of them. . . . I felt that it ought to be reported to the division commander although I myself was not in a position where I could do it. It made me more aware of civilian rights in a war zone.

Forcing civilians to provide intelligence information

Some respondents noted that villagers were often coerced into giving information on the movement of the Vietcong. A black veteran who served for army intelligence reported the following incident:

> A couple of the intelligence agents that were stationed with us would go into different villages at night to talk with the village chief, finding out if there were any Vietcong in the area. And the village chief would say "no." They'd say "it is obvious he does not want to cooperate." So the next night they go in and the chief ends up with his throat cut.

Withholding medical assistance from wounded or starving civilians

The narrative material also provides evidence that wounded civilians were often left unattended. A black army infantryman who participated in abusive violence reported:

> We were riding down a dirt road and there were mountaineers . . . working in the rice paddy. And one of the guys opened fire. The rest of the company just automatically went into a defensive move and they hit a few people before they realized what they were doing. And the captain just said, "to hell with it—let's go." . . . There were a couple of people wounded, I'm quite sure.

Although many veterans shared some of their food with starving civilians, others expressed a total disregard for the suffering of the people. A white veteran who witnessed abusive violence reported:

> I got into a hassle with my platoon leader at one time about cruelty. There were some kids around and they were starving. He would not give them C-rations. The way he looked at it was that they would be giving it to some Vietcong later. In my opinion the kids just wanted something to eat.

Blowing up family boats on rivers in civilian areas

Some veterans serving in the navy were involved in blowing up boats on rivers, an action which sometimes resulted in civilian casualties. A white veteran remembered:

> The navy's mission there, at least the squadron I was in, was to stop boats that were going South with the ammo and supplies. Any boat going south we just did not let it get there. We would blow it up. It did not bother me too much . . . blowing up the family boats. There were a couple of incidents in which we knew they were family boats and did not have any bombs on board but we hit them anyway. We never fired the guns without permission of the captain and so the captain of the ships had given permission.

Killing and wounding civilians

The killing and maiming of innocent civilians, especially children, women, and old men, is unavoidable in any war and often assumes even more tragic proportions in a guerrilla war.

As noted earlier, there was a tendency among Vietnam veterans directly involved in acts of abusive violence against civilians, especially white participants, to justify their actions or to suppress their feelings. Some of these respondents also expressed a studied indifference to the value of Vietnamese life.

Another group of Vietnam veterans who witnessed the killing of innocent civilians did not condone the violence, but did not feel strongly about it either. A white army infantry sergeant noted:

> One day on a search and destroy mission—this old lady was in a hooch and wouldn't come out. Somebody set the hooch on fire around her and I guess she finally came out with burns and all. . . . It's something that started when I was there—but I didn't actually see her come out. . . . I didn't condone it—I didn't stop it either. But of course I wasn't in a position to stop it.

Other Vietnam veterans who saw the suffering inflicted on civilians often expressed feelings of sadness or anger. They pointed out that fighting the enemy was one thing, but that to be involved in the killing of people that Americans were supposed to be protecting was unacceptable. This attitude is especially prevalent among those who served in Vietnam after the Tet offensive. A white marine who was in Vietnam after 1967 reported:

> I was in a place where they were bringing in wounded from villages that had been bombed by Americans. To see the women and the kids—little kids—that got to me so fast. I knew they were not Americans. But that did not matter. They

were people that had been hurt. To kill people that we were supposed to be protecting, I could not agree with that.

Respondents also explained how they became increasingly aware of what was happening in Vietnam and eventually concluded that Americans were killing the Vietnamese for no good reason. This is evident from the following remarks made by a white veteran who served during the post-Tet period:

> It was pitiful. I saw some kids, 8-, 10-year-old kids get bombed. I saw an old man killed. He was working in a rice paddy and we rode by on our patrol. The sergeant said he had a gun and told us to open fire. I did not see a gun. I did not shoot. Our fire just about tore him in half. That was depressing to see. We were killing them for no good reason.

A substantial number of veterans tried to compensate for some of the havoc wreaked on the civilian environment. A white army engineer noted:

> Our own units fired by mistake on a Vietnamese village. The next morning we had to go in. When we went there we saw pieces of skulls from Vietnamese still on the ground and a lot of skin and bones. It fazed me out completely. I felt as if I [had to] do something to alleviate the damage. We started building a hospital and a couple of the houses, but I was limited by what I could do really in the war. I think it gave me an appreciation of human life.

Many Vietnam veterans knew kids and cared for them. They admit that often when they see their own children sick or in pain, they think about the Vietnamese children. A white navy seabee remains haunted by the terrible fate of the young Vietnamese. He recounts:

> We used to do a lot of work for the orphanages. That was a bad scene. You see kids there who have had their faces shot off, crippled. They will never get old, these kids. They will never have a life. I would love to get every politician, put him against the wall and blow his head off. Because they are the ones who caused it.

War against the environment

As noted earlier, Vietnam veterans are least inclined to consider acts against the environment unlawful. While expressing concern for the devastation of land and crops, they generally consider this an unavoidable part of war. A substantial minority, however, pointed out that the defoliation of large parts of the country-side of South Vietnam was a clearly illegal act. For example, a white veteran when asked whether he was ever directly exposed to "the dirty side of the war" explained his affirmative answer this way:

> When you see what happens when napalm hits the civilians and see what it did
> to them. . . . The defoliage . . . to the countryside . . . that is a sad thing
> because people live off the land. I mean that is the Vietnamese . . . way of life.
> The bombs that were dropped . . . they dropped so many . . . just ruined the
> whole countryside. I felt sorry for the people.

Two additional types of abusive violence are reported that must be considered as personal crimes unrelated to the war effort: terrorizing civilians and raping young girls and women.

Terrorizing civilians

Some of the most brutal accounts found in the narratives deal with acts of terror against civilians, incidents that were committed out of sheer meanness. A white army veteran explained:

> I can remember shooting dogs and cats and water buffalo and other animals,
> farm animals, pigs, chickens, goats. We would be half drunk riding down the
> road in a jeep and we would see this civilian obviously working in a rice paddy.
> You would pick up your rifle and take a couple of pot shots at him just to scare
> the shit out of him.

A black marine reported:

> Action against civilians? We used to frighten them. The dudes, we might beat
> them up and throw them in rice paddies. Why did we do that? I don't know. Just
> mean, I guess.

A white marine commented:

> [I saw a] thing—just American sheer meanness. They were marines. It was on
> one of my many trips—Vietnamese kids would run up and ask for food. . . .
> The guys would take the C-ration cans and try to hit these kids and one guy, I
> swear to God—must have killed this kid. He hit him right in the head and the kid
> went out just like that.

Raping young girls and women

Vietnam veterans admit that rape was a common occurrence. A black army sergeant told us:

We went through a village and we were supposed to just search through it and they got a couple of 15-year-old girls and raped them. I tried to stop them at first, but when you've got about six or seven guys, there isn't too much you can do.

Responses to the War against Civilians

The narrative material, like the statistical data, indicates that a minority of Vietnam veterans denied that American forces engaged in abusive violence against the Vietnamese people. A white veteran had the following to say:

We put ourselves in chains. We were so strapped by the legal requirements and by very careful adhering to all the Geneva Conventions that we hampered our own efforts in a war with people who were not signatories to the treaties. We were fighting by one set of rules and the enemy was fighting by another. In that sort of situation I do not know that we really had to adhere to the Geneva Conventions. When we refused to bomb a dyke that would have caused North Vietnam to surrender at almost any moment, when we held back on bombing cities and bombing the oil reserves until the enemy had time to move them, well it really puts us in a very ridiculous situation.

A majority, especially of those who served after the Tet offensive, admitted that American forces had engaged in acts of abusive violence. But a substantial number felt that the American war against Vietnamese civilians was not only justified but necessary. They argued that the character of the war and the scope of guerrilla activity often placed the noncombatant status of Vietnamese civilians in question. The inability to differentiate clearly between noncombatants and the enemy strained the relations between the U.S. serviceman and the population he was defending and with which he was formally allied. The dual character of many Vietnamese, pretending to be allies but in reality often friendly to the Vietcong, placed additional strains on the American forces. As a result of the complexity of the war experience, noncombatants were often treated as the enemy and subjected to systematic violence. In addition, veterans explained that this ''war against civilians'' was caused by the pervasive threat to life American troops faced, or feared, in the context of a guerrilla war. The violent acts against civilians reflected the anger, fear, and anxiety of American troops in a situation where personal survival was continuously threatened.

Some respondents admitted that their attitude toward killing civilians drastically changed because of what the enemy troops did to the Americans. In this regard, a black army sergeant talked about his response to atrocities committed by the Vietcong:

People wonder why the GIs would open up and shoot babies and females. You can't help it when you see a buddy all chopped up in pieces. [Did your attitude toward killing people change as time went on?] Yes. I started liking it. The American GI can be one of the most savage of creatures. You go on a search and destroy mission. You search and destroy everybody you catch. You hold them for interrogation or if you are really mad, you pull the trigger and hey, too bad, he's dead.

These veterans also often felt that the war against civilians should have been intensified. The latter view is clearly expressed in the words of a white veteran who served in the army:

Well, we were too kind . . . we used kid gloves with them. We tried to be nice to the civilians and it got us absolutely nothing except losing more lives. I don't mean going out and slaughtering innocent civilians and children and all, but we should have been a lot tougher. Everyone in the country knew there was a war going on—so if a civilian was somewhere he shouldn't have been . . . common sense should have told them not to get around the perimeter, that they're even liable to get shot. . . . There were times when we weren't allowed to fire. . . . We were just way too easy going and we got whipped for it.

But a plurality of those who acknowledged American acts of abusive violence professed sadness about the "dirty" side of war. They argued that although the character of the Vietnam War created a very difficult situation for the American forces, many of the acts of abusive violence committed against the civilian population were not related to military necessity. They were critical of the "war against civilians" and concluded that the American forces carry a burden of responsibility for much of the unnecessary suffering of the people. A black infantryman provides an insight into the moral decline and the growing sense of guilt that so many veterans experienced:

Did I ever do anything? Yeah. I joined in the practice, because the guys kept on ribbing me. I raped a girl one time and I prayed: "God forgive me for doing that," because I knew that I was losing my mind. It made me think that I was just another animal, just like everybody else. Killing . . . that was all they thought about . . . tearing up . . . destroying everything.

Nonveterans' Perspectives on the Conduct of the War

Antiwar activism has an important and consistent effect on estimates of the frequency of the misconduct by the VC/NVA and the American forces. Activists estimate that the VC/NVA are less likely and the American forces more likely to engage in these types of actions than their nonactivist peers who did not enter the military. Since, as reported above, Vietnam veterans felt that misconduct occurred less frequently than did nonveterans, there is a significant difference between how Vietnam veterans and antiwar activists view the conduct of the war.

Activists are less charitable in their assessment of the conduct of the ARVN and U.S. forces toward civilians than are their peers. In addition, they describe VC/NVA conduct as less remorselessly abusive. As table 6.28 shows, the high activists see relatively little difference between the behavior of the ARVN and the VC/NVA. Indeed, the activists perceive the VC/NVA to have frequently abused civilians only slightly more than the ARVN (50% vs. 43%). In table 6.29, however, we find a very large difference between the activists' perception of the conduct of the U.S. forces and the VC/NVA. Only 20% of high activists believe that the U.S. forces frequently mistreated civilians compared to the VC/NVA (50%). High activists generally believe that U.S. forces sometimes mistreated civilians (69%) compared to 48% of their low activist peers. Thus, we see that activists are more likely than any other group to believe that all parties to the conflict were relatively unconcerned with the protection of civilians from abuse.

Antiwar activists perceive the American military as having extensively utilized bombing for terror compared to the VC/NVA. Table 6.30 shows that the highly engaged antiwar activists conclude that Americans more frequently resorted to the bombing and shelling of cities than do the low activists (34% vs. 23%). The NVA/VC were seen frequently to resort to this type of warfare by only 18% of the most involved antiwar activists, compared to 39% of the low activists.

The different views of the frequency with which the United States used environmental warfare are highlighted when we compare antiwar activists with Vietnam veterans. As indicated in table 6.31, none of the highly involved antiwar activists believe the United States infrequently (seldom) resorted to environmental warfare, while 70% believe the Americans relied very frequently on such aggression. Since only 26% of the Vietnam veterans come to this latter conclusion, it would appear that how our respondents experienced the war significantly affects their views of the conduct of the military during the Vietnam War.

In tables 6.32 and 6.33, we see that nonveterans who supported the war were more likely than their nonveteran peers who opposed the war to perceive the enemy forces as frequently culpable of acts of abuse of civilians or the use of terror bombing. The ARVN was seen as decidedly more prone to abuse civilians than the U.S. forces but less apt to utilize terror bombing. Estimates by prowar nonveterans of U.S. forces' frequent abuse of civilians (6%) were identical with those of Vietnam veterans and substantially lower than the estimates of the moderate (22%) and high antiwar activists (20%). The prowar nonveterans' estimates of the frequent use of terror bombing by the U.S. forces (20%) were also much lower than those of the antiwar activists (34%). Finally, in table 6.34, we see the same pattern regarding the frequency of U.S. forces' use of environmental warfare. Supporters of the war (43%) are less likely to believe that the United States frequently resorted to environmental warfare than those who opposed the war (51%) and those active in the antiwar movement (70%). Thus, we see clear evidence in the nonveteran population of ideology influencing perceptions of behavior.

Prowar nonveterans

In the narrative material, a minority of prowar nonveterans seemed equally concerned about acts of abusive violence committed by the enemy and by allied and American forces against the civilian population of Vietnam. While supporting the American involvement in the war, they had negative feelings about the way the war was fought. A nonveteran expressed this view as follows:

> The NVA and the VC's way of fighting left one very angry that man could do that to another man. . . . I feel negative that the war had to be fought on the basis that it was fought at . . . things that were being reported, like My Lai. You really wonder about some of those things our soldiers were doing. . . . My father said things will happen over there that you won't believe would happen. He said, don't think that the American soldier is a nice person when it comes to killing. He can be one of the worst there is if he's forced to be. . . . I think it really made me think about what one person could do to another person.

Some of these respondents also pointed out that the American Army was allowing acts that were worse than questionable. The Calley case seems to be the focus of their concern. A nonveteran observed:

> I have always had a vision of the army as being very structured. And yet here these things were being allowed which were basically illegal. A "nothing sacred" type of thing is going on. In many ways I felt that Lieutenant Calley was a fall guy. It was of concern to me that he could go ahead and take an order like that and kill innocent people and by the same token it was of concern to me that there were others that could issue that order and still not be touched and that he was the only one who was really punished.

A second small group of prowar respondents expressed little or no concern about the issue of abusive violence. They simply noted that abusive violence is an unavoidable part of war. A respondent made this attitude clear:

> I felt the VC and NVA were the enemy and there were a lot of atrocities they committed. . . . You see how dirty the war gets: the terrorizing of civilians, torturing of prisoners. It was never publicized much about that occurring in the

previous wars, this is the first time I realized how much of that goes on in a war. . . . I figured it was a part of war, you had to accept it.

A majority of prowar nonveterans seemed to be concerned only about the abusive violence committed by the enemy forces. They pointed out that the NVA and VC used inhumane guerrilla tactics and felt that the American forces had to take retaliatory measures. According to these respondents, the Communists had to be defeated and the Americans should not have had to fight the war according to the rules of humanitarian law. A respondent presented this view:

> If these people don't want to be under Communist rule then we really should be there helping them out. But, by the same token, we shouldn't fight the war according to some crazy rules made up by some conference somewhere.

Since from their perspective the North Vietnamese and the Vietcong were the aggressors, the American and South Vietnamese forces were not at fault for killing civilians. A nonveteran noted:

> I do feel that the Vietcong and the North Vietnamese were the aggressors in that war and we tried to save a country that wanted to rule themselves and not be under a Communist domination. I knew we were killing civilians over there, but I really didn't feel that the American soldiers that were doing the killing were doing anything wrong.

The narrative material indicates that there is one dominant theme for most of the prowar nonveterans: the enemy committed atrocities against the civilians. These respondents considered VC and NVA tactics of fighting to be inhuman and without conscience. A respondent provided this assessment:

> The North Vietnamese soldiers, the Vietcong soldiers, they seemed to have a terrible disregard for human life and human dignity. They tortured people. . . . I felt that our involvement there was just, I thought it was to protect . . . the Vietnamese people.

Antiwar activists

Activists commented that acts of abusive violence against civilians were being committed by *all* parties to the conflict. A high activist noted:

> There's no such thing as a clean war anymore, but this was a particularly dirty and brutal one. The craziness of it, for instance, children coming out with grenades and destroying soldiers. We would use that to justify our attacks on civilians because "you never knew who the enemy was." The Vietnamese

saying, "you want to play war, we're going to teach you it really dirty." They got down to it and our side got down to it, the barbaric, simple, out-and-out get even type philosophy.

Another high activist added:

I felt, getting back to the atrocities committed, that some of the things I mentioned—like the terror bombing—the Vietcong couldn't do, because they didn't have the resources to do it. I felt that if they could they would have. The United States didn't commit a lot of the atrocities because they had the ARVN to do it for them. In terms of bombing the cities, the ARVN didn't do it because they had the United States to do it for them. . . . I saw pictures of North Vietnamese prisons, where the cells were like 12 inches from the ground and guys were laying there for months—so it affected my view of the war. I figured both sides were brutal, inhumane. . . . I became sickened by what was going on.

Despite their awareness that acts of abusive violence were committed by all parties to the conflict, in the narrative material antiwar activists, like their Vietnam veteran peers, talked primarily about the American involvement in "the dirty side of war." Four types of activities seemed to concern them most: indiscriminate bombing of towns and villages, terrorization of the civilian population, My Lai type of attacks on villages, and defoliation of the countryside.

Respondents pointed out that during the early stage of the war there was significant military and political cover-up surrounding the U.S. bombings. But by the late sixties, media focus on American actions in Vietnam had become intensive and as a result opposition to the war escalated. The following remarks by a high activist illustrate this attitude:

The coverage and extent of the war increased dramatically year by year from '66 on. In '65 we were led to believe [that the war] was a small kind of guerrilla operation. By '70 it was a matter of a full-scale invasion with much greater coverage, so that I grew more negative the more I learned about what we were actually doing.

The dropping of bombs on the civilian population, especially in nonstrategic, undefended localities, was considered needlessly cruel by many respondents. A high activist observed:

I thought that the bombings were extremely unnecessary . . . they weren't even sure if they were only using them on the NVA and Vietcong or on civilians. It seemed like every other week I was reading how another plane had dropped the bombs on civilians . . . some peaceful little town and blew it sky high.

Respondents pointed out that the whole population of Vietnam was being attacked indiscriminately and people who had no effect on the outcome of the war were being killed. A high activist noted:

> The war was being conducted in a way which was almost genocidal. The whole population of Vietnam was being attacked. The countryside was being essentially wasted. They were trying to destroy entire jungles. There was indiscriminate saturation bombing from B 52's.

Activists not only were concerned about the bombing of civilians in South Vietnam, but were equally upset about the attacks on North Vietnam, especially the carpet bombing of Hanoi and the Christmas bombing in 1972. A high activist expressed this view:

> I think it was tearing me apart . . . that the country which I do love was committing acts of genocide and imperialism. As the war grew on the problems simply compounded themselves. [What concerned you most?] The napalm and the bombing of North Vietnam.

Respondents also pointed out that a strategy of terrorism directed against the civilian population was part of the official American policy in Vietnam. A high activist explained:

> The whole war was ordered by the people in power. . . . The war was against a guerrilla movement. So they wanted to terrorize the population, scare them out of supporting them and that couldn't be just.

Respondents also referred to My Lai and "whatever other My Lais may have occurred." A moderate activist explained what upset him most about the war:

> The mass murders . . . I got really disgusted with Calley. . . . Reading of other similar sorts of things and reading about the amount of people getting killed there on all sides. I felt that our being there and killing anyone who was innocent was just a sad moral implication to our society.

Respondents noted that the My Lai massacre also destroyed their belief in "how the American military might act in a combat situation." A moderate activist recalled:

> I saw when the American planes dropped bombs on a village, I think by mistake, and this little child was on fire—she was burning. That was awful. How could you kill thousands of people and My Lai—the guy Calley. How

could he live after that? We should be the best—we should be democratic—but we were doing the same dirty work as them.

Many activists felt that the fault lies primarily at the top, not at the bottom. A high activist reported:

I became more concerned because of the atrocities, the My Lai things; I was highly outraged by those activities. But at the same time, as was seen in most of the antiwar movement, we never blamed the GIs. We always disassociated the men in the field from U.S. military policy. That was an important thing to do.

Respondents argued that it was shameful for our country to be involved in waging a war that was so unnecessarily cruel. One high activist expressed this feeling as follows:

It really was a time of a loss of innocence in viewing of our society. Going from a society that we thought was constantly on the side of good and right and justice, to a more realistic view of the fact that we operate many times in a selfish, hostile, and corrupt way. It underscored for me the psychopathic mentality at work in waging this war, and it meant that we were literally no better than anybody else. I think America's only salvation is not in our military power or military might but in our sense of fairness. The world should respect us because we're a just and fair society.

Antiwar activists also often presented a strong plea that in future wars international legal rules protecting civilians should be respected. A high activist stated:

I felt that we were indiscriminately murdering people for goals or for reasons which I couldn't understand. . . . I don't think the United States followed very many, if any, of those established rules of conduct. . . . I think that what ought to be done is that everybody ought to make the effort to see that these rules if they ever have to be followed in another war should be followed, that by not doing something, we are permitting evil to exist.

Conclusion

A central unifying theme in this chapter is the consensus among our respondents in terms of what they perceive to be acceptable or unacceptable conduct in wartime. Actions against individuals are condemned by 90% of the sample, bombing or shelling of cities to terrorize the civilian population by 75%, while only a bare majority of the sample oppose environmental warfare as unlawful.

A second unifying theme is the assertion by all groups of respondents that the enemy forces were more likely than other combatants to abuse civilians, that the South Vietnamese forces also commonly but less frequently engaged in such abuses, but that this behavior was comparatively uncommon for American forces. Furthermore, except among the high antiwar activists, terror bombing and shelling was more often attributed to the enemy than to the Americans. However, the degree of difference on this issue is less dramatic than on the abuse of civilians.

We also found that Vietnam veterans generally attribute *less* abusive violence to all military forces in Vietnam than their peers. There is, however, no absence of evidence presented by Vietnam veterans that abuse and terrorization were common in the Vietnam War. Involvement in the violence of the war, combat, and witnessing of and participation in abusive violence generally tend to increase estimates of the rate at which U.S. forces abused civilians. Again, however, the pattern of attribution of violence against civilians remains as described above, even among those exposed to the war's brutality.

From the transcript material, we see that Vietnam veterans who experienced the violence of war are emphatic about their assertion that abuse of civilians was endemic among the indigenous forces. They point out that the exercise of violence by enemy forces was pervasive and methodical. The Vietcong and North Vietnamese Army, they contend, assassinated innocent civilians and employed military strategies geared to cause death and injury indiscriminantly. They further argue that the number of civilians killed and wounded, through deliberate attacks on inhabited areas, was large indeed.

It is also commonly observed that the ARVN troops and commanders seemed oblivious to the devastation and suffering they inflicted on the civilian population. South Vietnamese forces are reported to have terrorized, tortured, and killed a great number of innocent civilians. While many veterans are shocked by the brutality of ARVN behavior, others justify such action as militarily necessary.

As noted earlier, in the narrative material respondents most often talked about cases in which U.S. forces were involved. Two arguments were presented explaining the occurrence of American acts of abusive violence. One group of veterans noted that these act were inherent not in the men but in the circumstances under which they had to live and fight. The conflict in Vietnam combined civil war, revolution, and jungle warfare. It was a guerrilla war without fronts, and this created an environment especially conducive to abusive violence. American servicemen in Vietnam experienced both frustration and fear. Troops would tramp through alien swamps and impenetrable jungles, or lie in irrigated rice paddies covered by mud and leeches, scorched by the sun, drenched by the rain of the monsoon, without making contact with the elusive enemy. Ties of friendship were woven by dangers and privation shared. Meanwhile they endured the deadly ravages of enemy ambushes, snipers, booby traps, and mines. They lived with the smell of death, the loss of friends, the desultory violence of endless war, yet there was no visible enemy on whom one could revenge these losses. Apparent civilians were actually combatants; women and children engaged in hostile acts. Gradually the whole Vietnamese population became cause for fear. Our sample noted that men who do not expect to receive mercy eventually lose their inclination to grant it. The hostility toward the enemy was often transferred to the civilian population. In such a scenario, respondents argued, the need to prosecute the war against the enemy which hid among the people legitimized the use of a broad range of action against civilians. The torture of noncombatants in order to obtain information was also defended as necessary for self-protection in an environment where the enemy was often unseen but omnipresent.

A counterargument was presented by another group of Vietnam veterans who reacted with horror to American acts of abusive violence against civilians. Sensitive to the suffering of civilians in the war, they stressed the human consequences of violence and pointed out that though some of the abuse was unavoidable, most of it could have been prevented or stopped. They often blamed military and political leaders for their unwillingness to forgo certain military strategies directed against civilians and for their indifference to the human costs involved. They also stressed that the damage done to Vietnamese society by allied military operations was a serious handicap to pacification and winning the support of the Vietnamese people. They further stated that some American military techniques were counterproductive in terms of "winning hearts and minds." Moreover, they observed that American and allied acts of abusive violence against innocent men, women, and children gave the Vietcong and North Vietnamese Army a propaganda tool which resulted in increasing loss of support for the South Vietnamese government.

Nonveterans, especially antiwar activists, also acknowledged the reciprocal brutality of the indigenous forces and the participation of American troops in the violence against the civilian population. For them, this pattern of violence against the civilians became the basis for arguing that a war fought under such conditions cannot be justified, that it degraded the American soldier and made the mission of the U.S. forces hopeless. Activists also noted that the American methods of counterinsurgency warfare in a Vietnam-type setting frequently do not accomplish their objectives and indeed may play a negative role.

CHAPTER SEVEN

THE USE OF UNNECESSARILY CRUEL WEAPONS

The attempt to control the production and use of unnecessarily cruel weapons is another form of recognition of the inhumanity in warfare.[1] As early as the twelfth century, Pope Innocent II became one of the first critics of "modern" weapons when he condemned the use of the crossbow as too deadly for Christian warfare. The elaborate codes of conduct used by feudal armies when engaged in combat offer further evidence of man's early desire to control the tactics of war. During the Middle Ages, war was viewed as a purposeful and honorable endeavor; deviations from the norms of battle were deemed ignoble.

Today, this philosophical tradition is reflected in the arguments of those who support international legal efforts to regulate cruel weapons. They attest that the use of such devices is, like former deviations from feudal norms, unnecessary, disadvantageous, and unworthy. Moreover, as technological advancements in weaponry increase the degree and level of suffering inflicted upon combatants and civilians alike, the control of unnecessarily cruel weapons becomes increasingly imperative.

This chapter explores the modern regulation of unnecessarily cruel weapons and briefly describes their use during the Vietnam conflict. The views of the Vietnam Generation are then presented regarding the cruelty of specified weapons, the conditions under which they can be used, and the respondents' personal exposure to their use.

Control of Unnecessarily Cruel Weapons

Modern regulation of the use of cruel weapons has followed two distinct, yet inherently complementary, paths. One approach lays down *general principles* concerning broad and unspecified categories of weapons; the other imposes *restraints on specific weapons.*[2]

Antonio Cassese, in his authoritative study of humanitarian law, has said that the first approach, used alone, is the less satisfactory.[3]

An examination of customary and conventional international law finds three general tenets concerning weapons use: 1) belligerents do not have an unlimited right to choose the means of injuring the enemy; 2) weapons causing unnecessary suffering are to be avoided; and 3) weapons that are indiscriminate in effects are to be shunned.[4] Clearly, such prohibitions are easier to negotiate since vast categories of weapons are covered and application is couched in vague terms. Interpretation and implementation of these prohibitions is left to the belligerents.

Banning specific weapons has two important advantages over the general prohibitory conventions. First, all parties are certain about the kind of weapons outlawed; second, the use of these weapons is forbidden regardless of the circumstances.[5] Cassese argues, however, that because specific bans are neutralized by new and more sophisticated weapons, the linking of general prohibitions with the enactment of specific bans strengthens both approaches.[6]

Just as the Declaration of St. Petersburg of 1868 pioneered the protection of civilian rights, so it was the first ruling to control the use of weapons.[7] The main concern of the declaration was the establishment of *general rules* regarding weapons that cause unnecessary suffering to their victims. It lists as contrary to humanity those weapons that "uselessly aggravate the sufferings of disabled men, or render their death inevitable." At the same time, the declaration prohibited explosive or charged projectiles weighing less than 14 ounces. These bullets, which exploded on contact with human flesh, were regarded as an inhuman instrument of war.

The first international codification of the laws of war took place some thirty years later with the Hague Conventions of 1899 and 1907, which linked specific bans and general principles. The "Law of the Hague," embodied in the Hague Conventions of Land Warfare and their annexed "Regulations," set forth the general principle that the belligerent does not have an unlimited choice in the means of injuring the enemy. It also forbade belligerents from employing poisoned weapons and any other weapons calculated to cause unnecessary suffering.[8] Another early limitation on armaments, the Declaration Respecting Expanding Bullets of 1899, prohibited projectiles that readily grow or flatten (the so-called dum-dum bullet), ripping through flesh.

The ban against poisonous weapons was elaborated in a protocol signed in 1925, which prohibited the use in war of asphyxiating, poisonous, and other gases and all analogous liquids, materials, or devices. Bacteriological methods of warfare were also outlawed.[9] During the Second World War, the protocol was generally observed by all nations. More recently, in 1972, the Convention on the Prohibitions of the Development, Production and Stockpiling of Bacteriological (Biological) and Toxic Weapons and on Their Destruction was signed. This convention, which entered into force in 1975, constitutes an important step toward agreement on biological weapons and on their elimination from the arsenals of all states.

As technology advanced, air power became increasingly important, and the explosive and incendiary shell or bomb was used more and more frequently. In the Korean and the Vietnam conflicts, the United States resorted to napalm, an incendiary device more effective and devastating than the Second World War's flamethrower. In an attempt to halt this practice, the General Assembly of the United Nations has passed a number of resolutions condemning the use of napalm and other incendiary weapons in armed conflicts in circumstances where they may affect human beings or may cause damage to the environment or natural resources.[10] Napalm bombing has also been attacked by the 1968 International Conference on Human Rights.[11]

Nuclear weapons present a complicated problem. It should be noted that the two major antagonists in the world have each, while avowing their own restraint, recognized the possibility of the use of these devices. Since both the Soviet Union and the United States perceive nuclear arms to be essential to their defensive power, it is likely that their use would be determined by the demands of military strategy rather than the prescriptions of international law. Arguments that employment of these weapons is contrary to international law usually cite the 1868 Declaration of St. Petersburg, the 1907 Hague Regulations, and the 1925 Geneva Protocol.[12] In 1961, the General Assembly passed a resolution declaring that the use of nuclear devices constitutes a violation of the United Nations Charter and of international law.[13] Difficulty in determining the precise requirements of international law has led to the proposal that a new convention be adopted to outlaw the use of nuclear arms.

New Initiatives

Protocol I Additional to the Geneva Conventions, adopted in 1977 and entered into force in 1978, states clearly that in any armed conflict, the right to choose methods or means of warfare is not unlimited. It is, for example, prohibited to employ weapons, projectiles, and material and methods of warfare that could cause superfluous injury or unnecessary suffering. In adopting a new weapon, means, or method of warfare, a party is also obligated to determine whether its employment would be prohibited by this protocol or by any other rule of international law applicable to the party to the conflict.[14]

The year 1981 marked the signing of a treaty to protect civilians from certain conventional weapons regarded as inhumane. The treaty, which entered into force in 1983,[15] along with its three attached protocols, was the product of two years of negotiations in Geneva. Although it offers soldiers only limited protection from cruel weapons, focusing rather on sparing civilians from the indiscriminate use of such devices, the convention remains a significant step forward by the international community. It stands as a positive example of the possibility of reaching agreements regarding weapons restriction despite a complex international situation.

Protocol I of the convention prohibits the use of plastic grenade bombs, whose fragments are difficult to detect with an X-ray, and establishes the principle that weapons that cause untreatable wounds should be banned. A major weakness of the protocol is that it does not outlaw the destructive cluster bombs that spew out thousands of steel pellets.

The most important provision of the second protocol, which governs mines and booby traps, prohibits the seeding of an area with mines, either fired by artillery or dropped from planes, unless the region contains a genuine military objective. Even then, the protocol requires that records be kept of landmine emplacements so that the devices may be rendered harmless when the fighting is over, unless they self-destruct after a certain time. It also forbids such ruses as the attaching of booby traps to children, the sick or wounded, toys, kitchen utensils, and food and drink, as well as the concealment of these devices at grave sites or medical facilities. If further seeks to prevent the mass production of booby traps by banning those that take the form of an "apparently harmless portable object."

Protocol III prohibits the use against civilians of weapons like napalm, flame throwers, and bombs dropped to start fire storms. More important, it bars the delivery of incendiary weapons from the air against any military target "within a concentration of civilians." This would appear to prohibit the starting of fire storms in cities or dropping napalm on villages or towns. However, the protocol does not limit the use of either flame throwers or napalm against soldiers, even in an open area.

The treaty and its protocols are applicable not only to wars between nations but also to conflicts in which "peoples are fighting against colonial domination and alien occupation and against racist regimes in the exercise of self-determination."

Assessment and Prospects

The fact that existing treaties regarding weapons use are replete with loopholes, that many arms remain excluded from international provisions, and that treaties currently in force do not guarantee their prohibition, suggests that international law does not yet effectively govern weapons control. One important obstacle to international regulation of cruel weapons derives from the fact that when a means of destruction is viewed as highly effective, states refrain from outlawing it.[16] Indeed, military effectiveness still overrides humanitarian concerns. Furthermore, industrially advanced states do not like to submit their technological prowess to regulation, nor do small countries favor restrictions on means of combat that may prove effective in fighting larger invading enemy forces.

Still, the restatement of general principles found in Protocol I reaffirms a commitment to developing humanitarian law. As evidenced by the 1981 treaty, there also appears to be a growing consensus recognizing the utility of limiting the use of unnecessarily cruel ''conventional weapons.'' What is needed is more effective enforcement machinery. Recent developments give reason for optimism about the evolution of humanitarian law, but there is a long way to go before cruel weapons disappear from the arsenals of the world's nations.

United States Rules of Engagement in Vietnam

The complexity that characterizes most legal documents makes them difficult for the military commander in the field to interpret and apply. The problem is to draw up rules regulating the use of weapons that are adequate to the task of protecting the civilian population, comprehensive enough to apply to all conceivable situations without providing loopholes that reduce their efficacy, yet specific enough to be applied by field commanders in a tactical situation.

While the United States Rules of Engagement in Vietnam do not go beyond the provisions of the armed conflict conventions accepted by the United States, they do represent an attempt to draw up more specific rules applicable in a field situation. The American attempt to apply the principles to tactical conditions is therefore worth a short commentary.[17]

On June 6, 1975, extracts of the Rules of Engagement applicable to United States forces in Vietnam appeared in the *Congressional Record*.[18] This was the first time these rules were published, and they are of considerable interest. However, since the published versions are incomplete and originate from various periods of the Vietnam War, they must be interpreted with care.

The directives state that indiscriminate effects of firepower on the civilian population are to be avoided. Certain weapons such as incendiary and chemical munitions and blast and fragmentation weapons are prohibited for use within stated ranges of inhabited places. Military commanders are explicitly instructed that military operations should be carried out as far as possible according to the general principle of avoiding indiscriminate effects.

Taken at face value, there is considerable evidence in the documents for an underlying norm intended to minimize suffering. But the actual instructions regarding the use of specific weapons contain several escape clauses. For example, one U.S. Military Assistance directive instructs that:

> The use of incendiary type munitions (napalm and phosphorus) in inhabited or urban areas will be avoided unless friendly survival is at stake or is necessary for the accomplishment of the commander's mission.[19]

In the case of herbicide use, the directive requires that ''the inhabitants must be warned by leaflets, loudspeakers, or other appropriate means prior to the attack and given sufficient time to evacuate the area.'' However, two important exceptions are cited:

> If the attack on an inhabited area from which enemy fire is being received is deemed necessary, and is executed in conjunction with a ground operation involving the movement of ground forces through the area, and if in the judgment of the battalion or higher commander his mission would be jeopardized by prior warning, the attack may be made without such warning or delay.

Further,

> An exception may be made for herbicide missions in cases where prior warning may jeopardize the safety of the spray aircraft.[20]

Use of Unnecessarily Cruel Weapons in Vietnam

All of the combatants used cruel weaponry during the Vietnam War. The United States' employment of the chemical agents DM, CN, and CS clearly amounted to gas warfare. All three agents have the potential to cause death and have also been linked to carcinogenic, mutagenic, and teratogenic reactions.[21] Despite advanced methods of delivery, these agents proved to be threatening to nonhostile forces.

In addition to chemical gas agents, the United States used napalm and white phosphorus in Vietnam. Napalm is a jellied gasoline that produces an incendiary effect and burns and kills. Morris Greenspan has attested to its cruelty:

> To burn a man to death or disable him by burning must in *all* circumstances cause the victim agonizing pain and suffering. Burning can never offer an instantaneous and comparatively painless death.[22]

Additionally, it has been reported that napalm burns can lead to the development of tumorous growths.

In the early part of 1967, phosphorus bombs came into use. Phosphorus, like napalm, is an incendiary weapon. Moreover, phosphorus remains inside the wound and continues to burn; this slow combustion may last up to fifteen days.

The United States Army does not categorize napalm or white phosphorus as violative of international law. Jurists have argued, however, that napalm and white phosphorus cause "unnecessary suffering" and thus are illegal.

The M-16 rifle used by the United States in Vietnam has also been considered a cruel weapon.[23] The high power of the rifle causes the bullet to tumble on contact. This tumbling causes horrible wounds. There appears to be a marked similarity between the M-16 projectile and the banned dum-dum bullet. The effects of the M-16 additionally include a partial metal "splatter."

The United States also tested and employed various forms of fragmentation devices in Vietnam. The "Lazy Dog," consisting of a drum that exploded above the enemy and scattered steel pellets in a buckshot effect, was one such weapon. A similar arm, the CBU (cluster bomb unit), was used during the war. The cluster bomb unit opened in mid-air and released various types of munitions over a wide area. Numerous variations on the Lazy Dog and cluster bomb unit were utilized as well.

Finally, the United States engaged in the deployment of herbicides to defoliate the forests of Vietnam. Defoliation was considered to be a strategic necessity since the Vietcong hid from their attackers beneath the heavy greenery. The three primary defoliants used were Agents Orange, White, and Blue. Between 1962 and 1970, a total of 5,065,600 acres were sprayed with millions of gallons of herbicides from planes at tree-top level to strip away the Vietnamese jungle cover. As noted in the previous chapter, herbicide use resulted in the destruction of land and in the deaths of many Vietnamese peasants as well as livestock.[24] There is also increasing evidence that the defoliants cause teratogenic and carcinogenic problems in humans.

The Vietcong and NVA, while lacking the technological capabilities of the United States, had their own forms of unnecessarily cruel weapons. For example, the Vietcong employed pungee sticks: bamboo stakes, tipped with poison, placed at the bottom of pits covered with grass. They also hid steel spikes, driven through wood, in rice paddies. Harrison Salisbury describes another horribly cruel weapon:

> . . . a ghastly device—a kind of bird cage with movable crosswires to which were fitted a set of jagged fishhooks. The bird cage was buried on a trail and covered with a light scattering of leaves. When a man came down the trail his leg would thrust down into the cage and the fishhooks would dig in. If he tried to lift this limb or struggle out, each pull would drive them deeper, more cruelly into the flesh. The barbs could not be removed except by a surgeon's knife. . . . This was not a weapon of the past. This was a deadly device being set out . . . every day in the jungle trails of the South where the Americans were seeking to flush out the Viet Cong strongholds.[25]

It seems apparent that the use of cruel and unusual weapons in Vietnam was rampant. Each side clearly violated the rules of war set down in all of the treaties directed at bringing to a halt the use of unnecessarily cruel weapons.

Views of the Vietnam Generation

The Vietnam War intensified the concern about unnecessarily cruel weapons and accelerated the work being done in this area, not only at the United Nations, but also in specialized conferences. While historians, philosophers, and other concerned observers once again raised the fundamental question of unnecessary brutality in war, the generation most directly involved in the Vietnam War was developing and expressing its own perspectives on this issue. As Richard Baxter has noted:

> If the law of war is to be applied, it must speak with certainty and authority and directness to the great diversity of persons who will be called upon to give effect to it. . . . The course is set for more law, and one can only hope that it may serve the cause of humanity.[26]

In this regard, the views of those who came of age during the Vietnam War, especially Vietnam veterans, on the issue of unnecessarily cruel weapons are crucial for the future.

The issue of firepower was central to the Vietnam War controversy. American strategic thinking assumed that guerrilla forces, supplemented or even supplanted by main force North Vietnamese regulars, could not endure the punishment the array of sophisticated weaponry contained in the United States arsenal could bring to bear on the conflict. The reliance on firepower against the enemy forces led necessarily to the development and use of ever more destructive weaponry as the war continued.

The wisdom of relying on firepower and technological warfare was challenged on both military and moral-ethical grounds. As the war accelerated, the weaponry deployed in Vietnam became a key issue in the debate over the legitimacy of the American involvement in the conflict.

The limited access of the guerrillas to sophisticated technological weaponry led to the use of primitive weapons like those noted above whose consequences were gruesome indeed. As did some of the sophisticated weapons in the United State arsenal, these devices left their victims permanently disabled and disfigured.

In questioning the Vietnam Generation about their reactions toward a range of weapons employed in the war, our objective was to clarify their feelings about the use of cruel devices and to examine the conditions under which certain types of weapons, in the opinion of the generation, could be used. These two issues were central elements in the debate that developed over the United States' role in the Vietnam War.

In an attempt to analyze the issue of weapons use, we asked our respondents to tell us whether seven types of weapons were or were not unnecessarily cruel, and under which of the four categories of use each weapon belonged.[27] Although our weapons list does not exhaust the very broad range of weapons used by either side in Vietnam, we took care to include devices that reflect the unique dimensions of the war, as well as one weapon category—germ warfare—that to the best of our knowledge was never employed in Vietnam. The range of weaponry cited runs the gamut from high-technology warfare to the most primitive weaponry used over the centuries. Some of these weapons such as plastic bombs and "simple weapons," share a common ground, for example, that treatment of the wounded is often impossible or extremely difficult.

Generational Perspectives

Table 7.1 summarizes our respondents' attitudes toward the seven weapons we asked them to evaluate, ranked in descending order of cruelty. About 80% or more of the nonveterans and Vietnam era veterans agree that germ warfare, chemical warfare, mines and booby traps, and primitive weapons are unnecessarily cruel. Napalm and plastic bombs are considered unnecessarily cruel by somewhat fewer Vietnam era veterans (64%) and nonveterans (76% and 74%). Vietnam era veterans (57%) and nonveterans (64%) are more likely than Vietnam veterans (46%) to consider dum-dum bullets as unnecessarily cruel. Overall, nonveterans' threshold of acceptance of the weapons in consistently lower than that of Vietnam era veterans.

Vietnam veterans, generally, share their peers' view of the cruelty of germ warfare (87%), mines and booby traps (81%), primitive weapons (73%), and chemical warfare (70%). However, the proportion of Vietnam veterans who consider chemical warfare and primitive weapons unnecessarily cruel is substantially less than found among the other groups in the study.

Larger differences, which reflect qualitatively different judgments, are to be found between Vietnam veterans' and era and nonveterans' views of napalm, plastic bombs, and dum-dum bullets. U.S. soldiers in Vietnam frequently used both napalm and dum-dum bullets. Napalm, epitomized in the movie "Winning Hearts and Minds" by a young girl running down a road ablaze, was a weapon whose use stirred outrage in the United States. Only a minority of Vietnam veterans considered the above three weapons to be unnecessarily cruel. As table 7.1 shows, 48% put napalm, 49% plastic bombs, and 46% dum-dum bullets into that category. Comparing Vietnam veterans' perceptions of those weapons they considered most and least unnecessarily cruel, we find a strong tendency to view those weapons most easily available to the enemy—mines and booby traps and primitive weapons—adversely. Contrarily, the weapons used by the U.S. soldier—napalm and dum-dum bullets—are least likely to be judged as unnecessarily cruel. Not suprisingly, the weapons our respondents were most likely to legitimate were those that they feel helped ensure their own safety. Other weapons in the United States arsenal, such as chemical warfare (Agent Orange), used extensively in Vietnam but whose advantages were not as immediately evident, did not receive the same level of acceptance.

Table 7.2 shows that not only are there important differences between the perceptions of Vietnam veterans and their peers regarding the cruelty of particular weapons, but both era and nonveterans are much more likely than Vietnam veterans to categorize *all* the weapons as unnecessarily cruel. Only 24% of the

Vietnam veterans compared to 43% of the era veterans and 49% of the nonveterans considered all seven weapons as unnecessarily cruel. Thus the range of weaponry Vietnam veterans find acceptable is broader than that accepted by their peers.

Among Vietnam veterans we find that four weapons, napalm, dum-dum bullets, mines and booby traps, and primitive weapons, generate the most disagreement regarding their cruelty. Three dimensions of the war experience account for these differences: branch of service, combat, and exposure to abusive violence. As table 7.3 indicates, marines are significantly less prone to consider three of these weapons—dum-dum bullets, napalm, and primitive weapons—unnecessarily cruel than either the army or air force/navy veterans. The smallest difference between the marines and the other branches of the military is over the cruelty of napalm; the largest difference is over the cruelty of primitive weapons. Marines (57%) are less likely to consider primitive weapons cruel than other veterans (75%); and they are also substantially less likely (32%) to consider dum-dum bullets unnecessarily cruel than their army (54%) or navy/air force (52%) counterparts.

Combat also affects attitudes toward napalm and mines and booby traps. As table 7.4 shows, while some slight differences exist between heavy- and low-combat veterans in this regard, there is a significant attitudinal difference toward weapons' cruelty between the moderate-combat veterans and those with little combat experience. Men in the former category are much more prone to view both napalm and mines and booby traps as unnecessarily cruel than either of the other combat categories.

A majority of the veterans who saw moderate combat (57%) describe napalm as unnecessarily cruel, while only 45% of the low combat and 42% of the high combat groups share this attitude. Similarly, 92% of the moderate-combat groups compared to 74% of the low-combat and 80% of the high-combat group see mines and booby traps as unnecessarily cruel.

Finally, we find substantial disagreement regarding the cruelty of napalm, dum-dum bullets, and mines and booby traps between veterans who were and were not involved with abusive violence. Table 7.5 shows that those respondents who witnessed abusive violence are most likely to judge napalm, dum-dum bullets, and mines and booby traps as unnecessarily cruel. There is a systematic pattern to the findings worth noting. We see that participants in abusive violence least often perceive the weapons cited as unnecessarily cruel; the not-exposed group considers the weapons substantially more cruel than the participant group; and the veterans who witnessed abusive violence most often judge the weapons unnecessarily cruel.

In table 7.5 the most important differences are found between the veterans who witnessed and participated in abusive violence. About 55% of the veterans who witnessed abusive violence considered napalm and dum-dum bullets unnecessarily cruel. Among the participants, however, only 40% placed napalm and

32% dum-dum bullets in that category. Furthermore, only 63% of the participants, compared to 89% of veterans who witnessed abusive violence, viewed mines and booby traps as cruel weaponry. This is a clear indication that participants in abusive violence most often saw the war in terms of unrestricted violence. Indeed, their orientation toward "cruel" weapons is consistent with and reflects a justification for their conduct.

Perceptions of weaponry among nonveterans, as seen in tables 7.6 through 7.9, also show variations. Generally, as table 7.6 makes clear, high and moderate antiwar activists are more likely to define individual weapons as unnecessarily cruel than are the low activists. We find that napalm (30%), plastic bombs (29%), and dum-dum bullets (42%) are the weapons most acceptable to the low activists. The high activists reject napalm (87%), plastic bombs (86%), and dum-dum bullets (82%) as unnecessarily cruel. There is also a substantial difference between perceptions of chemical weapons between these two groups: 96% of the high activists compared to 82% of the low activists considered such devices unnecessarily cruel. Overall, as table 7.7 shows, there is a step-wise progression from low to high activists in the proportion who consider *all* weapons unnecessarily cruel. Almost two-thirds of the high activists compared to 56% of the moderate and 45% of the low activists place all the weapons in this category.

Those who supported the war, as seen in tables 7.8 and 7.9, are substantially less likely to view these weapons as unnecessarily cruel. Table 7.8 shows that except for germ warfare, mines and booby traps, and primitive weapons, there is a consistent tendency for supporters of the war to consider all weapons less cruel than those who opposed the war; and if we compare their responses with the antiwar activists we see significant differences between the two groups. In regard to three weapons, however—napalm, plastic bombs, and dum-dum bullets—we find the attitudes of supporters of the war distinctly and significantly different from those of their nonveteran peers and very much like the Vietnam veterans. Only 43% of the prowar group felt that dum-dum bullets, 54% that napalm, and 58% that plastic bombs were unnecessarily cruel. Contrarily, supporters of the war are as likely as their peers to consider weapons such as mines and booby traps (84%) and primitive weapons (80%) unnecessarily cruel. Thus, again, we find those weapons available to the enemy to be most often perceived as unnecessarily cruel. Indeed, we need to emphasize that in response to items 5 and 7 (plastic bombs and primitive weapons) dealing with treatment complications, supporters of the war apparently are substantially more concerned with this problem if the victims are Americans. Finally, as table 7.9 demonstrates, there is a very substantial difference between nonveteran prowar supporters (41%) on the one side and their peers who were opposed to the war (69%) on the other in terms of judging all the weapons listed as unnecessariy cruel.

The use of unnecessarily cruel weapons is an important issue in the narrative material. The transcripts also illustrate the substantial differences of opinion that existed among respondents.

Vietnam Veterans and Unnecessarily Cruel Weapons

Many Vietnam veterans were exposed to the use of unnecessarily cruel weapons; the narrative material is rich with descriptions of these exposures and of the effects the experiences had on respondents.

Use of cruel weapons by enemy forces

Weapons that make treatment of victims nearly impossible and cause death or mutilation are most commonly cited by veterans. A captain in the marines noted:

> Pungee sticks, glass bombs, boot busters . . . the steel plates on the ground with the spikes in them that they'd bury under the leaves that would penetrate your boots. . . . They had some phenomenal neat little land mines they used to plant. . . . Garbage mines—they used to make them out of tin cans and pipe bombs, some of that was pretty nasty.

Cruel weapons were also used by Vietcong sympathizers. A veteran who served in the navy noted:

> We were told not to drink water with ice in it in Vietnam unless it was prepared in our base because the VC sympathizers would put ground glass in the ice. They were also selling Zippo lighters that said "made in USA" on it and the second time you would strike it, it would blow up in your hand, right in front of your face.

Veterans also pointed out that while these "primitive" weapons were intended for American forces, the civilians often became their victims. A veteran who served in the army airborne remembered:

> I saw some kids get fucked up on pungee sticks at a dump. . . . The Vietcong had put them there because the dump was outside of our base camp. The kids would go there to eat up our leftovers, and somebody put pungee sticks in a pit and covered it up and the kid fell on it and they brought him into the medevac. And I thought that was bad—that they would do that. But it was meant for us, it wasn't meant for the kid. The kids just stumbled on it. . . . That poison goes all the way up in you, he's probably crippled.

Another veteran reported the casualties caused by booby traps set by the Vietcong in areas travelled by both the military and civilians:

> We went to pick up some infantry soldiers up north. They had stepped on booby

traps and got their feet blown off. . . . I have seen the booby traps that the Vietcong had set up after they had been used. It really made you mad especially to see a four- or five-year-old kid with an arm blown off or missing a leg or something like that . . . especially when it was from a booby trap.

While many of those exposed to primitive weapons strongly condemned their use, others were less critical. While not denying that such weapons were cruel, they argued that they were all the Vietcong had to use. An army infantry-man who was in heavy combat presented the following view:

I guess the VC had to use these primitive weapons because they were not as advanced as we were in terms of weapons. They had to use different things. Nobody likes the dirty side of war but, I guess, you have got to put up with whatever they throw at you.

American forces and cruel weapons

The American weapons most often mentioned by veteran respondents are na-palm, white phosphorus, gas, flame throwers, beehives and other fragmentation weapons, and mines and booby traps. Almost half of all Vietnam veterans consid-ered the use of napalm by American forces as unnecessarily cruel. It was noted that civilians often became the victims of napalm attacks. A sergeant in the marines reported:

Worst incident I saw was when they called in an air strike on a village . . . and when they first dropped . . . bombs at the far end of the village . . . everybody started running across a bridge that spanned the river and the bridge was just packed with civilians and maybe a few Vietcong—it would be hard to tell in all the confusion, and then they come in with the next strike and it was napalm and one of the bombs hit the bridge and it just incinerated everything on it.

There were frequent reports on napalm being dropped by mistake on American forces. An infantryman who was in heavy combat remembered:

I had napalm dropped on my entire squad. . . . The scout dog that was next to me was on fire. I had four people in my squad that were next to me . . . they got third degree burns and were medevaced to Japan. So I would say I was just lucky. . . . I have seen most of my own people destroyed by their own medi-cine. Ninety percent of the people that got wounded, got wounded by ourselves.

The use of white phosphorus was also often mentioned. A veteran who was in the navy recalled:

During a naval bombardment, we used what they called white phosphorus to burn the houses. But in those houses were people. I was the one doing it . . . the shooting. We would fire a high explosive to splatter the house and we would shoot the white phosphorus to make it burn. At the time I did not think about it at all. It was part of the job that I had to do. I have changed in knowing that people over there were being subjected to things that they did not want to be subjected to. I would probably call it cruelty now.

Other veterans talked about their exposure to the use of flame throwers. An army sergeant reported his reactions as follows:

Charlie started firing on us through the bush and no one could spot them. We threw in grenades and they still kept firing on us. We had flame throwers on our tanks, and they shot in flames and burned them alive. At the time I was glad they were doing it, but I just thought it was a terrible way to burn. . . . I never went to look at anybody. I didn't want to. Some guys would go and examine them and see what they could get off somebody. I never went to look.

A heavy-combat army infantryman who was involved in throwing gas into enemy bunkers added:

We had gas and we would throw it in the bunkers. I thought that was unnecessarily cruel because we could throw a smoke bomb in there and they would come out. But a lot of times the guys would throw gas in there to kill or burn them.

Many veterans also considered fragmentation weapons unnecessarily cruel. An army man described the use of beehives this way:

It was fired from a tank and you could set the explosion of the projectile to go off at a certain distance and when it exploded it would burn an area of foliage. It would spray an area with little hard plastic arrows. If you have ever seen anybody pinned by about five hundred needles . . . that was something a little unnecessary.

And an air force lieutenant observed:

The stuff I used to drop? It was called bluies. They were bombs in cannisters that broke open when they hit a certain target above the ground and they would spin and you would have a bunch of these little sharp fragmentation pellets in them . . . antipersonnel, for . . . troop concentrations. Now that was one cruel weapon I thought then.

An army man who was in heavy combat talked about his exposure to flechettes:

> It is like a nail and instead of a head on it, it has little wings. . . . When fired properly, you get a coverage of at least one per square foot in the area the size of a football field per rocket. They penetrate your body and hurt badly.

A captain in the marines presented an officer's view of the cruelty of certain weapons used by American forces:

> One of the very nasty things were the small pea bombs, I think they used to call them. Little metal inch-and-a-half long, 3-ounce metal bombs. They'd drop a million out of a plane because those things would hit you in the arm and take your arm off—hit you in the head—they'd kill you. You'd end up getting mutilated by the damn things. The M-16 was a garbage gun. We'd been better off with a 30–06 that killed instantly. I almost think we were cruel in the weaponry we were using on the ground. . . . It doesn't do you any good to have some little slug go ripping into your heart and take a chunk of it out and you sit there and think about dying for a half hour and then drop dead. That type of stuff. In our fire power—the actual weapons that were issued to American troops were too low a caliber. The Vietcong were better set up, as far as that. They were using a more humane weapon than we were, literally.

Veterans were also exposed to the use of cruel weapons by allied forces, especially the Koreans and South Vietnamese. A corporal in the marines who was in heavy combat and served four months with a Korean unit reported:

> The Koreans were the hardest and dirtiest fighting guys I ever saw in my life. They would take a 106 and fire it into a friendly village. They did not care about the people at all. They were not following any special set of rules. A 106 is an antitank weapon and we used them a lot against foot troops. We weren't supposed to, it was against the Geneva Conventions.

U.S. versus enemy cruelty

Some veterans felt that the enemy was using unnecessarily cruel weapons against the American forces, while the United States was respecting the laws of warfare. One Vietnam veteran, who served as a sergeant in the infantry and was in heavy combat, reflected:

> I think the United States went about the war wrong. The Vietcong foot soldiers could use all of their cruel weapons against us, they obeyed no rules. But the

Geneva Conventions and other treaties prohibited us from using certain types of weapons. At that time I was ready to break all rules. We needed all the weapons we could get to fight the Communists off. The United States was too soft on them: if they had wiped the place out and killed the enemy, it would have saved a lot of our guys' lives, you know.

But most veterans pointed out that *all* parties to the conflict used unnecessarily cruel weapons and the civilians suffered most from both sides. An army man who was wounded by a pungee stick provides this account of the effects of that primitive weapon:

I got a pungee stick in my leg and I pulled it out myself and I did not think much of it. A week later I brushed my leg against a bush and the pain was awful. I had a major infection. They had to lance it in the hospital and drain it. I almost lost my leg. But then, we napalmed a village that did not need to be napalmed. We threw grenades in caves, instead of taking the Vietcong alive.

And a navy man who was involved in the use of unnecessarily cruel weapons against civilians described his feelings this way:

We used to do things that were against the Geneva Conventions. Like . . . plant booby traps in civilian areas. The Vietcong used some doozies too, like a Malasian whip—the bamboo thing that whips across and catches you in the chest with the spikes. But a war is a war. How can you make rules on a war?

Nonveterans and Unnecessarily Cruel Weapons

Prowar nonveterans

In the narrative material, a minority of respondents in this group expressed concern about the use of cruel weapons by *all parties* to the conflict, including American forces. One nonveteran had the following to say:

In Vietnam everybody used cruel weapons. I realize that it's a little tough to fight a war under the rules. You're not always going to be able to follow the rules. But treating a person humanely, God, that's the least you can do. And as far as the weapons are concerned, using weapons that are really not necessary or do harm or create injuries that put people to a lot of suffering, I can't see it. You know if it's going to kill them, kill them. OK. But you're not going to make the guy suffer for the rest of his life because of it.

The majority of these respondents expressed a low level of interest in cruel weaponry and only condemned the use of these weapons by enemy forces. Some argued that guerrilla warfare is always based on unethical terrorist tactics.

Antiwar activists

In the narrative material, the antiwar activists were generally extremely critical of the use of cruel weaponry. While pointing out that the North Vietnamese and the Vietcong used a wide range of such weapons, their greatest concern was focused on the American use of these devices. They observed that in 1961, the United States military expected that a limited number of men could fight the jungle war with conventional weapons. By 1964, the military knew they could not win with these tactics and they developed a new weapons program intended to overcome the Vietcong's guerrilla strategies. In addition, they used existing weapons, such as the B-52, by adjusting them to the "realities" in Vietnam.

Many of the weapons and strategies used were, as far as antiwar activists were concerned, unnecessarily cruel and in violation of humanitarian law. It was because of this type of warfare that a substantial number of nonveterans joined the antiwar movement.

Many activists were upset by the saturation bombing of regions containing numerous villages but few permanent military installations. Others cited the "highly technologized barbarianism" of the new weapons that were developed for Vietnam. As one antiwar activist put it:

> It was insane—napalm, cluster bombs, plastic bombs that you can't find by X-ray. It's just impossible for me to comprehend why anybody would want to invent so many different ways to kill somebody so brutally.

Conditions under Which Unnecessarily Cruel Weapons Can Be Used

In response to our question, asking under what conditions cruel weapons can be used, our respondents indicate that such devices may only be employed outside the battle zone infrequently or should never be utilized (table 7.10).

The findings indicate that if we state the issue in terms of three categories of use for these weapons—use in urban areas, the battle zone, and never—we can more intelligently interpret the response to this question in the general population. Thus, for purposes of the discussion we will combine the responses of those who accept the use of these weapons anytime and those who accept their use in urban areas, i.e., we assume that "anytime" also includes urban areas. This approach to the data shows more clearly the profound differences between Vietnam veterans and their peers on the appropriate use of cruel weapons.

Among Vietnam veterans, three weapons—napalm (18%), plastic bombs (25%), and dum-dum bullets (30%)—are considered usable in urban areas. Only dum-dum bullets are considered comparably by the era veterans (16%) and the nonveterans (26%). Clearly, the bombing of urban areas, whether the weapon is napalm or plastic bombs, is more acceptable to Vietnam veterans than to their peers.

Attitudes toward the use of all the cited weapons in the battle zone are roughly the same among era and Vietnam veterans, while nonveterans are generally less likely to accept the use of cruel devices on the battlefield. This is especially true of the use of napalm. Only 35% of the nonveterans compared to 51% of the era veterans and 58% of the Vietnam veterans are prepared to accept the use of napalm even in the fighting zone.

Finally, when we turn to the proportion of our respondents who say these weapons can never be used, we see that Vietnam veterans would resist eliminating napalm (24%), plastic bombs (34%), and dum-dum bullets (38%) from their arsenal. Vietnam era veterans too are quite reluctant to abolish the use of napalm: only 38% agree to never using it. However, nearly 50% would ban dum-dum bullets and plastic bombs. More than 50% of the nonveterans would ban all the weapons cited, and 54% would eliminate napalm.

Combat, as table 7.11 demonstrates, leads to a greater tolerance for the use of four weapons: napalm, plastic bombs, mines and booby traps, and primitive weapons. Heavy-combat veterans are consistently less likely to reject totally the use of these weapons than are veterans who saw moderate or little combat. For example, heavy-combat veterans (24%) accept the use of napalm in urban areas or anytime more often than their counterparts who saw moderate (17%) or little combat (14%).

The conditions of use that differentiate heavy- and moderate-combat veterans from Vietnam veterans who saw little combat are most evident regarding napalm, dum-dum bullets, and plastic bombs. Vietnam veterans who saw heavy and moderate combat are substantially more likely than veterans who saw little combat to accept broad employment of these weapons, i.e., in urban areas or anytime. Acceptance of the relatively unrestricted use of these weapons among heavy-combat veterans is substantial, napalm 24%, plastic bombs 32%, and dum-dum bullets 27%; comparable figures for moderate-combat veterans are napalm 17%, plastic bombs 24%, and dum-dum bullets 37%. Veterans who saw little combat are in each instance somewhat less willing to accept broad use of these weapons (napalm 14%, plastic bombs 20%, and dum-dum bullets 23%). The differences between heavy and low groups in combat veterans are greatest on the use of napalm and plastic bombs, while low- and moderate-combat veterans differ most regarding dum-dum bullets.

Finally, among all three categories of combat veterans, as with Vietnam veterans generally, we find that there is markedly stronger opposition to the use of mines and booby traps and primitive weaponry than to napalm, dum-dum bullets, or plastic bombs. Again, the level of opposition to what we refer to as weapons in the enemy arsenal (mines and booby traps and primitive weapons) is weakest too among heavy-combat veterans. For each of the above devices, about 8% fewer heavy-combat veterans also reject the idea that the weapons should never be used. Among the heavy-combat veterans, we find a 14% disparity in the "never use" category of attitudes toward plastic bombs and primitive weapons, which emphasizes the difficulty of treatment subsequent to the weapon's entry into the human body. Weapons that make tending of wounds more arduous for the enemy (plastic bombs) are less objectionable than those that hinder the treatment of Americans (primitive weapons). Finally, the acceptance of American weapons versus enemy weapons is highlighted by the fact that the moderate- and low-combat veterans reject the use of mines and booby traps more than 60% of the time, and 55% reject ever using primitive weapons.

Exposure to abusive violence also has an impact on attitudes about the conditions under which cruel weapons can be used. There is a statistically significant difference between witnesses and the not exposed group on all five weapons in table 7.12, but with the exception of mines and booby traps, which participants are more likely to accept, there are no significant differences between the participants and the not exposed groups in the study. Table 7.12 shows perceptibly different patterns of acceptance of the use of all weapons between the witnessed and the not exposed groups except for the conditions under which napalm can be used. In more powerful statistical models that adjust for background characteristics, the differences between the witnessed and not exposed veterans becomes even greater. This is one of the few instances in the study where the weighted percentages understate the differences between groups. As noted in the methodological appendix, all our findings are based on the results of statistical models that adjust for background characteristics. Usually, we find the tables clearly reflect the findings of these models. Occasionally, as in this case, we find some variation between the descriptive statistics and the more sophisticated analyses. Table 7.12 shows the general pattern. The important finding is that witnesses of abusive violence are more restrictive of the use of the weapons cited than are their peers. It should also be emphasized that this pattern cuts across weaponry available to enemy and U.S. forces. Thus, witnesses to abusive violence are more strongly opposed to the use of weapons in the armories of all the combatants than their peers.

The conditions under which any of these weapons can acceptably be used differ systematically among nonveterans based on the degree of participation in the antiwar movement. As table 7.13 indicates, the key difference lies in the proportion of high and moderate activists who feel these weapons should never be used as compared to the low activists who more often accept the use of such devices in the battle zone. In addition, a small proportion of low activists is more likely than either the moderate or very active group to accept the use of some of these weapons anytime or in urban areas.

There is unanimous agreement among the hard-core antiwar activists that germ warfare, chemical warfare, mines and booby traps, and napalm may not be used freely or in urban areas. These respondents are almost equally opposed to the use of plastic bombs (4%), dum-dum bullets (3%), and primitive weapons (6%) in urban areas. The moderate activists' views on the use of these weapons are relatively similar to those of high activists on all the weapons described above except mines and booby traps, whose use in urban areas 10% could accept; only from 4% to 7% of the moderate activists would accept the use of the other weapons in urban areas. Among low activists, the broad use of these weapons is somewhat more acceptable. Napalm (14%), plastic bombs (15%), dum-dum bullets (21%), and primitive weapons (6%) are considered acceptable for use in urban areas, while chemical warfare and mines and booby traps are considered usable in urban areas about 10% of the time. The low activists hold similar views to those of the moderate activists on the use of germ warfare, and 6% of both groups consider primitive weapons usable at least in urban areas.

As seen in table 7.13, each group has a relatively similar hierarchy of which weapons may be used in the battle zone or never. The response to when these weapons can and cannot be used, however, shows that the more actively involved in the antiwar movement a group of respondents is, the higher the proportion who consider these weapons unusable under any circumstances. Thus, for each weapon, except primitive devices, there is a higher proportion of high activists who consider these arms unusable than there are moderate activists, who in turn reject the weapon's use more often than do low activists. The sharpest disagreements over the conditions of use involve napalm, plastic bombs, and dum-dum bullets. The low activists totally reject the use of these weapons only about half of the time (50%) while two-thirds (67%) of the moderate activists and three-quarters (75%) of the high activists are against ever using these devices.

The low activists' attitudes toward the use of the weapons cited are closer to the attitudes found among Vietnam era veterans, except for the use of primitive weapons. Thus, Vietnam veterans and antiwar activists occupy the two poles of opinion regarding the conditions under which the weapons could be used. The most extreme differences are found on their competing views of the conditions under which napalm, plastic bombs, and dum-dum bullets can and cannot be used. Nonveteran activists totally reject the use of napalm three times as often as Vietnam veterans (75% vs. 24%), plastic bombs by more than a two-to-one margin (79% vs. 34%), and dum-dum bullets twice as often as Vietnam veterans (77% vs. 38%).

Table 7.14 demonstrates how fundamentally at odds the nonveteran supporters of the war are with their antiwar peers and illustrates their general concurrence with Vietnam veterans. Prowar nonveterans are generally more willing to use all weapons in the arsenal of any of the armies. Four weapons— chemical warfare, napalm, plastic bombs, and dum-dum bullets—are considered particularly usable. Absolute restriction of these weapons in the prowar group is much lower for each of these weapons than is characteristic of the nonveterans. Only 34% would never use napalm or dum-dum bullets, and only 38% would prohibit the use of plastic bombs, while a bare majority, 52%, would unequivocally resist the use of chemical weapons. If we compare the findings in table 7.13 and 7.14, we see that there is a 15% to 30% difference between the prowar nonveterans and antiwar activists on the prohibition of all these weapons in

Vietnam. The striking differences between these groups suggest that fundamental divisions over the conduct of war persist today.

As we have noted, exposure to the weapons of war has a significant effect on respondents' perceptions of their cruelty. We find that proximity to the war also influences views of the conditions under which these weapons can be employed. Combat and witnessing of and participation in abusive violence exhibit patterned relationships to feelings about weapons use. Regardless of war experience, however, only a relatively small minority of Vietnam veterans accept the use of any of these weapons outside the battle zone.

Vietnam Veterans

The narrative material reaffirms that veterans responded in different ways to the use of the weapons cited. A short analysis of the three main responses follows.

Use of unnecessarily cruel weapons was permissible or unavoidable

Some Vietnam veterans justified the use of these weapons and argued in support of minimal or no restrictions on their use. Many of these respondents, especially heavy-combat veterans, argued that while some of the American weapons were extremely cruel, their use against enemy forces was permissible since they worked efficiently and no more humane, alternative devices were available. A veteran who served in the army described the type of weapon he saw used:

> Napalm. It was used by the United States Air Force jets. They would drop them down on the enemy bunkers. I feel it was an unnecessarily cruel weapon but I couldn't come up with a better weapon to do the same job. I think it made me have a little bit more respect for people, a little bit more feeling towards other humans. I wouldn't want anyone to drop napalm on me, or my friends.

Veterans in this group often stressed the fact that a guerrilla war creates a very difficult situation where rules regulating weaponry are unavoidably violated. The following statement by one Vietnam veteran, who was a 1st lieutenant in the infantry and saw combat, illustrates this view:

> The North Vietnamese and the Vietcong taught us a whole new type of warfare. Guerrilla warfare does not entail massive battles between two well-organized forces. Pungee sticks and some of the more deceptive types of weapons and some more lethal type situations they were experts in—and we learned from them. We developed and used a range of weapons that were extremely cruel.

Substantial limitations on the use of unnecessarily cruel weapons are necessary

Vietnam veterans who supported substantial restrictions on the use of the weapons cited argued that a war should be fought against military objects and military personnel but not against the civilian population. One army man who served in a helicopter medical outfit felt that napalm should never be used in a civilian area. He explained why:

> I told you about the young kid earlier. He was a victim of napalm. I think the civilian population suffers just as much as the military because you are dumping napalm and civilians have no way out. They are just victims of it—We go in and wipe out an area, we are talking about the military strength of this area, but what about the civilians, they are the ones to suffer. They're the ones that are maimed.

An army infantryman echoed this view, stating:

> I saw civilians get hit with napalm. Can you imagine liquid fire hitting you? It should never be used against civilians.

It was also considered unneccessarily cruel to place mines and booby traps in civilian areas. As one marine put it, "We should not have used them in there."

Full restrictions should be made on the use of unnecessarily cruel weapons

Some Vietnam veterans who supported total bans on the use of unnecessarily cruel weapons argued that only a total prohibition of these weapons would provide the civilian population with the protection they deserved. In this regard, a sergeant in the marines made the following remarks about napalm:

> I think it is one of the worst things we could ever use. Very indiscriminant. There's no way they can use it without endangering civilians, anybody else in the general area, it destroys everything. I have seen napalm dropped in many villages where the Vietcong were. It would be only a handful and they'd come in and drop napalm and just burn everything to the ground—that sounds cruel to me. It seems to me there could be another way. It should not be permitted.

Others stressed that combatants in the battle zone should not be exposed to unnecessarily cruel weapons. An army man commented:

> You see so many people suffer unnecessarily. After all you would not want them to do the same thing to you, when you dropped in chemicals or napalm especially. You figure you give the guy the same chance you got with conventional weapons if they are going to fight. They should outlaw all this chemical warfare.

Another army man stressed the mutilation of victims resulting from the use of ''cruel'' weapons:

> As far as napalm goes, the disfigurement, the body being burned, . . . even plastic surgery could not probably make them look human again. As far as some of the others go, chemical warfare and dum-dum bullets, booby traps . . . it is just more ways of mutilating a person. I mean, you can kill him, but this is like overkilling.

Vietnam veterans who were not in heavy combat often had no exposure to unnecessarily cruel weapons but heard reports about their use. While many had no strong feelings on the matter, a substantial number became highly critical of the types of weapons used in Vietnam and supported full restriction of their use. The following remarks by a navy veteran are typical of the latter response pattern:

> You heard the reports since television cameras were right there. We actually say napalming of dense civilian populations. . . . They talked about the defoliating agents, Agent Orange. I do not think those things are necessary. You do not know the effects of chemical warfare and five years later somebody has children that are horribly deformed. . . . I just do not believe the kind of warfare that mutilates bodies is necessary. If you have to kill the enemy, fine, but you do not have to mutilate them. I have seen, from working in the mortuaries, our boys sent home dead. It is probably a little bit easier if your son comes home dead rather than shredded or poisoned.

Nonveterans

As noted earlier, the major concern of most of the prowar nonveterans was to stop the Communist movement. In the narrative material they often argued that the American forces were doing their duty and that to win a war you have to use every weapon you have without restrictions.. The following response typifies this attitude:

> It was primarily their [NVA and Vietcong] tactics of fighting . . . their booby-trapping and how they bring little kids with bombs up to a bunch of GIs and blow them up or some of the other things that you heard about, that seemed almost inhuman, it was just like they had no soul or no conscience. . . . I felt that we were pussy-footing around and that we should take a stand and do whatever we had to do to win the war. That was probably the most frustrating thing about the whole war.

Many prowar nonveterans therefore either ignored or defended as a necessary part of combat the American use of unnecessarily cruel weapons. One
respondent summarized the latter attitude as follows: "In combat . . . the only
way you make headway is by getting rid of the opposing team."

There is almost unanimous agreement among antiwar activists that unnecessarily cruel weapons should never be used against civilian populations and in
urban areas. A minority argued that while the weapons listed in our interview
were unnecessarily cruel, they might have to be used against enemy forces if
survival was at stake.

A substantial majority of activists felt that neither military forces nor the
civilian population should be exposed to the brutality of these weapons. As a
moderate activist put it:

> I was against the type of warfare that was being employed in Vietnam, the use
> of defoliants and other unnecessarily cruel weapons. During the war, I became
> more interested in historical abuses of warfare in general, from spears to
> defoliants. I did become more aware of how people fought. . . . You are in
> there to win, whether for right or wrong and so sometimes you might have to do
> a certain thing to get what you want. But if you're going to shoot a guy, you
> don't have to tear his stomach out with a dum-dum bullet, you don't have to
> make the dying even more painful.

A majority of the antiwar activists took some form of action to reenforce
their beliefs. Some wrote letters to Congress and to the manufacturers of certain
weapons. Others boycotted products or picketed the principal manufacturers of
contested weapons. Ther prevailing sentiment among many antiwar respondents
is expressed by the following two statements. One activist recalled:

> I was already against the war, because I thought it was against the principles of
> America and it was immoral, and just how immoral it was became more and
> more apparent to me by the obscene weapons being used . . . I boycotted
> several products being made by manufacturers who made the napalm chemicals
> that were used.

And a moderate activist commented:

> These cruel weapons influenced my opposition to the war. If it was a clean war,
> as opposed to a dirty war, I'd probably still be opposed but not as strongly. . . .
> Dow Chemical was a real top concern at the time, because they were the
> principal manufacturer of napalm and when they came to recruit on campus for
> prospective employees there was a lot of picketing going on and I participated
> in that.

Conclusion

The findings in this chapter indicate that our respondents' views of the weapons cited and their conditions of use are based on a variety of considerations, including the implications of the weapons for civilians and the suffering they cause combatants, the availability of equally effective alternative weapon systems, successful prosecution of military objectives, personal safety, and retaliation. In reviewing the findings, what stands out is that the definition of weapons as unnecessarily cruel and their conditions of use in the generation is divided along two fundamental lines: military experience and attitude toward the war. The latter is largely a question of ideology, while the former reflects the concrete experiences of combatants as opposed to those who experienced the war at a distance. In our view, it is the difference between men who went to war and those who did not that is paramount in grappling with the issues raised by the concept of unnecessarily cruel weaponry and the conditions under which weapon systems may be used.

Our data show that none of the combatants had a monopoly on the use of unnecessarily cruel weaponry, or the use of these weapons under conditions that unnecessarily turned them on civilians, causing grievous suffering. Furthermore, the data indicate that there is full awareness of these facts among Vietnam veterans. There is also ample evidence that Vietnam veterans are often traumatized by the suffering these weapons inflicted on their fellow units, enemy soldiers, and civilians. Nonetheless, most Vietnam veterans are reluctant to renounce totally the use of these weapons. Their dilemma, as evidenced by the transcripts, arises from the fact that ''cruel'' weapons were often perceived as protecting respondents from harm, the enemy's use of equally brutal weapons required retaliation, or the success of the mission depended on the use of these devices.

For most weapon systems the pattern is consistent: Vietnam veterans are less likely to consider the weapon system cruel if it appears to provide immediate protection against the enemy than either Vietnam era veterans or nonveterans. From their viewpoint, in a wide range of situations such weapons are useful or even indispensable. A minority of Vietnam veterans would prohibit the use of these weapons entirely, on the grounds that suitable substitute weapons are available that are not unnecessarily cruel. There is, however, a general acceptance among Vietnam veterans that the use of these weapons in civilian areas should be prohibited. The majority of Vietnam veterans would limit the use of these weapons to the battlefield. There were generally fewer differences between Vietnam veterans and their peers in their characterizations of weapon systems that were readily available to the enemy as unnecessarily cruel.

Among nonveterans, with the exception of the prowar group, we generally find a stronger emphasis on humanitarian considerations. This is most pronounced among the antiwar activists. The underlying concern in the nonveteran population, especially among activists, is issues such as the unnecessary suffering caused by such weapons, their indiscriminate effects, and the perfidy of such weapons. In light of these considerations we find stronger support here for the banning of "cruel" devices. The use of these weapons even against military personnel is rejected outright, in part because of the suffering they cause and also because the battlefield in Vietnam often blurred the distinctions between civilians and combatants.

In interpreting the findings, we need to reflect on the extent to which the needs of the military situation pose fundamental contradictions between humanitarian objectives and choice of weapon systems. For example, Vietnam veterans routinely complained that the enemy forces had infiltrated the civilian population. American soldiers were, therefore, at greater risk because they could not readily differentiate friend from foe. The question that arises here is whether the weapon systems employed by U.S. forces increased or decreased the hostility of the civilian population. To the extent that weapon systems were more likely to magnify the damage to and suffering of the civilians, hostility to the U.S. presence may have increased and support for the enemy risen. In this context, the use of certain weapon systems, such as napalm, perceived by Vietnam veterans to enhance their safety, may well have done the reverse, increasing their exposure to enemy actions.

In assessing the military necessity or personal safety thesis, it is important to keep in mind that military objectives support political objectives. The relevant question, then, is whether or not humanitarian or tactical concerns are more likely to further the political aims of the combatants. In the case of those who argue for the humanitarian use of weapons, it is necessary to keep in mind that in war, decisions about which weapon systems to use are often perceived to be dictated by circumstances. A war's losers often receive little mercy from either history or the victors. The problem, as this chapter demonstrates, is that in war cruelty is commonplace. It is often exceedingly difficult to get combatants to acknowledge that escalating the level of violence or inflicting maximum pain on the enemy may only increase the level of violence and suffering without appreciably altering the relative military position of the combatants. Yet, our data clearly show that there is genuine concern that the weapons of war in Vietnam, sophisticated and primitive, often did little more than increase the general pain. In that sense, we can interpret our findings as evidence that even among the men at war there is serious concern for the issues raised by the cruelty of weaponry, even when it is accompanied by a heightened sensitivity to their own vulnerability.

CHAPTER EIGHT

TREATMENT OF PRISONERS OF WAR

The treatment of prisoners of war during the Vietnam conflict was a profoundly disturbing part of the war. There is little doubt, as the pages that follow show, that the combatants were deeply concerned about their fate should they fall into enemy hands. Their preoccupation with this aspect of the combat makes the issue of how to treat POWs an important part of our study. We begin this chapter with a discussion of the historical foundation for the rights POWs have slowly attained and next demonstrate that these rights were routinely violated by all parties in Vietnam. We then examine three important related issues: whether or not Vietnam veterans fundamentally differ with their peers on the nature of POW rights, whether they feel, given the character of the war, that guerrillas were entitled to the same protection as regular soldiers, and how Vietnam veterans perceive what happened to certain captives.

Rights of Prisoners of War

A group of rulings called "Regulations," annexed to the Convention Respecting the Law and Customs of War on Land, 1907, comprised one of the first provisions for the humane treatment of prisoners. These regulations did little, however, to ease the privations that prisoners suffered during World War I. The main short-comings of the rulings were lack of preciseness, failure to foresee the problems that arose in the First World War, and lack of any enforcement mechanism. On July 27, 1929, a conference at Geneva adopted a new set of rules, more elaborate than those previously in force: the Convention Relating to the Treatment of Prisoners of War (IInd Geneva Convention of 1929). Like the prior regulations, these rulings did not anticipate the new types of warfare used in the world war that followed their acceptance. A later ruling, the Geneva Convention Relative to the Treatment of Prisoners of War, dated August 12, 1949, stands as the authoritative statement on POW rights (IIIrd Geneva Convention of 1949).

Under current international law, full and primary responsibility for the treatment of prisoners of war falls upon the detaining power. The rulings state that at the time of detention, the prisoner is required to provide only his surname, first name and rank, date of birth, and army, regimental, personal, or serial number. No form of coercion may be inflicted upon him to secure additional information. He may retain his personal effects. Prisoners must be evacuated, as soon as possible after their capture, to camps situated in an area far enough from the combat zone to ensure their safety.

Prisoners of war shall in all circumstances be treated humanely, the rulings continue. They will be dealt with alike, regardless of race, color, religion, faith, or sex. To this end, the following acts are prohibited: violence to life and persons, in particular murder of all kinds; cruel treatment and torture; outrages upon personal dignity, in particular humiliating and degrading treatment. POWs must receive maintenance and medical attention, and any unlawful act or omission seriously endangering the health of a prisoner is prohibited. In particular no prisoner of war may be subjected to physical mutilation or to medical or scientific experiments of any kind. Likewise, prisoners of war must be protected against acts of intimidation and against insults and public curiosity. Measures of reprisal against them are prohibited.

Conditions at the camps of detention must meet standards provided in the Geneva Conventions. The work that the prisoner is required to perform must not be inherently dangerous, humiliating, or directly connected with the operations of the war. The prisoner must be permitted contact with his family and correspondence privileges. Procedures must be established for registering complaints against the administration of the detention camp.

Penal and disciplinary sanctions, including procedures for determining guilt, are also provided by the Geneva Conventions. Parties to the Conventions are obligated to search out and penalize those persons alleged to have committed breaches of the established norms. After the cessation of active hostilities, prisoners of war shall be released and repatriated without delay.

Combatant and Prisoner-of-War Status

Until 1949, groups known as guerrillas, partisans, or simply as "the underground" were not considered legitimate combatants under the prevailing rules. Hence, resistance movements possessed no customary or conventional right to demand the privileges usually accorded to regular soldiers.

During the Second World War, a large number of such "underground" groups were established in the many occupied countries. Their activities contributed substantially to the victory of the Allies but were declared illegal by the Axis Powers, who penalized guerrillas severely whenever punishment could be imposed. Most resistance groups were recognized by their legitimate government and received support in the form of air drops of weapons, medical supplies, food, and often allied intelligence agents.[1]

In view of the important role played by the underground in World War II, the status of this type of armed resistance was reevaluated at war's end. Many observers felt that guerrilla forces were entitled to the status of lawful combatants and should be given the customary and conventional rights of prisoners of war upon capture of any of their members.[2]

Thus it was understandable that the Diplomatic Conference of Geneva in 1949 should deal with the rights of resistance movements. Article 4A (2) of the Third Geneva Convention of 1949 (Treatment of Prisoners of War) provides that among the groups to be treated as prisoners of war upon capture are members of organized resistance groups, belonging to a belligerent and operating in or outside of their own territory, even if the latter is occupied.

The article in question, however, retains the traditional limitation that such rights shall be subject to the fulfillment of four specific conditions: command of a person responsible for his subordinates, distinctive insignia recognizable at a distance, open carrying of arms, and conduct of operations in accordance with the laws and customs of war. Only those resistance groups satisfying these four conditions were considered lawful combatants.

In the sixties, Third World states began to demand a new legal principle that would protect all participants in a wide variety of conflicts. These situations included armed conflicts in which people fight against colonial domination, alien occupation, and racist regimes in the exercise of the right of self-determination.

In the early seventies, the Thirld World states were granted the rulings they sought in the form of Protocol I Additional to the Geneva Conventions of 1949. The protocol also extends the category of persons who, in the event of capture, are entitled to benefit from prisoner-of-war treatment. Article 43 provides that the armed forces of a party to the conflict consist of ''all organized armed forces, groups and units which are under a command responsible to the Party for the conduct of its subordinates, even if that Party is represented by a government or an authority not recognized by an adverse Party.'' Such armed forces (including resistance, guerrilla, and liberation movements) ''shall be subject to an internal disciplinary system which, inter alia, shall enforce compliance with the rules of international law applicable in armed conflict.''

To promote the protection of the civilian population from the effects of hostilities, Protocol I provides that combatants are obliged to distinguish themselves from the civilian population. Recognizing, however, that there are situations in armed conflicts where, owing to the nature of the hostilities, a combatant cannot always make his identity known, he will retain his status as a combatant, provided that he carries his arms openly during each military engagement.

According to the protocol, a participant in hostilities who falls into the power of an adverse party shall be presumed to be a prisoner of war. If he claims POW status, or if he appears to be entitled to such status, or if the party on which he depends claims such status on his behalf by notification, he will be protected by the Third Geneva Convention. Should any doubt arise as to whether an individual is entitled to POW status, he shall retain that status until it has been revoked by a competent tribunal.

Members of a resistance or a guerrilla movement who are not entitled to prisoner-of-war status, as well as other persons having taken part individually in hostilities, shall be regarded as civilians. They shall not be placed at the discretion of their captors but shall be entitled to the guarantees of the Fourth Geneva Convention as supplemented by Article 75 of Protocol I.[3]

Civil War and the Rights of Guerrilla Fighters

In the case of a civil war, the situation becomes more complex. At what points should a group of rebels (or secessionists) be granted the same protection as regular soldiers? The answer has traditionally been that any significant degree of popular support entitles the guerrillas to their war rights and that recognition of these rights follows upon the establishment by the rebels of a secure territorial base that enables them to carry out sustained and concerted military operations.[4]

Protocol II Additional to the Geneva Conventions of 1949 adopted in 1977 attempts to protect *all* persons not taking a direct part in the hostilities, or who have ceased to take part in hostilities, without setting up categories of protected persons enjoying special treatment. It does not set any distinction between the treatment of members of armed forces who have fallen into the hands of the adverse party and that of civilians whose liberty has been restricted. Guerrilla fighters are entitled to all the guarantees contained in articles 4, 5, and 6 of the protocol.

This protocol constitutes a first step toward the protection of prisoners of war in a civil war situation. But its impact will probably remain limited within the immediate future, since its enforcement in a civil war poses enormous problems.

Prisoners of War in the Vietnam Conflict

During the course of the war, all of the major parties to the conflict violated the rules protecting prisoners of war.[5] Both North Vietnam (a party to the Geneva Conventions of 1949) and the Vietcong, while defending their "humane" treatment of captured opponents, declined to admit that they were legally obligated under the Third Geneva Convention. In practice, neither of the two fully respected the Geneva Convention. Indeed, North Vietnam in particular refused to comply with the reporting, correspondence, and neutral inspection provisions relating to prisoners of war. There have been many reports of cruel treatment of American prisoners in the North Vietnamese POW camps. In 1966 and 1967 the North Vietnamese marched American pilots through the streets of Hanoi and subjected them to insults and public curiosity. In retaliation for American bombing of North Vietnamese villages, the North Vietnamese repeatedly threatened to try captured Americans as war criminals. It has also been reported that the Vietcong mistreated American POWs in their detention camps. In 1965 the Vietcong announced the killing of three American prisoners, in retaliation for South Vietnamese executions of several Vietcong soldiers.[6]

United States and South Vietnamese treatment of prisoners of war also often violated international law. Although both parties were signatories to the 1949 Convention, there is evidence that American soldiers and officers mistreated prisoners of war and that killing enemy POWs was a common practice. A policy of refusal to take prisoners has long been condemned by customary and conventional laws of war.

The International Committee of the Red Cross in Geneva, to which the Third Geneva Convention gave the right to visit POWs and insure their proper treatment, publicly protested United States treatment of prisoners in Vietnam. Indeed, the I.C.R.C.'s representative in Saigon was not permitted to visit prisoners taken by American and South Vietnamese troops. But, when the North Vietnamese government threatened to try captured United States airmen as war criminals, the United States declared any such move as a violation of the Geneva Conventions. This led a former executive of the International Committee of the Red Cross to comment: "The Viet Cong fighters are as protected by the Geneva Conventions as the American G.I.'s are. It is utterly hypocritical to condone wholesale violations of the Red Cross principles on one side and protest reprisals against the other."[7]

The American forces did not keep permanent custody of the prisoners they took, but transferred them to camps controlled by the South Vietnamese. As Telford Taylor has noted:

> Article 12 of the Geneva Convention authorizes such transfers, but only if the transferring power "has satisfied itself of the willingness and ability" of the receiving power to observe the requirements of the Convention. If, after transfer, the receiving power does not do so, then the original captor power must "take effective steps to correct the situation or shall request the return of the prisoners."[8]

In view of the documented South Vietnamese mistreatment of POWs the American transfers violated these provisions.

The South Vietnamese used many ways to kill their prisoners. According to witnesses, at Fu Quoc, an island prison until 1972, when the inmates demanded better food, machine guns carried on jeeps fired on the protesters, resulting in dozens of dead and wounded. And there were other ways of killing people: by starvation, by rationing their water, by beating them, by torturing them, by leaving them in tiger cages.

The testimony of Jean-Pierre Debris and Andre Menras, two young French teachers arrested on July 25, 1970, by ARVN military police and taken to the Chi Hoa prison in Saigon, where they remained until December 29, 1972, is an authentic non-Vietnamese statement concerning the fate of prisoners in South Vietnamese prisons. In February 1971, they reported as follows on the condition of the prisoners who had been brought back from the tiger cages in Poulo Condor:

> Normally, they were never allowed to go out into the sunlight; but were kept in solitary confinement, in cells without windows or light. But that day, the first day of Tet, they could come down into the prison yard. So we saw, the whole jail saw, for the first time, these hundred prisoners from the tiger cages. And in what condition! They had to crawl down, because they could not walk anymore; their knees had been broken. They dragged themselves along the ground with little wooden benches they had made. In the sun they had to close their eyes completely because they had been blinded from so many years of darkness. Their faces were haggard and lined, their bodies gaunt and emaciated. No one made a sound when they arrived. Even the trustees who guarded them were astonished.[9]

Perspectives of the Vietnam Generation

Given the ferocity of the Vietnam War, the issue of the rights of prisoners of war was a matter of considerable concern to Americans in general and the Vietnam Generation in particular. The above-mentioned U.S. pattern of handing over POWs to the South Vietnamese Army, and the documented mistreatment of these prisoners by the ARVN, politicized the issue in the United States and created deep concern among antiwar activists. At the same time there was clear documentation that American soldiers were abused and tortured by the enemy (Vietcong and North Vietnamese) forces.

In light of the problems of mistreatment, torture, and murder of POWs in the Vietnam War, we asked our respondents the following, regarding the rights of POWs and the treatment of guerrilla fighters:

> Prisoners of war have many internationally guaranteed rights. Please tell me whether you agree or disagree that prisoners should have these rights:
> Prisoners of war may not be treated better or worse on the basis of race or political beliefs.
> Prisoners of war must be permitted to contact their families and to write letters to them.
> Prisoners of war should not be forced to do work that directly supports war.

Prisoners of war must be allowed to formally put their complaints against the administration of the camp in writing.

Prison camps rules and punishments must meet the standards of international agreements.

Captured members of resistance movements and guerrilla organizations have the same rights as other prisoners of war.

The consistency of the responses to these queries led us to aggregate the first five items cited above into a single measure, which we called POW rights. We placed the sixth item, concerning guerrilla fighters, in a category of its own because it is a conceptually distinct question. Thus, our findings here revolve around two areas. First we discuss views of POW rights and then attitudes toward guerrilla fighters.

POW Rights

As table 8.1 shows, there are no real differences in the views of Vietnam veterans and their era or nonveteran peers on the rights to which POWs are entitled. Approximately 70% of the sample believe that POWs should be accorded all of the five rights listed. Furthermore, there are no differences in the views of men who saw combat, witnessed or participated in abusive violence, enlisted, or were drafted. Nor did branch of service or rank change perceptions of POW rights. Finally, we find that neither antiwar activism nor support of or opposition to the war causes significant variation in attitudes toward the above-listed items. A substantial majority of all our respondents agree that prisoners of war need to be afforded protection and may not be abused.

Treatment of Guerrilla Fighters

Although, as table 8.2 demonstrates, there is overwhelming support among our respondents for treating guerrilla fighters as POWs, the uniformity of agreement that we found on POW rights is less apparent here. Again, we find no real differences between Vietnam veterans and their peers overall. At least 80% of the respondents agree that guerrilla fighters should be treated as POWs. As table 8.3 shows, however, among Vietnam veterans, moderate- and heavy-combat veterans (23%) are more likely than low-combat veterans (14%) to disagree that guerrilla fighters should be granted POW status. Furthermore, as table 8.4 indicates, those who witnessed abusive violence (87%) are significantly more likely to argue that guerrilla fighters should be treated as POWs than those who were not exposed to such abuse (82%).

Finally, among nonveterans, both participation in the antiwar movement and support for the Vietnam War led to varying assessments of the extension of POW rights to guerrilla fighters. Active involvement in the antiwar movement leads to substantially greater support for treating guerrillas as POWs. As table

8.5 shows, among those most involved in the antiwar movement, 98% agree that guerrillas should be treated as POWs compared to only 75% of the low activists. In table 8.6 we find that the supporters of the war (67%) are the least likely of any group in the study to be willing to accord POW status to guerrilla fighters. This finding is important in light of the fact that 84% of the Vietnam veterans would treat guerrilla fighters as POWs. Since the nonveteran supporters of the war are often in closer agreement with Vietnam veterans on most issues than are the antiwar activists, it suggests that being in Vietnam created a distinctive outlook in this case.

The conclusion we can draw from our findings is clearcut. Our respondents overwhelmingly support protecting POW rights, and guerrilla fighters are judged to have the same prerogatives as regular soldiers. As noted, Vietnam veterans generally are sympathetic to the rights of guerrilla fighters. This may in part be explained by their often positive attitude toward the Vietcong, a mixture of respect for the VC as soldiers and fear of them as the enemy. In sum, there is virtually no support in our study for the common and brutal mistreatment of prisoners, regular forces or guerrilla fighters, in the Vietnam War.

Views of Vietnam Veterans

In light of the above findings, why was the mistreatment of POWs by all parties so pervasive in the Vietnam War? In reviewing the testimony of our respondents, the behavior of the enemy and of American units and their allies seems fathomable only in terms of the Vietnam War's reciprocal and often limitless violence. It would appear that some men confronted by the brutality of "enemy" and "ally" came to see such behavior as retributory and even justifiable when they in turn held prisoners.

Indeed, although our data suggest that brutality toward POWs is uncharacteristic of the veteran population, the transcripts show that revulsion was not sufficient to stop the cycle of barbarism in war. Apparently, men's attitudes often counted little or not at all in contexts involving the torture or killing of POWs.

In considering the views of our respondents, it is important to remember that Vietnam veterans were the only ones who faced the possibility of becoming POWs. Their vulnerability to capture increased their concern with POW rights and led them to talk extensively about what they had seen and experienced. Their testimony offers unique and chilling insight into one of the darkest sides of the Vietnam conflict.

Our discussion centers around three issues: the pattern of abuse of POWs; the pattern of responses to these abuses; and the perceived effects of the experience. In the pages that follow, we deal mainly with Vietnam veterans who personally witnessed abusive events or directly participated in the mistreatment of POWs (about 30% of all Vietnam veterans). Occasionally, we include the reactions of Vietnam veterans who saw the effects of POW mistreatment but did not witness the abuses.

Mistreatment of POWs by the Vietcong and North Vietnamese Army

American soldiers deeply feared falling into enemy hands. Those who did not see the actual remains of captured prisoners heard ominous accounts from the field about mutilation and torture of Americans by the VC or NVA. Vietnam veterans who were directly exposed to the mistreatment of Americans by enemy forces harbored vivid images of enemy brutality. A white heavy-combat veteran observed:

> You hated the Vietcong because they did not believe in taking prisoners and they tortured our men. One day we found one of our patrols and their heads and arms and legs were cut off and they were just hung up on a tree like a Christmas decoration.

A black army sergeant added:

> The only way I really did not want to die was to be caught by the Vietcong. If they caught you and did not feel like taking you back, they would nail you to a tree and castrate you right there. Chop you off. And if they had time, they would hang around and just watch you suffer.

As noted, many Vietnam veterans in our sample although not directly exposed to the mistreatment of American POWs by enemy forces were aware of this mistreatment and saw some of its consequences. A white veteran who was in the Green Berets reported:

> I have seen some of our men who escaped from prisoner-of-war camps. They had been starved and beaten and had their fingers cut off by the Vietcong.

NVA prisoner-of-war camps were also occasionally liberated by American forces. A black veteran who worked in a hospital commented:

> As far as treatment of American prisoners . . . they overran this NVA camp and they brought in the hospital some of our guys that were interned there and they were in pretty bad shape.

Mistreament of POWs by South Vietnamese forces

The VC/NVA had no monopoly on cruelty toward prisoners. The South Vietnamese Army (ARVN) replicated in spirit and practice the VC/NVA disregard for the lives and safety of their prisoners. Veterans witnessed the cruel treatment of POWs by the South Vietnamese Army. An army infantryman described his experiences as follows:

There was some torturing used to obtain information from the Vietcong. They were beaten up. The South Vietnamese have some water tortures that they used. They would get someone and pour water in their mouths and hold their throat shut and it would be as if they were drowning.

Mutilation and murder of POWs was also evident in the ARVN's handling of POWs. A veteran who was in the air force explained what he observed:

One, they just shot in cold blood, because he didn't give up information. . . . Another one, they were using a couple of torture techniques . . . pulling a fingernail off . . . strap a man to a chair and take a pair of pliers and just pull his finger off and other things. Use a wire and loop it around his balls and slowly twist it. . . . They would continue until he passed out from shock or something—torture is to gradually break down a guy.

The murder of POWs by the ARVN described above was not, as indicated below by a paratrooper, a unique event:

Once I saw a Vietnamese shoot another Vietnamese. We had Vietnamese interpreters with us and we had captured a North Vietnamese. We had been interrogating him all that night and all the next day. That afternoon they told me to get a couple of men and an interpreter and escort the prisoner to a helicopter. I was in charge and I was walking beside him. All of a sudden the interpreter grabbed me and pushed me away. He pulled out his 45 and shot the North Vietnamese right in the head.

Brutality toward prisoners by the ARVN was not limited to torture in situations where information was sought from prisoners. The abuse of POWs appears to have been systematically extended to those held captive by the South Vietnamese in detention centers. A navy seabee commented:

There was a VC camp not far from us. The way these people were treated, they were put in cages. They were given a bowl of rice to eat. That was their meal for the day. They were mistreated badly. The Vietnamese personnel took charge of the prisoners. They were the worst.

Mistreatment of POWs by Korean Forces

Brutalization of captives by the Koreans was also reported. A veteran who was in the navy noted:

A number of Vietcong prisoners were captured by the forces of the Republic of Korea. They were interrogating this group of men and they were not getting anywhere. So they grabbed this one that looked like he was the youngest and they put his hand on the table. This ROK lieutenant started on his little finger with a knife, put it on the first joint of his finger and asked him the question. The kid refused to answer so they hit the knife with a hammer and started taking the joints of his fingers until he started talking. The ROK marines were a strange group of people, very cruel. I saw several instances of this type of mistreatment of prisoners.

Another example of violence against POWs is described by an army infantryman:

They had a little VC and we had Koreans with us. He was supposed to show them where a division was. After three days, they didn't find the division. They cut the little man's head off.

Mistreatment of POWs by American Forces

American forces were also involved in the abuse and murder of POWs. The most common incidents described are: a general unwillingness to take captives, the killing of badly wounded enemy soldiers, and various forms of torture in order to obtain information.

Some veterans involved in or witness to the killing of POWs reported that it was American military policy not to take prisoners. A black veteran who was a participant in abusive violence against POWs explained this policy as follows:

He was running and then he saw us, and we opened up fire and we had just wounded him at first, and then we just came up and put a bullet in his head, because we didn't take any prisoners. That was the policy. First of all, because the prisoner will do anything to get away and if he runs into any of his own people, he is going to try to get their attention. Then your life is in danger. . . . Sometimes the company commander would say: "we're going through the search and destroy, we're not taking time to take any prisoners." The only time we took prisoners was when somebody real big came. . . . But if they caught somebody who doesn't have any information of value, you got rid of him.

A white marine who participated in abusive violence of POWs explained the treatment given to many badly wounded enemy soldiers:

What happened was that everybody had so many prisoners, it was impossible and they had to cut it out. Prisoners were getting killed. We really did not kill them unless they were badly wounded. . . . Of course, if you were in a firefight and a guy came out with his hands up, well, you ain't letting him walk in—you kill him.

Veterans also talked about the unauthorized killing of prisoners after they had been captured and were on their way to a POW camp. A white marine described the following incident:

> I remember trying to save eleven of them once. We had captured them and we found a small building. They were under constant surveillance. In the rest of the building we stored gasoline barrels, fifteen to twenty 55-gallon drums. I would try to talk to them. I could see that they feared for their lives. We had an interpreter tell them that they were going to be taken to Saigon for interrogation purposes and then they would be put into a POW camp. I think someone set fire to the gasoline drums that night. A whole bunch of us ran over and saw them trying to get out of the window and the window was barb-wired up so they could not escape. The flames were just too much and there was no way we could get to them. I remember the lieutenant saying, okay get your rifles and open up on them. Just to put them out of their misery because there was no way to rescue them. I mean they were burning to death.

Respondents also discussed the difficulties that arise when captured enemy soldiers must be transported to POW camps. A white sergeant in the marines who participated in the mistreatment of an NVA colonel recounts:

> We were sitting on a trail and there was a fork in the trail and two NVA colonels, one on either fork, just walked right in the middle of us. We killed one and captured the other. It took us three days to get out. We kept a bag over his head, tied . . . running him into trees, and beating on him. By the time we finally got back with him his face was so disfigured that you couldn't tell what he was. The main reason he was treated this way is because the NVA were in the area and were trying to locate us with indiscriminate mortar fire. And we had to keep him quiet because if we didn't out lives would be a stake, and every time he would try and make a sound he would be hit.

The use of various forms of torture to obtain information was also reported. Many veterans gave accounts of prisoners who were taken out of interrogation centers and thrown alive out of helicopters. This is one of the most recurrent themes about the American treatment of POWs. The stated objective was to kill one or two to force the others to provide intelligence information. A black veteran witnessed the following event:

> I think it was a major or colonel, he took them up in a helicopter ride, and he wanted each one to talk, and the first one would not talk and so he threw him out. And the second one did not talk and so he was thrown out. And by this time, the third one, he was talking—and after he told him what he wanted, he threw him out too. I just looked up and I did not know what was going on at

first. I saw a helicopter just circling around the same area. Then they told me when he came down. He was gungho. . . . If you have some people that are gungho and overdo things, what can you say?

Response Patterns to the Mistreatment of POWs

The above testimonies help to understand what Vietnam veterans witnessed in regard to the mistreatment of prisoners of war. Their responses to that experience take three widely differing forms: mistreatment of POWs is justified, abuse of POWs is impermissible, and abusive violence could have been controlled.

Mistreatment of POWs was justified

Although our data provide evidence only for the allied forces, the information assembled contributes to our general understanding of the logic of abuse of POWs in guerrilla warfare. In answering the question why did such abuse occur, we are confronted by several different rationales that constitute a justification for the torture and/or murder of POWs. The two most consistent themes we found are the necessity of obtaining information that could save American lives and revenge for enemy treatment of prisoners. We also find that for some veterans war was hell and in hell there is not protection, while others simply felt guerrillas were not entitled to protection. On occasion there is evidence of cruelty for its own sake.

Finally, a number of veterans felt that if one of the participants in an armed conflict violates the rules, all other parties are freed from their obligations. They argued that since the NVA and Vietcong ignored international rules and mistreated their prisoners, Americans and their allies could do the same. Enemy prisoners were forced to talk, mistreated, and killed. But if the enemy had respected POWs' rights things would have been different.

In guerrilla war, the unseen enemy, the hidden sniper, the unit lurking nearby pose a constant threat to survival of the soldier. Knowledge of the enemy's location in such a war is invaluable. Access to such information is difficult since the enemy draws his strength from camouflaging his identity as well as his postion. Prisoners, in these circumstances, offer a matchless source of information. Since they are unlikely to divulge the whereabouts of their comrades voluntarily coercion becomes a ready solution to the dilemma of acquiring "security enhancing" data. Once the option of POW mistreatment is exercised it becomes, as our data demonstrate, increasingly easier to move to ever grosser abuses in the name of security.

Veterans who justified abuse through the "military necessity-security" argument outlined above believed that in war, military strategy is determined by strategic considerations and lies beyond the strictures of humanitarian law. In war, they noted, the rights of soldiers can be ignored if need be for military reasons, and the torture and/or killing of prisoners is justified if it is necessary for military success. As one veteran observed, "It was our survival against theirs." Another respondent, a white army infantry sergeant, echoed this feeling:

> They had an intelligence team come out to the base camp that we were in. They used torture on this guy who they thought was a Vietcong to find out what they wanted to know. I did not do anything. I mean it was not anything terrible and if they found out what they wanted to know it might have saved some lives.

Another response, from an American adviser to the ARVN, indicates that those whom he perceived to have useful information were more likely to be spared excessive torture, while soldiers he thought knew little of value were left to their fate at the hands of the ARVN interrogators. He presented the following account:

> In the function of an adviser I felt obliged to witness interrogations of suspected Vietcong, almost all of whom were soldiers. They were not infrastructure . . . meaning it was a POW situation and not a political one. The methods employed by the Vietnamese would be usually sticks, hoses, electrodes applied to various parts of the body. Occasionally beatings would get to the point of reprisal . . . a personal vendetta by the interrogation officer. I did not provide any direct assistance . . . only indirectly, in terms of money and space made available. For POWs that may have had some intelligence information I was somewhat effective in reducing their torture . . . any kind of abusive interrogation.

The importance attached to information as a vital element in survival is clearly illustrated by the reports of two veterans. The first, a white veteran who served in the navy and participated in abusive violence against POWs, provides the general security rationale for POW abuse:

> If you catch one guy wandering around . . . where there is one, you know there are more. You try to find out where and if these guys do not talk, you are going to have to use measures to make them talk. . . . If you do not find out information and get them before they get you . . . you are going to get it sooner or later. So it is a matter of survival. You do not do it because you enjoy it.

In the second illustration, a black marine gave a self-defense justification for his participation in the mistreatment of a prisoner, based on an immediate crisis in the field:

> We got this one prisoner of war, and he would not tell us what we wanted to know, so we dropped him in the well and we used this pole and kept dunking his head under the water until he told us what we wanted to know. See in the bush

you did not have time. We were supposed to strip him, put him on the helicopter and send him to the rear. . . . We thought we had a cause for it. It was getting information, keeping our guys from getting killed.

The second type of justification for brutality against POWs is revenge for similar actions by the enemy against friends or other Americans. Nothing so swiftly alters the perspective of the soldier as exposure to evidence of enemy savagery against his own kind, especially in the case of a buddy. The navy veteran cited earlier who described the Korean torture of a POW noted how his attitude toward mistreatment changed as a result of the mutilation of a close friend:

The first time I saw [brutality] I could not believe that anybody could have such a disregard for a human being, such contempt for the rules protecting prisoners. But then my attitude changed. And it goes back to the death of my friend, he was killed and we only found his hand. If we had to send his mother his hand, we could take the hand of a Vietcong to shorten the war or at least get some of our guys home.

A white marine explained his involvement in the torture of prisoners as follows:

Well, first of all you are under a lot of pressure. I mean you are like an animal. It is nothing to kill somebody. You see your friends die, you want revenge. What are you going to do with the gook. You want information. Well I guess it was torture. Scare him with a knife or gun, shit like that.

Finally, we find that in the heat of battle, anger directed at the losses of one's own men generates rage at the enemy. In the aftermath of the battle, as men vent their anger at the losses endured, abusive violence occurs. An example of this pattern is provided by the following description given by a white army man who participated in abusive violence against POWs:

In one day of combat we killed, by body count, 881 NVAs. We did not take any prisoners at all. And it was just a hate because A company was wiped out. . . . We were reprimanded through a chain of command for not taking any prisoners because we were right in the middle of an NVA regiment and we could have learned a lot through prisoners. But there weren't any, so what the fuck?

A small number of veterans felt that international rules laid down in conventions play no role in war and mistreatment of prisoners simply cannot be avoided in a wartime situation. A white veteran who witnessed abusive violence explained this position as follows:

To me mistreatment is just part of war, I do not know how you could have a clean war. . . . Whenever we captured one of the enemy, I am sure his treatment was not as described in any of these regulations. He was obviously not treated the way I would have liked to have been treated, but he was the enemy. It is unreasonable to expect to be treated like you have just checked into the Conrad Hilton. They were treated roughly and I do not know what could be done about it. It had no effect on me, it just unfolded exactly as I would have expected it to.

Other respondents upheld the validity of the Geneva Conventions but argued that the rulings did not apply to guerrilla fighters. In this regard, a white veteran noted:

I remember one day when the South Vietnamese had captured a Vietcong. They had beat him and they had his wrists lashed so tight that his hands were turning blue. And they interrogated him at a village and when they were through with him they just threw him up against a tree and shot him. That, I was told, was because the South Vietnamese were not bound by the Geneva Convention on POWs because it was a civil war. And the Vietcong were guerrilla fighters, not regular soldiers, they had no rights.

We also find evidence that war loosens the constraints on human behavior and encourages acts whose only purpose is to increase pain and suffering. A black veteran who was in the army describes his experiences with such brutality:

The back door of our vehicle was grated and hot air from the engine comes out and that deck gets to be 600 degrees after a while. And you can not stand there. It will burn through your shoes. That is where we would put our prisoners. Rope them, tie them, just throw them down there like a piece of steer, piece of cattle. That is unnecessarily cruel—you did not have to do that. And that was just for transportation. It was not specifically to torture them. The Green Berets used to get jump cables and attach them to their ears, turn the engine on.

Violence against POWs is not permissible

A majority of Vietnam veterans considered international rules important and insisted that the rights of POWs must be protected. They argued that these rules apply to all forms of armed international conflict, including the Vietnam War, and must be obeyed by all parties. Military necessity, in their view, provides no excuse for the mistreatment of POWs. A white marine sergeant noted:

I know of several instances where guards claimed to have murdered prisoners or taken away their rights. I feel that this violates international rules and all of the principles of why we were fighting the war to begin with and it changes it from warfare to gestapo-like tactics. I felt that I ought to do something about it but I never did. Voicing my opinion would not have been good for me at the time.

Veterans who insisted that POW rights must be respected often presented a strong self-interest argument, i.e., "if we mistreat enemy prisoners they will do the same to us." They admitted that taking prisoners of war in Vietnam created a difficult situation. Sometimes wounded Vietcong had to be carried for a long way through the jungle to the helicopter pick-up place. Often, enemy forces would not allow themselves to be captured, fighting back when approached. Despite these difficulties, for many respondents, like the black marine quoted below, the self-interest argument prevailed:

Once the tank company in the marine corp dragged a couple of Vietcong on the back of their tank. Another time the marines pushed this dude out of the helicopter because he did not tell them where the location of the VC was. It gave me a bad effect, because I felt this way. If we were doing that to them, then I know they are going to be doing it to us. Then if I get captured, they are going to give me the same treatment that we gave them. I did not like it, but it made me more resistant to being captured. If I were surrounded, I would probably have to fight to death, instead of just surrendering, knowing how I will be treated as a prisoner of war.

Others, like the veteran who witnessed the execution of a NVA prisoner, argued that mistreatment is not permissible because it is inhumane:

That was terrible . . . to see the look on the man's face, a second before he was shot. I saw the bullet going through his head and I saw him fall. I do not think anybody could ever forget that saw it.

Abusive action against POWs could have been controlled

The rejection of torture and murder of POWs, including guerrilla fighters, found in our study is reflected in the responses to these actions discussed above. Overall, we find little evidence among respondents who objected to or were repulsed by the treatment of POWs that they could or would have acted to halt such abuse. Indeed, our transcripts bear grim witness to the difficulty of stopping mistreatment of POWs once that practice has become part of the fabric of the war.

Veterans reported witnessing cruel incidents that they are unable to forget. At the time, however, they felt helpless and/or were prevented from taking any action. The veteran cited earlier who expressed disgust at the torture methods of the ARVN felt there was no one he could turn to for support. As he put it: "I didn't think I had a choice, who could I complain to? Some of my superiors were there, people over me, so I didn't say anything."

A similar response was given by the veteran who described the torture of POWs by the Green Berets, "I was witness to it. I felt that I should do something about it, but it was such an American custom that I couldn't possibly reach anybody, so I didn't do it."

Another response was to block out the experience, as did the veteran who saw an American colonel drop POWs out of a helicopter: "I guess you justify it to yourself. You say: I'm glad it was not me. [Did you ever feel you should do something about these things?]: Nope. It makes me appreciate life more. That is all."

Others simply did nothing, even though they personally disagreed with what was occurring, as was the case of the veteran who observed the use of torture by the ARVN: "I knew what was going on. I was not involved. I disagreed with it. But I never did anything about it."

Finally, there were instances where men did act or attempted to act to prevent violence against a POW. A case in point is the veteran who observed the Koreans cut off the head of a prisoner. Thereafter, as he put it: "I said that I didn't want any more Koreans working with me. . . . It was the Koreans, it was their way."

Several incidents, however, indicate how difficult it can be to stop violence against POWs, especially among one's own men. The dilemma faced by those who attempted to intervene when mistreatment occurred is illustrated in the following two statements. A white army infantry squad leader described the following experience:

> The biggest effect the Vietnam War had on my life is something that I personally experienced. I still have frequent nightmares about it. . . . I was a squad leader at that time and a few guys in my squad had captured a Vietcong. He was unarmed and instead of bringing him to intelligence, turning him in as a prisoner, they executed him. A couple of guys held me down as I screamed for them not to do it. This went against the Geneva Convention. . . . I could not report them because they were guys I worked with. My life depended on them and their life depended on me. We worked together as a team. However, even though I protested, I was outnumbered. They murdered him right there in front of me. I think that is the biggest horror that I experienced. I was in charge and they went against me. But I could never turn them in or pursue any kind of disciplinary punishment for them.

A white army captain witnessed mistreatment of prisoners of war but was afraid to say anything because, as he noted, mistreatment was acceptable to higher commanders and he feared his disapproval might cost him his life. He explained his apprehensions as follows:

Mistreatment of prisoners of war? Yes . . . I was exposed to actions taken by our people. . . . [Did you ever do anything about it?] . . . I wanted to but I felt helpless because I might get shot for saying anything. [You were relatively sure that you would have been shot?] Oh yes, that was one of the first things I was learning about what they called "the fragging" in Vietnam and I was pretty much aware what fragging was and I kept that in the back of my mind. Also it was the general assumption that mistreatment of prisoners was acceptable by our higher commanders. I never heard anyone else talking about those actions being bad so I kept my mouth shut. I'll never forget these actions . . . they're very vivid to this day and they'll always be.

Some veterans reported what while they witnessed inhumane treatment of prisoners, they personally tried to treat captives with respect. A black veteran, who was an interrogator for army intelligence, described some of his personal exposure to mistreatment of prisoners of war as follows:

We had a guy investigated by the Red Cross because of his illegal doings in his interrogations. I resented that for the things he did he more or less got a slap on the hand. This guy brought five prisoners back to the unit, singled one guy out and shot him, just to show them that you mean business. . . . I used a different technique. I'd give the guy a cigarette and sit next to him and talk. I got the information. Maybe I didn't get all I could have gotten out of him. But that is the way I saw I had to do it.

Other veterans reported that they took some form of action when they witnessed the mistreatment of POWs. A white army infantryman described his efforts this way:

I said to one of the POW guards: "That's fucked up what you're doing." When they'd just walk around and kick the person for no reason. Guys, they'd just sit there on their haunches, not doing nothing but eating and they'd come and kick their food out of their hands—kick them in their face . . . I told our platoon leader "that's not right" and he'd say "well that's none of your business." I didn't go any higher. It taught me that we weren't the good guys that I thought we were. . . . When I first got out of the service I'd have dreams and think about it a lot.

In spite of the hazards involved, intervention in cases of POW abuse could produce official response if pursued. However, even when there was subsequent official action, it often came too late to help the victims. The evidence presented below shows that it was extremely difficult to stop torture once underway. A black army infantry sergeant explained how little he could do when faced with violence involving Vietnamese women:

Our support unit had captured some medical personnel. They were interrogating these prisoners and most of them were women, nurses. And we had this captain. He spoke Vietnamese very fluent and he told these women, maybe ten or fifteen, if they didn't give up the information that he wanted, he was going to turn the whole unit loose on them. . . . Now this I couldn't dig. I told the guys in my platoon. "You touch any of these women, I'll have you court-martialed. I'll report you when I get back to the rear." Thank God, the dudes had enough respect for me. The nurses were beaten and raped and eventually killed because they wouldn't give information which I don't believe they had. [They killed these women?] They had to kill them. Because if they would have brought them back to the rear, they would have been interrogated. That means that all these dudes are going to be brought up on charges. The Americans fought the war under the Geneva Convention, mostly . . . [What did you do or didn't do?] I reported to the brigade commander in charge. And he took action against the officers in charge of the unit. [What happened to them?] I really couldn't say.

Impact of Abuse of POWs

We turn now to the effects veterans felt that abusive experiences had on them. The transcripts indicate several distinct reactions to the torture of POWs. One type of response to abuse was denial of any reaction at all, as in the case of a veteran who, when queried about the effect of killing wounded prisoners, replied: "Effect? None at all. Never thought about it."

A second response was concern over what respondents considered to be an "unholy" alliance with the South Vietnamese. As this group saw it, the United States was partly responsible for the mistreatment of POWs by the South Vietnamese because we should never have turned our prisoners over to them.

A third response, as noted, is traumatization at the time, followed by either nightmares or memories of the abuse after returning home. Thus, for some of these veterans, exposure to abuse left psychological scars that have not yet healed. Among those who did not openly acknowledge the psychological impact of what they saw, traumatization is evident by such remarks as "What I experienced gave me a greater appreciation for life" and "The cruelty that I witnessed taught me exactly what war is." Indeed, evidence of psychological scarring consistently accompanies the searing descriptions of veterans who witnessed deliberate savagery against prisoners of war.

Nonveterans and the Treatment of Prisoners of War

Generally, in the transcript material, the issue of POW rights and their abuse does not seem as important to nonveterans as abusive violence against civilians and the use of unnecessarily cruel weapons. But here again, there is a difference in perspective between the prowar nonveterans and the antiwar activists. Those nonveterans who supported the American involvement in the war seem to show less interest in the fate of POWs than antiwar activists. Indeed, only a small minority of prowar respondents criticized the violations of the rights of prisoners during the war. One nonveteran presented this concerned view as follows:

> Under the category of the prisoners rights, I feel that a lot of these rights were violated during the war, which shouldn't happen. I realize that it's a little tough to fight a war under rules. You're not always going to be able to follow the rules. But treating a POW humanely, God that's the least you can do.

The majority of prowar respondents showed little or no concern for the treatment of POWs. They even ignore the issue of the handling of American POWs by the North Vietnamese. The following example seems typical of the attitude of a plurality of prowar nonveterans:

> You see how dirty the war gets . . . torturing of prisoners. This is the first time I realized how much of that goes on in a war. . . . I figured it was a part of war, you had to accept it. If you're going to fight a war you're going to have that kind of thing happen.

Again, antiwar activists seemed more concerned than prowar nonveterans about the treatment of POWs, including the Vietcong guerrilla fighters. The following remarks by a high activist are typical of their response pattern.

> You hear horror stories of prisoners being thrown out of helicopters and crowded into ships in a harbor and left there. I saw pictures of North Vietnamese prisons, where the cells were like 12 inches from the ground and guys were laying there for months. . . . I figured both sides were brutal, inhumane.

Other activists stressed the American mistreatment of POWs, an issue which for some became one of the main reasons for their increasing opposition to the war. A high activist explained this attitude:

> [Why did you become more concerned with why we were in Vietnam?] Well as far as what *we* were doing in Vietnam . . . I think a couple of things that struck me were the stories you would hear about torturing prisoners.

Some nonveterans who originally had supported the United States involvement in the war changed their minds after they saw photographs documenting certain American practices. This shift in attitude is evident from the following remarks made by a high activist:

[Why did you change your view of the war?] I think the way they covered up the entire war. . . . And pictures of Americans pushing prisoners out of a helicopter at four thousand feet, you know that changed my mind. [Did you ever do anything about it?] I wrote my congressman.

Conclusion

In this chapter we find evidence for two conclusions. First, there is broad support for the humane treatment of prisoners of war among Vietnam veterans and their peers. Second, there was widespread abuse of POWs in Vietnam, including American mistreatment of enemy prisoners. Hence, it is clear that the wish to protect POWs does not necessarily lead to the desired outcome.

The long, painstaking struggle to establish POW rights springs from a history of failure among combatants to respect the rights of their captives. Thus, Vietnam was in many ways simply one case in a long chain of conflicts during which protection of disarmed combatants failed to materialize. Since the hostilities in Vietnam, other struggles around the world have resulted in similar failures. The important issues here are why prisoners of war in Vietnam were not better protected, how exposure to abuses of POWs has affected combatants, and whether the prospects seem favorable for protecting POWs in future situations.

Our data indicate several root causes for the persistent abuse of POWs in Vietnam. The two major factors seem to be intertwined. At the same time that the North and its allies generally refused to accept obligations under existing treaties on the treatment of POWs, the South chose to define VC guerrillas as rebels not entitled to protection under existing covenants and generally treated NVA regulars as if they, too, were subversives. These concurrent views of the situation contributed to an environment in which all combatants, including Americans, could reasonably assume the worst if captured. Since the worst more often than not seems to have occurred when enemies fell into each other's hands, especially among the Vietnamese factions, there was built into the situation a cycle of violence against captured soldiers that fed on itself and escalated as fear of what might happen and revenge for what did occur mounted.

The context of a guerrilla war also reenforced the established pattern of violence against POWs. The ubiquity of the enemy made intelligence about its whereabouts precious and hard to come by. The generalized tendency to obtain scarce information "that might save lives" through virtually any means was compounded by the treatment of each side's buddies by the enemy. However, even if the enemy had been less savage in its treatment of captured soldiers, the torture of POWs in a guerrilla war appears endemic to the more traditional military forces. Extracting information from POWs about the location of the enemy and its supporters in the population is in the eyes of the antiguerrilla forces one of the few ways of remedying their own dangerous and perpetual vulnerability to surprise attack.

But, as our study indicates, there are heavy costs associated with the torture of POWs. First, the allied practice of abuses against enemy POWs contributed to reducing support for the war among U.S. forces. In particular, ARVN abuses helped alienate American soldiers from their Vietnamese allies. Second, the abuse of American POWs by the NVA and VC increased fear and anxiety among U.S. units and potentially inhibited risk taking on their part. In addition, there were psychological costs to those who witnessed or came into contact with the victims as well as trauma to those who practiced violence. The memory of these experiences lives on long after the event. Finally, there is the cost in pain and suffering as well as death to those who actually became POWs. During the Vietnam War the price of failure to protect POWs was fearsome indeed.

In reviewing our findings, we find little comfort in the general attitudes supporting humane treatment for POWs. True, improved outside inspection and verification might somewhat alleviate the suffering of POWs. But unless it is possible to persuade soldiers that their safety may not be enhanced by the torture of their prisoners, there seems little reason to hope that the pattern of violations as it existed in Vietnam will be altered. The acceptance of the costs of mistreatment of POWs to all parties in an armed conflict, i.e., motivation through enlightened self-interest, seems the only hope for moving away from an ever-increasing cruelty toward those who become prisoners of war.

CHAPTER NINE

PERSPECTIVES ON INDIVIDUAL RESPONSIBILITY IN WAR

One important aspect of individual responsibility is the principle that individuals are criminally responsible for violations of the rules of war.[1] In most countries, the laws of war are part of the law of the land and may be enforced against both soldiers and civilians.

The formalization of military structure in the eighteenth century resulted in the creation of military courts, authorized to try violations of the laws of war as well as other offenses by soldiers. Since the mid-nineteenth century, states have used military courts with increasing frequency for the trial of persons accused of war crimes. A more controversial aspect of individual responsibility is the question of an international criminal liability for war crimes under a generally accepted international penal code.

This chapter begins by examining the historical development of international liability for violations of the rules of war. Against this background, it then focuses on the views of the Vietnam Generation regarding individual responsibility. Special attention is given to their levels of awareness of humanitarian law and their views on what caused violations of existing international rules. The generation's attitudes toward the responsibility of soldiers, officers, and governments in time of war are also analyzed.

Attitudes Toward War Crimes: A Historical Overview

Ancient literature contains numerous condemnations of war crimes. In more recent times, religious humanitarianism became the foundation for declaring grave breaches of humanitarian law, when committed willfully, to be war crimes. In the seventeenth century, the question of individual responsibility for the conduct of war was discussed in learned writings, especially those of the Dutch jurist-philosopher Hugo Grotius. In 1863, the United States took the lead in writing the concept of war crimes into its military code. That year, in the midst of the Civil War, President Lincoln encouraged the proclamation by the War Department of "Instructions for the Government of Armies of the United States in the Field." These "Instructions" comprised 159 articles, including such subjects as "punishment of crimes against the inhabitants of hostile countries."

The late nineteenth century was marked by a movement to incorporate the concept of "war crimes" into international agreements. The most important results of that thrust were the Hague Conventions of 1899 and 1907, the Geneva Conventions of 1949, and the war crimes trials of the Second World War. The system of penal procedure adopted in the Geneva Conventions of 1949 is based on three essential obligations laid upon each contracting party: to enact special legislation; to search for persons alleged to have committed breaches of the Conventions; and to bring such persons before its own courts or, if the contracting party prefers, to hand them over for trial to one of the other contracting parties concerned.[2]

The penal provisions of the Geneva Conventions constitute an important step forward in the development of international penal law, by formally defining "war crimes" as international crimes.[3] They provide a list of "grave breaches" of humanitarian law including the following acts against protected persons (prisoners of war, the wounded, sick, shipwrecked, medical or religious personnel, refugees and stateless persons, and the civilian population) and objects:

> Willful killing, torture, or inhuman treatment, including biological experiments, willfully causing great suffering or serious injury to body or health;
> Extensive destruction and appropriation of property, not justified by military necessity and carried out unlawfully and wantonly;
> Compelling a prisoner of war to serve in the forces of the hostile power, or willfully depriving him of the rights of fair and regular trial prescribed in the Convention;
> Unlawful deportation or transfer or unlawful confinement of a protected person, compelling a protected person to serve in the forces of a hostile power, or willfully depriving a protected person of the rights of fair and regular trial prescribed by the Convention, taking of hostages.

Protocol I additional to the Geneva Conventions of 1949, adopted in 1977 and entered into force in 1978, provides a supplementary list of grave breaches that are considered war crimes, thus granting further protection to civilians and other protected persons.[4] These additions include launching an indiscriminate attack affecting the civilian population or civilian objects in the knowledge that such attack will cause excessive loss of life, injury to civilians, or damage to civilian objects; practices of apartheid and other inhuman and degrading practices involving outrages upon personal dignity, based on racial discrimination; and the infliction of heavy damage on clearly recognized historic monuments, works of art, or places of worship which constitute the cultural or spiritual heritage of peoples, when these targets are not located in the immediate proximity of military objectives.

International Criminal Liability for War Crimes

Article III of the Hague Convention of 1907 prescribes that "A belligerent party which violates the provisions of the said regulations shall, if the case demands, be liable to pay compensation." The article goes on to confirm a longtime principle of international law by stating that a belligerent "shall be responsible for all acts committed by persons forming part of its armed forces." The incorporation of the principle of responsibility into the Hague treaty was important because it formalized the idea that a state was accountable for all acts undertaken by its military. From the international perspective, the responsibility established by Article III is civil, not penal in character. Violations of Article III are to be satisfied by the payment of money. There is no provision regarding a trial and punishment of the officers and men responsible for the actual commission of the violations of the Hague regulations.

As Telford Taylor has observed, the action taken by Germany following its defeat in the First World War illustrates the view that neither individuals nor states could incur a criminal liability under international treaty (conventional) law. When the Allies insisted that nearly 900 Germans accused of war crimes, including military and political leaders, be surrendered to them for trial on war crimes charges, the Germans replied that jurisdiction over so-called war crimes was vested in the national courts of the accused state. In the end, they were allowed to try their own "war criminals." From the Allied standpoint, the trials in 1921 and 1922 were a failure. Only a small number of the accused were tried, and of these nearly all were found not guilty or allowed to escape their minimal prison sentences.[5]

However, the argument that all members of armed forces were released from personal international liability and punishment did not appear defensible even before the Second World War. It is widely accepted by concerned observers that criminal responsibility did exist under customary international law for violations of that law. In addition, even under pre-1945 rules of law, offending members of an occupant's armed forces would seem to have been accountable on a personal basis to the state that had been wronged. This is shown by the provisions of many military manuals which specified that commanders ordering acts in violation of international law could be punished by the wronged belligerent if they fell into his hands.

During World War II, a large number of violations of customary and conventional law were committed along with many acts not specifically prohibited in treaty law but objectionable on humane grounds. The rising protest in Allied countries against the practice of genocide in Axis-occupied territories indicated long before the end of the war that punishment for acts committed in pursuit of genocide and other "conventional" war crimes would be demanded at the conclusion of hostilities. On January 13, 1942, an "Inter Allied Conference on the Punishment of War Crimes" adopted the "Declaration of St. James," a document expressly stating that the signatory powers would "place among their principal war aims the punishment through channels of organized justice, of those guilty of or responsible for these crimes." In 1943, the United Nations War Crimes Commission was established in London, to serve as a depository of proof concerning war crimes and to make plans for the trial of those accused.[6]

By 1945, various declarations made it clear that individual responsibility for war crimes was accepted by the Allied powers and that prosecution of accused persons would be instituted. Indeed, most of the important Germans and Japanese accused of war crimes were tried at Nuremberg and Tokyo before courts created "under international authority, and quite outside the usual channels of military justice." In addition, some 1,600 German defendants "were tried before United States Army military commissions and military government courts" for crimes committed against American troops, or in Nazi concentration camps liberated by American forces. Over 250 death sentences were carried out. About an equal number of enemy offenders "were tried by British, French, and other military courts established by the countries that had been occupied by Germany." Further trials were held by the Soviet Union and China. Hundreds more offenders have been and still are being tried before West German and other national courts. These trials were primarily concerned with mistreatment either of prisoners of war or of civilian populations of occupied countries.[7]

By 1945, the International Military Tribunal was established by the "London Agreement" between the United States, the United Kingdom, France, and the Soviet Union. Its jurisdiction was defined by the "Charter of the International Military Tribunal," an annex to the agreement. Nineteen other states adhered to the agreement. The Nuremberg trials of the major German war criminals began in November 1945 and the tribunal gave its judgment in September 1946.

During that first trial, it was argued on behalf of the defendants that they were operating under the command of Hitler and therefore could not be held responsible for acts committed in response to his orders. However, the charter provided in Article 8: "The fact that the defendant acted pursuant to order of his government or of a superior shall not free him from responsibility." The tribunal pointed out:

> The provisions of this article are in conformity with the law of all nations. That a soldier was ordered to kill or torture in violation of the international law of war has never been recognized as a defense to such acts of brutality, though, as the Charter . . . provides, the order may be urged in mitigation of the punishment. The true test, which is found in varying degrees in the criminal law of most nations, is not the existence of the order, but whether moral choice was in fact possible.

The Nuremberg trials helped significantly to develop the principle that individuals may be held criminally responsible under international law, even though their behavior was legal under domestic law. Before Nuremberg, the laws of war had been enforced primarily against ordinary soldiers or officers of middle or low rank. At Nuremberg and Tokyo, however, nearly all the defendants were top military or civilian officials. Their punishment made it clear that the primary responsibility for war crimes rests on those who gave the orders.[8]

The problem of responsibility for war crimes, including genocide, has continued to engage the attention of both governments and legal experts. In a resolution adopted on December 13, 1946, the U.N. General Assembly, by unanimous vote, affirmed the principles of international law recognized in the Nuremberg Charter and Judgment. It also took note of the fact that similar principles had been adopted in 1945 in the Charter of the International Military Tribunal at Tokyo.[9] In 1950, the International Law Commission, pursuant to a request from the General Assembly, prepared a Draft Code of Offenses against the Peace and Security of Mankind, defined as crimes under international law for which individuals would be responsible. The commission formulated the following principles in a draft code.[10]

Principle I

Any person who commits an act which constitutes a crime under international law is responsible therefore and liable to punishment.

Principle II

The fact that internal law does not impose a penalty for an act which constitutes a crime under international law does not relieve the person who committed the act from responsibility under international law.

Principle III

The fact that a person who committed an act which constitutes a crime under international law acted as Head of State or responsible government official does not relieve him from responsibility under international law.

Principle IV
     The fact that a person acted pursuant to order of his Government or of a superior does not relieve him from responsibility under international law, provided a moral choice was in fact possible to him.

As noted, the question of individual responsibility had played an important part in the deliberations of the Diplomatic Conference at Geneva in 1949, and punishment of war crimes was embodied in the Geneva Conventions adopted that year. The signatory states undertook to enact any legislation necessary to provide effective penal sanctions for persons committing, or ordering to be committed, grave breaches of the Conventions and accepted the obligation to search for persons alleged to have committed, or to have ordered to be committed, such grave breaches. According to the Conventions, such persons, regardless of their nationality, must be brought before its own courts or may also be handed over for trial to another concerned state.[11]
     Central to humanitarian law is the duty it imposes on an army commander to take such appropriate measures as are within his power to control the troops under his command. The problem is defining how far this responsibility goes. Should the guilt for a crime be limited to he who commits it and he who orders it to be committed? At Nuremberg, the International Military Tribunal neglected an important aspect of criminality: the responsibility for an omission to act and to prevent war crimes. In the Tokyo Trial it was different. There, during the trial of General Yamashita, the tribunal decided that responsibility exists for failure to act. Furthermore, Article 86 of Protocol I additional to the Geneva Conventions of 1949 clearly provides that responsibility for omission exists.[12]
     Unfortunately, despite the above legislation, events since 1949 indicate that men and nations continue to ignore the rules enacted to limit the practice of warfare. In Vietnam, as elsewhere, although conflict had led to flagrant war crimes, alleged offenders have seldom been arraigned.

Dissemination and Teaching of Humanitarian Law: The Legal Obligation

Public awareness of a system of humanitarian law operative in wartime is a powerful tool and can perhaps in the long run do more to secure better treatment of the individual in time of armed conflict than judicial action. The teaching of humanitarian rules is, therefore, a necessity.
     In addition, concerned observers have noted that awareness of humanitarian law may reduce the demoralization of soldiers and lessen the destructive effect of war on the participants by fostering respect for human life and limiting injuries inflicted to those strictly necessary. Unless soldiers are trained to revere

human values, they may lose this respect permanently and inflict harm on the peacetime society. Indeed, as noted earlier in this study, recent research has demonstrated that participation in abusive violence has had long-term disruptive effects on Vietnam veterans' lives.[13]

The duty to give instruction in the rules of warfare has been incorporated in many international treaties.[14] The Hague Convention on Land Warfare of 1907 provided in Article I that "The Contracting Powers shall issue instructions to their armed land forces which shall be in conformity with the Regulations respecting the laws and customs of war on land, annexed to the present Convention."

In addition, there is an obligation on the contracting parties in the Geneva Conventions of 1949 to secure a wider dissemination of the text of the Conventions—in time of peace as in time of war—and to include the study thereof in their programs of military and, *if possible*, civil instruction, so that the principles may become known to the entire population. The Conventions also state that the instruction of military personnel should include the distribution of a complete collection of international legal texts.

Additional Protocol I strengthens the duty to disseminate the knowledge of fundamental principles of humanitarian law and provides for increased military as well as civilian instruction. In regard to the civilian population, the protocol goes further than the Geneva Conventions and deletes the words "if possible."

The Vietnam Generation and Individual Responsibility

Through history, people have remained largely insensitive to the violation of humanitarian law. Even at the end of the Second World War, the war crimes trials were unwilling to consider certain acts of the victors, including the mass bombings of Dresden, Tokyo, or Hiroshima and Nagasaki. Indeed, in that conflict, aerial bombardment and submarine warfare were practiced so extensively on both the Allied and Axis sides that charges surrounding this type of warfare were excluded from the trials.

Robert Jay Lifton commented as follows on moral issues raised by these acts of mass destruction:[15]

> I became impressed with the increasing gap we face between our technological capacity for perpetrating atrocities and our imaginative ability to confront their full actuality. . . . As Hiroshima took me to Auschwitz and Treblinka, however, I was struck mostly by the similarities and parallels in the overall psychology of atrocity. . . . With Hiroshima and Auschwitz now part of man's historical experience, it is dangerously naive to insist that our imaginative relationship to world-destruction can remain unchanged. . . . There is therefore a danger . . . for all of us . . . of being immobilized and totally unable or unwilling to participate in essential day-by-day struggles to counter atrocity.

Indeed, the moral and political questions raised by the nature of American involvement in the Vietnam War have taken their toll on the national psyche. After details of the My Lai massacre were revealed, enormous interest centered on the war crimes issue for several weeks. But the issues involved were soon forgotten by many Americans.

Today in the mid-1980s the Vietnam War stands as a disturbing image that can be neither fully confronted nor ignored. The conflict brought the question of individual responsibility before the conscience of an entire generation and became an important step in its personal development. As that generation continues to grapple with images of the war, the time has come to examine how it views responsibility for inhumane actions in battle.

Level of Awareness of Humanitarian Law

Conventions dealing with military conduct in wartime

To tap general awareness of the major issues in the area of humanitarian law in armed conflict we proceeded as follows: our respondents were asked to tell us something about their familiarity with some of the legal instruments and concepts in international law concerned with the treatment of combatants and noncombatants alike. We chose the Geneva Conventions of 1949 because they have been incorporated into the Uniform Code of Military Justice (UCMJ); the Nuremberg Principles because the Nuremberg Trials of 1945–46, a landmark in judicial history, have become part of the common political and moral culture of the Western world; and, finally, the Genocide Convention of 1948, because it affirms that genocide is a crime under international law. In each case, respondents were asked if they had "never heard of," had "heard of," or were "familiar with" the ruling.

Our findings (table 9.1) not surprisingly show that the Genocide Convention is the least known, indeed well over 60% of all veterans and nonveterans have never heard of it; and in table 9.2 we see that only 11% of the officers questioned report they are familiar with the ruling. The Nuremberg Principles (table 9.3) are slightly more familiar to veterans and nonveterans alike, with about 50% reporting that they have heard of these precepts. Among officers, the group in the veteran population who claim most knowledge of these principles, only 16% claim they are familiar with them (table 9.4). Thus, it would appear that real knowledge of the concepts behind the Nuremberg Principles and the Genocide Convention is very rare in this population.

The Geneva Conventions, on the other hand, are clearly more familiar to our veteran and nonveteran respondents (table 9.5). Only about 2% of the veterans and 9% of the nonveterans have never heard of them. Furthermore, almost 50% of the veterans and 27% of the nonveterans claim some familiarity with these rules. Officers (60%) are substantially more likely than enlisted men (47%) to report familiarity with these treaties (table 9.6).

However, when we asked our veteran respondents who said they were familiar with these codes to specify what they thought were the important ideas in the conventions, the response was generally vague or very limited. It appears that what they meant in stating "familiarity" was a general understanding that these rules involved constraints on the conduct of war. More specifically, the most relevant knowledge they carried with them about the impact of the conventions is that they offered them some protection in the event they fell into enemy hands. The above findings suggest that American soldiers were poorly prepared as regards their legal obligations in the war zone to civilians, enemy soldiers, and even enemy prisoners of war.

Americans civilians, too, appear generally poorly informed about the treaties dealing with the conduct of war. As table 9.7 demonstrates, only a minority (43%) of even the antiwar activists report that they are familiar with the Geneva Conventions, and the proportion of those supporting the war who claim familiarity with the Geneva Conventions is slightly more than one-third of this population. The greatest difference between the activists and the prowar nonveterans is in familiarity with the Nuremberg Principles. The magnitude of the difference reflects the extent to which the issues raised at Nuremberg became an important factor in the antiwar movement.

Military training and the Vietnam experience

It has often been stated that two events weaken the level of awareness of soldiers to international humanitarian law. One is military training and the other is the adjustment to the realities of warfare, as they emerge in actual combat.

During basic training, the recruit is encouraged to reject his preexisting civilian identity, values, and expectations. He must accept a new institutional persona and incorporate the value system of the military organization. He must learn to obey orders, accept a submissive role, and develop respect for superiors and for the army. Peter G. Bourne has observed:

> Military training and particularly Basic Training embody the concrete realization of attitudes and activities that are diametrically opposed to the practice and spirit of democracy. Obedience, the keystone of military order, is incompatible with the candid expression of opinion and the right to question and critically examine courses of action. . . . Obedience instilled in Basic Training leads effectively to dependence with a reliance upon and acceptance of the will of others. Responsibility for one's own welfare and for the consequences of one's acts is relinquished and remains habitually in the hands of superiors.[16]

Within the basic training framework, the time devoted to learning the laws of warfare is a matter of some debate. Peter Karsten has noted that "prior to My

Lai, United States ground forces received only one hour of training in the laws of warfare before being sent into combat, and the Air Force received no instruction whatsoever.''[17]

In contrast, General James Woolnough, who was responsible for the army's school system in the late 1960s, felt that this minimal allocation was overgenerous since the time devoted to such training "has to be taken from something else" and is "not profitably spent" inasmuch as "you cannot teach judgment. There is no black-and-white rule you can lay down."[18]

In the narrative material, a substantial number of our respondents stressed that basic training shapes the soldier's response to combat. Vietnam veterans responded in many different ways to military training. A majority, notably marines, had a positive response to basic training. One marine respondent had the following to say:

> In basic training I felt wonderful. I felt physically perfect, mentally alert. And well naturally there was a certain amount of brainwashing that goes through basic. They would constantly pound it into you that you have to kill to survive. You know, you are going to Vietnam and you are going to fight a war and all you are going to do is kill, kill, kill, kill.

A substantial minority argued that the military destroyed their individuality. They pointed out that when you throw a person into a totally alien environment, tell him that he is a soldier, teach him to hate, and hand him a gun, he will probably shoot at anything. An army man reported:

> They wanted you to be more or less like robots. You reacted on command only. You did not use any of your logic or reasoning. You had to do what they told you. It was very hard because a lot of these things went against our grain. I was very naive at that time and also very scared. They are so authoritative. I tried to do everything the best way they wanted.

A navy man remarked:

> I was completely stripped of my identity and made to look like a thousand other fellows. Remodeled into a regimented military person. They have a really unique way of doing it. At first, they kick the shit out of you and attack you. When you have turned into a military robot they pat you on the back.

When the soldier arrives on the battlefield, he undergoes brutalizing experiences. He is thrown into an environment where killing and the struggle for survival are a daily fact of life. Students of warfare contend that the more frightening the environment, the more the soldier is willing to submerge his civilian identity in the military organization. Even if he has knowledge of international humanitarian law, he may abandon previous values and beliefs for the sake of survival. However, in the battlefield and after his return to civilian society, his awareness of the principles of humanity may shield him against a total deterioration of his own personality.[19]

Instruction in international rules of conduct in wartime

When querying veterans about the instruction in humanitarian law they received, we asked them the following: 1) Were you given a card stating the rules about what you cannot do to people in war? 2) Did you receive written material explaining what was on the card? and 3) Did you attend a lecture on the rules?

The most common form of instruction reported by these veterans was receiving a card stating the rules (83%). Only about 10% reported receiving an explanation of the card through written materials, and barely 3% of the veterans reported receiving lectures on the rules. Furthermore, it was primarily the officers and to a lesser extent the noncommissioned officers who reported receiving any degree of instruction about the rules of warfare.

Given the relatively low rate of response to the last two questions, we created a simple measure of whether or not soldiers received *any* instruction in the rules of warfare. Among all veterans in the total sample, slightly more than two-thirds reported having received any training in the rules of conduct in military operations. Vietnam veterans are the most likely to indicate that they were exposed to some type of instruction. Table 9.8 shows that there is a small difference in education received between Vietnam veterans and Vietnam era veterans. However, tables 9.9 and 9.10 indicate larger differences in terms of branch of service in which respondents served and whether or not the subjects were officers or enlisted men.

As noted, commissioned officers were most likely to receive some type of instruction in the rules of war (91%); and noncommissioned officers were second in receiving such instruction (81%). It is noteworthy, however, that among enlisted men only 64% reported receiving any training at all. Overall, those most actively engaged on the battlefield, the army (76%) and especially the marines (83%), were significantly more likely to report having received some training in how to conduct themselves in war.

In general, in the narrative material, our respondents did not talk much about the type of instruction they received about the rules of conduct during wartime. Those who did discuss such training presented three response patterns: a minority insisted that they had received no instruction of this kind; the majority indicated that they had received some training but only on what their legal rights would be if they were captured as prisoners of war by enemy forces; and a very small number of Vietnam veterans mentioned that they had received instructions in how to treat the civilian population as well as enemy POWs.

Knowledge of the rules of conduct in wartime

The question that arises from the above discussion is how aware Vietnam veterans thought they had become about how to treat the people they would encounter in the war zone. In this context we asked our respondents five questions:

1. How aware would you say this/these instruction(s) made you about how you are supposed to treat the enemy during wartime?

2. How aware would you say this/these instruction(s) made you about how you are supposed to treat civilians during wartime?

3. How aware would you say this/these instruction(s) made you about how you are supposed to treat the sick and wounded during wartime?

4. How aware would you say this/these instruction(s) made you about how you are supposed to treat enemy prisoners of war?

5. How aware would you say this/these instruction(s) made you about how to act if you were a prisoner of war?

Veterans could respond that the instruction made them thoroughly aware, somewhat aware, or not really aware of the rules at all. As table 9.11 shows, Vietnam veterans, because of their military training, report being slightly more aware of how to treat civilians and the enemy than Vietnam era veterans. However, the most impressive finding in the table is the clarity with which everybody sees their rights as POWs. Fully 70% of the veterans report they were thoroughly aware of how to act if they were taken prisoner. Yet only 31% to 39% of Vietnam veterans admit a thorough awareness of how to treat Vietnamese civilians, the sick and wounded, or enemy soldiers and enemy POWs they might encounter.

In our analysis, we have combined the four items that deal with the treatment of the Vietnamese into a single measure—the awareness American soldiers had of their legal responsibilities.[20] As table 9.12 shows, the evidence indicates that, except for officers, a thorough awareness of how to behave in the battlefield was low. Among enlisted men, who compose more than 60% of the veteran sample, only 27% report that they were thoroughly aware of the rules governing their conduct, while 33% say they were unaware of how they were meant to act.

The only other significant difference in level of awareness of appropriate conduct in war is that, as with degree of instruction received, marines, and to a slightly lesser extent the soldiers who served in the army, are significantly more aware of how to behave in a war zone than those who went into the navy or air force (table 9.13). The difference between the marines and navy/air force veterans is most notable in the extremes. Marines are almost half as likely to report thorough ignorance of how to behave and by 39% to 24% to say they were thoroughly aware of the rules of conduct in wartime. However, as table 9.11 makes clear, the most dramatic finding in this area is how strongly veterans feel their instruction was weighted toward increasing awareness of *their* rights compared to those of anyone else in the battle zone.

As table 9.14 indicates, among nonveterans overall awareness of how to treat the enemy (36%), civilians (36%), the sick and wounded (38%), and POWs (44%) is relatively low. Those involved in antiwar activism, however, claim considerably more knowledge of these issues. Indeed, we find a stepwise impact of activism on self-reported knowledge of the rules of conduct. Among the high activists, more than 60% report that they were informed about treatment of the enemy, civilians, and the sick and wounded; comparable levels of awareness among the moderate activists are above 40%, while only about 30% of low activists claim a similar awareness. As in the case of veterans (see table 9.11), reported knowledge of the rules of conduct governing the treatment of POWs is greater among nonveterans than for any of the other items, reaching a high of 74% of the high activists and a low of 36% in the low-activist group. In table 9.15, we see that prowar nonveterans express a comparable level of awareness to that of their low-activist peers.

We next explored how nonveterans acquired their knowledge about the conduct of war. In table 9.16, we see that the mass media (36%) and general reading (24%) are the two most common sources of this information. There are, however, some important differences between the nonveterans that deserve attention. The educational system, with the exception of the high activists (41%), appears to have contributed relatively little to the knowledge acquired by our nonveteran respondents. Indeed, the discrepancy between the reports of the high activists and the rest of the sample raises the question of whether the contribution of the educational system to the knowledge of the activists came through the formal structure of the school system. It is, of course, possible that the activists were more sensitive to the material made available, but we suspect that the difference may well be accounted for by the extracurricular opportunities schools provide. Interestingly, friends seem to have offered a minimal source of information for all groups including the high activists (24%). Indeed, given the evidence in table 9.16 that the high activists made extensive use of the media (63%) and general reading (46%), the proportion who identify friends as sources of information is remarkably low. Among the moderate activists, we find the mass media (51%) and general reading (37%) are the primary sources of information; the findings indicate that the low activists were essentially dependent on the mass media for what information they possess. The sources of information that the war's supporters drew on for knowledge of the rules of conduct in warfare, as shown in table 9.17, are essentially the same as those used by the low activists.

Reasons Behind the Occurrence of Unlawful Acts

The actual operation of international humanitarian law is shaped by the interaction between two principles: the principle of military necessity,[21] which justifies the use of any amount of force deemed necessary for the purpose of winning the war; and the dictates of humanity, which state that certain kinds and degrees of violence are not permissible and that a degree of fairness toward civilians and a mutual respect between opposing forces must be maintained. Interaction between these principles is skewed by the difficulty of defining "military necessity" in a combat situation. The following example illustrates this problem.

The United States Army Field Manual, the Law of Land Warfare, 1956, provides that:

> Under the Constitution of the United States, treaties constitute part of the "Supreme Law of the Land." . . . In consequence, treaties relating to the law of war have a force equal to that of laws enacted by the Congress. Their provisions must be observed by both military and civilian personnel. . . . The unwritten or customary law of war is binding upon all nations. It will be strictly observed by United States forces. . . . The customary law of war is part of the law of the United States and, insofar as it is not inconsistent with any treaty to which this country is a party or with a controlling executive or legislative act, is binding upon the United States, citizens of the United States, and other persons serving this country.[22]

The purpose of the Field Manual is to provide authoritative guidance to military personnel on the law applicable to the conduct of warfare on land. The manual defines war crimes as every violation of the law of war, and deals with responsibility for illegal acts and punishment of war crimes.

However, the statement of the rule of military necessity is unclear and weakens the general validity of the manual:

> The law of war places limits on the exercise of a belligerent's power . . . and requires that belligerents refrain from employing any kind or degree of violence which is not actually necessary for military purposes and that they conduct hostilities with regard for the principles of humanity and chivalry. The prohibitory effect of the law of war is not minimized by "military necessity," which has been defined as that principle which justifies those measures not forbidden by international law which are indispensable for securing the complete submission of the enemy as soon as possible. Military necessity has been generally rejected as a defense for acts forbidden by the customary and conventional laws of war inasmuch as the latter have been developed and framed with consideration for the concept of military necessity.[23]

The Rules of Engagement Applicable to United States Forces in Vietnam were not prohibitions but restrictions that in no case prevented the commander from using a particular munition, for example napalm, if he judged it necessary for the accomplishment of his mission, or if not using it would jeopardize the success of the operation. For example, the rules state:

> Nothing shall infringe on the inherent right of a commander to exercise self-

defense. The commander may take immediate action against an attacking force with all means available; however, every possible safeguard short of endangering life will be used to avoid non-combatant casualties and the destruction of private property. Firepower will be brought to bear on enemy in populated areas only to the extent necessary to accomplish an assigned mission.[24]

An interesting account of the operation of the rules was written by two staff members of the United States Senate Foreign Relations Committee. The committee published a censured version of their report in 1971.[25] According to that document:

> Given the apparent stringency of these rules of engagement, it is difficult to see how roads with civilian traffic, villages and groups of civilians could have been bombed, rocketed, or napalmed. . . . Nevertheless there are plenty of instances known to American civilian employees in which targets have been bombed.[26]

The report then indicates several reasons for this discrepancy, which may be summarized as follows:

(i) mistakes do happen (especially when Forward Air Controllers begin flying missions as soon as they arrive in Laos);

(ii) some pilots have deliberately violated the rules of engagement expending ordnance against unauthorized targets (the town of Khang Khay being a notable example);

(iii) the effort to provide in the rules of engagement for every contingency appears to create obvious loopholes;

(iv) the system itself is so complicated that it cannot possibly be foolproof.

Explanations of Abuses in Vietnam by the Vietnam Generation

If our respondents show little awareness of the rules of war, how then do they explain what they perceive to be abuses by American soldiers? We asked our sample to determine which of the seven explanations below they thought most often accounted for the violations of the rules of war in Vietnam.

1. The actions were a result of an order by someone in power.

2. It happened because everyone knew they did not have to worry about punishment.

3. Some soldiers deliberately violated the rules of war and attacked unauthorized targets on their own.

4. Some soldiers are not fully aware of the rules of war.

5. The U.S. rules are not laws but guidelines which can be ignored if necessary for military reasons.

6. Mistakes do happen.

7. There's an evil side to war.

As table 9.18 shows, Vietnam veterans (40%), Vietnam era veterans (40%), and nonveterans (39%) agree that the principal explanation for abuses that occurred is adherence to "orders from above." "Lack of punishment" is the second most common explanation for violations of the rules of war in Vietnam given by Vietnam veterans (17%). Vietnam era veterans (24%) and nonveterans (21%) believe that the "evil side of war" is the second leading cause of abuses; and Vietnam veterans rank the "evil side of war" (15%) as the third most important explanation for violations during the war. None of the other explanations is selected by more than 7 or 8 percent of the Vietnam veteran sample, and only military necessity (11%) is ranked higher by the era veterans and the nonveterans. Thus, the major difference between Vietnam veterans and their peers is that the former emphasize the "lack of punishment" as a leading factor in explaining the causes of violations of the rules of war. It is noteworthy that all major subgroups in the study seem to emphasize institutional features of the military or structural characteristics of warfare rather than individual responsibility as the source of abuses during wartime.

Vietnam Veterans

Table 9.19 documents dramatic differences in opinion between Vietnam veterans who served in different branches of the military services. Army veterans (42%) and those who served in the navy or air force (44%) emphasize that "orders from above" is the major cause of the abuses that occurred in Vietnam. In this regard, an army artillery man had the following to say:

> I feel that if a man is told what to do he has to do it. He probably would get court-martialed or something else for not carrying out the order. So I would say someone always leads the parade and he is always the last one caught.

Marines (36%), on the other hand, cite the "evil side of war" as the primary cause of military misconduct. Indeed, only 21% of the marines accept the "orders from above" explanation. Marines who emphasized the "evil side of war" often argue that when the enemy fights dirty you cannot act civilized in return. People under pressure, they note, lose control. A marine captain who witnessed abusive violence reported:

> Well, the guidelines of the Geneva Conventions, like the Nuremberg Principles, were really fine until bullets are coming at you from all sorts of different

directions. And then the attitude of self preservation has got to take over. . . . I don't think you can expect anybody who sees his best friend get killed and who captured the guy who just did it to take him behind the lines and put him in a prison camp. They'd blow his head off, right there on the spot, and I would also. In other words, you became judge, jury, and executioner all in one.

Only army veterans (20%) feel that the "lack of punishment" theme is important. An army man commented:

You are 15,000 miles away from home. You are out in the field, you see a village. You say, "Okay, let us go in and kill everybody and shoot the place up." Who is going to know but you? You are not going to get punished.

Marines (9%) and navy/air force veterans (10%) downgrade the significance of punishment as an issue. It is noteworthy, however, that the marines (9%) are almost twice as likely to see abuses stemming from "deliberate acts" of soldiers than veterans from other branches (5%); and they are also the most likely to select "ignorance of the rules" (12%) as a significant factor. One marine explained:

We get our orders. Now they say to us, there are VC in that village. We got to destroy the village and we were under orders to do that. You may not like it, but if you turn against it, they could file charges. Some soldiers are not fully aware of the rules of the war, they do not tell you anything. They just tell you your job is this. I am the commander in chief and I say do it, if not, you will be court martialed.

As might be expected, rank plays an important part in respondents' perceptions of the causes of misconduct in Vietnam (table 9.20). Enlisted men (47%) and noncommissioned officers (34%) assert that "orders from above" was the most important factor in explaining abuses. An army sergeant who participated in abusive violence commented:

Look at Calley. He is the one in jail, but it was higher-ups. But they all claim it was a mistake on his part. It is a good way to cover up. I mean the man did what he was told. Now he is the scapegoat.

Among officers, the explanation "orders from above" ranks third (19%). This group emphasizes "mistakes" (26%) and the "evil side of war" (23%) as the most important factors in violations of the rules of war. Officers (17%) also emphasize "deliberate acts" as significant in explaining misconduct in war. Their tendency to blame the combat soldiers for acts violating the rules of war in Vietnam is exemplified by a marine captain who observed:

> I think that in the real world, the field soldiers are the ones that actually commit the acts. Any order comes out from a long chain of command and is subject to interpretations and, along the line, eager beavers make changes—modifications or their own interpretations to those rules. Some soldiers, in the spirit of what they feel is right, that they say is for the military good, . . . modify the guidelines.

Finally, none of the officers queried accepted the "lack of punishment" theme as relevant to military abuses during the Vietnam War. Enlisted men rank the issue of "lack of punishment" (17%) and the "evil side of war" (18%) as two major explanations for misconduct. The noncommissioned officers (19%) share the enlisted men's view of the importance of "lack of punishment," but do not agree that the "evil side of war" (8%) is a useful concept in understanding what happens in war. Rather, they rank "military necessity" (12%) and "ignorance of the rules" (11%) as the third and fourth major arguments. A marine sergeant who witnessed abusive violence explained the "military necessity" approach as follows:

> I feel that any unlawful acts of war that happened on the part of the Americans over there were a result of a reaction under stress in order to survive . . . it could have been a lieutenant, or a sergeant like myself, who made a decision that something had to be done right there at the spot and the legality of it did not enter into the picture. It was just "damn it, let's do it." Get it over with because it has to be done. More of a survival type reaction than anything else.

In short, the most important difference between the officers and other Vietnam veterans is that enlisted men and the NCOs emphasize the institutional explanations for the violations of military rules while the officers focus on volitional misconduct and personal shortcomings of the men under their command. Officers also stress the deus ex machina explanation for "the evil side of war." Thus, they stand as the first group in our study to point the finger of responsibility at individuals rather than the system.

Degree of combat experience seems to create some interesting differences of opinion as to why the rules of conduct are violated. As table 9.21 demonstrates, heavy-combat veterans (7%) do not accept the "evil side of war" explanation for abuses that occur. Rather it is the low-combat veterans who stress this argument. Veterans in all three combat categories agree that "orders from above" ranks as the most important explanation for violations of these rules. However, the low- (47%) and high- (42%) combat veterans emphasize this issue more strongly than those who saw moderate combat (33%). The moderate-combat veterans (27%) are the most likely to believe that "lack of punishment" is a major factor in the abuses that occurred in Vietnam, compared to the low- (12%) and high- (11%) combat veterans. Finally, it should be noted that only the high-combat veterans

(15%) view "military necessity" as a significant factor in assessing the behavior of United States troops in Vietnam.

With table 9.22, we turn to the issue of how men who witnessed and participated in abusive violence explain misconduct in the war. Again, "orders from above" is the most commonly presented explanation for military violations of the rules of war. As might be expected, however, those not exposed to abusive violence follow the Vietnam veteran pattern of emphasizing both "lack of punishment" (18%) and the "evil side of war" (17%) as the second ranking reasons for violations. Among witnesses to abusive violence, the "deliberate" theme stands as the second most important factor in explaining the roots of abuses in Vietnam.

This latter group argued that certain units went out and engaged in abusive acts because they were "into violence" or "just plain mean." An army infantry-man who witnessed abusive violence against civilians pointed out:

> It depends upon who the individual is . . . who's giving you instructions. . . . They might have their own selfish reasons for not giving you the full effect or value of the law or rules. Some people, they might just be gungho. They might just dig war and just dig killing people.

Participants, on the other hand, strongly support the thesis that it is "lack of punishment" (24%) that explains why soldiers violate the rules of conduct. A marine observed:

> I feel an order could come down and no matter what the order was, they knew they would not have to worry about being punished. Unfortunately there were some people there like myself who got to the point where they got a kick out of it at times. We did not have to answer for our actions.

The third factor in the estimation of the witnessed group is "lack of punishment" (12%), while the participants (14%) select the "evil side of war" argument.

Nonveterans

Among nonveterans, as shown in table 9.23, there is little diversity in the ranking of explanations for military violations of the rules of warfare. But while all three groups place "orders from above" first, the major difference to be found among nonveteran respondents is the relatively low proportion of the high activists (27%) who select this explanation compared to the moderate (47%) and low (40%) activists. The White House was often blamed for illegal acts. One high activist argued:

The overriding factor in military life is that you obey orders. And I think, for instance, in the obvious case of My Lai, it's pretty clear that there were orders or indications coming down from farther up as to what should be done. In the case of the hospitals, in the December bombing—that order obviously came from the White House. Not to hit the hospital but to undertake the carpet bombing—it's an anticivilian tactic.

The high activists are almost equally likely to select the "evil side of war" as the central explanation behind military violations; while the moderate activists (30%) rank this explanation a clear second. Since all three groups viewed the American involvement in the war as unjust, it is not surprising that they saw the situation as one where normal restraints would crumble. One activist expressed this view as follows:

Once people start realizing that the main reason they're there doesn't make any sense, then all the other things, all rules and regulations, well, they can all be broken too. Since we're not there for any solid reason—nothing else makes any sense either.

High activists (17%) also emphasized the "military necessity" argument as an important factor while 13% stressed the role of "lack of punishment." Ten percent of low and 11% of moderate activists see "military necessity" as relevant to understanding the patterns of violations by United States military forces in Vietnam.

As table 9.24 shows, the rank order of explanations for abuses among the prowar group is virtually identical with that of high activists, i.e., "the evil side of war" (28%) is the most often selected explanation, followed by "orders from above" (20%) and "military necessity" (16%). This finding is interesting because it suggests that ideological opponents share a common view of why abuses occurred in Vietnam. Again, we see an almost exclusive emphasis on institutional and structural characteristics as the prime motivating factors.

The most remarkable finding regarding perceived motivations for abuse is the extraordinarily small proportion of the generation who imagine that individual soldiers have any control over their behavior. The exceptions to that rule come from men faced with command responsibility and those acquainted directly with abuses. But even here, institutional explanations predominate.

Accountability for Violations of Rules of Conduct in War

We now turn to the question of who should be held responsible or accountable for the violations of the rules of military conduct that occurred in Vietnam. Our respondents were asked to indicate whether they thought political leaders, senior officers, officers directly in command, or the individual soldier in the field should be prosecuted for the acts deemed unlawful. As table 9.25 shows, there is broad agreement here; more than 60% of the Vietnam veterans, era veterans, and nonveterans agree that political leaders should be prosecuted. There is also reasonable consensus that senior officers should be held accountable, with Vietnam veterans (67%) least likely and nonveterans (79%) most likely to support prosecution of this group. Agreement, however, begins to break down around the issue of the prosecution of officers with field commands. Although a healthy majority of Vietnam veterans (58%) agree to the prosecution of these officers, this number is substantially less than the proportions of era veterans (70%) and nonveterans (74%) favoring the prosecution of leaders in the field. Conversely, all three groups are significantly less inclined to extend prosecution for violations to the level of the individual soldier. Nonveterans (40%) are most inclined and Vietnam veterans (28%) least likely to support prosecution of this group, with era veterans (35%) falling between the two. Thus, we see a clear reluctance among respondents to favor punishment of those at the bottom of the chain of command.

Vietnam Veterans

In the narrative material, Vietnam veterans were most likely to favor the prosecution of responsible political leaders and senior officers for acts deemed unlawful. In this regard, a veteran who served in the navy reported:

> Lt. Calley, I think he got a very raw deal. I think they sold him out. I think it is a common consensus of opinion that the war was dirty. It was fought dirty. We were the big bad guy in the end. But what a lot of people do not realize, it was our big bad politicians and our generals and our admirals or whatever. They were the ones who made the rules. You disobey a direct order in time of war, and you were subject to being shot or however they decided to do you in. I think the all-American male got the shaft.

To a lesser degree it was felt that officers directly in charge of an operation shared some of the responsibility for its outcome. The perceived collusion of officers in certain practices is demonstrated by an army infantryman who witnessed abusive violence:

> Whenever we were out in the field we always had Vietnamese with us. And so to speak, the backs of our officers would be turned if they wanted information. They would not take the responsibility of torturing someone, or beating someone; that would be given to the Vietnamese to do and they would just sort of wash their hands of it and let someone else do it. But they were responsible.

Again, there was consensus that, as one respondent put it, "The enlisted man, who is doing the best he can, should not be punished.''

Nonveterans

Activism, as shown in table 9.26, alters the picture described above in two ways. Among the high activists, support for prosecution ranges from 83% for political leaders to 90% for senior military officers and 95% for field officers. Among the moderate activists, we see the same general pattern, with the proportion favoring prosection for political leaders and officers in the 80% range. Among the low activists, only 61% favor prosecuting political leaders while about 70% favor prosecuting officers. Thus, in all three groups there is a tendency to favor prosecution for military officers regardless of rank over political leaders. However, there is a major difference, as table 9.26 demonstrates, between the perspective of the high activists and that of both the moderate and low activists on whether or not individual soldiers should be prosecuted for their misconduct in military operations. Only a minority of the low (35%) and moderate (42%) activists are prepared to prosecute those at the bottom of the chain of command. Yet those most active in the antiwar movement are unwilling by a substantial 66% majority to allow individual soldiers to escape prosecution.

The view of individual responsibility held by the high activists puts them in dramatic contrast with their Vietnam veteran peers, only 28% of whom believe enlisted men should be held legally responsible for their behavior. The almost 40% difference between these two groups on the issue of prosecution of individual soldiers suggests that the sympathy the activists generally exhibit for the plight of Vietnam veterans does not extend to those who were actively engaged in violations of the rules of military conduct in Vietnam.

Respondents who supported the war offer two distinctive responses to the question of prosecution. As tables 9.26 and 9.27 demonstrate, they are more likely than the low activists to accept the idea of prosecuting the individual soldier (45%). However, they are the least supportive of prosecuting political leaders (53%) of all three subgroups in table 9.27. Examining their response pattern, we find them singling out the officers as having the primary responsibility for abuses. For this group, only a bare majority indicate that they are willing to hold political leaders responsible for misconduct in the field; i.e., they tend to differentiate between the war's legitimacy and the means by which the war was fought. This position, we suspect, leads them to be less tolerant than either veterans or the low activist group of misconduct by soldiers.

Individual Responsibility and the American Forces in Vietnam

The provisions of the United States Army Field Manual of 1956 describe the extent to which American soldiers are held criminally accountable for compliance with the laws of war. Violations of these rulings usually constitute violations of the Uniform Code of Military Justice and as such are subject to prosecution under that code. Commanding officers of United States troops must insure that war crimes committed by members of their forces against enemy personnel are promptly and adequately punished.

In regard to "Superior Orders" the manual contains the following provisions:

Defense of Superior Orders

a. The fact that the law of war has been violated pursuant to an order of a superior authority, whether military or civil, does not deprive the act in question of its character of a war crime, nor does it constitute a defense in the trial of an accused individual, unless he did not know and could not reasonably have been expected to know that the act ordered was unlawful. In all cases where the order is held not to constitute a defense to an allegation of war crime, the fact that the individual was acting pursuant to orders may be considered in mitigation of punishment.

b. In considering the question whether a superior order constitutes a valid defense, the court shall take into consideration the fact that obedience to lawful military orders is the duty of every member of the armed forces; that the latter cannot be expected, in conditions of war discipline, to weigh scrupulously the legal merits of the orders received; that certain rules of warfare may be controversial; or that an act otherwise amounting to a war crime may be done in obedience to orders conceived as a measure of reprisal. At the same time it must be borne in mind that members of the armed forces are bound to obey only lawful orders (e.g., UCMJ, Art. 92).[27]

The manual also explicitly provides that a military commander not only is responsible for criminal acts committed in pursuance of his orders, but "is also responsible if he has actual knowledge, or should have knowledge . . . that troops or other persons subject to his control are about to commit or have committed a war crime and he fails to take the necessary and reasonable steps to insure compliance with the law of war or to punish violations thereof."[28]

The manual also provides that the fact that domestic law does not impose a penalty for an act that constitutes a crime under international law does not relieve the person who committed the act from responsibility under international law.

Despite these provisions, American forces in Vietnam violated the rules of war. As noted earlier, the Rules of Engagement Applicable to United States Forces in Vietnam were not prohibitions but restrictions that in no case prevented the commander from using a particular munition, for example napalm, if it was judged necessary for the accomplishment of his mission, or if not using it would jeopardize a mission's success. Similarly, precautions such as warning the civilian population of impending attack were only obligatory where they could be carried out without jeopardizing the success of the operation.

The circumstances of the war in Vietnam often pushed men to the limit of endurance, as illustrated by what happened at My Lai. In brief, a company of American soldiers entered a Vietnamese village, found only civilians, old men, women, and children, and began to kill them, not stopping until they had murdered between four and five hundred people.[29]

It has been argued on behalf of these soldiers that they acted in the context of a cruel war which was in fact a war against the Vietnamese people as a whole. They had been encouraged to kill, it was said, without making careful distinctions, by their own officers and compelled to do so by their enemies, who fought among the civilian population.

As Seymour Hersh has noted, the orders of Captain Medina, the company commander, had in fact been unclear. The men who heard them could not agree afterward as to whether or not they had been told to "waste" the inhabitants of My Lai. Lieutenant Calley, who led the unit, gave more specific orders, commanding his men to kill civilians.[30] The army's judicial system singled him out for punishment, although he claimed that he was only following Medina's orders. The enlisted men who did what Calley commanded were never charged.[31]

Even under these circumstances, however, there is considerable proof that the soldiers at My Lai knew that this was an unjustified massacre. For while most of them joined in the killing, a few refused to fire their guns and others simply ran away.

The effectiveness of the law of war in combat situations depends, above all else, on holding those in command and in policy-making positions responsible for the behavior of the combat soldier on the field of battle. Uncontrolled troop behavior is nearly always indirectly authorized by commanding officers—if only in the sense of creating the impression that acts of abusive violence will not be punished. In discussing the responsiblility of the higher officers in Vietnam, Telford Taylor has concluded:

> Given the circumstances and purposes of the war . . . it should have been a matter of the highest priority to insure, by indoctrination and subsequent policing, that the troops should treat the Vietnamese as human beings with lives worth preserving . . . the Son My courts martial are shaping the question [of individual responsibility] for us, and they can not be fairly determined without full inquiry into the higher responsibilities. Little as the leaders of the Army seem to realize it, this is the only road to the Army's salvation, for its moral health will not be recovered until its leaders are willing to scrutinize their behavior by the same standards that their revered predecessors applied to Tomayuki Yamashita 25 years ago[32]

Individual responsibility for conduct in war

We turn now to the views of the Vietnam Generation on individual responsibility for the conduct in war and whether or not military necessity should take precedence in determining the choice of weapons and strategies. In an attempt to tap the influence of moral-ethical standards in wartime, we asked our respondents five specific questions.

1. If you do something that is a crime under international law, you are guilty and should be punished even if your country does not consider your act a crime.

2. No one should be punished by his government for refusing to carry out an order that seriously violates international rules of war.

3. In a war, only military necessity, not international rules of war, should determine the choice of strategies and weapons.

4. An officer whose men violate international rules of war is legally responsible if he could have known about it and did not try to stop them.

5. Let's say you violated a rule of war. Acting under orders is no excuse, if you had a chance to know about those international laws and had had an opportunity to disobey.

Four of these questions deal clearly with different aspects of individual culpability. Question three, on military necessity, basically involves decisions of men at higher levels of command. However, relatively junior officers and NCOs are often forced to make judgments in the field about whether to use certain strategies and available weapons in particular circumstances that clearly involve individual choices for which the actors assume responsibility. Finally, some weapons, such as explosive bullets, are used at the discretion of individual soldiers without resorting to the command structure for guidance. Thus, we have included issues revolving around question three in our study.

Our data show that 53% of the population reject and 36% accept item three, which states that "only military necessity should determine strategy and weapons in wartime." We also find support among 60% or more of the population for the idea (item one) that international law imposes obligations beyond those contained in national codes.

The concept that individuals are answerable to higher laws than those of the nation, and that acting under orders is no defense, under carefully defined conditions where the soldier is afforded the opportunity to exercise their right of refusal (item five), is accepted by 63% of the sample. Refusal to obey orders by appealing to a higher law (item two) also finds support from a large majority (71%) of the population. Finally, the idea that officers have a responsibility to prevent and to seek out the misconduct of their men (item four) is acceptable to 84% of the respondents.

As seen in table 9.28, Vietnam veterans (51%) are significantly less likely to support the concept of criminal liability for actions considered illegal under international law than either Vietnam era veterans (59%) or nonveterans (68%). In addition, Vietnam veterans (49%) are more likely than their peers (43% and

31%) to accept the thesis that military necessity dictates choice of strategy and weapons in war.

Table 9.29 underlines the different perspectives on the conduct of war among officers who served in Vietnam, compared to NCOs and enlisted men. The military-necessity argument is overwhelmingly rejected by officers (90%), but accepted by soldiers (50%) and NCOs (54%). Indeed, only 5% of the officers unequivocally adopt the military necessity stance. The difference between officers and their men regarding military necessity demonstrates, we think, the significance of some in-depth knowledge of the rules of war.

Table 9.30 looks at the questions from the vantage point of the antiwar activists and the supporters of the Vietnam War. Except for query two, which deals with punishment of individuals who refuse to carry out an order that seriously violates international law, there is a systematic pattern of disagreement between these two groups. The two areas of greatest contrast are on the military necessity question and item five, which challenges the "acting under orders" defense where the opportunity to disobey an illegal order was present. The antiwar activists (78%) overwhelmingly reject the military necessity argument, while only a bare majority of the prowar respondents reject this thesis (51%) and 37% accept it. A similar pattern is found among antiwar activists concerning item five, with 76% of that group arguing that the acting under orders defense is no excuse, while only 49% of the prowar respondents take a similar position. Much less dramatically, we find supporters of the war somewhat more likely to reject the responsibility of officers to seek out wrongdoing (14%) than antiwar activists (1%); and to protect soldiers from prosecution for conduct illegal solely under international law (21% vs. 11%).

It should be noted that most of the five questions include clauses containing conditions that our respondents generally did not believe were met in Vietnam. Thus, we find support for rejecting the illegal orders when disobedience is feasible, but our respondents' previous responses suggest that they generally do not believe the conditions for refusal of orders were present. Finally, although not the major theme, lack of punishment for violations is cited as an important reason for abuses, indicating that our respondents do not see much likelihood of prosecution.

In sum, the tables presented above seem to indicate that by and large this generation accepts the concepts of individual responsibility under international law and the primacy of international over national law, and by a modest margin rejects the idea that in war military necessity determines behavior.

Reactions to Violations of International Law

Resistance to Abuse among Vietnam Veterans Who Witnessed Abusive Violence

Although individual resistance to abuse in combat often isolates the soldier from his superiors or fellow units, such incidents do occur. We conclude this chapter by examining the Vietnam veterans who witnessed abusive violence and responded to our query about their reaction. We limit ourselves to the responses of those veterans who directly witnessed abusive violence, because although some of the participants in fact expressed qualms about their involvement, they were on the whole less likely to articulate the issue of resistance to abuses.

We asked those who witnessed abusive violence about their reactions to what they saw. Three primary responses were provided by this group regarding possible action. One group rejects the idea that they should have intervened; a second group discusses the difficulty of acting in such situations; and the third reports that they tried to step in and stop the violence to which they were being exposed.

Witnesses who took no action

Among those veterans who observed these acts but did nothing, 16% felt no compulsion to intervene. A veteran who served in the navy noted:

> Our unit picked up five Vietnamese civilians that were supposedly giving information to the Vietcong. We took them into the helicopter. First they talked to one old man and asked him a question and he kept shaking his head and they booted him right out of the door. They did this right down the line until all five were gone. I just stood there and watched.

Observers who felt powerless or immobilized

A second group of observers who took no action (26%) felt that they were powerless to intervene. There are two ways these veterans explain their behavior. One type of response focused on the likelihood that intervention would not help and the fear of retaliation from their own troops. An army captain described his response to abusive violence this way:

> I wanted to do something about it, but I felt helpless because I might get shot for saying something. Action would have been taken against me.

A second response suggests that some men felt that they should have acted, but somehow felt immobilized by what they had seen. One veteran explained this reaction as follows:

> We napalmed a village that did not need to be napalmed. We threw grenades in caves, instead of taking the Vietcong alive. We threw prisoners out of helicopters or drowned them in tubs of water. I could have stopped the people from doing it. I should have stopped it, but I did not.

Witnesses who took action against abusive violence

Finally we come to that small group (14%) who when faced with abusive violence took direct action to stop it. The narrative indicates why so few men attempted to intervene. Generally, these men found that their efforts at intervention were ignored and that the violence continued unabated. A helicopter pilot who was severely traumatized by the abusive violence he witnessed noted:

> A number of times I encountered situations where people were killed needlessly and I spoke out and got very angry and screamed and it did nothing. And I thought that I was a victim of some invisible man somewhere who made these decisions.

Conclusion: The Basis of the Acceptance of Individual Responsibility

In the narrative, a clear distinction is consistently made between the responsibility of soldiers on the one side and officers and political leaders on the other.[33] Our respondents generally agreed that the latter group have clear obligations and are legally liable. At the same time, it was noted that it is unlikely that political leaders will ever be prosecuted for unlawful acts through national channels, since it cannot be expected that a national judge will pass sentences for illegal action committed by responsible authorities. The initiation of disciplinary or penal action against military commanders was considered equally doubtful.

A majority of those respondents who discussed the responsibility of combat soldiers noted that judgments and decisions are extremely difficult for soldiers in the field. Moreover, the conditions of war supply an abundance of excuses for misconduct: survival, fear, coercion, ignorance, shell shock. Respondents tend to accept the defenses commonly offered for specific violations of the rules of war by combat soldiers: military necessity, the disciplinary system of the army and the obedience it requires, the loss of individuality implicit in warfare, the soldier's lack of freedom of choice, and, above all, the intensity and stress of battle. Our sample presents the following main arguments surrounding the issue of individual responsibility.

Adherence to Superior Orders

As noted earlier, while it is the soldier's duty to obey lawful orders, he may—and indeed must, under certain circumstances—disobey unlawful orders. Realistic appraisals by respondents throughout the sample, veterans as well as nonveterans, recognized that a soldier is often in no position to establish the legality or illegality of an order, and that the very nature of military service requires prompt obedience. It was pointed out that many soldiers stress their duty to follow orders and argue that when they take the army oath, they surrender individual responsibility for what they do. Indeed, army training encourages this view, even though soldiers are also informed that they must refuse "unlawful orders."[34]

Two specific defenses for violations of the rules of war by combat soldiers were presented: the claim of ignorance and the claim of duress. It was noted that unfamiliarity with the rules of war is the enlisted man's common lot. Furthermore, soldiers can argue that they do not know whether the military action in which they are engaged is central to the cause of victory, or whether it has been planned so as to protect the lives of innocent civilians. In addition, the laws of war are often vague, especially when they relate to the realities of combat. Some orders are so abusive that the soldier can reasonably be expected to sense that they should not be obeyed. But, especially in combat situations, the legitimacy of many commands may depend on the prevailing circumstances, which the soldier is not always well prepared to judge.

Moreover, even when a soldier is aware that an order violates the rules of war, and some form of disobedience becomes necessary, our respondents find his available options are limited. Methods of reacting to an order, short of obeying it, include avoidance and intentional misunderstanding; but the realities of combat will most likely discourage their use. Besides, our respondents recognized that the soldier is often confronted by a superior who reenforces his command with the threat of severe punishment. Risking serious penalties for the sake of principles requires a high level of moral as well as physical courage.

The "Heat of the Battle" Argument

A substantial number of respondents stressed that the adjustment to war itself that takes place when the soldier arrives in the combat zone shapes his response. Most soldiers, they argue, do not question the orders that lead them to kill women and children. The killing of the enemy is a necessary job, and few complain about the way it is done.

While the inherent right to exercise self-defense was recognized by many respondents, others pointed out that soldiers should take some risks rather than kill innocent civilians. Self-protection, they argued, is not an excuse for serious violations of the rules of war. The "in the heat of the battle" argument suggests an escalation of violence that begins in legitimate combat and ends in murder, with the difference between the extremes often forgotten by the individual soldier. Most respondents agreed that under special circumstances some allowance may have to be made for what individual soldiers do "in the heat of the battle," especially if they have been under severe strain and are close to nervous exhaustion. While as a general rule combat soldiers should be held responsible for their actions, it was also recognized that during battle only a minority of soldiers and officers react with awareness and a sense of individual responsibility. Many respondents would agree with J. Glenn Gray, who wrote in his diary of the Second World War:

The sober fact appears to be that the great majority of veterans . . . are able to free themselves of responsibility with ease after the event, and frequently while they are performing it. Many a pilot or artilleryman who has destroyed untold numbers of terrified noncombatants has never felt any need for repentance or regret. Many a general who has won his laurels at a terrible cost in human life . . . can endure the review of his career with great inner satisfaction. . . . So long as the soldier . . . identifies himself with his unit, army, and nation, his conscience is unlikely to waken . . . nevertheless . . . guilt is incurred in conflict and made present to the conscience of the minority. . . . It is a crucial moment in a soldier's life when he is ordered to perform a deed that he finds completely at variance with his own notions of right and good . . . He discovers that an act someone else thinks to be necessary is for him criminal. His whole being rouses itself in protest. . . . What this means in the midst of battle can only inadequately be imagined by those who have not experienced it themselves. It means to set oneself against others. Suddenly the soldier feels himself abandoned and cast off from all security. Conscience has isolated him.[35]

Our findings on the issue of individual responsibility under international law suggest that our respondents, including Vietnam veterans, generally see a need for constraints in the conduct of warfare. Concerning the individual items, we continue to witness support for the responsibility of officers to control their men. Indeed, Vietnam veterans like all other respondents are prepared to impose demanding requirements on officers, but they feel that international law should supersede national law by a relatively small margin when their own responsibility is in question. Vietnam veterans are also the most willing to license the use of whatever weapons will work regardless of the rules of war. The magnitude of their differences with officers on this issue is dramatic. Thus, they ask two things from officers: that they control their men and that they protect those under their command from harm regardless of the rules of war.

Our findings suggest a paradoxical conclusion. Institutional failures in teaching soldiers about their obligations in warfare are mitigated by the cultural values of American society and the socialization process of childhood and adolescence. Moreover, our respondents generally accept the concept of individual responsibility and are prepared to acknowledge a significant role for international law in the management of international conflict. The limitations our respondents place on individual responsibility, with the exception of the antiwar activists, relate to the culpability of those at the bottom of the chain of command. Although there is a high degree of acceptance of the right of the common soldier to refuse illegal orders, there is a stated assumption that conditions in Vietnam were not generally conducive to the exercise of such discretion. Consequently, a majority of our respondents oppose the prosecution of the foot soldier for questionable actions and emphasize the liability of the command structure. Indeed, our findings indicate that those abuses that *did* occur are overwhelmingly interpreted as the outcome of command decisions, by either political or military leaders, and of the institutional characteristics of the military system and warfare.

The perceived effectiveness of the military socialization process and the social pressures in Vietnam are, in the judgment of this generation, factors mitigating the responsibility of the common soldier and heightening the responsibility of those who politically and militarily created the conditions for the war. Our culture's insistence on individual responsibility for actions translates in our study into a demand for personal accountability on the part of those who are perceived as having actively stripped individual soldiers of control over their behavior, i.e., political and military leaders.

PART
FOUR

VIETNAM
AND BEYOND

CHAPTER TEN

THE POLITICAL LEGACY OF VIETNAM

In the preceding pages, we have attempted to show how a generation viewed its war and the scars that war has left on their lives and psyches. A generation's images of combat, its memories and reflections, as we have tried to demonstrate, are not pictures stored in albums of the mind to be pulled out during moments of curiosity. Rather, the images of the Vietnam War are part of living memory that influence lives. Vietnam veterans, more so than others, as these pages have attested, continue to search their wartime experience for meaning and understanding, in quest of connective tissue between past and present.

The question with which we conclude this book involves how these experiences and images influence perceptions of the fundamental issue of military intervention by U.S. forces in situations similar to Vietnam. When we conducted our study this question was not as clearly in the forefront of public consciousness as it is today. The debate evoked by the idea of sending U.S. troops to Central America or using American troops in Grenada and Lebanon, along with the threat of U.S. military force in the Straits of Hormuz, resonates with the echoes of Vietnam.

In this concluding chapter we focus on attitudes toward potential U.S. military intervention and public resistance to participation in military actions already underway. Our approach to these issues is distinct from the approach we have used in the rest of the book. As chapter 1 demonstrated, particular aspects of the war experience help us understand the imagery of the war and its personal consequences. We have limited the analysis to those particular indicators in the previous chapters. In this chapter we ask a somewhat different question: Is it the experience of war men endure or the images of war they acquire that constitute the prisms through which they filter the lessons they learn from conflict? To answer this question we have tested a series of analytic models, which include a broad range of the imagery of the war discussed in the previous chapters. We limit our discussion here to those indicators that consistently help us to explain our respondents' views of questions related to future military interventions.

The Question of Intervention

The Vietnam War opened up a series of issues about citizens' rights and government powers in deciding whether or not to wage war and the obligations to serve in a war once undertaken, officially or unofficially. The issue of personal liability, as David Surrey points out, is hardly a new one in American history.[1] However, after World War II, where resistance to military service was based primarily on religious grounds, the political nature of the resistance to participation in Vietnam came as a profound shock to American society. Thus, we have included as part of the assessment of attitudes about future military intervention the issue of how our respondents view resistance past and future. At the same time, we examine the issue of support for military intervention per se by asking questions about unstable situations where at the time of the study there was some public debate or concern about the possible use of American forces. We also asked whether or not men would wish their sons to serve in the military in a war like Vietnam. This question we felt requires the respondent more fundamentally to face his feelings about sending U.S. troops into another land. Such an approach also allows us to address the question of future intervention in both the general and specific terms and to differentiate our respondents' willingness to intervene in principle and to accept personally a role in the process of intervention.

Factors Influencing Attitudes Toward Future Interventions

Not surprisingly, our analysis found that in order to interpret respondents' feelings about future intervention, we had to look at the Vietnam veteran and nonveteran populations separately. Our first finding was that Vietnam status generally is significantly associated with distinct attitudes toward issues of future intervention. Second, we discovered that the war experiences of Vietnam veterans and to a lesser extent antiwar activism among nonveterans were less important in explaining current views toward intervention than were *perceptions* of how the war had been fought. Third, with one exception, attitude toward the war (WARATT), the imagery of the war that predicts attitudes toward intervention-related questions is not the same for Vietnam veterans and nonveterans. In light of these findings we have organized the presentation of our inquiry in terms of how veteran status contributes to attitudes surrounding intervention. We also present the key predictors on this question for Vietnam veterans and nonveterans. Finally, as elsewhere in this volume, we focus on those predictors that are consistently related to the issues of intervention.

General Orientation Toward Intervention by U.S. Troops

As table 10.1 shows, there is very little support among our respondents for sending U.S. troops to intervene in Third World countries. Nonveterans (84%) are most opposed to using American soldiers abroad in situations that involve internal conflicts, even though these confrontations incorporate elements of the East-West conflict. Vietnam era and Vietnam veterans (71%) are significantly less likely to oppose the use of troops in these conflicts; still, seven out of ten veterans oppose the use of U.S. forces in Third World conflicts.

As tables 10.2 and 10.3 indicate, Vietnam veterans (40%) and nonveterans (32%) who supported the war are more likely than their peers to advocate the deployment of American troops abroad. Among Vietnam veterans the only other factor that differentiates levels of support for future military intervention is the amount of education the veteran has acquired. The greater his education, the less likely the veteran is to support United States intervention abroad.

Among nonveterans, as table 10.4 shows, we find that the issue of abusive violence influences attitudes toward future intervention. Of those who said that abusive violence turned them against the war (TRNAGNST), 90% reject the use of force by the United States in foreign conflicts, while only 78% of the nonveterans who were not decisively influenced by acts of abuse against civilians oppose intervention in these situations.

Overall, we can see that perceptions of the Vietnam experience appear to have created profound resistance to the use of American troops to resolve conflicts in foreign countries even where there are overtones of a Communist threat.

Vietnam Veterans' Views of Future Military Interventions

A substantial majority of Vietnam veterans (71%) are against future United States military involvement in conflicts like Vietnam, with only 29% supporting such actions. In the narrative material, many respondents cite the lessons they have learned from Vietnam. There is only one legitimate type of war, they explain, "a war to protect your homeland against aggression." "If the United States' survival was really threatened," and "if enemy forces would land on our shores or invade our allies," they would be among the first to take a rifle in a defensive action, but they strongly oppose any future "offensive war" or "immoral war" like Vietnam, where "Americans go out and destroy other people" in order to control that nation's strategic position, natural resources, or political structures. A black Vietnam veteran, who witnessed abusive violence by American forces, explained what he learned from Vietnam as follows:

> I would say it gave me new insights on life and living. . . . It brought home to me how important it was for the social order to be changed—because I saw . . . graphically the impact that America had on little countries around the world. And it really drove home the fact that this shouldn't keep going on like this.

. . . I saw America was just using these people there.

Some veterans who turned against the American involvement in Vietnam are worried about the "advance of world Communism," but argue that if we are going to oppose Communism, it should not be done militarily. A white veteran who witnessed abusive violence, commented:

> Before I went to Vietnam I did not understand the war. After I got there, we looked around and investigated towns and villages. . . . We Americans were fighting a war against an enemy backed by Russians. But the Russians did not want physically to participate in the fighting. . . . I started thinking and felt that if we are going to fight a war against Communism, it should not be fought on a physical level. This terrible war was draining America of some of its best manpower.

A number of Vietnam veterans pointed out that the United States fights too many useless wars. They feel that the United States has a war-based economy, "when we are out of war we cannot survive, the big companies cannot sell their military goods." They observed that military and political leaders keep developing new weapons and that "one day soon they will want to test them out." They further noted that "the military will get frustrated with peace and then it will happen all over again." From their point of view "we are always preparing for future interventions like Vietnam." They questioned whether Vietnam has in fact taught us a lesson. A white veteran, who witnessed abusive violence, shared his concerns this way:

> What frightens me most is our government's lack of interest in what is happening to our country. It is paying more attention to other countries. . . . It seems like the economy of this country is based on war. We always have to have a little war going on someplace.

Vietnam veterans also made it clear that they do not want to become involved in any future Vietnam-type situation. They observed that "these days all you hear about again is helping other countries fight against Communism," but in reality "we do not really help them: we dictate to them." They feel that "the American people should somehow get the American government to understand that they want peace." An army infantryman who saw heavy combat expressed a common sentiment among many Vietnam veterans when he commented:

> The Vietnam War gave me knowledge of what I would do if the situation ever came up again. There wouldn't be any doubt what I would do or how I would feel about it . . . I would actively oppose it. I guess the war didn't have the effect that the government wanted it to have which would be that I would've

turned out like a robot with one thing in mind, to kill and attack the enemy. I
guess I'm not a good product of infantry training.

Nonveterans' Attitudes Toward Future Interventions

Only a minority of those nonveterans who supported the American involvement in
the war while it was going on have now turned against it. One of them explained
his shift in attitude this way:

> At the time I thought that we should have been there to stop Communism, that
> was the big single purpose. I was all for it. At the time when I was in college I
> didn't understand why all these people were resisting and dodging the draft but
> now, you know, looking back I can see the reasons. Now I think, we shouldn't
> have been there.

But a plurality still defend the war and are upset that the United States did
not defeat the enemy. They are also more likely than their peers to support future
military interventions in situations like Vietnam. They view the United States
foreign policy as an important issue, and many voice the complaint that we have
"gone soft on Communism." One nonveteran noted:

> We made a big mistake in Vietnam. Now that we're out of Vietnam, the
> Communists have systematically taken over Laos, Cambodia, and probably in
> the future Thailand; they're moving into Africa, South America, and the Ori-
> ent.

And another respondent stated:

> We don't seem to have any backbone anymore. I see a lot of countries with
> Communism becoming dominant and we probably will not get involved be-
> cause of the big scare of Vietnam. Politicians don't want to get involved
> anymore. I don't really think that's too good. We should get involved and it's
> really too bad that Vietnam happened, because it's scaring us away from that.
> That really bothers me, that because of Vietnam, some countries are inevitably
> going to go Communist and we probably won't do a damn thing about it.

As was to be expected, in the narrative material antiwar activists presented
strong arguments against future interventions like Vietnam. The Vietnam War
made them become determined "to try and stop anything like that from happening again," to make sure that if a war like that reoccurs, they would once more
"conscientiously object to it." A high activist commented:

> I don't think people should feel that the antiwar movement was a temporary

political feeling on their part. I still feel strongly about Vietnam, the experience, and I don't know if I would act any different today than I did at that time. Occasionally you hear people, like your parents, say to you "well, you've certainly grown up now, you won't get into any of this hell raising anymore." And that's not really the point, if this country ever did become involved in another episode like Vietnam, I think a great many people, probably even more than before, would come out against it. I certainly think the country's politicians should be aware of that.

And another high activist made the following observation:

If the Vietnam War would start today, I believe that I would oppose it more than I did then. I believe that what happened then should be a lesson for American history, for us to keep out and not let a thing like that happen again.

Attitude Toward Resisters

During the Vietnam War the question of resistance to military service became a major issue in the debate surrounding the war and a significant component of the antiwar movement. One of the issues raised by resisters was their right to refuse to participate in a war as a matter of conscience. Men who went into the military and especially those who went to Vietnam found their own behavior directly challenged by such resistance. By asking our respondents how they now viewed the resisters, we raised, in our view, the question of the legitimacy of resistance to participation in such ventures.

As table 10.5 demonstrates, there are significant differences in attitude between veterans and their nonveteran peers regarding resistance. Vietnam (43%) and Vietnam era (42%) veterans say they oppose the resisters compared to only 24% of the nonveterans. The two categories, support and respect for resisters, show that only about one-third of the veterans were sympathetic to resisters while nearly half of the nonveterans indicated acceptance of the resisters' posture. However, it is also possible to read this table somewhat differently. Even among Vietnam veterans there appears to be a residue of resentment to the war which makes hostility to resisters, the most common response, a minority position; indeed, only about four in ten Vietnam veterans appear truly angry at those who refused to fight. Moreover, among nonveterans only 24% express hostility at resisters.

The relationship between the perception of the war and the views of resisters is evident in the Vietnam veteran population. Three factors—attitude toward the war, perception of the frequency of U.S. forces' abuse of civilians, and perceptions of and attitudes toward the enemy—lead Vietnam veterans to very different positions on the resisters. Vietnam veterans who opposed the war were the most sympathetic to the resisters (47%), while 50% of the veterans who supported the war expressed opposition to resisters (table 10.6). Even more dramatically, we see, in table 10.7, that of Vietnam veterans who said that U.S. forces frequently abused civilians (USABPERS), 67% expressed support or respect for resisters, while only 24% of the veterans who asserted such abuses occurred infrequently expressed similar views of resisters.

Views of the enemy also played an important role in Vietnam veterans' perceptions of resisters. Veterans who defined the guerrilla forces as being entitled to be treated as prisoners of war (37%) were significantly more likely than those who rejected such treatment of enemy troops (17%) to express approval for resisters (table 10.8).

In table 10.9 we find that Vietnam veterans who expressed the most hostile view of the enemy (VC/NVA) (47%) as well as those who indicated ambivalence (46%) were significantly more hostile to resisters than veterans who reported positive perceptions of the enemy (30%). Interestingly, we find about 24% of all three groups expressing ambivalence toward resisters. Only a plurality of those who held negative or ambivalent views of the enemy express opposition to resisters.

Thus, we see that how Vietnam veterans perceive resisters is significantly influenced by their images of the war and their views of the enemy. It may be that acknowledging respect for the enemy implies some legitimation of the conflict as a civil war, as veterans who opposed the war are also more likely to express positive views of the enemy forces.

The nonveterans' perceptions of resisters, as tables 10.10–10.15 show, are more strongly influenced by their view of war (WARATT), the conduct of the war (TRNAGNST and USABPERS), involvement in the antiwar movement (ACTIVISM), and their educational attainments. Views of the enemy play no role in the nonveteran response to resisters.

In tables 10.10 and 10.13 we find that WARATT and ACTIVISM play decisive roles in views of resisters. Nonveteran supporters of the war (44%), like veterans, are the most hostile to resisters, while more than 70% of the antiwar activists, both moderate and high, strongly support or respect resisters. Nonveterans opposed to the war (59%) are also quite supportive of resisters, while those who were only slightly involved in the antiwar movement (37%) are much less supportive than their antiwar counterparts, but are still more accepting than those who supported the war (25%).

The significance of the conduct of the war is evident in tables 10.11 and 10.12. Table 10.11 shows that those whose view of the war was determined by abusive violence (63%) are much more supportive and respectful of resisters than respondents whose view of the war did not turn on this issue (38%). We see a similar pattern in table 10.12 when we examine the relationship between perceptions of the frequency of civilian abuse (USPERS) and support for resisters. Fully 55% of those who thought such abuses were frequent indicate "support" for resisters compared to 20% of the respondents who thought such abuses infrequent. An additional 7% of the frequent and 20% of the infrequent groups reported that they respected resisters. Thus 62% of the respondents who said such abuse was frequent, compared to 40% who said that abuse was infrequent, indicated support for resisters.

Finally, among nonveterans, level of education has a profound effect on attitudes to resisters. In table 10.14 we find that respondents with less than a high school diploma (57%) and those with a high school diploma (42%) are the most hostile to resisters. Entry into college substantially reduces hostility toward those who refused to fight. Only 25% of the men with some college, 15% of college graduates, and 12% with postgraduate training are opposed to the resisters. And, as table 10.14 demonstrates, there is a substantial jump in support for resisters among men with postgraduate training (68%) compared to college graduates (51%).

Vietnam Veterans' Views of Resisters

As was to be expected, we find Vietnam veterans are more opposed to resisters than nonveterans. From the critics' point of view, national military service must be performed by everybody. They believe that what the resisters did was wrong and cowardly and that they should be duly punished. Some explanations for this view are provided below. A marine officer remarked:

> I do not feel that anybody should be allowed to resist military service to the country. I feel strongly that these people should have been punished for resistance. By allowing them to resist the whole military organization and discipline had a direct hit. It was very difficult to maintain order within the military organization while others were free to resist.

A veteran who served in the air force commented:

> Well, a lot of them just can't hack it I guess. I feel that if I was good enough to go in and do what I had to, why not them? I had to leave whatever I had behind to do it and so did hundreds of thousands of others, so why couldn't they? We were in the same boat. . . . If everybody felt the same way there'd be nobody to fight.

Veterans also reported that most resisters did not understand what was happening in Vietnam and therefore did not have the right to resist. As one navy engineer noted:

> A lot of them were out marching and rallying. I really think a lot of them did not know what they were talking about. They read a couple of magazines, they read what they wanted to read about Vietnam. They did not know what was going on

over there so I didn't think they had the right to march, burn their draft cards, carry signs telling that we were killing innocent people over there.

Respondents also argued that those who left the country "cannot ever come back." Once they made the decision to go, resisters were obligated to accept the consequences. From this group's point of view "there is no place for them in this country any longer." Resisters, they insist, could have legally fought it out in our court system and served a sentence in jail in lieu of service. But once they escaped to a foreign country, they forfeited their rights as citizens. An air force officer remarked:

> I feel that those who did not follow the legal route available to them . . . that is to say, those who simply protested and left the country . . . abdicated their right to citizenship in the country. I think an individual who cannot work within the framework of law provided by the constitution does not deserve citizenship in the country.

Still, a substantial number of Vietnam veterans held a positive view of resisters. They pointed out that before they went to Vietnam they had felt that everyone should be obligated "to make themselves available for service to fight for freedom, to protect democracy." It was simply "a moral duty as a citizen." But when they got over there and saw what was going on, they turned against the war and felt that the resisters were doing the right thing. Some even felt that they too should have resisted the war. An army infantryman who was in heavy combat recalled:

> I guess it is the thing I should have done actually. I can see their point of view. I gave it absolutely no thought. Maybe they were the brave ones because they were the ones that risked jail, risked ridicule of their friends and neighbors. Maybe they were the ones that had all the courage. If more of us had had it, we would never have got so much involved into the Vietnam War.

An army infantryman, who was exposed to abusive violence against civilians by American forces and turned against the war, presented the following observation:

> I think they are probably better examples of humanity than I was . . . knowing that you can make that strong a decision considering what happens. I would say that they were a little ahead of the rest.

Another infantryman who was also exposed to abusive violence and opposed to the war remarked:

In spite of the fact that they're said to be cowards and not very brave, I think it takes a lot of guts to resist the laws of this country. To me it takes courage to get up and leave the country to evade the draft . . . to leave your home and your family. That's the kind of courage that I didn't have at the time. That's why I couldn't do it. . . . The resisters resisted for what they believed in. . . . I really don't know what problems a person living in Canada has. I've never done it. But I would think it's a heavy experience.

A heavy-combat veteran, who enlisted in the marines and went to Vietnam as a volunteer, expressed the following attitude:

Those guys must have had crystal balls. . . . They are in a much better frame of mind than any veteran—by not going there. I wish I had been at the time intelligent enough to do the same thing they did. From what I have experienced in Vietnam, and being a veteran now, I raise my hand to these guys.

Some respondents also pointed out that there are no pat answers. Each case must be examined carefully and its merits or demerits must be judged individually. A veteran who served in the army made this point as follows:

They should be dealt with on an individual basis. If they did not have a serious objection to the war I could see them still serving in a noncombatant role in the military here at home. Or in a civilian type of work project or community betterment type of project if they opt not to be involved with the military at all. For others open resistance would be the only answer because they would consider nonaction a form of support . . . and I give them credit for doing what they believe they should do.

Finally, a veteran who served in the navy and who turned against the war because of his concern over abusive violence made the following remarks:

Insofar as it really had to do with opposition to the war, I had pretty general sympathy with them. Insofar as many of them, I think, did it out of cowardice, I do not have much sympathy at all. I have a suspicion that a lot of them could easily tell the difference themselves. I helped a number of these people and counseled draft evasion if they were trying to avoid participating in something that they really did not go along with.

Nonveterans' Attitude Toward Resisters

Only 25% of our respondents who supported the war expressed a tolerant attitude toward resisters. One such nonveteran argued:

I feel they have to be judged on an individual basis. If a person was honestly a conscientious objector, I can see no reason why he should have to serve in the military, in a fighting capacity. I think there could have been room made for these people in other areas, be it administration or medical or whatever.

Most of those nonveterans who supported American involvement in the war were hostile to resisters (44%) or expressed an ambivalent attitude (31%). They considered them traitors to the cause of a "free world" and the defeat of "the evils of Communism." One nonveteran noted:

I think you should serve your country in the best way you can and if you can't do that then you should be deported. I don't have any respect for them.

And another observed:

Resisters? I think they should be treated as traitors . . . take whatever punishment that being a traitor goes with.

The antiwar movement was also often condemned for creating problems for the country. One prowar nonveteran expressed his dissatisfaction as follows:

Kent State seemed to be all out of proportion to what was really going on. I felt the resisters were creating a problem here that did not exist, and it came down to martyrdom for a few, to get more publicity for the movement. And I was definitely against it, I felt it was wrong.

As was to be expected, the *prevailing sentiment* among antiwar activists was a feeling of respect for resisters. They were perceived to be acting in harmony with democratic principles and to be fully justified in resisting military service. This sentiment is expressed by a high activist in the following statement:

I feel they were right. I think that history has shown that they were right. Or if you define democracy as getting the most number of people to agree with you, then, according to democratic principles, they were fully justified in taking the stance they did.

A minority of activists, however, felt that resisters should not have left the United States but should have stayed here and fought against the war. A moderate activist remarked:

I didn't see anything wrong with them resisting, but I disagree with them leaving this country, going to another country. I felt if they felt strong enough against it, that it was worth staying here fighting against . . . fighting for. Stay here and resist and fight it. Go through the proper channels.

Sending a Son to Fight a War like Vietnam

We asked our respondents two questions that tapped the extent to which members of this generation were willing to have their children personally involved in future interventions like Vietnam. The first question asked was whether the respondent would want his son to enter the military in such a war. We next inquired whether the respondent would want his son to go into the military or go to Canada if that were the only way to avoid going into the military.

The response to the first item, "Would you want your son to enter the military during a war like Vietnam?" (table 10.15), indicates little enthusiasm in our population for having their children go through a Vietnam type of war. Vietnam veterans (38%) and Vietnam era veterans (28%) are significantly more willing to have their children participate in a future war of this type than non-veterans (20%). Nonetheless, 62% of the Vietnam veterans do not want to have their children enter the military during such a war.

Table 10.16, however, indicates that the idea of going to Canada to avoid military service is considerably less acceptable. Only 26% of the Vietnam veterans and 28% of the Vietnam era veterans would encourage their children to resist in this fashion; though an additional 13% would leave the choice to their children. Among nonveterans, however, the idea of such resistance has considerably greater acceptance. Fully 44% of the nonveterans would encourage their children to leave the country, and another 11% would leave the choice up to their children. The key finding, in our view, is that only 60% of the veterans would insist that their children enter the military under these circumstances, as would only 45% of the nonveterans. It appears that the idea of resistance to military service in an unpopular war has taken root in this generation.

Vietnam veterans' feelings about the participation of their children in the military during Vietnam-type interventions are influenced by their perception of the Vietcong (POWGUER). Among those who were prepared to grant the guerrillas military status, 65% did not want their sons to enter the military; while 51% of the veterans who rejected the idea of giving the guerrillas recognition as soldiers wanted their sons to sign up (table 10.17). Clearly, how the veterans defined the character of the enemy forces plays a key role in their view of future participation in military intervention.

As table 10.18 shows, whether or not Vietnam veterans thought they received public support also plays a role in their feelings about what they would want their children to do. The effects of support for veterans' military service, however, are less clearcut than is evident in the previous discussion. Those who felt that they received little support and those who say they received high levels of support (32%) from the public and the government for their service to the country are substantially more likely to have their children avoid entering the military during a Vietnam type of intervention. Only the veterans who report they received moderate levels of support are more likely to encourage their children to enter the military.

In tables 10.19–10.20, we see that attitudes about the war, perceptions of the enemy (POWGUER), and feelings about how military service is supported have substantial effects on views toward resistance to military service for one's offspring.

Opposition to the war provides a reason for encouraging sons' resistance (35%) or allowing them to decide for themselves (21%) (table 10.19). Indeed, only among Vietnam veterans opposed to the war do we find less than 50% who would want their sons to enter the military during a Vietnam type of intervention. Contrarily, 69% of the Vietnam veterans who supported the war affirm the responsibility of their sons to fulfill their military obligations if they are called.

Vietnam veterans who accepted the military status of the guerrillas are much more likely to encourage their sons to resist (29%) or let them make their own decision (13%). Contrarily, 78% of those who do not accept the guerrillas as having the status of soldiers would insist their children go into the military (table 10.20).

Finally, in table 10.21, we see that feeling the people and the country failed to provide support for their sacrifices leads men to encourage their children to resist (39%) or let them make up their own minds (8%).

In the nonveteran population we find that attitude toward the war, perception of the conduct of the war, the issue of individual responsibility, and educational attainment are the key factors affecting avoidance of and resistance to military service in a war like Vietnam. In tables 10.22–10.25, we find with few exceptions little enthusiasm for having one's children enter the military during a Vietnam-like intervention. Avoidance of military service is preferred by a majority of all the nonveterans in every category. However, there are important differences in how strongly some groups support avoidance of military service by their children.

In table 10.22 we see that among supporters of the war, only 58% opt for avoidance compared to 86% of their peers who opposed the war. Men who believe the U.S. forces frequently abused civilians support avoidance more than 90% of the time, compared to 70% of those who report that USABPERS was infrequent (table 10.23). Respondents who express high levels of support for individual responsibility in wartime also support avoidance nearly 90% of the time, while 69% who express little support for this concept would encourage their children to avoid service (table 10.24). [2] Finally, in table 10.25, we see the dramatic effects of education on supporting avoidance of military service by one's children. Only 51% of the respondents with less than a high school diploma support avoidance of military service, while 94% of those with postgraduate education would encourage their children to stay out of the military in a future intervention like Vietnam. As table 10.25 demonstrates, there are significant stepwise increments in levels of support for avoidance between high school graduates and those with some college or college graduates and between college men and postgraduates.

In tables 10.26–10.30, we see that levels of support for going to Canada to avoid service vary dramatically in light of perceptions of the war. Nonveterans who supported the war (74%) overwhelmingly affirm that they want their sons to go into the military if called, while 54% of those opposed to or ambivalent about the war would encourage their sons to resist (table 10.26). In table 10.27 we find that perceived frequency of U.S. abuse of civilians has a similar impact. Fully 60% of the respondents who said such abuses were frequent and 51% who said they sometimes occurred support resistance, while 60% of those who said such actions were infrequent want their sons to enter the military. Table 10.28 shows that support for the concept of individual responsibility likewise differentiates support for and opposition to resistance. Strong supporters of the concept of individual responsibility are prepared to encourage their children to go to Canada (56%) or let the son make the decision (10%), and even respondents who express moderate levels of support for the concept are quite likely to support resistance (49%) or let the son make the decision (11%). However, among men who exhibit little support for the idea of individual responsibility, 61% would urge their sons to enter the military.

Activism provides the most striking illustration of the different positions on resistance in the event of another Vietnam-type intervention. Eighty-five percent of the high activists would urge their children to leave the country rather than serve in the military, compared to 59% of the moderate activists; and 53% of the low activists would send their children into the military (table 10.29).

In table 10.30, we see once again the strong impact of educational attainment on views of resistance. Men with a high school diploma or less would push their children into the military (68%). Respondents with some college education or college degrees appear evenly divided between wanting their sons to enter the military, about 40%, and encouraging resistance, approximately 45%, with about 12% opting to let their children decide the issue for themselves. Finally, nonveterans with postgraduate training (63%) clearly prefer their children to resist military service if the United States were to intervene in another war like Vietnam.

Vietnam Veterans' Views of Military Service in a War like Vietnam

Proinvolvement veterans

When asked, "Would you want your son to go into the military in a war like Vietnam?" a minority of Vietnam veterans (38%), and especially those who supported the American involvement in Vietnam, argued that it would be the duty of their son "to fight to keep this country a free democracy." An army infantry sergeant remarked:

> I would want him to go in the service. This maybe sounds old fashioned but I do believe you got to fight for what you believe in. My only hope would be that the whole country believed in what we were fighting for at the time and there wouldn't be some . . . protesting the war that he's over there fighting for.

Another veteran noted:

> I would think that my son after I raised him would automatically take that stance of going in. I would bring him up to the best of my ability to accept responsibility and to accept authority and I feel he would be intelligent enough to make his own decision to go in. We owe a lot to the country because of the way we live. We live under a free democracy. I do not see why I would want him out because then I would be throwing a monkey wrench into everything I believe in.

Some veterans in this minority group, especially those who remain strongly in support of the American involvement in Vietnam, argued that the draft must be restored because "the country is in danger." An army man explained why his son should serve in a war like Vietnam:

> I feel that somebody has to go—somebody has to protect the country. I think our military is on the downward swing. I think they are definitely in trouble, morale wise and personnel wise. I think our army, our military is just weakening. I am sorry that they abolished the draft. I really think it is a necessary part of the military.

Other proinvolvement veterans argued that fighting in a war like Vietnam would teach their sons to cope with difficult situations and toughen them. A navy man observed:

> I think it would be a worthwhile life experience for my eldest son. There should be some type of military conscription, immediately after high school, to have everyone experience the order and regimentation. Show them the necessity for following orders. Those people who have been in are usually more able to cope with adverse situations than those who have not. The military can provide an individual with a basic strength and fortitude, if you call it guts, to rely on himself and to rely on others in a given situation.

And a marine captain who supported the American involvement in Vietnam presented this view:

I think that my son might benefit from his experiences to see what it's like. . . .
There are so many functions that you can serve in the military where you'll
never even be exposed to doing anything that would be a vicious act and so I
would say, go ahead.

Veterans Opposed to Son's Military Service

Two main themes are presented by those veterans who do not want their son to
serve in a future war like Vietnam (62%).

A minority of those veterans who are opposed to having their sons serve in a
Vietnam-type conflict pointed out that the war was conducted the wrong way and
could have been won. They also argued that there was no national support for the
war. Under those conditions they would not want their sons to become involved in
any future military conflict. An army lieutenant observed:

I would be opposed to having my son serve in the armed forces if a war was
conducted the way we conducted this war, which was to lose it by politicians
frustrating generals and adhering to rules which our enemy was not willing to
adhere to. We . . . were willing to callously lose lives week after week just to
stay where we were and to go nowhere. . . . A nation at war should have acted
decisively and effectively either to stay in or get out.

A veteran who served in the navy stated:

I believe that we all have responsibilities to our country. We have to respond to
its call and we have to make sacrifices. The people that went into World War I,
World War II, the Korean War did so because they felt that this was the cause
they had to support. But the Vietnam War was different. You know, we could
have won the war, but suddenly after all the people have died just to pull out and
leave everything, that was wrong. No, I would never want to go back to another
Vietnam with the kind of disgrace we veterans got. What keeps the average
military man in the service going when he is in a place like Vietnam is that deep
down inside you feel that you are supported by your country. I would never ever
want anybody to go through that again.

And an army captain who supported the war gave this bitter response:

Thinking of all the dead and disabled veterans . . . I suppose millions and
millions of dollars spent in Vietnam for nothing—the crummy way that we left
leaving all the equipment behind us. To me it was the epitome of stupidity on
our government's part and I would not want my son going anywhere and going
through the same thing that I did for good intentions and wind up with nothing.

But the majority of those who felt that their sons should not serve in a war like Vietnam pointed out that we should not become militarily involved in an internal conflict in another country. All of these respondents had gradually turned against the American involvement in Vietnam. A veteran who served in the navy responded:

> No, not if it were a war like Vietnam where we did not belong to begin with, it was just a waste. I would not mind it if we were fighting in a war that had some meaning, like World War II. Not for a meaningless conflict where even if we win, we lose. I do not believe the United States belongs in a war like that any more. I totally disagree with our stance in Vietnam. I disagree with our stance that we now maintain. It is a very dangerous one. We are asking for it again.

And a marine commented:

> See, I went through it and I would not want him to go through it, because he might not survive it. And I do not think it is right anymore. Fighting, you know, in a civil war in another country . . . like Vietnam.

Many of these veterans not only do not want their sons to serve in a war like Vietnam, but are hopeful that they would participate in a resistance movement against such an involvement. An army airborne who witnessed abusive violence against civilians by American forces and developed a strong ideological opposition to the war while still in Vietnam explained why he would not want his son to go:

> Because I think there's so little that you can do to influence the course of events in the world and when a war comes that you don't agree with—this is one of the few times where you can actually do something concrete. And say, no, I won't go, on a personal level. And I think if that's how you feel, you shouldn't do it. You should stand up and say no, I'm not going. Because it is one of the few opportunities you will ever have to make a difference.

Reactions to the Canadian Alternative

From the above responses, we may conclude that Vietnam veterans are generally reluctant to have their children serve in a Vietnam-type conflict. However, support for entering the military goes up substantially when the alternative is going to Canada. Under those conditions, 60% of Vietnam veterans are likely to encourage their children to join the military, 26% are prepared to urge them to leave the country for Canada rather than enter the military, and 13% feel that it should be the son's own decision.

The narrative material provides some explanation of why a substantial number of Vietnam veterans who would not like their son to serve in a war like Vietnam reject the Canada option. One group is afraid that if their son went to Canada, he could never return and live a normal life. In Canada his life would be "all messed up," and if he tried to come back to the United States "in one form or another he would always be persecuted." Thus, he should probably join the military and "hope for the best."

An army engineer who has vivid memories of the death and dying of Americans as well as Vietnamese and turned against the war toward the end of his stay in Vietnam explained why his son should not go to Canada:

> I am looking at it from a long-term point of view. I would not want his life to be ruined. I think that from looking at what happened to the people that fled to Sweden and Canada, you know, their life is ruined. They do not have any kind of an ability to fit into society. You are in a different environment. You can't make a success of yourself. It is much more difficult. So I think it is regrettable. If I am a parent and I love my child, I would not want him to go into the army. . . . But I think it is something that he has to do . . . if the only option is to go to Canada.

Another group argued that their son should not go to Canada, but should remain in the United States and actively resist the war. They noted that "he would not be doing himself and his country any good at all by running away," "he should stay here and face the problem." A navy seabee, who is still haunted by memories of the war, had the following to say:

> I would not want him to go to Canada. Stay here and fight it. Because I have seen what Vietnam was, I would not want my son to go there and get shot for nothing. . . . I am worried about the government. I think there is going to be another war eventually. That is one of my biggest concerns. When it does come, it is going to be bad. What bothers me most is bringing up kids to meet that. I brought a son into the world. What is going to happen to him? I would not like him to get caught up in a situation like that. I would have nothing against him going to war . . . an honest war, where you are fighting for something, but a situation like Vietnam, forget it.

Those Vietnam veterans who would support their sons' going to Canada express several views. Again, some respondents point out that we did not try to win the war in Vietnam and under those conditions Americans should not serve. A marine captain argued:

> Why I would rather have him not go in and go to Canada? Well, most GIs in this war were in the regular army. The infantry. And that was a very bloody, gory,

complete mess. There was no organization—there was no commitment to fight a war. It was like a big farcical game that was being played. If you're going to fight a war you go in like we did in World War II and you fight a war. And if you're not going to fight a war, then you don't belong there. So if it was a Vietnam-type thing and I had a son that was going to go in . . . then I'd recommend he go to Canada. If I thought that we might win and we're really going to have a war then I'd say—fight the war.

Others stressed that the country did not appreciate the sacrifice made by Vietnam veterans and denied them a hero's welcome. Why then should their sons serve in a similar war? A veteran explained why he would want his son to go to Canada:

I feel that way because of what the war and the whole system has done to the person in the war. I was happy to serve my country, but after I have seen what has gone on there and having a family and having two boys . . . after the way I was treated after I got out of the war, I would never want my son to go into the war and receive the same treatment I did.

And a marine remarked:

I would take my son to Canada if another Vietnam were to break out. I feel that I would not want to subject him to what I've been through to this point because of Vietnam. I also feel that the military is a necessity for the defense of our country and if a foreign nation were to invade I'd probably go and reup again because I feel this country is worth saving. But for a place like Vietnam, no way, why put my son in jeopardy.

In fact, the majority in this group expressed strong opposition to American involvement in Vietnam-style wars. An antiwar army man reflected:

And now that I'm 30 and my son is 4 1/2 years old . . . I kind of wish my father had the foresight to say "man, don't go." And if the only way of not going was going to Canada until this thing blew over or Sweden or wherever I'd be accepted I would go . . . if the situation was the same as Vietnam. . . . If there was another war to break out like Vietnam, my son, John, I would . . . chain him to the plumbing before he would go. Because I would be very much against it.

Many veterans observed that while they would prefer their son to stay here and fight American military involvement, if Canada were the only option they would encourage him to go rather than serving in the war. An ex-intelligence veteran, who also advised village chiefs, has since turned against the Vietnam

War and strongly opposes future interventions. He responded:

> In case of a future Vietnam I would support resistance. I would not encourage
> my son to go to Canada, I would encourage him to remain here. . . . But if
> Canada was the only option I would encourage him to go as opposed to going to
> Vietnam.

Nonveterans' Attitudes Toward Military Service in a War Like Vietnam

A majority of the prowar respondents argued that their son should not serve in a war like the Vietnam War. The motivation for this argument is often the same: the United States lost the war in Vietnam, but if we had been victorious the involvement would have been worth it. A nonveteran makes this attitude clear:

> Why I would want him to go to Canada? Basically all we did over there is just
> waste a lot of lives. We pulled out. If we would have kept South Vietnam and it
> would have been an American extension state, then it would have been worth it
> and if my son would have gone over there to serve and was killed, there would
> have been a definite difference there.

But a minority (42%) of the prowar respondents would want their son to join the military in a Vietnam-type conflict. They believed in the war effort then and continue to argue that we must fight Communism everywhere in the world. This attitude is evident from the following two remarks. One nonveteran commented:

> I would want him to love his country enough to go and fight for it. I would hate
> to see him go but you have to make the sacrifice because someday he might have
> a child and I'd hate to see that child raised under Communist rule just because
> we were too lazy to go and fight.

And another respondent observed:

> He would have a moral obligation to go. I think Vietnam wasn't as bad as we
> thought. I think the American people were to a great extent brainwashed by the
> press. I think we were actually fighting for the liberty of people. Circumstances
> subsequent to the Vietnam War indicated we did the right thing, except we
> didn't try to win the war.

Like many prowar Vietnam veterans, these respondents also pointed out that "this is the best country in the world," and citizens owe it something other than just paying taxes. A nonveteran explained why he would want his son to serve:

I think it's your duty. I'm really adamant on that—this country gave everybody everything they have and I think a lot of people should take some trips and go to some places and see what other people live like and then they're really going to see how many things people just take for granted in this country. And let's face it . . . most people in this country have it pretty good.

Prowar respondents also argued that their son should go into the military because, as citizens, we must adhere to the law:

I would want him to go in the military, because I think you have got to obey your country's rules. If everybody broke the rules we'd be in a pretty bad situation. If everybody deserted we would have anarchy. I never did really care for somebody that ran when things got going tough.

When asked, "If your son were called to serve in the armed forces in a war *like* Vietnam, would you want him to go into the military or stay out of it?" antiwar activists generally agreed that their son should not serve and nearly nine out of ten would encourage their son to resist. One high activist reflected:

There's no reason to go into the military if his thoughts were strongly against it. If his morals were against it, I would say that is what you should follow. I think that to fight against a war that you feel is wrong or against an idea that you think is wrong is strengthening, if gives as much strength to the American ideal as to fight for patriotism, in fact it takes more courage at times. It's part of the fabric of society.

And a moderate activist pointed out:

No, he should not go. . . . Basically, I would put myself in that place and I felt that because of the immorality of the war, and the fact that we really had no purpose being there, why should I or my son in this case risk our lives for something like that.

Activists also pointed out that while they would prefer their son to stay out of the military in a Vietnam-type war, they would expect him to serve in a legitimate conflict. A moderate activist commented:

Well in the case of it being a war like Vietnam my own inclination would be that I would hope that he would not agree to participate in such a racist, genocidal act. If on the other hand it were a war that I felt that our country should be engaged in, I think I would disagree vigorously if he chose not to do what I consider to be his duty to his country.

A number of activists observed that their son would have to make his own decision. A moderate activist noted:

I wouldn't want to make decisions for him if I had a son. It's not my life, it's his life. I would prefer he stay out of the military, but I'm not an authoritarian, if he'd be my son, I would raise him the best way I know how to and if he felt he had to go in the army and felt comfortable going in the army, it's his decision. I have to respect his decision.

The answer to the question, "If the only way he could avoid service in the military was going to Canada, would you want him to go to Canada?" was somewhat more difficult for many activists. A minority felt that in that case their son should probably go into the military. A moderate activist explained:

It's a rough thing . . . once these people have left this country there's no way back and there's always something of a fear that someone's going to arrest them or somebody's going to be after them. It's more of a fear of the future . . . the old bugaboo about a man without a country, never really being at home. That would be a constant fear that that would happen to him, that he could never come back. . . . I don't know what I would do but I would say probably to try the military and hope for the best.

A majority agreed that their son should go to Canada in the case of a war *like* Vietnam. This attitude is demonstrated by the following reply by a high activist:

Because it would keep him out of the military. It's probably of all the ways of staying out of the military, the one which provided the best possibility for continuing to maintain some sort of freedom. All the other alternatives were ones which limited your freedom—either by being in jail, or by going underground, or something else which prevented an individual to have freedom, plus it also would afford an opportunity to continue opposition to the war publicly.

Another high activist concluded:

If he had a strong moral and legal objection to the war and that was the only way to implement that objection, and he recognized the disadvantages, essentially giving up your citizenship, then I would support him because it's more important to follow your conscience.

Conclusion

The findings in this chapter emphasize the relevance of the Vietnam experience in the politics of contemporary America. The crystallized imagery of the war profoundly influences attitudes about the relationship of the United States to social change and upheavals in the Third World. The role of the United States in the world today constantly demands that its leaders and the nation take positions on violent conflicts around the globe. Whether these conflicts are defined in terms of the East-West conflict or internal social and economic crises plays an important role in how the U.S. government responds. Unlike the early days of Vietnam, however, there is no longer a general political consensus on how to define or respond to social revolution. Fundamental fissures have emerged within the national political leadership and are reflected by the general population in national polls. There is considerable resistance to military intervention and a deep reluctance to use of U.S. troops to achieve political objectives in resolving social conflicts abroad.

Our data show that the divisions on the use of U.S. troops to resolve distant conflicts are deeply affected by the interpretation of the Vietnam experience by the Vietnam Generation. Our respondents focus on a variety of issues surrounding the Vietnam War, including the definition of the conflict, the nature of warfare in that setting, and the motivation of the indigenous combatants. Nonveterans focus more often on the larger socio-political factors and the character of antiguerrilla wars, while Vietnam veterans appear to be strongly influenced by the motivation and conduct of military forces they were called upon to aid or fight.

In our view, the Vietnam veterans' concerns about the military forces with which they interacted is vital and often overlooked in understanding their response to the war. The willingness of forces the U.S. seeks to aid to carry the burden of the war, or at least fight as well as their opponents, is a critical factor in the response of American soldiers to the Vietnam War. These feelings about the enemy and the allies also influence their feelings about future use of U.S. troops in similar situations.

Finally, it is evident from our findings that there is no single interpretation of the Vietnam experience. Indeed, the divisions we find so many years after the war suggest that the imagery of Vietnam will play a continuing and important role in the debates over how to respond to social change and revolution in the Third World for the foreseeable future. Vietnam was for this generation a watershed event and serves as a referent for interpreting the world in which we live. The contradictory meanings drawn from this experience promise to intensify political controversy in our society over foreign policy. No single interpretation of the Vietnam War is soon likely to become a consensually accepted version. It appears that the battle over the legacy of the war will be even more protracted than the war itself.

EPILOGUE

Wars, as our study shows, do not simply fade away when the guns are silenced. Returning soldiers carry home their memories of battle. Nor do the civilian population's imagery and feelings about a conflict vanish at war's end, although public responses may become less visible. After the termination of hostilities, the war that was is gradually replaced by the images of war as they are committed to individual and collective memory. It is this body of perceptions, recollections, and responses that combine to form the accepted truth about a war and its meaning for the nation that fought it.

These images of past wars influence subsequent generations confronted with the need to manage a world fraught with peril. World War I left a bitter taste, and in its aftermath that "war to end all wars" was perceived as a largely futile endeavor instigated by political leaders whose shortsightedness resulted in a tragic loss of young lives. For years afterward, peace movements flourished which, even in the face of Hitler's Nazism, could only perceive issues in terms of the "Great War." Indeed, it took the shock of Pearl Harbor to end America's isolationary stance toward entanglement in the "corruption" of European political life.

World War II, and to a much lesser extent Korea, changed the image of war in America and in the following decades dominated U.S. attitudes toward military intervention. The horrors of the Holocaust and Japanese brutality combined to legitimate in American society, and for a time in much of the world, the role of the United States as an international peacekeeper and policeman. Whereas World War I created an image of war that served to tie the hands of Franklin Roosevelt in his efforts to help the British repel Nazi military might, World War II freed American presidents to carry out national policy objectives forcibly overseas. Lyndon Johnson's allusion to America' role in Vietnam as "preventing another Munich" graphically illustrates the hold past wars can have upon the future.

War as a Central Organizing Experience

War is an especially powerful organizing experience for men and women who come of age during a major conflict. The Vietnam War, like the two world wars before it, was a conflict that defined war for a generation. Unlike those previous wars, it was not fought on a broad international battlefield but rather in a narrow stretch of land far distant from America. Moreover, as our study shows, it left not a single overwhelming image, but conflicting visions and meanings over which we continue to fight, though less stridently than at the height of that bitterly divisive conflict.

Within the Vietnam Generation, one finds a dominant sense of the American involvement in the war as a grave mistake. Yet, upon deeper probing, varying interpretations of the nature of that error emerge. At the same time, certain threads are common to the body of images resulting from the war. In sifting through the thoughts and feelings of the generation, we are constantly reminded that what is essential here is not what actually happened, but what is believed to have occurred. It is those impressions, fixed in memory, that form the bedrock from which a generation draws its conslusions about the legacy of war.

Effects of Vietnam on Its Veterans

The organization and focus of our study emphasize a crucial element of the Vietnam conflict, the consensus concerning the effects of the war on those who fought it. Indeed, for nearly a decade, the story of the Vietnam War has centered on its veterans, men who were originally ignored or denigrated. There is every evidence that we as a society finally agree that in some way the men we sent off to fight in Vietnam were sacrificed without sufficient thought to whether the objectives of the war warranted the price they were forced to pay. The story of the continuing pain of Vietnam veterans has become central to the national story of the war. If the Vietnam War challenged the established image of the United States and its global role, the Vietnam veteran has recast the image of war and its warriors. It is the continued replay of the conflict in the minds and lives of Vietnam veterans that keeps the issue at the forefront of national concern. And it is in the hearts and minds of those in the Vietnam Generation who did not serve that the pain of the Vietnam veterans finds its clearest resonance.

Despite the many books that describe the Vietnam War in political, moral, or strategic terms, what has caught the public imagination in recent years is how the war was experienced by American soldiers. The reality of Vietnam in the hearts and minds of its veterans has shocked and dismayed our nation and elicited a sense of obligation to veterans of that conflict. This study shows the extent to which the Vietnam War continues to shape the direction of its veterans' lives. As we have seen, the veterans most adversely affected by the war are those who experienced high levels of war stress. Heavy-combat veterans and veterans who participated in or witnessed abusive violence are particularly marked by their war experiences.

The Vietnam Generation's Views of the War

Our data show that among Vietnam veterans and their peers certain aspects of the war experience have become major predictors in determining feelings about the United States' role in the world and in future interventions. In this respect, it is noteworthy that while a small minority of our sample justified the American involvement in the war as necessary to the struggle against Communist aggression, U.S. participation as seen through the eyes of the majority of the generation was unjustifiable. While there are some differences in perspective among Vietnam veterans, era veterans, and nonveterans, respondents generally agree that the conflict was a revolutionary struggle in which the United States should not have become involved. They maintain that we did not have sufficient legitimate interests to defend in the area to merit our level of sacrifice in terms of dead and wounded Americans. In addition, they observe that the regime in South Vietnam did not merit our support, citing the serious wartime problems caused by widespread corruption within all levels of the South Vietnamese government. Respondents also note that the government practiced graft and favoritism and lacked the support of the people, few of whom identified with the regime. Vietnam veterans are especially bitter. Many recount that upon arrival in Vietnam, they saw themselves as champions of a cause that was just and would triumph. They had come as allies, helping a people confronted by aggression. But after facing a determined enemy and receiving little support from the Vietnamese population, they realized that they were involved in an exhausting, indecisive war in which their major cause was personal survival. This loss of a sense of mission was profoundly demoralizing and deeply resented by many of the men who fought the war. From their perspective, the American involvement in the conflict was reduced to a senseless loss of life, limb, friends, and self-image. Indeed, it appears from the transcripts and statistical findings that future American military involvement in this type of conflict is viewed with a great deal of wariness across the generation.

Perceptions of Allies

For Vietnam veterans, even more than for nonveterans or era veterans, the caliber of their military allies remains a central traumatizing element of the Vietnam conflict. American soldiers initially assumed that the South Vietnamese Army was committed to fighting the war. Throughout the years of the American involvement in Vietnam, American policymakers repeatedly stressed that the objective of U.S. intervention was to assist the South Vietnamese defend themselves and that ultimately South Vietnam would carry on alone its battle for freedom and independence from the North. Vietnam veterans agreed that the final outcome of the war depended on the commitment of the South Vietnamese government and the ARVN. They pointed out that in fact this basic reality was largely disregarded and the war was fought as an American war, with the South Vietnamese performing an unimportant role.

The causes for the Americanization of the war were complex. An important reason was the years of dissatisfaction experienced by the American forces in Vietnam caused by ARVN inefficiency. The ARVN officer corps, by and large, came from the middle and upper classes of South Vietnam's urban society and had little in common with its soldiers, who were primarily of peasant origin. Moreover, despite notable exceptions, many of the officers lacked determination and leadership capacity, preferring safe rear-area locations to combat commands. Thus, the American military concluded that fighting the war themselves would prevent needless enmity and avoid unnecessary frustration.

As our transcripts indicate, the failure of the South Vietnamese soldiers to carry their weight contributed heavily to veterans' lack of regard for their ally as well as their sense of the war as a shameful farce with Americans carrying the burden of the tragic costs of the war. Veterans risking their lives too often found that those they were ostensibly there to help failed to show the will to help themselves. The degree of their resentment over the ARVN's behavior has been greatly underestimated by the general public as well as by political leaders.

Reactions to Abusive Violence

Our study also demonstrates that the way the war was fought by the combatants made a major impression on Vietnam veterans and nonveterans and, indeed, for many became the main reason they turned against American involvement in the conflict. This feeling is especially strong in regard to acts of abusive violence directed against civilians. A central unifying theme in our study is the consensus among our respondents in terms of what they perceive to be acceptable or unacceptable conduct in wartime. As we have seen, actions against civilians including terrorizing civilians, attacking hospitals, withholding medical treatment from wounded civilians, killing of hostages, mutilation of the dead, and rape are condemned by 90% of the sample, while 75% oppose bombing or shelling of cities to terrorize the civilian population and 51% cite environmental warfare as unlawful.

The frequent brutality by all parties to the conflict toward civilians, the routine torture of prisoners, and the use of cruel weaponry that marked the prosecution of the war left a profound imprint on the generation, especially Vietnam veterans. From the transcript material, we see that those men who directly experienced the violence of war emphatically assert that abuse of civilians was endemic among the indigenous forces. They also note that the ARVN's characteristically low regard for human life and suffering caused many civilians to fear the army that was supposedly defending them as much or more than the enemy.

Vietnam veterans also spoke openly about the occurrence of American acts of abusive violence. One group noted that these acts were inherent in the circumstances under which they were forced to live and fight. The conflict in Vietnam was a guerrilla war without fronts, they argued, and this created a setting conducive to abuse. The need to prosecute the war against an enemy that hid among civilians legitimized the use of a broad range of actions against noncombatants. But other Vietnam veterans pointed out that most of the abusive violence could have been prevented and that not enough was done to stop it. They also noted that the American war against civilians was a serious handicap to "winning the hearts and minds" of the Vietnamese people.

Another aspect of the stigma surrounding the Vietnam War is the feeling expressed by Vietnam veterans who were exposed to the persistent brutality of the conflict that such wars ought not to become an American concern. Nonveterans, especially antiwar activists, share this perspective and argue that American involvement in a war fought under these conditions cannot be justified.

Role of Individual Responsibility

Our findings on the issue of individual responsibility in war suggest that our respondents, including Vietnam veterans, generally see a need for constraints in the conduct of warfare. But a clear distinction is consistently made between the responsibility for soldiers on the one side and officers and political leaders on the other. Our sample generally agreed that the latter group have clear obligations and are legally liable. Moreover, while a majority of those respondents who discussed the responsibility of combat soldiers noted that judgments and decisions are extremely difficult for soldiers in the field, we witnessed remarkably strong support for the responsibility of officers to control their men. We also found a consensus in the generation that in the final analysis law alone cannot assure protection of basic human values. It was often noted that humane conduct will depend on recognition by the military leadership that violations of the law of war, especially in a guerrilla war setting, are often counterproductive and do not contribute to the attainment of military objectives. The hope was also expressed, especially by antiwar activists, that the tragic experience of Vietnam will motivate American political leaders in future military conflicts to pay greater heed to considerations of humane conduct.

Attitudes Toward Future Vietnam-type Interventions

Our data further suggest that the question of participation in future wars like Vietnam will be carefully scrutinized. The traditional given, that when one's country called one went to war, has been seriously undermined by the experience of Vietnam. It appears that participation in any future military ventures will require persuasion by the political leadership that the purposes of the action are consonant with the national interest as seen by those who are called upon to fight or to abandon their children to war. If the legitimacy of a conflict is generally accepted, we expect that the military will have little problem in recruitment. But Vietnam has shifted the burden of decision from the political and military leaders to those who are eligible for service as well as those whose young would be required to fight. Our data indicate that compliance with national leaders' directives can no longer be taken for granted. Moreover, fundamental fissures have emerged within the national political leadership regarding the propriety of future interventions, and there is a deep reluctance to involve United States troops in Third World countries.

The Vietnam Generation seems to articulate this general caution toward intervention by U.S. troops. As our study shows, there is very little support among our respondents for sending U.S. troops to intervene in situations like Vietnam. Nonveterans (84%) are most opposed to utilizing American soldiers abroad in situations that involve internal conflicts even though these confrontations incorporate elements of the East-West conflict. Vietnam era and Vietnam veterans (71%) are significantly less likely to oppose the use of troops in these conflicts; still, seven out of ten veterans oppose the use of U.S. forces in Third World conflicts. Supporters of the Vietnam War, both veterans and nonveterans, generally encourage future interventions and continue to argue that "we must fight Communism everywhere." But the general picture that emerges of the Vietnam Generation is one of consistent opposition to military intervention in situations like Vietnam, accompanied by legitimation of resistance to military service. This orientation carries over to how these men would counsel their children to deal with subsequent situations that recall Vietnam.

Finally, our data deny that a national reconciliation around the war has taken place. Rather, the experiences and attitudes that have emerged during the conflict and its aftermath indicate that the legacy of Vietnam will remain a source of debate during the foreseeable future. The Vietnam War has clearly undermined the national consensus that emerged from World War II, making the burden for legitimating future interventions within the Vietnam Generation extremely difficult. This is a generation that wants to evaluate the costs and benefits of military actions before committing itself. The long and painful struggle of Vietnam veterans to cope with the effects of war is central to how the generation perceives the conflict and a key barrier to sending future U.S. military forays into uncharted terrain.

TABLES[a]

Chapter 1

Table 1.1

Proportion of Veterans Who Enlisted or Were Drafted into the Armed Forces during the Vietnam Era

	Enlisted	Drafted
Vietnam veterans	65	35
Vietnam era veterans	66	34
N[b]	443	229

No test of statistical significance was performed on this table.

Table 1.2–Panel A

Proportion of Vietnam Veterans by Branch of Service

Vietnam Veterans	Army	Marines	Air Force	Navy
Enlisted	50	75	93	95
Drafted	50	25	7	5
N	199	43	25	58

No test of statistical significance was performed on this table.

Table 1.2–Panel B

Proportion of Vietnam Era Veterans by Branch of Service

Vietnam Era Veterans	Army	Marines	Air Force	Navy
Enlisted	42	78	94	93
Drafted	58	22	6	7
N	188	23	65	61

No test of statistical significance was performed on this table.

---

a. All percentages in the tables are based on weighted data. Due to rounding procedures not all the percentages in the tables sum to 100%.

b. This column or row shows the unweighted N (total in each category).

Table 1.3

Proportion of Veterans Who Served in Each Branch of Military during the Vietnam Era

	Army	Marines	Air Force	Navy	N
Vietnam veterans	61	11	8	20	326
Vietnam era veterans	51	6	23	18	341

No test of statistical significance was performed on this table.

Table 1.4

Proportion of Veterans in the Vietnam Era Military by Rank

	Privates	NCO's	Officers	N
Vietnam veterans	57	36	7	326
Vietnam era veterans	69	25	6	341

No test of statistical significance was performed on this table.

Table 1.5–Panel A

Proportion of Vietnam Veterans in the Vietnam Era Military by Rank

Vietnam Veterans	Army	Marines	Air Force	Navy
Privates	50	60	68	74
NCO's	43	29	22	22
Officers	7	11	10	4
N	199	43	25	58

No test of statistical significance was performed on this table.

Table 1.5–Panel B

Proportion of Vietnam Era Veterans in the Vietnam Era Military by Rank

Vietnam Era Veterans	Army	Marines	Air Force	Navy
Privates	65	87	75	70
NCO's	28	13	19	27
Officers	7	—	6	3
N	188	23	65	61

No test of statistical significance was performed on this table.

Table 1.6

Subjective Reactions to Traumatic Experiences

Panel A Group Who Saw Americans Killed (N = 189)		Panel B Group Who Saw Vietnamese Killed (N = 204)		Panel C Group Who Experienced Combat (N = 317)	
Felt anger seeing Americans killed	21%	Felt death of Vietnamese was justified	22%	Felt fear in combat	17%
Felt sadness seeing Americans killed	42%	Felt indifference to the death of Vietnamese	28%	Concerned with self- preservation in combat	20%
Felt shock seeing Americans killed	24%	Felt sadness seeing Vietnamese killed	36%	Had no feelings in combat	20%
Had no feelings seeing Americans killed	14%	Felt fear seeing Vietnamese killed	3%	Felt frustrated by constraints in combat	6%
Accepted the deaths of Americans	12%				
Reported a reaction to this experience	72%	Reported a reaction to this experience	74%	Reported a reaction to this experience	51%

Note: The columns do not total to 100% because codes developed for these items allowed for two responses; and some responses were too idiosyncratic to be used in the analysis.

Table 1.7

Proportion of Whites and Blacks Who Participated in the Antiwar Movement among Nonveterans

	Whites	Blacks
Low activists	67	89
Moderate activists	18	9
High activists	14	3
N	401	191

The relationship between these two variables is significant at p < .001.

Table 1.8

Parental Educational Attainment Among Nonveteran Antiwar Activists

	Less than H.S.	H.S. graduate	Some college	College graduate	Postgrad training	N
Low activists	29	38	17	11	6	438
Moderate activists	19	33	18	17	14	82
High activists	13	19	20	20	27	56

The linear relationship between these two variables is significant at p < .001.

Table 1.9

Proportion of Nonveterans Who Participated in the Antiwar Movement by Age

	Low activism	Moderate activism	High activism	N
Thirty and under	62	21	17	269
Thirty-one and over	83	11	6	323

The relationship between these two variables is significant at p < .001.

Table 1.10

Proportion of Nonveterans Who Expressed Positive Feelings about the Military by Participation in the Antiwar Movement

	Expressed positive feelings toward the military	Did not express positive feelings toward the military	N
Low activists	31	69	454
Moderate activists	12	88	82
High activists	9	91	56

The relationship between these two variables is significant at $p < .001$.

Table 1.11

Proportion of Nonveterans Who Expressed Negative Feelings about the Military by Participation in the Antiwar Movement

	Expressed negative feelings toward the military	Did not express negative feelings toward the military	N
Low activists	39	61	454
Moderate activists	66	36	82
High activists	64	36	56

The relationship between these two variables is significant at $p < .001$.

Table 1.12

Proportion of Nonveterans Who Felt There Were No Advantages to Military Service by Participation in the Antiwar Movement

	Felt there were no advantages to military service	Did not feel there were no advantages to military service	N
Low activists	20	80	324
Moderate activists	33	67	48
High activists	39	61	43

The relationship between these two variables is significant at $p < .01$.

Table 1.13

Proportion of Nonveterans Aware of Alternative Means of Avoiding Military Service by Participation in the Antiwar Movement

	Aware of no alts.	Aware of one alt.	Aware of 2–3 alts.	Aware of 4–5 alts.	Aware of 6–7 alts.	N
Low activists	13	16	28	23	21	454
Moderate activists	8	4	20	26	42	82
High activists	5	8	14	23	51	56

The relationship between these two variables is significant at $p < .001$.

Table 1.14

Proportion of Whites and Blacks Who Supported the War among Nonveterans

	Whites	Blacks
Opposed war	64	78
Ambivalent	14	13
Supported war	22	10
N	316	156

The relationship between these two variables is significant at $p < .001$.

Table 1.15

Parental Educational Attainment among Nonveterans Who Supported the War

	Less than H.S.	H.S. graduate	Some college	College graduate	Postgrad training	N
Opposed war	25	32	19	11	13	315
Ambivalent	20	42	22	11	5	58
Supported war	32	36	15	12	6	87

The relationship between these two variables is significant at $p < .05$.

Table 1.16

Proportion of Nonveterans Who Expressed Negative Feelings about the Military by Support for the War

	Expressed negative feelings toward the military	Did not express negative feelings toward the military	N
Opposed war	55	45	323
Ambivalent	46	54	59
Supported war	32	68	90

The relationship between these two variables is significant at $p < .01$.

Table 1.17

Proportion of Nonveterans Who Saw No Advantage to Military Service by Support for the War

	Felt there were no advantages to military service	Did not feel there were no advantages to military service	N
Opposed war	31	70	211
Ambivalent	41	59	36
Supported war	13	88	73

The relationship between these two variables is significant at $p < .01$.

Table 1.18

Proportion of Nonveterans Who Saw the Military as a Career Disruption by Support for the War

	Saw military service as career disruption	Did not see military service as career disruption	N
Opposed war	40	60	211
Ambivalent	47	53	36
Supported war	56	44	73

The relationship between these two variables is significant at $p < .01$.

Chapter 2

Table 2.1

Felt Isolated upon Returning Home, by Combat Experience

	Felt very isolated	Somewhat isolated	Not isolated	N
Little combat	35	49	16	(111)
Moderate combat	27	66	7	(122)
Heavy combat	39	56	5	(92)

The linear relationship between combat experience and feelings of isolation is significant at $p < .10$.

Table 2.2

Felt Isolated Upon Returning Home, by Combat Experience, after 1967

Post-1967	Very isolated	Somewhat isolated	Not isolated	N
Little combat	41	44	15	(49)
Moderate combat	45	43	8	(68)
Heavy combat	49	44	11	(48)

The linear relationship between combat experience and feelings of isolation in the post-1967 period is significant at $p < .10$.

Table 2.3

Perceived Support by U.S. Government and Public, by Veteran Status

	Low	Moderate	High	N
Vietnam veteran	41	35	24	(324)
Vietnam era veteran	36	40	24	(335)

Table 2.4

Perceived Support by U.S. Government and Public, by Exposure to Abusive Violence, after 1967

Post-1967	Low	Moderate	High	N
Not exposed	45	26	29	(108)
Witnessed*	69	20	12	(38)
Participated	40	43	17	(19)

*This group differs significantly from the not exposed group at p < .05.

Table 2.5

Confidence and Trust in Governmental Institutions to Serve the Public Interest, by Veteran Status

	Low alienation	Moderate alienation	High alienation	N
Vietnam veteran	27	33	40	(325)
Vietnam era veteran	24	42	35	(337)
Nonveterans*	37	36	27	(592)

*This group differs significantly from veterans at p < .01.

Table 2.6

Confidence and Trust in Governmental Institutions to Serve the Public Interest, by Exposure to Abusive Violence

	Low alienation	Moderate alienation	High alienation	N
Not exposed	30	30	41	(221)
Witnessed*	23	36	41	(75)
Participated	20	45	34	(29)

*This group differs significantly from the not exposed group at p < .05.

Table 2.7

Talked about What You Had Just Been Through, by Veteran Status

	Kept pretty much to self	Talked about it some	Talked a lot about it	N
Vietnam veteran	60	29	11	(325)
Vietnam era veteran	29	49	22	(339)

These groups differ significantly at $p < .01$.

Table 2.8

Talked about What You Had Just Been Through, by Combat

	Kept pretty much to self	Talked about it some	Talked a lot about it	N
Low combat	53	32	15	(111)
Moderate combat	63	29	8	(121)
Heavy combat	66	26	7	(93)

Table 2.9

Talked about What You Had Just Been Through, by Exposure to Abusive Violence

	Kept pretty much to self	Talked about it some	Talked a lot about it	N
Not exposed	59	30	12	(220)
Witnessed	65	28	7	(76)
Participated	70	28	2	(29)

Table 2.10

After Return Home, Anxious to Get Involved in Everything or Did Not Want to Participate in Things with Other People, by Exposure to Abusive Violence, after 1967

Post 1967	Reluctant	Eager	N
Not exposed*	48	51	(107)
Witnessed	62	38	(38)
Participated	59	42	(19)

*This group differs significantly from those who witnessed and participated in abusive violence at $p < .05$.

Table 2.11

How Things Actually Worked Out Regarding Your Plans When You Got Home, by Combat, after 1967

Post-1967	Better than expected	About as expected	Worse than expected	N
Low combat	18	58	24	(49)
Moderate combat	18	41	41	(67)
Heavy combat	14	29	57	(48)

The linear relationship between combat and how things worked out is significant at $p < .10$.

Table 2.12

How Things Actually Worked Out Regarding Your Plans When You Got Home, by Exposure to Abusive Violence, after 1967

Post-1967	Better than expected	About as expected	Worse than expected	N
Not exposed	17	52	31	(108)
Witnessed*	14	22	62	(37)
Participated	22	25	53	(19)

*This group differs significantly from the not exposed group at $p < .05$.

Table 2.13

Mean Scores on PERI Symptom Scales, by Race and Exposure to Abusive Violence

Demoralization—Mean Scores			*N*
White			
	Not exposed	17.97	(154)
	Witnessed	21.13	(52)
	Participated	15.52	(19)
Black			
	Not exposed	18.99	(67)
	Witnessed	20.89	(23)
	Participated	27.25	(10)
Perceived Hostility—Mean Scores			
White			
	Not exposed	19.49	(152)
	Witnessed	20.53	(53)
	Participated	19.70	(19)
Black			
	Not exposed	28.67	(67)
	Witnessed	27.41	(23)
	Participated	35.03	(10)
Active Hostility—Mean Scores			
White			
	Not exposed	41.12	(154)
	Witnessed	41.00	(52)
	Participated	37.93	(19)
Black			
	Not exposed	34.59	(66)
	Witnessed	39.32	(23)
	Participated	49.32	(10)
Angry Feelings—Mean Scores			
White			
	Not exposed	33.47	(154)
	Witnessed	37.31	(53)
	Participated	31.59	(19)
Black			
	Not exposed	33.00	(67)
	Witnessed	31.43	(23)
	Participated	43.67	(10)
Guilt—Mean Scores			
White			
	Not exposed	19.11	(153)
	Witnessed	22.65	(52)
	Participated	14.89	(19)
Black			
	Not exposed	17.67	(67)
	Witnessed	21.56	(23)
	Participated	28.42	(10)

Table 2.14

Breakdown of Varieties of PTSD by Selected Experiences[a]

Part I: Prevalence of PTSD by Levels of Combat Experience among Vietnam Veterans[b]

	Reexperiencing PTSD	Denial PTSD
Low combat (N = 82)	22%	10%
Moderate (N = 92)	24%	22%
Heavy (N = 71)	32%	22%

The linear relationship between combat and Reexperiencing PTSD is significant at $p < .05$. The relationship between combat and Denial PTSD is not statistically significant.

Part II: Prevalence of PTSD by Types of Exposure to Abusive Violence among Vietnam Veterans

	Reexperiencing PTSD	Denial PTSD
No exposure (N = 171)	19%	15%
Witnessed[b] (N = 55)	40%	20%
Participated[b] (N = 19)	38%	41%[c]

a. There is no statistically significant relationship between witnessing or participation in abusive violence and Reexperiencing PTSD.

b. The percentages represent the proportion of respondents in this group (defined by the row category) who reported this form of stress disorder (defined by the column).

c. This group differs significantly from the not exposed group on Denial PTSD at $p < .001$.

Table 2.15

Is There Anything about Your Experience in the Military—Anything You Saw or Did—that You Find Yourself Trying to Forget? by Combat Experience

	Yes	No	N
Low combat	34	64	(111)
Moderate combat	49	51	(122)
Heavy combat	56	44	(93)

The linear relationship between combat exposure and presence of memories the veteran wants to forget is significant at $p < .001$.

Chapter 3

Table 3.1

Feelings about U.S. Involvement in Vietnam, by Veteran Status

	Supported	Confused	Opposed	N
Vietnam veteran	46	10	45	(227)
Vietnam era veteran	32	19	49	(260)
Nonveteran*	19	14	67	(472)

*Nonveterans are significantly different from both Vietnam and Vietnam era veterans at p < .001.

Table 3.2

Feelings About U.S. Involvement in Vietnam, by Race

	Supported	Confused	Opposed	N
White	29	14	57	(657)
Black	13	15	73	(302)

The relationship is significant at p < .001.

Table 3.3

Feelings about U.S. Involvement in Vietnam by Period of Service or Eligibility for Military Service

	Supported	Confused	Opposed	N
Pre-1968	34	11	55	(454)
Post-1967	20	16	64	(505)

The relationship between these two variables is significant at p < .001.

Table 3.4

Feelings about U.S. Involvement in Vietnam by Period of Service among Vietnam Vets

	Supported	Confused	Opposed	N
Pre-1968	55	9	36	(109)
Post-1967	36	10	54	(118)

The relationship between these two variables is significant at p < .05.

Table 3.5

Feelings about U.S. Involvement in Vietnam, by Branch of Service among Vietnam Veterans

	Supported	Confused	Opposed	N
Army	44	7	49	(139)
Marines*	66	11	23	(31)
Navy/Air Force	41	16	44	(56)

*This group is significantly different in feelings about U.S. involvement than those who served in the navy or air force, $p < .01$.

Table 3.6

Feelings about U.S. Involvement in Vietnam by Antiwar Activism among Nonveterans

	Supported	Confused	Opposed	N
Low activists	25	16	60	(353)
Moderate activists	11	15	74	(70)
High activists	3	4	93	(49)

The linear relationship between these two variables is significant, $p < .01$

Table 3.7

Was Your Personal View of the War Influenced by Abusive Violence?

	Abusive violence did affect view of war	Abusive violence did not effect view of war	N
Vietnam veteran	54	46	(250)
Vietnam era veteran	60	41	(326)
Nonveteran	62	39	(574)

Table 3.8

Was Your Personal View of the War Influenced by Abusive Violence? by Race

	Abusive violence did affect view of war	Abusive violence did not effect view of war	N
White	65	35	(793)
Black	40	60	(357)

The relationship between these two variables is significant, p < .001

Table 3.9

Was Your Personal View of the War Influenced by Abusive Violence? by Exposure to or Participation in Abusive Violence

	Abusive violence did affect view of war	Abusive violence did not affect view of war	N
Not exposed to abusive violence	47%	53%	(174)
Witnessed abusive violence	67%	33%	(56)
*Participated in abusive violence	83%	17%	(20)

*This group is significantly different from those not exposed to abusive violence, p < .05

Table 3.10

Was Your Personal View of the War Influenced by Abusive Violence? by Antiwar Activism

	Yes	No	N
Low activists	54	46	(441)
Moderate activists	82	18	(80)
High activists	85	15	(53)

The relationship between antiwar activism and being influenced by abusive violence is significant at p < .05.

Table 3.11

Awareness of Abusive Violence Led to Opposition to the War, by Race

	Turned against war because of abusive violence	Did not turn against war because of abusive violence	N
White	46	54	(860)
Black	22	78	(399)

This relationship between these two variables is significant, p < .001

Table 3.12

Awareness of Abusive Violence Led to Opposition to the War, by Exposure to Abusive Violence

	Turned against war because of abusive violence	Did not turn against war because of abusive violence	N
Not exposed to abusive violence	32	68	(221)
Witnessed abusive violence*	57	43	(76)
Participated in abusive violence	44	56	(29)

*This group is significantly different from the not exposed group at p < .001

Table 3.13

Awareness of Abusive Violence Led to Opposition to the War, by Antiwar Activism

	Yes	No	N
Low antiwar activists	33	67	(454)
Moderate antiwar activists	64	36	(82)
High antiwar activists	56	44	(56)

The relationship between antiwar activism and turning against the war because of abusive violence is significant at p < .10.

Chapter 4

Table 4.1

Attitudes toward the South Vietnamese Army (ARVN), by Veteran Status

	Positive	Mixed/ conflicted	Negative	N
Vietnam veterans	8	42	50	(319)
Vietnam era veterans	7	60	33	(334)
Nonveterans	5	56	37	(588)

Table 4.2

Attitudes toward the Vietcong and North Vietnamese Forces (VC/NVA), by Veteran Status

	Positive	Mixed/ conflicted	Negative	N
Vietnam veterans*	24	38	37	(316)
Vietnam era veterans	13	50	38	(331)
Nonveterans	19	46	34	(581)

*Vietnam veterans are significantly different from nonveterans, p < .10

Table 4.3

Attitudes toward the ARVN, by Branch of Service Among Vietnam Veterans

	Positive	Mixed/ conflicted	Negative	N
Army*	8	33	59	(193)
Marines	0	44	56	(43)
Navy/ Air Force	14	59	28	(82)

*Army veterans are signficantly different from air force and navy veterans, p < .01.

Table 4.4

Attitudes toward the ARVN, by Race

	Positive	Mixed/ conflicted	Negative	N
White	8	52	41	(846)
Black	7	63	30	(395)

The relationship between these two variables is significant, p < .05.

Table 4.5

Attitudes toward the VC/NVA, by Race

	Positive	Mixed/ conflicted	Negative	N
White	18	42	40	(839)
Black	23	60	17	(389)

The relationship between these two variables is significant, p < .001.

Table 4.6

Attitudes toward the ARVN, by Period of Service among Vietnam Veterans

	Positive	Mixed/ conflicted	Negative	N
Pre-1968	13	49	39	(154)
Post-1967	5	35	60	(165)

The relationship between these two variables is significant, p < .05.

Table 4.7

Attitudes toward the VC/NVA, by Combat Experience

	Positive	Mixed/ conflicted	Negative	N
Low combat	12	44	44	(107)
Moderate combat	32	40	27	(119)
Heavy combat	30	29	41	(90)

The linear relationship between these two variables is significant, p < .05.

Table 4.8

Attitudes toward the ARVN, by Activism among Nonveterans

	Positive	Mixed/ conflicted	Negative	N
Low activists	9	61	30	(450)
Moderate activists	7	34	59	(82)
High activists	1	50	49	(56)

The linear relationship between these two variables is significant, $p < .001$.

Table 4.9

Attitudes toward the ARVN, by Support for the Vietnam War among Nonveterans

	Positive	Mixed/ conflicted	Negative	N
Supported war	21	41	38	(88)
Ambivalent	9	70	22	(58)
Opposed war	3	53	44	(322)

The linear relationship between these two variables is significant, $p < .001$.

Table 4.10

Attitudes toward the VC/NVA, by Activism among Nonveterans

	Positive	Mixed/ conflicted	Negative	N
Low activists	12	52	36	(444)
Moderate activists	26	37	36	(81)
High activists	56	24	20	(56)

The linear relationship between these two variables is significant, $p < .001$.

Table 4.11

Attitudes toward the VC/NVA, by support for the Vietnam War among Nonveterans

	Positive	Conflicted	Negative	N
Supported war	14	25	61	(89)
Ambivalent	15	54	31	(58)
Opposed war	25	47	28	(317)

The linear relationship between these two variables is significant, $p < .001$.

Chapter 5

Table 5.1

Feelings toward the Vietnamese, by Veteran Status

	Positive	Ambivalent	Negative	N
Vietnam veterans	37	31	31	(266)
Vietnam era veterans	54	21	25	(185)
Nonveterans*	72	16	12	(394)

*This group significantly differs from Vietnam and Vietnam era veterans at $p < .001$.

Table 5.2

Feelings toward the Vietnamese, by Antiwar Activism among Nonveterans

	Positive	Ambivalent	Negative	N
Low activists	71	15	14	(280)
Moderate activists	75	16	9	(69)
High activists	74	20	6	(45)

Table 5.3

Feelings toward the Vietnamese, by Race among Vietnam Veterans

	Positive	Ambivalent	Negative	N
White	35	29	36	(194)
Black	49	41	10	(72)

The relationship between these two variables is significant at $p < .01$.

Table 5.4

Feelings toward the Vietnamese, by Whether of Not the Veteran Knew Vietnamese Personally among Vietnam Veterans

	Positive	Ambivalent	Negative	N
Knew Vietnamese	46	31	22	(155)
Didn't know Vietnamese	29	32	41	(108)

The relationship between these two variables is significant at $p < .10$.

Table 5.5

Feelings toward the Vietnamese, by Combat, Among Veterans Who Were Neither Exposed to nor Participated in Abusive Violence

	Positive	Ambivalent	Negative	N
Low combat	37	28	35	(73)
Moderate combat	32	28	40	(63)
Heavy combat	18	54	29	(35)

Table 5.6

Feelings toward the Vietnamese, by Exposure to and Participation in Abusive Violence

	Positive	Ambivalent	Negative	N
Not exposed to abusive violence	33	32	34	(171)
Witnessed abusive violence*	46	33	21	(69)
Participated in abusive violence	41	18	41	(26)

*This group significantly differs from the not exposed group at p < .05

Table 5.7

Perception of Vietnamese Feelings toward U.S. Military, by Veteran Status

	Positive	Ambivalent	Negative	N
Vietnam veterans*	41	28	34	(220)
Vietnam era veterans	30	22	48	(214)
Nonveterans	25	23	52	(395)

This group differs significantly from nonveterans at p < .001

Table 5.8

Perceptions of Vietnamese Feelings toward U.S. Military, by Attitude toward the War among Nonveterans

	Positive	Ambivalent	Negative	N
Supported	42	27	31	(70)
Ambivalent	42	14	44	(40)
Opposed	17	22	61	(225)

The linear relationship between these two variables is significant at $p < .001$.

Table 5.9

Effect of the War on Vietnamese Society and the Vietnamese People, by Veteran Status

	Positive	Positive/ negative	Negative	N
Vietnam veterans	41	26	34	(278)
Vietnam era veterans	14	18	68	(292)
Nonveterans*	10	12	77	(544)

*This group differs significantly from Vietnam era veterans at $p < .05$ and from Vietnam veterans at $p < .001$.

Table 5.10

Effect of the War on Vietnamese Society and the Vietnamese People, by Activism

	Positive	Positive/ negative	Negative	N
Low activists	14	13	73	(409)
Moderate activists	5	9	86	(82)
High activists	2	9	90	(53)

The linear relationship between these two variables is significant at $p < .001$.

Table 5.11

Effect of the War on Vietnamese Society and the Vietnamese People, by Heavy-Combat Experience and Race

	Positive	Positive/ negative	Negative	N
White, heavy combat	40	28	32	(50)
Black, heavy combat	29	20	51	(28)

The relationship between combat and the perception of the effects of the war among blacks and whites differs significantly at $p < .10$.

Table 5.12

Effect on the War on Vietnamese Society and the Vietnamese People, by Exposure to and Participation in Abusive Violence among Whites

	Positive	Positive/ negative	Negative	N
Not exposed to abusive violence	40	32	29	(133)
Witnessed abusive violence	34	23	43	(50)
Participated in abusive violence*	40	7	53	(16)

*This group differs significantly from the not exposed group at $p < .01$.

Chapter 6

Table 6.1

The Frequency with which the Military Forces in Vietnam Engaged in Abuse of Civilians and Environmental Warfare

	Mean	Median	N
NVABPERS	70.42	71.49	(1143)
SVABPERS	53.19	55.75	(1111)
USABPERS	35.22	32.15	(1158)
NVTERBOMB	6.88	7.23	(1139)
SVTERBOMB	5.23	5.65	(1096)
USTERBOMB	5.43	5.86	(1136)
USENVWAR	52.32	50.44	(1023)

Table 6.2

Perceptions of the Commonality of Actions Against Civilians and the Environment during the Vietnam War by the North Vietnamese/Vietcong, South Vietnamese, and American Forces, by Veteran Status and Antiwar Activism[a] and Support for U.S. Involvement

MEAN SCORES

	NVA/VC[d] ABPERS	ARVN[b] ABPERS	U.S.[b] ABPERS	NVA/VC[c] TERBOMB	ARVN[c] TERBOMB	U.S.[c] TERBOMB	U.S.[b] ENVWAR
Vietnam veterans[d]	68.99 (N=295)	*** 47.32 (N=287)	*** 26.86 (N=300)	* 6.37 (N=307)	*** 3.99 (N=282)	*** 4.28 (N=296)	43.91 (N=267)
Vietnam era veterans	71.93 (N=314)	54.46 (N=300)	34.26 (N=313)	6.99 (N=303)	5.51 (N=298)	5.49 (N=301)	55.95 (N=273)
Nonveterans	69.34 (N=534)	56.97 (N=524)	41.20 (N=545)	6.82 (N=529)	5.60 (N=516)	5.90 (N=539)	58.91 (N=483)
	***	***	***		***	***	***
Low activists[e]	71.81 (N=405)	55.01 (N=395)	38.35 (N=414)	7.00 (N=401)	5.46 (N=387)	5.47 (N=407)	55.16 (N=364)
Moderate activists	64.30 (N=78)	60.55 (N=78)	47.78 (N=77)	6.94 (N=75)	6.20 (N=77)	6.88 (N=78)	63.35 (N=73)
High activists	61.83 (N=51)	61.68 (N=51)	48.34 (N=54)	5.66 (N=53)	5.49 (N=52)	6.91 (N=54)	73.68 (N=46)
Supported the war	75.42 (N=82)	53.00 (N=82)	32.26 (N=83)	7.49 (N=84)	5.05 (N=82)	4.89 (N=83)	54.99 (N=76)

[a]The higher the score, the more commonly the group attributes this behavior to the combatants military forces.
[b]The possible scores range from 0 to 100.
[c]The possible scores range from 0 to 9.
[d]Statistically significant differences are indicated only when differences exist between Vietnam veterans or era veterans, and nonveterans: * = less than .10; ** = less than .05; *** = less than .01
[e]Statistically significant differences are indicated only where a linear association exists between antiwar activism and the measure represented by the column.

Table 6.3

Perceived Frequency with which Vietcong or North Vietnamese Army (VC/NVA) Engaged in Direct Mistreatment of South Vietnamese Civilians, by Veteran Status

	Seldom	Sometimes	Frequently	N
Vietnam veteran	4	34	63	(295)
Era veteran	2	28	70	(314)
Nonveteran	3	33	65	(534)

Table 6.4

Perceived Frequency with which South Vietnamese Army (ARVN) Engaged in Direct Mistreatment of South Vietnamese Civilians, by Veteran Status

	Seldom	Sometimes	Frequently	N
Vietnam veteran*	21	56	23	(287)
Era veteran	10	57	33	(300)
Nonveteran	10	52	39	(524)

This group differs significantly from nonveterans at p < .01.

Table 6.5

Perceived Frequency with which U.S. Forces Engaged in Direct Mistreatment of South Vietnamese Civilians, by Veteran Status

	Seldom	Sometimes	Frequently	N
Vietnam veteran	55	39	6	(300)
Era veteran	47	42	11	(313)
Nonveteran*	31	53	17	(545)

*This group differs significantly from Vietnam and Vietnam era veterans at p < .01.

Table 6.6

Proportions of Veteran Status Groups who Believe the Military Forces to the Conflict *Seldom* Used Bombing and Shelling to Terrorize Civilian Populations

	VC/NVA	ARVN	U.S. Forces
Vietnam veteran	15 (N = 307)	42 (N = 282)	41 (N = 296)
Era veteran	7 (N = 303)	20 (N = 298)	21 (N = 301)
Nonveteran	9 (N = 529)	19 (N = 516)	18 (N = 539)

Table 6.7

Perceived Frequency with which U.S. Military Forces in Vietnam Employed Environmental Warfare, by Veteran Status

	Seldom	Sometimes	Frequently	N
Vietnam veterans*	36	39	26	(267)
Vietnam era veterans	19	38	44	(273)
Nonveterans	17	37	46	(483)

*This group significantly differs from nonveterans at p < .01.

Table 6.8

Perceived Frequency of Abuse of South Vietnamese Civilians by North Vietnamese Army and Vietcong, by Period and Heavy-Combat Experience

	Seldom	Sometimes	Frequently	N
Heavy-combat exposure—pre-l968	3	40	57	(44)
Heavy-combat exposure—post-1967	4	24	73	(40)

These groups differ significantly at p < .10.

Table 6.9

Perceived Frequency of VC/NVA Bombing and Shelling of Cities to Terrorize the Population, by Period and Heavy-Combat Exposure

	Seldom	Sometimes	Frequently	N
Heavy-combat exposure—pre-1968	16	53	30	(44)
Heavy-combat exposure—post-1967	11	48	42	(46)

The relationship between combat and perception of VC, NVA actions is significantly different in the two periods at p < .05.

Table 6.10

Perceived Frequency of VC/NVA Bombing and Shelling of Cities to Terrorize the Population, by Race and Participation in Abusive Violence

	Seldom	Sometimes	Frequently	N
White participants in abusive violence	14	19	67	(16)
Black participants in abusive violence	18	40	43	(9)

The relationship between participation in abusive violence and perceptions of VC/NVA actions is significantly different in the two races at p < .05.

Table 6.11

Perceived Frequency of Abuse of South Vietnamese Civilians by South Vietnamese Army (ARVN), by Period of Service among Vietnam Veterans

	Seldom	Sometimes	Frequently	N
Served prior to 1968	21	60	19	(146)
Served after 1967	22	52	27	(141)

The relationship between these two variables is significant at p < .05.

Table 6.12

Perceived Frequency of Abuse of South Vietnamese Civilians by South Vietnamese Army (ARVN), by Branch of Service among Vietnam Veterans

	Seldom	Sometimes	Frequently	N
Army	23	59	19	(179)
Marines	28	59	13	(36)
Navy/Air Force*	16	53	31	(71)

*This group is significantly different from those who served in the army or marines at p < .10.

Table 6.13

Perceived Frequency of Abuse of South Vietnamese Civilians by South Vietnamese Army (ARVN), by Race and Combat Exposure

	Seldom	Sometimes	Frequently	N
White				
Low combat	16	62	22	(77)
Moderate combat	16	56	28	(73)
Heavy combat	18	56	26	(51)
Black				
Low combat	41	57	3	(24)
Moderate combat	50	29	21	(31)
Heavy combat	23	57	20	(31)

The relationship between SVABPERS and combat differs significantly among whites and blacks at $p < .05$.

Table 6.14

Perceived Frequency of South Vietnamese Army Use of Bombing and Shelling of Cities to Terrorize Civilian Population, by Combat among White Vietnam Veterans

	Seldom	Sometimes	Frequently	N
Low combat	38	54	9	(76)
Moderate combat	38	55	7	(70)
Heavy combat	51	44	5	(52)

The linear relationship between these variables is significant at $p < .10$.

Table 6.15

Perceived Frequency of South Vietnamese Army Use of Bombing and Shelling of Cities to Terrorize Civilian Population, by Exposure to Abusive Violence

	Seldom	Sometimes	Frequently	N
Not exposed to abusive violence	46	47	7	(192)
Witnessed abusive violence*	34	59	7	(65)
Participated in abusive violence	35	48	17	(25)

*This group is significantly different from the not exposed group at $p < .05$.

Table 6.16

Perceived Frequency with which U.S. Forces Abused South Vietnamese Civilians, by Period of Service among Vietnam Veterans

	Seldom	Sometimes	Frequently	N
Served prior to 1968	67	29	4	(149)
Served after 1967	42	50	8	(151)

The relationship between these two variables is significant at p < .05.

Table 6.17

Perceived Frequency with which U.S. Forces Abused South Vietnamese Civilians, by Combat

	Seldom	Sometimes	Frequently	N
Low combat	51	45	4	(103)
Moderate combat	49	46	5	(110)
Heavy combat	65	25	10	(87)

The linear relationship between these two variables is significant at p < .05.

Table 6.18

Perceived Frequency with which U.S. Forces Abused South Vietnamese Civilians, by Witnessing of and Participation in Abusive Violence

	Seldom	Sometimes	Frequently	N
Not exposed	59	38	3	(202)
Witnessed	53	35	12	(71)
Participated*	24	64	12	(27)

*This group is significantly different from those not exposed at p < .001.

Table 6.19

Perceived Frequency with which U.S. Forces Abused South Vietnamese Civilians, among Whites Who Witnessed or Participated in Abusive Violence

	Seldom	Sometimes	Frequently	N
Not exposed	54	43	4	(141)
Witnessed*	51	35	13	(51)
Participated**	34	63	3	(17)

*This group is significantly different from those not exposed at p < .05.
**This group is significantly different from those not exposed at p < .01.

Table 6.20

Perceived Frequency with which U.S. Forces Abused South Vietnamese Civilians, among Blacks Who Witnessed or Participated in Abusive Violence

	Seldom	Sometimes	Frequently	N
Not exposed	77	21	2	(61)
Witnessed	60	33	8	(20)
Participated*	4	65	31	(10)

*This group is significantly different from those not exposed at p < .05.

Table 6.21

Perceived Frequency with which U.S. Forces Abused South Vietnamese Civilians, by Period and Witnessing of Abusive Violence

	Seldom	Sometimes	Frequently	N
Witnessed before 1968	60	28	12	(36)
Witnessed after 1967	43	44	13	(35)

The relationship between witnessing of abusive violence and perceptions of the U.S. abuse of civilians is significantly different in the two periods at p < .05.

Table 6.22

Perceived Frequency with which U.S. Forces Bombed and Shelled Cities to Terrorize Civilian Population, by Combat among Whites

	Seldom	Sometimes	Frequently	N
Low combat	40	43	17	(75)
Moderate combat	39	48	12	(75)
Heavy combat	41	37	21	(57)

The linear relationship between these two variables is significant at $p < .01$.

Table 6.23

Perceived Frequency with which U.S. Forces Bombed and Shelled Cities to Terrorize Civilian Population, by Witnessing of and Participation in Abusive Violence

	Seldom	Sometimes	Frequently	N
Not exposed	47	40	13	(197)
Witnessed	33	45	22	(73)
Participated*	19	51	30	(26)

*This group is significantly different from those not exposed at $p < .05$.

Table 6.24

Perceived Frequency with which U.S. Forces Employed Environmental Warfare, by Branch of Service among Vietnam Veterans

	Seldom	Sometimes	Frequently	N
Army	42	38	21	(170)
Marines	48	33	19	(31)
Navy/Air force*	17	43	40	(65)

*This group is significantly different from those who served in the army and marines at $p < .01$.

Table 6.25

Perceived Frequency with which U.S. Forces Employed Environmental Warfare, by Combat

	Seldom	Sometimes	Frequently	N
Low combat	35	35	30	(93)
Moderate combat	50	21	29	(100)
Heavy combat	46	38	16	(74)

The linear relationship between these two variables is significant at $p < .01$.

Table 6.26

Perceived Frequency with which U.S. Forces Employed Environmental Warfare, by Combat among Whites

	Seldom	Sometimes	Frequently	N
Low combat	22	42	36	(69)
Moderate combat	48	27	25	(69)
Heavy combat	30	54	16	(46)

The linear relationship between these two variables is significant at p < .01.

Table 6.27

Perceived Frequency with which U.S. Forces Employed Environmental Warfare, by Witnessing of and Participation in Abusive Violence

	Seldom	Sometimes	Frequently	N
Not exposed	45	29	26	(181)
Witnessed	39	33	28	(63)
Participated*	42	37	22	(23)

*This group differs significantly from the not exposed group at p < .10.

Table 6.28

Proportions of Activists who Perceived the Military Forces in Vietnam *Frequently* Engaged in Abuse of Vietnamese Civilians

	VC/NVA	ARVN	U.S. Forces
Low activists	70 (N = 405)	37 (N = 395)	15 (N = 414)
Moderate activists	55 (N = 78)	44 (N = 78)	22 (N = 77)
High activists	50 (N = 51)	43 (N = 51)	20 (N = 54)

Table 6.29

Perceived Frequency with which the U.S. Forces Engaged in Mistreatment of South Vietnamese Civilians by Antiwar Activism

	Seldom	Sometimes	Often	N
Low activists	37	48	15	(414)
Moderate activists	20	59	22	(77)
High activists	11	69	20	(54)

The linear relationship between these two variables is significant at p < .01.

Table 6.30

Proportions of Nonveterans who Believed the U.S. and VC/NVA Frequently Used Bombing and Shelling to Terrorize the Civilian Population, by Activism

	VC/NVA	U.S. Forces
Low activists	39 (N = 401)	23 (N = 407)
Moderate activists	38 (N = 75)	34 (N = 78)
High activists	18 (N = 53)	34 (N = 54)

Table 6.31

Proportions of Nonveterans who Believed the U.S. Frequently Employed Environmental Warfare, by Activism

	Seldom	Sometimes	Frequently	N
Low activists	22	37	42	(364)
Moderate activists	12	42	46	(73)
High activists	0	30	70	(46)

The linear relationship between these two variables is significant at $p < .01$.

Table 6.32

Proportions of Supporters and Opponents of the War who Perceived the Military Forces in Vietnam *Frequently* Engaged in Abuse of South Vietnamese Civilians, among Nonveterans

	VC/NVA	ARVN	U.S. Forces
Supported war	74 (N = 82)	33 (N = 82)	6 (N = 83)
Ambivalent	71 (N = 52)	26 (N = 50)	12 (N = 51)
Opposed war	61 (N = 294)	44 (N = 287)	21 (N = 302)

Table 6.33

Proportions of Supporters and Opponents of the War who Perceived the Military Forces in Vietnam *Frequently* Used Bombing and Shelling of Cities to Terrorize the Civilian Population, among Nonveterans

	VC/NVA	ARVN	U.S. Forces
Supported war	48 (N = 84)	8 (N = 82)	20 (N = 83)
Ambivalent	38 (N = 52)	15 (N = 50)	26 (N = 53)
Opposed war	37 (N = 287)	23 (N = 277)	32 (N = 292)

Table 6.34

Perceived Frequency with which U.S. Forces Employed Environmental Warfare in Vietnam, by Support for the War

	Seldom	Sometimes	Frequently	N
Supported war	18	39	43	(76)
Ambivalent	27	36	37	(44)
Opposed war	14	35	51	(264)

The linear relationship between these two variables is significant at $p < .05$.

Chapter 7

Table 7.1

Weapons Considered Unnecessarily Cruel (I am going to read you a list of weapons that have been used in some places, including Vietnam, by one or both sides. Please tell me which of these weapons you think are unnecessarily cruel and which are not unnecessarily cruel.)[a]

	Cruel	Not cruel	N
Vietnam Veterans			
1. Germ warfare	87	13	(317)
2. Chemical weapons	70	30	(319)
3. Mines & booby traps	81	19	(321)
4. Napalm	48	52	(322)
5. Plastic bombs	49	51	(302)
6. Dum-dum bullets	46	54	(313)
7. Primitive weapons	73	27	(323)
Vietnam Era Veterans			
1. Germ warfare	86	14	(337)
2. Chemical weapons	78	22	(334)
3. Mines & booby traps	88	12	(337)
4. Napalm	64	36	(336)
5. Plastic bombs	64	36	(330)
6. Dum-dum bullets	57	43	(327)
7. Primitive weapons	79	21	(335)
Nonveterans			
1. Germ warfare	94	6	(582)
2. Chemical weapons	85	15	(580)
3. Mines & booby traps	87	13	(578)
4. Napalm	76	24	(571)
5. Plastic bombs	74	26	(567)
6. Dum-dum bullets	64	36	(554)
7. Primitive weapons	80	20	(580)

[a]In chapter 7 we examine general patterns of response to the perception of cruelty of weapons and the conditions under which weapons may, in the opinion of our respondents, be used. We do not generally present tables in terms of statistical differences but focus instead on distinct patterns of response across a range of weapons. However, we did perform statistical tests, and the patterns on which we focus broadly reflect statistically significant differences between groups on these issues.

Table 7.2

Number of Weapons Considered Unnecessarily Cruel, by Veteran Status

	0	1-6	7	N
Vietnam veterans*	4	71	24	(321)
Vietnam era veterans	4	53	43	(336)
Nonveterans	3	48	49	(577)

*This group differs significantly from nonveterans at p < .01.

Table 7.3

Weapons Considered Unnecessarily Cruel, by Branch of Service

	Cruel	Not cruel	N
Army			
1. Dum-dum bullets	54	47	(369)
2. Napalm	49	52	(380)
3. Primitive weapons	75	25	(384)
Air Force/Navy			
1. Dum-dum bullets	52	48	(201)
2. Napalm	47	53	(207)
3. Primitive weapons	75	25	(203)
Marines			
1. Dum-dum bullets	32	68	(65)
2. Napalm	43	57	(66)
3. Primitive weapons	57	43	(66)

Table 7.4

Weapons Considered Unnecessarily Cruel, by Combat

	Cruel	Not Cruel	N
Low combat			
Napalm	45	56	(109)
Booby traps	74	26	(109)
Moderate combat			
Napalm	57	43	(121)
Booby traps	92	9	(119)
Heavy combat			
Napalm	42	58	(92)
Booby traps	80	20	(93)

Table 7.5

Weapons Considered Unnecessarily Cruel, by Exposure to Abusive Violence

	Cruel	Not Cruel	N
Not exposed			
Napalm	47	54	(217)
Booby traps	81	20	(217)
Dum-dum bullets	46	54	(208)
Witnessed abusive violence			
Napalm	54	46	(76)
Booby traps	89	11	(76)
Dum-dum bullets	55	45	(76)
Participants in abusive violence			
Napalm	40	60	(29)
Booby traps	63	37	(28)
Dum-dum bullets	32	68	(29)

Table 7.6

Weapons Considered Unnecessarily Cruel, by Activism

	Cruel	Not Cruel	N
Low activists			
1. Germ warfare	93	7	(445)
2. Chemical weapons	82	18	(444)
3. Mines & booby traps	87	13	(442)
4. Napalm	71	30	(435)
5. Plastic bombs	71	29	(433)
6. Dum-dum bullets	58	42	(424)
7. Primitive weapons	80	20	(444)
Moderate activists			
1. Germ warfare	96	4	(82)
2. Chemical weapons	90	10	(82)
3. Mines & booby traps	86	14	(81)
4. Napalm	87	13	(81)
5. Plastic bombs	76	24	(79)
6. Dum-dum bullets	73	27	(75)
7. Primitive weapons	80	20	(81)
High activists			
1. Germ warfare	100	0	(55)
2. Chemical weapons	96	4	(54)
3. Mines & booby traps	85	15	(55)
4. Napalm	87	13	(55)
5. Plastic bombs	86	15	(55)
6. Dum-dum bullets	82	18	(55)
7. Primitive weapons	80	20	(55)

Table 7.7

Number of Weapons Considered Unnecessarily Cruel, by Activism

	0	1–6	7	N
Low activists	4	51	45	(445)
Moderate activists	2	42	56	(82)
High activists	0	35	65	(55)

The linear relationship between these two variables is significant, p < .01.

Table 7.8

Weapons Considered Unnecessarily Cruel, by Support for the Vietnam War among Nonveterans

	Cruel	Not Cruel	N
Supported the war			
1. Germ warfare	95	6	(90)
2. Chemical weapons	79	21	(88)
3. Mines & booby traps	84	16	(88)
4. Napalm	54	46	(88)
5. Plastic bombs	58	42	(89)
6. Dum-dum bullets	43	58	(85)
7. Primitive weapons	80	20	(89)
Ambivalent			
1. Germ warfare	90	10	(57)
2. Chemical weapons	85	15	(58)
3. Mines & booby traps	91	9	(57)
4. Napalm	72	28	(56)
5. Plastic bombs	70	30	(57)
6. Dum-dum bullets	75	25	(54)
7. Primitive weapons	81	19	(58)
Opposed the war			
1. Germ warfare	96	4	(317)
2. Chemical weapons	90	10	(318)
3. Mines & booby traps	87	14	(315)
4. Napalm	85	15	(313)
5. Plastic bombs	82	18	(307)
6. Dum-dum bullets	71	29	(303)
7. Primitive weapons	80	20	(315)

Table 7.9

Number of Weapons Considered Unnecessarily Cruel by Support for the Vietnam War among Nonveterans

	0	1–6	7	N
Supported the war	6	53	41	(89)
Ambivalent	2	33	66	(57)
Opposed the war	2	30	69	(314)

The linear relationship between these two variables is significant, p < .01.

Table 7.10

"Under What Conditions Do You Think These Weapons Can Be Used?" by Veteran Status

	Anytime	Urban areas	Battle zone	Never	N
Vietnam veterans					
1. Germ warfare	6	4	20	70	(297)
2. Chemical weapons	7	5	31	57	(298)
3. Mines & booby traps	7	4	29	60	(305)
4. Napalm	8	10	58	24	(276)
5. Plastic bombs	13	12	41	34	(262)
6. Dum-dum bullets	18	12	32	38	(267)
7. Primitive weapons	11	3	34	52	(292)
Vietnam era veterans					
1. Germ warfare	3	2	19	76	(320)
2. Chemical weapons	4	3	35	58	(316)
3. Mines & booby traps	3	4	27	66	(316)
4. Napalm	5	6	51	38	(304)
5. Plastic bombs	5	5	40	50	(299)
6. Dum-dum bullets	12	4	36	47	(290)
7. Primitive weapons	5	4	34	58	(302)
Nonveterans					
1. Germ warfare	3	3	13	81	(554)
2. Chemical weapons	3	4	25	68	(546)
3. Mines & booby traps	4	6	27	66	(547)
4. Napalm	4	7	35	54	(533)
5. Plastic bombs	7	5	29	59	(527)
6. Dum-dum bullets	18	8	30	54	(510)
7. Primitive weapons	6	5	24	65	(538)

Table 7.11

"Under What Conditions Do You Think These Weapons Can Be Used?" by Combat

	Anytime	Urban areas	Battle zone	Never	N
Heavy combat					
1. Mines & booby traps	7	4	36	54	(87)
2. Napalm	12	12	60	17	(78)
3. Plastic bombs	20	12	38	30	(80)
4. Dum-dum bullets	20	7	37	37	(79)
5. Primitive weapons	12	8	36	44	(86)
Moderate combat					
1. Mines & booby traps	8	3	28	61	(116)
2. Napalm	5	12	56	27	(105)
3. Plastic bombs	8	16	40	36	(96)
4. Dum-dum bullets	17	20	21	41	(100)
5. Primitive weapons	9	1	35	55	(108)
Low combat					
1. Mines & booby traps	8	5	25	63	(102)
2. Napalm	7	7	59	27	(93)
3. Plastic bombs	11	9	46	34	(86)
4. Dum-dum bullets	17	6	41	37	(88)
5. Primitive weapons	11	2	32	54	(98)

Table 7.12

"Under What Conditions Do You Think These Weapons Can be Used?" by Exposure to Abusive Violence

	Anytime	Urban areas	Battle zone	Never	N
Not exposed					
1. Mines & booby traps	9	4	29	59	(210)
2. Napalm	8	11	59	22	(189)
3. Plastic bombs	12	15	42	31	(181)
4. Dum-dum bullets	18	16	29	38	(181)
5. Primitive weapons	13	3	36	49	(196)
Witnessed					
1. Mines & booby traps	5	1	30	64	(70)
2. Napalm	8	10	57	25	(65)
3. Plastic bombs	15	7	43	36	(62)
4. Dum-dum bullets	17	3	41	39	(65)
5. Primitive weapons	7	5	35	53	(70)

Note: There is no pattern of differences in the regression analysis between participants and those not exposed, therefore the responses of the participants are not discussed in the text or included in this table.

Table 7.13

"Under What Conditions Do You Think These Weapons Can Be Used?" by Activism

	Anytime	Urban areas	Battke zone	Never	N
High activists					
1. Germ warfare	—	—	7	93	(53)
2. Chemical weapons	—	—	15	85	(52)
3. Mines & booby traps	—	—	19	81	(50)
4. Napalm	—	—	25	75	(51)
5. Plastic bombs	4	—	17	79	(50)
6. Dum-dum bullets	2	1	20	77	(52)
7. Primitive weapons	4	2	19	75	(49)
Moderate activists					
1. Germ warfare	3	1	10	86	(79)
2. Chemical weapons	1	4	15	79	(79)
3. Mines & booby traps	1	10	16	74	(79)
4. Napalm	2	4	24	70	(78)
5. Plastic bombs	5	2	28	65	(76)
6. Dum-dum bullets	4	2	26	68	(72)
7. Primitive weapons	1	5	23	71	(78)
Low activists					
1. Germ warfare	3	3	15	78	(422)
2. Chemical weapons	5	5	29	62	(415)
3. Mines & booby traps	5	6	21	68	(418)
4. Napalm	6	8	39	47	(404)
5. Plastic bombs	8	7	32	53	(401)
6. Dum-dum bullets	11	10	37	47	(386)
7. Primitive weapons	4	2	19	75	(411)

Table 7.14

"Under What Conditions Do You Think These Weapons Can Be Used?" by Support for the Vietnam War among Nonveterans

	Anytime	Urban Urban areas	Battle Battle zone	Never	N
Supported the War					
1. Germ warfare	4	3	20	72	(87)
2. Chemical weapons	8	3	37	52	(85)
3. Mines & booby traps	6	5	21	68	(83)
4. Napalm	9	7	50	34	(81)
5. Plastic bombs	11	3	47	38	(80)
6. Dum-dum bullets	17	9	40	34	(79)
7. Primitive weapons	10	2	30	58	(83)
Ambivalent					
1. Germ warfare	2	2	13	84	(54)
2. Chemical weapons	2	1	23	74	(53)
3. Mines & booby traps	3	8	20	69	(56)
4. Napalm	3	—	37	60	(50)
5. Plastic bombs	2	2	23	74	(51)
6. Dum-dum bullets	5	2	22	71	(51)
7. Primitive weapons	7	—	18	75	(52)
Opposed the war					
1. Germ warfare	4	2	10	85	(304)
2. Chemical weapons	3	3	19	76	(299)
3. Mines & booby traps	5	4	19	73	(297)
4. Napalm	4	4	29	64	(295)
5. Plastic bombs	7	4	25	64	(292)
6. Dum-dum bullets	8	5	23	64	(277)
7. Primitive weapons	6	6	21	67	(293)

Chapter 8

Table 8.1

Are Prisoners of War Entitled to All the Rights Guaranteed under International Law, by Veteran Status

	All their rights	Less than all their rights	N
Vietnam veterans	73	27	(325)
Vietnam era veterans	70	30	(338)
Nonveterans	68	32	(586)

Table 8.2

Should Members of Resistance Movements and Guerrilla Organizations Have the Same Rights as Other Prisoners of War, by Veteran Status

	Yes	No	N
Vietnam veterans	84	16	(321)
Vietnam era veterans	85	15	(330)
Nonveterans	80	20	(565)

Table 8.3

Should Members of Resistance Movements and Guerrilla Organizations Have the Same Rights as Other Prisoners of War, by Combat

	Yes	No	N
Low combat	86	14	(108)
Moderate combat	78	23	(120)
Heavy combat	77	23	(93)

The linear relationship between these two variables is significant, $p < .05$.

Table 8.4

Should Members of Resistance Movements and Guerrilla Organizations Have the Same Rights as Other Prisoners of War, by Exposure to Abusive Violence

	Yes	No	N
Not exposed	82	18	(217)
Witnessed*	87	13	(76)
Participated	88	13	(28)

*This group differs significantly from the not exposed group, $p < .05$.

Table 8.5

Should Members of Resistance Movements and Guerrilla Organizations Have the Same Rights as Other Prisoners of War, by Antiwar Activism

	Yes	No	N
Low activists	75	25	(431)
Moderate activists	89	11	(80)
High activists	98	2	(54)

The linear relationship between these two variables is significant, $p < .10$.

Table 8.6

Should Members of Resistance Movements and Guerrilla Organizations Have the Same Rights as Other Prisoners of War, by Support for the War among Nonveterans

	Yes	No	N
Supported war	67	33	(86)
Ambivalent	86	14	(54)
Opposed war	84	16	(312)

The relationship between these two variables is significant, $p < .05$.

Chapter 9

Table 9.1

Familiar with, Heard of, or Never Heard of Genocide Convention, by Veteran Status

	Never heard	Heard	Familiar	N
Vietnam veteran	68	26	5	(324)
Era veteran	65	33	3	(333)
Nonveteran	66	28	6	(585)

Table 9.2

Familiarity with the Genocide Convention, by Rank

	Never heard	Heard	Familiar	N
Enlisted men	71	26	3	(435)
NCOs	62	35	3	(190)
Officers*	68	21	11	(32)

*This group significantly differs from enlisted men at $p < .05$.

Table 9.3

Familiar with, Heard of, or Never Heard of Nuremberg Principles, by Veteran Status

	Never heard	Heard	Familiar	N
Vietnam veteran*	49	43	7	(324)
Era veteran	41	53	5	(332)
Nonveteran	41	45	14	(587)

*This group significantly differs from nonveterans at p < .05.

Table 9.4

Familiarity with the Nuremberg Principles, by Rank

	Never heard	Heard	Familiar	N
Enlisted men	49	45	6	(434)
NCOs	46	48	6	(190)
Officers*	12	72	16	(32)

*This group significantly differs from enlisted men at p < .01.

Table 9.5

Familiar with, Heard of, or Never Heard of Geneva Conventions, by Veteran Status

	Never heard	Heard	Familiar	N
Vietnam veteran*	2	48	51	(326)
Era veteran*	2	51	47	(333)
Nonveteran	9	64	27	(581)

*This group significantly differs from nonveterans at p < .05.

Table 9.6

Familiarity with the Geneva Conventions, by Rank

	Never heard	Heard	Familiar	N
Enlisted men	2	53	47	(435)
NCOs	2	35	54	(191)
Officers	–	40	60	(33)

Table 9.7

Familiarity with Genocide Convention, Nuremberg Principles, and Geneva Conventions, among Antiwar Activists and Supporters of the Vietnam War

	Genocide			Nuremberg*			Geneva		
	Never heard	Heard	Familiar	Never heard	Heard	Familiar	Never heard	Heard	Familiar
Hight activists (N = 55)	61	21	19	11	48	41	8	49	43
Supporters of the war (N = 88)	66	31	3	34	57	10	9	56	36

*The differences between these two groups are significant on this variable at p < .01.

Table 9.8

Did Respondent Receive Instruction in Rules of Warfare during Period of Training or Entry into Vietnam, by Veteran Status

	Received instruction	Did not receive instruction	N
Vietnam veterans	75	25	(326)
Vietnam era veterans	68	33	(341)

Table 9.9

Did Respondent Receive Instruction in Rules of Warfare during Period of Training or Entry into Vietnam, by Branch of Service

	Received instruction	Did not receive instruction	N
Army*	76	24	(387)
Marines*	83	17	(66)
Navy/Air Force	61	40	(214)

*This group is significantly different from those who served in the navy and air force at p < .01.

Table 9.10

Did Respondent Receive Instruction in Rules of Warfare during the Period of Training or Entry into Vietnam, by Rank

	Received instruction	Did not receive instruction	N
Enlisted	64	36	(441)
NCOs	81	19	(193)
Officers*	91	9	(33)

*This group is significantly different from enlisted men at p < .01.

Table 9.11

Percentage of Vietnam and Vietnam Era Veterans Who Report Instruction Made Them Thoroughly Aware of How to Treat Vietnamese Civilians and Combatants and How to Act as a POW

	Enemy	Civilians	Sick and Wounded	Enemy POWs	Behave as POW
Vietnam veterans (N = 240)	35	31	38	39	70
Vietnam era veterans (N = 220)	26	25	37	39	69

Note: The rows do not total 100% because this is a summary table which only includes the veterans who responded ''thoroughly aware'' to each question.

Table 9.12

How Aware Did Your Instruction Make You of How to Treat Enemy Combatants and Noncombatants, by Rank

	Not aware	Somewhat aware	Thoroughly aware	N
Enlisted	33	40	27	(287)
NCOs*	28	37	36	(150)
Officers*	23	25	52	(29)

*This group is significantly different from enlisted men at p < .05.

Table 9.13

How Aware Did Your Instruction Make You of How to Treat Enemy Combatants and Noncombatants, by Branch of Service

	Not aware	Somewhat aware	Thoroughly aware	N
Army*	24	38	38	(286)
Marines*	22	39	39	(56)
Navy/Air Force	42	34	24	(124)

*This group is significantly different from those who served in the navy and air force at p < .05.

Table 9.14

Did You Ever Learn About the Rules of Conduct in Military Operations, about How to Treat Civilians, the Enemy, Sick or Wounded, or POWs, by Activism

	Enemy	Civilians	Sick and wounded	POWs
Nonveterans (N = 592)	36	36	38	44
Low activists (N = 454)	30	28	31	36
Moderate activists* (N = 82)	42	45	47	56
High activists* (N = 56)	62	65	64	74

*This group significantly differs from low activists at p < .01.
Note: The rows do not total 100% because this is a summary table which only includes nonveterans who responded they did learn about "rules of conduct in military operations."

Table 9.15

Did You Ever Learn about the Rules of Conduct in Military Operations, about How to Treat Civilians, the Enemy, Sick or Wounded, or POWs, by Support for Vietnam War among Nonveterans

	Enemy	Civilians	Sick & Wounded	POWs
Opposed (N = 323)	37	38	40	47
Ambivalent (N = 59)	34	38	36	40
Supported (N = 90)	33	37	37	37

Table 9.16

Did You Ever Learn about the Rules or Laws of Combat, about How to Treat Civilians, the Enemy, Sick or Wounded, or Prisoners of War in School, through the Mass Media, Friends, General Reading, or Other Places, by Activism

	Educational System	Mass media	Friends	General reading	Other
Nonveterans (N = 592)	18	36	16	24	10
Low activists (N = 454)	14	28	14	17	7
Moderate activists (N = 82)	21	51	22	37	8
High activists (N = 56)	41	63	24	46	25

The rows do not total to 100% because individuals could report learning the rules of combat from multiple sources.

Table 9.17

Did You Ever Learn about the Rules or Laws of Combat, about How to Treat Civilians, the Enemy, Sick or Wounded, or Prisoners of War in School, through the Mass Media, Friends, General Reading, or Other Places, by Support for the Vietnam War among Nonveterans

	School	Media	Friends	Reading	Other
Opposed (N = 323)	18	43	19	27	13
Ambivalent (N = 59)	13	34	13	13	1
Supported (N = 90)	19	31	19	21	8

Table 9.18

Which One of the Explanations for the Violations of the Rules of War in Vietnam Do You Think Most Often Accounted for These Violations, by Veteran Status

	Due to orders	Lack of punish.	Delib. acts	Ignorance of rules	Military necessity	Due to mistakes	Evil side of war
Vietnam veteran (N = 276)	40	17	6	8	8	6	15
Era veteran (N = 276)	40	7	7	8	11	4	24
Nonveteran (N = 513)	39	9	7	6	11	7	21

The differences among these groups were not tested for significance.

Table 9.19

Rank Order of Explanations for Violations of Rules of War, by Branch of Service

	Due to orders	Lack of punish.	Delib. acts	Ignorance of rules	Military necess.	Due to mistakes	Evil side of war
Army (N = 316)	42	20	5	9	8	7	9
Navy/ Air Force (N = 180)	44	10	5	8	8	5	21
Marines (N = 56)	21	9	9	12	7	6	36

The differences among these groups were not tested for significance.

Table 9.20

Rank Order of Explanations for Violations of Rules of War, by Rank

	Due to orders	Lack of punish.	Delib. acts	Ignorance of rules	Military necess.	Due to mistakes	Evil side of war
Enlisted men (N = 357)	47	17	2	6	6	3	18
NCOs (N = 163)	34	19	8	11	12	8	8
Officer (N = 32)	19	0	17	11	4	26	23

The differences among these groups were not tested for significance.

Table 9.21

Rank Order of Explanations for Violations of Rules of War, by Combat

	Due to orders	Lack of punish.	Delib. acts	Ignorance of rules	Military necessity	Due to mistakes	Evil side of war
Little, no combat (N = 93)	47	12	4	5	5	4	24
Moderate combat (N = 99)	33	27	5	11	7	6	12
Heavy combat (N = 84)	42	11	8	9	15	9	7

The differences among these groups were not tested for significance.

Table 9.22

Rank Order of Explanations for Violations of Rules of War, by Exposure to Abusive Violence

	Due to orders	Lack of punish.	Delib. acts	Ignorance of rules	Military necessity	Due to mistakes	Evil side of war
No exposure (N = 183)	40	18	3	8	7	7	17
Witnessed (N = 68)	38	12	16	9	10	6	9
Participated (N = 25)	44	24	0	5	13	0	14

The differences among these groups were not tested for significance.

Table 9.23

Rank Order of Explanations for Violations of Rules of War, by Activism

	Due to orders	Lack of punish.	Delib. acts	Ignorance of rules	Military necessity	Due to mistakes	Evil side of war
Low activists (N = 383)	40	9	8	7	10	7	19
Moderate activists (N = 78)	47	4	2	3	11	4	30
High activists (N = 52)	27	13	7	2	17	9	26

The differences among these groups were not tested for significance.

Table 9.24

Rank Order of Explanations for Violations of Rules of War, by Support for Vietnam War among Nonveterans

	Due to orders	Lack of punish.	Delib. acts	Ignorance of rules	Military necessity	Due to mistakes	Evil side of war
Opposed (N = 289)	45	7	5	5	10	6	23
Ambivalent (N = 47)	54	2	8	3	12	6	15
Supported (N = 80)	20	12	8	7	16	10	28

The differences among these groups were not tested for significance.

Table 9.25

Who Should Be Prosecuted for Unlawful Acts Committed in Vietnam War, by Veteran Status

	Politicians	Senior officers	Officers with operational command	Soldiers
Vietnam veterans (N = 278)	61	67	58	28
Era veterans (N = 297)	69	72	70	35
Nonveterans (N = 518)	66	79	74	40

Table 9.26

Who Should Be Prosecuted for Unlawful Acts Committed in Vietnam War, by Activism

	Politicians*	Senior officers*	Officers with operational command*	Soldiers
Low activists (N = 385)	61	76	69	35
Moderate activists (N = 79)	75	82	80	42
High activists (N = 50)	83	90	95	66

*The relationship between antiwar activism and this variable is significant at p < .01.

Table 9.27

Who Should Be Prosecuted for Unlawful Acts Committed in Vietnam War, by Support for Vietnam War among Nonveterans

	Politicians*	Senior officers*	Officers with operational command*	Soldiers*
Opposed (N = 286)	72	82	80	44
Ambivalent (N = 54)	68	73	68	28
Supported (N = 79)	53*	78	68	45

*The relationship between support for the war and this variable is significant at p < .01.

Table 9.28

Attitudes of Vietnam Generation toward Individual Responsibility for Conduct in War, by Veteran Status

	Violations of int'l law should be punished even if not a national crime			Refusal to obey is permissible if action prohibited by international law			Military necessity not int'l law should dictate strategy & weapons			Officer responsible for conduct of his troops' misbehavior if he could have known about it			Acting under orders is no excuse for violating int'l law if you could have done something about it		
	Agree	Neut.	Disag.	Agree	Neut.	Disag.	Agree	Neut.	Disag.	Agree	Neut.	Disag.	Agree	Neut.	Disag.
Vietnam veterans (N=310)	51*	13	36	72	8	19	49*	8	44	81*	6	13	63	10	28
Vietnam era veterans (N=332)	59*	13	29	72	6	28	43*	7	50	86	3	11	63*	7	29
Nonveterans (N=562)	68	10	22	70	8	22	31	12	56	85	6	9	67	11	24

*This group is significantly different from nonveterans on this attitude toward responsibility for the conduct of war at p < .05.

Table 9.29

In War Only Military Necessity, not International Rules of War, Should Determine Choice of Strategies and Weapons, by Rank

	Agree	Conflicted	Disagree	N
Enlisted men	50	10	40	(426)
NCOs	54	5	41	(186)
Officers*	5	5	90	(30)

* This group is significantly different from enlisted men at p < .001.

Table 9.30

Attitudes of Vietnam Generation toward Individual Responsibility for Conduct in War, by Antiwar Activism and Support for Vietnam War among Nonveterans

	Violations of int'l law should be punished even if not a national crime			Refusal to obey is permissible if action prohibited by international law			Military necessity not int'l law should dictate strategy & weapons*			Officer responsbile for conduct of his troops' misbehavior if he could have known about it			Acting under orders is no excuse for violating int'l law if you could have done something about it*		
	Agree	Neut.	Disag.	Agree	Neut.	Disag.	Agree	Neut.	Disag.	Agree	Neut.	Disag.	Agree	Neut.	Disag.
Supporters of the war (N = 86)	73	6	21	63	9	27	37	15	51	83	3	14	49	13	28
Antiwar activists (N = 54)	78	12	11	67	12	21	14	9	78	91	8	1	76	6	16

*The differences between these two groups on this variable are significant at p < .05.

Chapter 10

Table 10.1

Support for Future Military Intervention by U.S. Military Forces in the Third World, by Veteran Status

	No support	Support	N
Vietnam veterans*	71	29	314
Vietnam era veterans*	71	29	325
Nonveterans	84	17	553

*This group is significantly different from nonveterans at p < .001.

Table 10.2

Support for Future Military Intervention by U.S. Military Forces in the Third World, By Attitude toward the Vietnam War Among Vietnam Veterans

	No support	Support	N
Opposed war	75	26	101
Ambivalent	84	15	23
Supported war	62	40	95

The relationship between these two variables is significant at p < .001.

Table 10.3

Support for Future Military Intervention by U.S. Military Forces in the Third World, by Attitude toward the Vietnam War among Nonveterans

	No support	Support	N
Opposed war	89	11	305
Ambivalent	84	16	54
Supported war	68	32	83

The relationship between these two variables is significant at p < .001.

Table 10.4

Support for Future Military Intervention by U.S. Military Forces in the Third World, by Turning against the Vietnam War as a Result of Abusive Violence, among Nonveterans

	No support	Support	N
Did not turn against the war because of abusive violence	78	22	340
Did turn against the war because of abusive violence	90	10	213

The difference between these groups is significant at p < .05.

Table 10.5

Attitudes toward Resisters against the Vietnam War, by Veteran Status

	Supported resisters	Respected resisters	Ambivalent to resisters	Opposed resisters	N
Vietnam veterans*	20	14	23	43	295
Vietnam era veterans	13	19	27	42	307
Nonveterans	31	18	27	24	541

*This group differs significantly from nonveterans at p < .01.

Table 10.6

Attitudes toward Resisters against the Vietnam War, by Attitude toward the Vietnam War, among Vietnam Veterans

	Supported resisters	Respected resisters	Ambivalent to resisters	Opposed resisters	N
Opposed war	28	19	22	32	100
Ambivalent	7	29	29	43	23
Supported war	17	13	20	50	94

The relationship between these two variables is significant at p < .01.

Table 10.7

Attitudes toward Resisters against the Vietnam War, by Estimates of Frequency with which U.S. Forces Abused Civilians, among Vietnam Veterans

	Supported resisters	Respected resisters	Ambivalent to resisters	Opposed resisters	N
Not frequent	8	16	26	50	150
Sometimes	36	12	18	34	104
Frequently	50	17	25	8	17

The linear relationship between these two variables is significant at p < .01.

Table 10.8

Attitudes toward Resisters against the Vietnam War, by Attitudes towards the Rights of Guerrilla Fighters, among Vietnam Veterans

	Supported resisters	Respected resisters	Ambivalent to resisters	Opposed resisters	N
Disagree: Guerrillas' rights not same as POWs'	10	7	33	50	53
Agree: Guerrillas' rights same as POWs'	22	15	22	41	237

The difference between these groups is significant at p < .05.

Table 10.9

Attitudes toward Resisters against the Vietnam War, by Attitudes toward Vietcong/North Vietnamese Army, among Vietnam Veterans

	Supported resisters	Respected resisters	Ambivalent to resisters	Opposed resisters	N
Very negative	18	12	23	47	73
Mixed feelings	21	10	24	46	106
Very positive	20	26	24	30	109

The linear relationship between these two variables is significant at p < .05.

Table 10.10

Attitudes toward Resisters against the Vietnam War, by Attitudes Toward the War, among Nonveterans

	Supported resisters	Respected resisters	Ambivalent to resisters	Opposed resisters	N
Opposed war	42	17	22	18	311
Ambivalent	18	28	32	21	57
Supported war	9	16	31	44	87

The relationship between these two variables is significant at $p < .001$.

Table 10.11

Attitudes toward Resisters against the Vietnam War, by Turning against Vietnam War because of Abusive Violence, among Nonveterans

	Supported resisters	Respected resisters	Ambivalent to resisters	Opposed resisters	N
Did not turn against the war because of abusive violence	24	14	33	30	318
Did turn against the war because of abusive violence	40	23	20	17	223

These groups differ significantly at $p < .05$.

Table 10.12

Attitudes toward Resisters against the Vietnam War, by Estimates of Frequency with which U.S. Forces Abused Civilians, among Nonveterans

	Supported resisters	Respected resisters	Ambivalent to resisters	Opposed resisters	N
Not frequent	20	20	26	34	157
Sometimes	32	20	27	21	260
Very frequent	55	7	24	13	81

The linear relationship between these two variables is significant at $p < .01$.

Table 10.13

Attitudes toward Resisters against the Vietnam War, by Involvement in Antiwar Movement, among Nonveterans

	Supported resisters	Respected resisters	Ambivalent to resisters	Opposed resisters	N
Low activists	20	17	31	32	406
Moderate activists	49	23	23	5	82
High activists	60	15	15	9	53

The linear relationship between these two variables is significant at $p < .05$.

Table 10.14

Attitudes toward Resisters against the Vietnam War, by Current Level of Education, among Nonveterans

	Supported resisters	Respected resisters	Ambivalent to resisters	Opposed resisters	N
Less than H.S.	13	8	23	57	7
H.S. graduate	21	14	23	42	88
Some college	30	15	30	25	176
College graduate	37	14	35	15	83
Some postgraduate	41	27	20	12	127

The linear relationship between these two variables is significant at $p < .001$.

Table 10.15

Would You Want Your Son to Enter the Military in a War like Vietnam, by Veteran Status

	Son should enter military	Son should not enter military	N
Vietnam veteran	38	62	322
Vietnam era veteran	28	72	335
Nonveteran*	20	80	589

*Nonveterans differ significantly from veterans at $p < .01$.

Table 10.16

Would You Want Your Son to Enter the Military, not Influence His Decision, or Go to Canada if He Was Called to Military Duty in a War like Vietnam, by Veteran Status

	Go into military	Not influence decision	Go to Canada	N
Vietnam veteran	60	13	26	287
Vietnam era veteran	59	13	28	303
Nonveteran*	45	11	44	540

*Nonveterans differ significantly from veterans at p < .001.

Table 10.17

Would You Want Your Son to Enter the Military in a War like Vietnam, by Attitudes toward Rights of Guerrilla Fighters, among Vietnam Veterans

	Son should enter military	Son should not enter military	N
Disagree: Guerrillas' rights not same as POWs'	51	48	63
Agree: Guerrillas' rights same as POWs'	35	65	255

The differences between these groups is significant at p < .05.

Table 10.18

Would You Want Your Son to Enter the Military in a War like Vietnam, by Whether Veterans Were Supported by the Government and the Public after Returning Home, among Vietnam Veterans

	Son should enter military	Son should not enter military	N
Felt little support	32	68	112
Felt moderate support	45	55	119
Felt high support	32	68	89

The linear relationship between these two variables is significant at p < .01.

Table 10.19

Would You Want Your Son to Enter the Military, not Influence His Decision, or Go to Canada if He Was Called to Military Duty in a War like Vietnam, by Attitude toward Vietnam War, among Vietnam Veterans

	Go into military	Not influence decision	Go to Canada	N
Opposed war	45	21	35	103
Ambivalent	54	15	31	25
Supported war	69	9	20	96

The relationship between these two variables is significant at $p < .05$.

Table 10.20

Would You Want Your Son to Enter the Military, not Influence His Decision, or Go to Canada if He was Called to Military Duty in a War like Vietnam, by Attitude toward Rights of Guerrilla Fighters, among Vietnam Veterans

	Go into military	Not influence decision	Go to Canada	N
Disagree: Guerrillas' rights not same as POWs'	78	9	9	58
Agree: Guerrillas' rights same as POWs'	56	13	29	227

These groups differ significantly at $p < .01$.

Table 10.21

Would You Want Your Son to Enter the Military, not Influence His Decision, or Go to Canada if He Was Called to Military Duty in a War like Vietnam, by Whether Veterans Were Supported by the Government and Public after Returning Home, among Vietnam Veterans

	Go into military	Not influence decision	Go to Canada	N
Felt little support	51	8	39	102
Felt moderate support	67	7	26	109
Felt high support	61	25	13	75

The linear relationship between these two variables is significant at $p < .05$.

Table 10.22

Would You Want Your Son to Enter the Military in a War like Vietnam, by Attitude toward Vietnam War, among Nonveterans

	Son should enter military	Son should not enter military	N
Opposed war	14	86	321
Ambivalent	15	85	59
Supported war	42	58	90

The relationship between these two variables is significant at $p < .01$.

Table 10.23

Would You Want Your Son to Enter the Military in a War like Vietnam, by Estimates of Frequency with which U.S. Forces Abused Civilians, among Nonveterans

	Son should enter military	Son should not enter military	N
Not frequent	29	70	179
Sometimes	18	82	275
Very frequent	8	92	88

The linear relationship between these two variables is significant at $p < .01$.

Table 10.24

Would You Want Your Son to Enter the Military in a War like Vietnam, by Level of Support for Individual Reponsibility in War, among Nonveterans

	Son should enter military	Son should not enter military	N
Little support	31	69	132
Moderate support	20	80	212
High support	11	89	244

The linear relationship between these two variables is significant at $p < .05$.
Note: The five items measuring individual responsibility in war were used to construct a scale INDWAR (see Appendix-Methodology) which is the variable used in this and subsequent tables in the chapter.

Table 10.25

Would You Want Your Son to Enter the Military in a War like Vietnam, by Current Level of Education, among Nonveterans

	Son should enter military	Son should not enter military	N
Less than H.S.	49	51	64
H.S. graduate	33	67	104
Some college	17	83	188
College graduate	21	80	89
Some postgraduate	6	94	134

The linear relationship between these two variables is significant at p < .001.

Table 10.26

Would You Want Your Son to Enter the Military, not Influence His Decision, or Go to Canada if He Was Called to Military Duty in a War like Vietnam, by Attitude toward Vietnam War, among Nonveterans

	Go into military	Not influence decision	Go to Canada	N
Opposed war	35	11	54	295
Ambivalent	33	14	54	53
Supported war	74	8	18	83

The relationship between these two variables is significant at p < .001.

Table 10.27

Would You Want Your Son to Enter the Military, not Influence His Decision, or Go to Canada if He Was Called to Military Duty in a War like Vietnam, by Estimates of Frequency with which U.S. Forces Abused Civilians, among Nonveterans

	Go into military	Not influence decision	Go to Canada	N
Not frequent	60	13	27	179
Sometimes	37	12	51	275
Very frequent	32	8	60	88

The linear relationship between these two variables is significant at p < .01.

Table 10.28

Would You Want Your Son to Enter the Military, not Influence His Decision, or Go to Canada if He Was Called to Military Duty in a War like Vietnam, by Level of Support for Individual Responsibility, among Nonveterans

	Go into military	Not influence decision	Go to Canada	N
Little support	61	12	26	122
Moderate support	41	11	49	192
High support	34	10	56	225

The linear relationship between these two variables is significant at p < .01.

Table 10.29

Would You Want Your Son to Enter the Military, not Influence His Decision, or Go to Canada if He Was Called to Military Duty in a War like Vietnam, by Antiwar Activism

	Go into military	Not influence decision	Go to Canada	N
Low activists	53	13	34	410
Moderate activists	33	7	59	78
High activists	8	8	85	52

The linear relationship between these two variables is significant at p < .05

Table 10.30

Would You Want Your Son to Enter the Military, not Influence His Decision, or Go to Canada if He Was Called to Military Duty in a War like Vietnam, by Current Level of Education, among Nonveterans

	Go into military	Not influence decision	Go to Canada	N
Less than H.S.	68	9	23	62
H.S. graduate	67	14	19	94
Some college	43	12	44	170
College graduate	41	11	47	82
Some postgraduate	27	10	63	124

The linear relationship between these two variables is significant at p < .01.

METHODOLOGY
APPENDIX

I. The Sample

Our sample contains 1,259 men who were of draft-eligible age during the Vietnam War. The sample includes Vietnam veterans, era veterans, and nonveterans. The sample was drawn from ten sites[1] chosen to represent four sections of the country on matched economic and demographic characteristics and collected in two waves: the Northeast in 1977 (wave I, N=341) and the South, Midwest, and West in 1979 (wave II, N=918).[2] Though not a national probability sample, it does represent several regions and city sizes in the continental United States and does, at minimum, adequately represent the population in those ten sites.

The sample was stratified by veteran status, race, age, and education (the latter for wave I only). Our sample consists of a group of Vietnam veterans (N=326), Vietnam era veterans (N=341), and nonveterans (N=592). The sample contains 860 whites and 399 blacks. The men in the sample were born between 1940 and 1953; and the sample is divided into men who are 30 or younger (N=527) and those who are 31 or older (N=732).

Random digit-dialing techniques were used in each of the ten locations to screen individuals and collect the sample. If a male who fit an unfilled cell's characteristics lived in the household reached, he was selected for interviewing. The refusal rate to the screening calls was 7.8%; the refusal rate of the interviews was 17.5%. Sample selection by telephone screening continued until the required number in each site cell was obtained.[3]

Due to high costs of collecting a large sample of a relatively rare population, such as veterans who served during the Vietnam conflict, by random probability techniques, multiplicity sampling was used to increase the yield of veterans.[4] If the household contacted did not contain an eligible respondent, the screener asked if a brother, son, or nephew living in the sampling area was a veteran during the Vietnam War. In these cases the kinship unit, not the household unit, was being sampled. If an eligible candidate was obtained by this process and fit the sample requirements, he was interviewed and information was obtained on his kinship network in the area. This allowed the estimation of his probability of being nominated given the random method of selection in respect to those found by contacting households. The wave II sample contained 290 veterans obtained by contacting households and 213 veterans obtained by kin nomination.

II. Analysis

A. Regression Procedure

Throughout the analysis in this volume we use multiple regression procedures on unweighted data to differentiate the groups in our study. Multiple regression allows the statistical control of characteristics on which the sample was stratified. Also, previous work has shown that regression estimates are reliable and only marginally affected by changes in sampling variance produced by weighting. When summary characteristics such as means, percentages, and correlations are presented, however, they will be based on weighted data, adjusting for both the stratification design and the differential probability of selection in the multiplicity group, to make our sample comparable to the general site populations from which it was drawn.

B. Content Analysis

The major themes our respondents use to describe their feelings, attitudes, or experiences were elicited through open-ended questions. Each respondent chose his own words to reply to these questions. Each open-ended question was coded for specific content. The content coding of each question allowed us to create common response categories for descriptive cross-tabular analysis of the major themes for the entire sample. The procedure entailed analyzing each open-ended question, finding the main conceptual categories used by respondents, and then training coders consistently to place responses in the appropriate category. We achieved an inter-rater reliability at the .90–.95 level on every question. This was accomplished by daily supervised review of coding behavior. Chapters 3 and 4 and the section in chapter 1 on subjective responses to war rely on this type of data.

C. Thematic Analysis

A second approach we used to analyze the open-ended data was qualitative analysis of the major themes in the transcript material for each issue we examine in this volume. The procedure involved three steps. First, every transcript of the

Vietnam veterans, antiwar activists, and prowar nonveterans was read to identify the relevant material on the general issues to be covered in each chapter. Second, the relevant material was differentiated into thematic categories. The third step was to create a file by theme for each case. This was accomplished by using the respondent's I.D. and entering the material into a data file on a word processor.

Subsequently, the file was printed and a count of the number of times a particular theme came up was established to differentiate dominant themes on specific issues. This procedure was followed repetitively for each chapter in which transcript material is used to identify the underlying modes of response to the war experience. We selected from the files those quotes we felt best illustrated the point being made by our respondents.

We have also utilized thematic material illustratively, i.e., where the closed-ended material is used to carry the argument, we were able to exemplify the statistical point with a quotation from the transcripts.

The transcript material is used extensively in this volume. Indeed, it is the story our respondents tell, in their own words, that forms the core of this volume. The statistics in the volume are used to give the reader a sense of parameters of differences on the issues, but our intention is to get to the meanings behind the numbers. Thus, we have gone to considerable length to assure the accuracy of the thematic material.

III. The Variables

In using multiple regression analysis to test for the effects of cohort location, military and war experiences, psycho-social effects of and value orientations concerning the war, we control for the characteristics on which the sample was stratified as well as selected background characteristics. The predictor variables used in the equation were:

1) six variables representing the sites and age group of the respondent, these were variables on which the sample was stratified;

2) the respondent's race;

3) the Duncan SEI score of the parent with the highest occupation when the respondent was 16;

4) the level of educational attainment of the most educated parent;

5) whether the respondent had a history of juvenile problems;

6) the level of educational attainment of the respondent before he entered the military;

7) whether the respondent enlisted or was drafted;

8) the branch of service the respondent served in;

9) the highest rank the respondent attained in the service;

10) whether the respondent served in the military prior to or after the Tet offensive in 1968;

11) among Vietnam veterans, the extent of the respondent's combat experience;

12) whether or not the respondent witnessed abusive violence; and

13) whether or not the respondent participated in abusive violence.

For nonveterans, the military variables were replaced by two variables:

1) the extent of the respondent's participation in antiwar activism;

2) the respondent's reported attitude toward the Vietnam War during the years he was most concerned about the war.

The model described above was used in all chapters except chapter 10, on the political legacy of the war. In chapter 10, we retained the variables in the model described above. In addition, we compared the explanatory power of the perspectives on the war described in chapter 3 through 9 against that of the war experience measures to determine which had the more important effect on long-term attitudes about the war, military interventions, and related issues. We were interested in identifying those attitudes and experiences that consistently influenced current political attitudes toward future intervention, and to assess the relative significance of these factors.

IV. Statistical Significance

Throughout the volume we specify the level of statistical significance between variables in the tables where multivariate tests were performed. We have included several different kinds of tables in the volume. First and most important are those that identify statistically significant differences between groups at $p < .05$, $< .01$, or $< .001$. Second, we have at times also included tables where the level of statistical significance is $p < .10$. The reader needs to treat table differences between groups, but as clearly less compelling than those at $p < .05$ or lower. Third, we have included some tables where there are no significant differences between groups where we wish to emphasize that point. At the bottom of these tables the reader will find no statement about statistical significance. Fourth, there are tables throughout the volume where the reader will find the statement that no test of statistical significance was carried out. There are a variety of reasons for presenting such tables, e.g., illustrative purposes, collapsing of several distinct tables into a single table, or comparisons on individual items where we feel the issue should be discussed but where the statistical test is done on a scale built from these items.

Throughout the volume the reader will find statements about the nature of the relationship in the tables phrased in several distinct ways. The statement of statistical significance in each table is based on whether the independent variable, the predictor, was a dichotomous or a continuous measure in the regression model used to determine its significance.

V. Scales and Constructed Measures Used in the Study

Combat scale

The elements of the Combat Scale used in our analysis are:

	Weight
In an artillery unit that fired on the enemy	1
Flew in an aircraft over Vietnam	1
Stationed at a forward observation post	1
Received incoming fire	1
Encountered mines and boobytraps	1
Received sniper or sapper fire	1
Unit patrol was ambushed	2
Engaged VC in a firefight, and/or engaged NVA in a firefight	2
Saw Americans killed, and/or saw Vietnamese killed	2
Wounded	2
Maximum Total	14

There are two types of items in the scale, those receiving a single rating (six items) and those receiving a double rating (four items). The items receiving the double rating are weighted to reflect the greater exposure to physical threat the veteran faced. While the potential maximum score on this scale is 14, no one in our sample scored higher than 13.

The statistical characteristics of the Combat Scale in our sample of 350 Vietnam veterans are:

Frequencies

Code	0	1	2	3	4	5	6	7	8	9	10	11	12	13
N	33	27	41	16	22	14	29	23	22	24	38	32	11	18
96	9%	8%	12%	5%	6%	4%	8%	7%	6%	7%	11%	9%	3%	5%

The mean of the scale is 6.114, the median is 6, and the standard deviation is 4.07.

Abusive Violence Measures

In measuring exposure to abusive violence we used a set of open-ended questions in which the veteran was asked whether he experienced the dirty side of war and to describe the events in this category. We required that veterans had witnessed the event or had seen its consequences soon after its commission and to have clearly known who had carried it out. To make the measure an indicator of objective experiences we eliminated any events of which they had heard secondhand. In our sample roughly a third (32%) reported they were directly exposed to at least one episode. These episodes varied in character but the most often cited were: torture of prisoners, including pushing them from helicopters; physical mistreatment of civilians; use of napalm, white phosphorus, or cluster bombs on villages; death or maiming by booby trap; and mutilation of bodies. Most of the men who reported episodes described cases in which U.S. regulars were involved (82% of those exposed). Less than a third mentioned ones in which the Vietcong or N.V. regulars were involved (32% of all exposed). Another 15% reported cases involving the ARVN or Korean forces. (These three figures do not sum to 100% because over a third of those exposed mentioned more than one episode.)

Exposure to abusive violence is related to the level of combat exposure but it is not so strongly tied to it that it would lead us to entertain the possibility that they reflect the same dimension of war stress. The combat scale and the measure of exposure are moderately correlated ($r = .43$). The mean level of combat for those exposed is significantly higher than for veterans not exposed (8.4 vs. 4.7) but there is little difference on combat among those exposed between those who participated and those who did not (8.5 vs. 8.4).

Period of the War

The Vietnam War lasted many years and the political climate surrounding the war changed, as did the levels of American involvement and troop commitments. This led us to create a variable to analyze the effects of being in the military or exposed to the draft at varying stages of the conflict.[5] We divided the war into five major periods based on the number of American troops in Vietnam and the distinctive changes in the nature of the conflict. The periods we chose were 1) 1961–65, 2) 1966–67, 3) 1968–69, 4) 1970–71, and 5) 1972–75.

To assign respondents to each category we decided to use the midpoint of military service for all veterans. And, because the median years of service was 2.5 years and very few veterans in the sample served more than four years, we made the decision that no more than the first four years of service would be counted to establish the midpoint. Thus the task of assigning veterans to one of the four periods was relatively straightforward, based on the dates of entry and exit from active duty. The procedure used to define the equivalent to period served for nonveterans is somewhat more complex. In the interview we asked nonveterans

Century Month of Birth[a] by Veteran Status for Each Period of the War

Cohort	Vietnam veteran	Status Era veteran	Nonveteran
1961–65			
Mean	530.02	523.65	521.32
Standard deviation	20.47	17.76	13.49
Number	(41)	(74)	(183)
1966–67			
Mean	551.18	543.59	558.80
Standard deviation	22.99	21.82	6.72
Number	(93)	(75)	(97)
1968–69			
Mean	572.87	572.22	581.35
Standard deviation	21.14	22.21	6.69
Number	(123)	(68)	(119)
1970–71			
Mean	590.83	594.48	605.98
Standard deviation	20.93	26.72	6.91
Number	(83)	(89)	(120)
1972–74			
Mean	619.11	615.63	628.40
Standard deviation	24.21	19.99	6.56
Number	(9)	(54)	(110)
	—	—	—
	567.52	528.29	573.34
	30.11	39.20	40.65
	(349)	(360)	(629)

a. "Century month of birth" refers to the month in which a man was born, counting from the first month of this century. Thus, a man born in December 1901 was born in the twelfth century month. A man born in December 1950 was born in the 600th century month.

to date the two- or three-year period in which Vietnam most concerned them. This led to the initial finding that the nonveterans' period of greatest concern tended to be the later years of the war, a trend which would have made between-group comparisons impossible. We therefore decided to explore the draft histories of the nonveterans for the ages during which they appeared most vulnerable to conscription. From this analysis we determined that the nonveterans appeared most vulnerable to conscription between the ages of 18 and 21. Second, the median age at which veterans entered the military turned out to be 20. Thus, we decided to use the midpoint of the ages of greatest likelihood of being drafted, 20.5 years, to assign nonveterans to periods.

This gave us a reasonable facsimile of the veterans' midpoint of service

Distribution of Vietnam Veterans, Era Veterans, and Nonveterans According to Period of the War Served (Veterans) or Period of Greatest Draft Vulnerability (Nonveterans).

	1961–65	1966–67	1968–69	1970–71	1972–74	
Vietnam veterans						
Percent	11.7	26.6	35.2	23.8	2.6	100.0
(number)	(41)	(93)	(123)	(83)	(9)	(349)
Era veterans						
Percent	20.6	20.8	18.9	24.7	15.0	100.0
(number)	(74)	(75)	(68)	(89)	(54)	(360)
Nonveterans						
Percent	29.1	15.4	18.9	19.1	17.5	100.0
(number)	(183)	(97)	(119)	(120)	(110)	(629)

distribution and enabled us to do a meaningful comparative analysis of the effect of period of service on the dependent variables. Although we have done a substantial analysis of period effects, we have reported findings only where period served makes a significant difference.

ACTIVISM

Description: Antiwar Activism scale (only nonveterans)
Scoring: 0 to 18; simple count of of antiwar activities respondent participated pre
    period of greatest concern and during period of greatest concern
Item: *PPGC*
lectures
teach-in
local demonstrations
organization leader
national demonstration
picket recruiters
picket defense contracters
picket military base
civil disobedience
went to jail
other
PGC
local antiwar marches
Washington antiwar marches
active in antiwar organization
civil disobedience
jail
other

WARATT: Attitude toward the Vietnam War

Responses to the question of attitude toward the Vietnam War were part of an open-ended question that was content analyzed and the responses were coded (0–3):
(a) opposed the war
(b) confused/ambivalent
(c) supported the war

WARESULT: What were the consequences of the war

This measure was constructed out of an open-ended question that probed respondents' feelings about the consequences of the war, which were coded 1–7:
(a) mentioned three or more negative consequences to two or more positive consequences

ATTVIET: Attitude toward the Vietnamese

Responses to the question were part of an open-ended question that was content analyzed and the responses were coded (0–5).:
(a) made one or more positive statements about the Vietnamese
(b) made only ambivalent statements about the Vietnamese
(c) made one or more negative statements about the Vietnamese

ATTARVN: Attitude toward the South Vietnamese Army

ATTARVN was a single closed item asking respondents their feelings about the South Vietnamese Army coded:
   0 Felt very positive about the ARVN
   to 100 Felt very negative about the ARVN

VCNVA

   Description: Attitude toward Vietcong and North Vietnamese Army scale
   Scoring: 0 to 100; low score—positive attitude;
   high score—negative attitude
   Items: How did you feel about Vietcong
   How did you feel about NVA
   N.B. Don't knows in original items assigned a middle value
   No prorating

Navy/Air Force merged variable

In the analysis we present findings for the respondents who were in the navy and the air force in a single variable called Navy/Air Force. The logic for collapsing these categories of respondents into a single measure was that they were similar demographically, before entry into the military, their reasons for entering the military were also similar, and the similarity of responses persisted in terms of their exposure to war stress as well as their reactions to it. As these two groups individually represented small populations in the study, collapsing these two categories created a larger population and seemed an appropriate way to increase the stability of the findings.

The PERI Scales

The PERI scales we used differ slightly from the form published by their originators.[6] This is because we incorporated the PERI scales into our questionnaire before Bruce Dohrenwend and his colleagues had settled on their definitive form. In most cases, however, our scales are quite similar to the final version.

The Demoralization Scale consists of several component scales. Dohrenwend and his colleagues tried to develop these scales as distinct dimensions but found, in their sample, the scales were so highly intercorrelated that each was tapping the same dimension. We came to the same conclusion in our sample.

Demoralization Scale. The Demoralization Scale consists of a weighted total of five component scales, each of the five weighted equally. The five scales are listed below.

1. Poor Self Esteem
   a. In the last twelve months, how often have you felt confident?
      (0- very often; 25- fairly often; 50- sometimes; 75- almost never; 100- never)
   b. Think of a person who feels that he is a failure generally in life. Is this person
      (100- very much like you; 75- much like you; 50- somewhat like you; 25- very little like you; 0- not at all like you)
   c. In general, how satisfied are you with yourself?
      (0- very satisfied; 25- somewhat satisfied; 75- somewhat dissatisfied; 100- very dissatisfied)
   d. In general, how satisfied are you with your body?
      (0- very satisfied; 25- somewhat satisfied; 75- somewhat dissatisfied; 100- very dissatisfied)
   e. In general, if you had to compare yourself with the average (man/woman) your age, what grade would you give yourself?
      (0- excellent; 25- good; 50- average; 75- below average; 100- a lot below average)

2. Hopelessness-Helplessness
   a. In the last twelve months, how often have you felt nothing turns out for you the way you want it to, would you say?
      (100- very often; 75- fairly often; 50- sometimes; 25- almost never; 0- never)

b. In the last twelve months how often have you felt completely helpless?

(100- very often; 75- fairly often; 50- sometimes; 25- almost never; 0- never)

c. In the last twelve months, how often have you felt completely hopeless about everything, would you say?

(100- very often; 75- fairly often; 50- sometimes; 25- almost never; 0- never)

3. Anxiety

a. In the last twelve months, how often have you had personal worries that get you down physically, that is, make you physically ill?

(100- very often; 75- fairly often; 50- sometimes; 25- almost never; 0- never)

b. In the last twelve months, how often have you feared getting physically sick?

(100- very often; 75- fairly often; 50- sometimes; 25- almost never; 0- never)

c. In the last twelve months, how often have you felt anxious?

(100- very often; 75- fairly often; 50- sometimes; 25- almost never; 0- never)

d. In the last twelve months, how often have you been bothered by feelings of restlessness?

(100- very often; 75- fairly often; 50- sometimes; 25- almost never; 0- never)

e. In the last twelve months, how often have you feared being left all alone or abandoned?

(100- very often; 75- fairly often; 50- sometimes; 25- almost never; 0- never)

f. In the last twelve months, how often have you feared being robbed, attacked, or physically injured?

(100- very often; 75- fairly often; 50- sometimes; 25- almost never; 0- never)

g. Think of a person who is the worrying type—you know, a worrier. Is this person:

(100- very much like you; 75- much like you; 50- somewhat like you; 25- very little like you; 0- not at all like you)

4. Sadness

a. In the last twelve months, how often have you been in very low or low spirits?

(100- very often; 75- fairly often; 50- sometimes; 25- almost never; 0- never)

b. In the last twelve months, how often have you felt like crying?

(100- very often; 75- fairly often; 50- sometimes; 25- almost never; 0- never)

5. Psycho-Physical Symptoms

a. In the last twelve months, how often have you been bothered by acid or sour stomach several times a week, would you say?

(100- very often; 75- fairly often, 50- sometimes; 25- almost never; 0- never)

b. In the last twelve months, how often has your appetite been poor?

(100- very often; 75- fairly often; 50- sometimes; 25- almost never; 0- never)

c. In the last twelve months, how often have you been bothered by cold sweats?

(100- very often; 75- fairly often; 50- sometimes; 25- almost never; 0- never)

d. In the last twelve months, how often did your hands tremble enough to bother you, would you say?

(100- very often; 75- fairly often; 50- sometimes; 25- almost never; 0- never)

e. In the last twelve months, how often have you had trouble with constipation?

(100- very often; 75- fairly often; 50- sometimes; 25- almost never; 0- never)

Guilt Scale

1. In the last twelve months, how often have you felt you deserved to be punished?

(100- very often; 75- fairly often; 50- sometimes; 25- almost never; 0- never)

2. In the last twelve months, how often have you felt guilty about things you do or don't do?

(100- very often; 75- fairly often; 50- sometimes; 25- almost never; 0- never)

3. In the last twelve months, how often have you blamed yourself for everything that went wrong?

(100- very often; 75- fairly often; 50- sometimes; 25- almost never; 0- never)

Angry Feelings Scale

1. How often in the last twelve months have you felt angry?

(100- very often; 75- fairly often; 50- sometimes; 25- almost never; 0- never)

2. How often in the last twelve months have you felt like a powder keg ready to explode?

(100- very often; 75- fairly often; 50- sometimes; 25- almost never; 0- never)

3. How often in the last twelve months have you gotten easily irritated?

(100- very often; 75- fairly often; 50- sometimes; 25- almost never; 0- never)

Active Expression of Hostility Scale

Scoring notes: Questions 1–4, 6, 7, and 10 are scored on a five-point scale with the highest weight applied to the first response alternative. Questions 5, 8, and 9 are scored in the opposite direction with the highest weight applied to the last response alternative.

1. When you get angry, how often do you yell or shout?

(100- very often; 75- fairly often; 50- sometimes; 25- almost never; 0- never)

2. When you get angry, how often do you swear and curse?
(100- very often; 75- fairly often; 50- sometimes; 25- almost never; 0- never)

3. When you get angry, how often do you criticize someone?
(100- very often; 75- fairly often; 50- sometimes; 25- almost never; 0- never)

4. When you get angry, how often do you get into an argument?
(100- very often; 75- fairly often; 50- sometimes; 25- almost never; 0- never)

5. When you get angry, how often do you try to calmly explain your feelings or opinions?
(100- very often; 75- fairly often; 50- sometimes; 25- almost never; 0- never)

6. When you get angry, how often do you hit somebody?
(100- very often; 75- fairly often; 50- sometimes; 25- almost never; 0- never)

7. When you get angry, how often do you make a fist and show an angry expression?
(100- very often; 75- fairly often; 50- sometimes; 25- almost never; 0- never)

8. When you get angry, how often do you just stop talking, avoid arguing, and start to do something else?
(100- very often; 75- fairly often; 50- sometimes; 25- almost never; 0- never)

9. When you get angry, how often do you hide your anger, try not to show it?
(100- very often; 75- fairly often; 50- sometimes; 25- almost never; 0- never)

10. When you get angry, how often do you take out your anger by kicking things like a chair, giving a door a good slam, punching the wall, or looking for something to throw or smash?
(100- very often; 75- fairly often; 50- sometimes; 25- almost never, 0- never)

Perceived Hostility from Others Scale

1. In the last twelve months, how often have you felt that people were talking about you behind your back?
(100- very often; 75- fairly often; 50- sometimes; 25- almost never; 0- never)

2. In the last twelve months, how often have you felt that people were trying to cheat you?
(100- very often; 75- fairly often; 50- sometimes; 25- almost never; 0- never)

3. In the last twelve months, how often have you felt that people avoid you?
(100- very often; 75- fairly often; 50- sometimes; 25- almost never; 0- never)

4. In the last twelve months, how often have you felt that people were staring at you?
(100- very often; 75- fairly often; 50- sometimes; 25- almost never; 0- never)

5. In the last twelve months, how often have you felt that people were trying to pick quarrels or start arguments with you?
(100- very often; 75- fairly often; 50- sometimes; 25- almost never; 0- never)

Internal Consistency Reliability of PERI Scales (Alpha Coefficients).

	# of Items	Whole Sample	All Vets	Viet Vets	Era Vets	Non-vets
Demoralization	Five Scales	.86	.87	.87	.86	.84
Guilt	3	.58	.64	.69	.58	.50
Angry feelings	3	.67	.67	.69	.65	.65
Active expression of hostility	10	.69	.69	.69	.68	.70
Perceived hostility from others	5	.77	.77	.77	.77	.77

The Stress Scales[7]

The selection of items for the Stress scale was based on a review of the literature of traumatically stressed populations, Grinker and Spiegel's (1945) study of combat veterans from World War Two, Segal's (1973) findings with POWs from Korea, Krystal's (1968) studies of concentration camp survivors, Erikson's (1976) description of the survivors of the Buffalo Creek Dam Collapse, a number of early findings of studies of Vietnam veterans (Lifton, 1973; Horowitz, 1976; Shatan et al., 1977); and with reference to the working papers of D.S.M. III. Any symptom that had been mentioned 75 percent of the time was included on the Stress scale symptom checklist.

Twenty-two symptoms met this criterion. They were: (1) feelings of dizziness, (2) anxiety or tension, (3) headaches, (4) stomach troubles, (5) having trouble remembering things, (6) feeling numb, (7) loss of interest in usual activities, (8) feeling irritable or short tempered, (9) sleep disturbances (trouble staying asleep or oversleeping), (10) having frightening dreams or nightmares, (11) feeling sad, depressed, or blue, (12) feeling like lashing out, (13) tiring easily, (14) feeling that one might get out of control, (15) feeling jumpy or easily startled, (16) attacks of sudden fear or panic, (17) thoughts of how one might die, (18) feeling confused or having trouble thinking, (19) having difficulty trusting others, (20) feeling that life was not meaningful, (21) having flashbacks to specific events during the war,[8] (22) feeling that what other people care about does not make sense.

Respondents were asked if they had experienced any of these symptoms very often, fairly often, sometimes, almost never or never. If they answered in the affirmative (very often, fairly often, or sometimes), the time of the onset of the symptom was determined. The Stress-scale scores were derived simply by adding the number of affirmative responses together. The potential range was 0 to 22 for

Internal Consistency Reliability of Stress Scales (Alpha Coefficients)

	# of items	Whole Sample	Viet Vets	Era Vets	Non-vets
Stress scale	21	.72	.72	.72	.72
Intrusive imagery	3	.46	.62	.38	.25
Hyperarousal	6	.73	.75	.76	.68
Numbing	4	.48	.53	.39	.48
Cognitive difficulties	2	.57	.64	.61	.49

The entire analysis is based on the Vietnam veteran sample. Therefore the scale alphas that are below a minimum criterion of .50 for the nonveterans on intrusive imagery and cognitive difficulties, and for era veterans on intrusive imagery and numbing do not affect the reliability of the scales in this analysis.

Two Scales of Social Reintegration[a]

Feelings of Alienation at Homecoming (3 items)

1. People at home just didn't understand what you had been through in the armed forces.
2. Having been away for a while, you felt left out of everything that was going on at home.
3. Readjusting to civilian life was more difficult than most people imagine.

Belief that People and Government Support Veterans (5 Items)

1. Our presidents and their administrations have done and are doing all they can to help veterans return to civilian life.
2. The American people have done everything they can to make veterans feel at home again.
3. Most people at home respect you for having served your country in the armed forces.
4. When you got home, you did't want any thanks for what you had done for your country.
5. People at home made you feel proud to have served your country in the armed forces.

Each item is scored as follows:

Agree strongly	100
Agree mildly	75
Neither agree nor disagree	50
Disagree mildly	25
Disagree strongly	0

Each scale score is the mean of the item scores.

[a]The items were originally used in the 1971 Harris Survey, "A Study of the Problems Facing Vietnam Era Veterans: Their Readjustment to Civilian Life."

veterans and 0 to 21 for nonveterans. If a respondent had more than twelve missing values to his score, his whole score was declared missing. There were four missing scores out of 1,001 cases in wave II of our sample, for a percentage of .04.

Human Rights Scales

There are eleven major Human Rights scales. The following table is a summary of the names of the scales, the variables they include, their alpha coefficients of reliability, and the ranges of the scales. (Note: The ranges are standardized as 0 to 100, except for those scales that intrinsically are made up of countable units.)

Scale	Alpha	Range
1. AWARE	.88	0–100
2. INDWAR	.51	0–100
3. ABPERS	.83	0–6
4. ENVWAR	.79	0–3
5. NVABPERS	.85	0–100
6. SVABPERS	.88	0–100
7. USABPERS	.87	0–100
8. USENVWAR	.81	0–100
9. PROSECUT	.55	0–4
10. WEAPONS	.82	0–7
11. POWRIGHT	.55	0–5

The following pages will describe each of the scales separately, indicating what each scale is measuring and listing the variables of which the scale is composed.

1. AWARE—Awareness of the Rules of War. The AWARE scale, consisting of variables asked only of veterans who responded that they had received some type of instruction concerning rules of conduct in military operations, is concerned with awareness of international rules of war.

The scale consists of five questions:

(How aware would you say this instruction made you about how you . . .)

(1) are supposed to treat the enemy . . . (during military operations/wartime?)

(2) are supposed to treat civilians . . .

(3) are supposed to treat the sick and wounded . . .

(4) are supposed to treat enemy prisoners of war . . .

(5) were to act if you were a prisoner of war?

There were four available responses for each question:
(1) thoroughly aware of the rules
(2) somewhat aware of the rules
(3) not really aware of the rules at all
(4) don't remember (coded as missing)

The responses to these items were recoded and summed so that someone who was not aware of any of the five received a score of 0, while someone who was thoroughly aware of all five rules was given a score of 100.

2. INDWAR. The INDWAR scale, asked of everyone, measures the respondent's respect for individual responsibility in war. It consists of the following five questions:

(1) If you do something that is a crime under international law, you are guilty and should be punished even if your country does not consider your act a crime.

(2) No one should be punished by his government for refusing to carry out an order that seriously violates international law.

(3) In a war, only military necessity, not international rules of war, should determine the choice of strategies and weapons.

(4) An officer whose men violate international law is legally responsible if he could have known about it and did not try to stop them.

(5) Let us say you violated international law. Acting under orders is no excuse, if you had a chance to know about those international laws and had had an opportunity to disobey.

The responses were:
(1) strongly agree
(2) agree
(3) neither agree or disagree
(4) disagree
(5) strongly disagree
(9) not sure (coded as response 3)

As for the previous two scales, the responses for INDWAR were recoded and summed, with a score of 100 indicating the most respect for individual responsibility in war.

3. ABPERS. ABPERS is a six-item scale of how many of the acts of war against persons asked about are considered unlawful. All respondents were asked these six questions:

(Here is a list of things that sometimes happen in war. Please look at the list and tell me which of these actions against civilians you would consider unlawful.)

(3) terrorizing, assassinating, or torturing civilians for political or religious beliefs

(4) attacking hospitals and similar places

(5) not giving medical treatment to wounded civilians in battle area

(6) killing hostages

(10) mutilating bodies

(11) raping civilian women

The responses for these items were:

(1) unlawful

(2) not unlawful

(9) not sure (coded as missing)

The responses were recoded so that their sum represents the count of the items which the respondent considered unlawful—i.e., a score of 6 means that he felt all the items were unlawful.

4. ENVWAR. ENVWAR is a scale composed of three items (7), (8), and (9). It counts the number of environmental abuses directed primarily against the environment that are perceived as unlawful.

(7) . . . defoliating large parts of the countryside of South Vietnam

(8) . . . using chemicals to create rain to destroy the natural environment of the civilian population

(9) . . . destroying the dikes to create widespread flooding in civilian areas

The responses for these items were:

(1) unlawful

(2) not unlawful

(9) not sure (coded as missing)

The responses were recoded so that their sum represents the count of the items that the respondent considered unlawful—i.e., a score of 3 means that he felt all the items were unlawful.

5. NVABPERS. NVABPERS measures actions against the people, committed by the Vietcong and North Vietnamese Army.

The exact wording is:

How commonly do you think the following were done by the Vietcong and North Vietnamese Army? (acts of unlawfulness items)

The responses were:

(1) very common

(2) common

(3) occasionally

(4) hardly ever
(5) never
(9) don't know (coded as missing)

These responses were recoded and summed, so that a score of 0 would represent that the respondent felt all of the acts were never committed by this group, and a score of 100 would mean the respondent felt that all of the acts were very commonly done by the Vietcong and the North Vietnamese Army.

6. *SVABPERS*. This scale is exactly analogous to NVABPERS in response to the question: How commonly do you think these things were done by the South Vietnamese Army?

7. *USABPERS*. This scale is exactly analogous to NVABPERS and SVABPERS with the question of interest being: How commonly do you think these things were done by the American armed forces?

8. *USENVWAR*. USENVWAR measures the perception of the frequency of the five actions directed against the environment.

9. *PROSECUT*. Count of who should be held responsible for acts of abusive violence. This scale, asked of everyone who responded that anything was unlawful and done by the United States, is concerned with the persons whom the respondents feel should be held responsible for actions against the law of armed conflict. It consists of four items:

Whom do you think should be prosecuted for those acts you said were unlawful?
(1) the combat soldier on the ground
(2) officers directly in charge of the operation
(3) senior officers with overall responsibility
(4) responsible political leaders

The available responses were:
(1) yes
(2) no
(9) not sure (coded as missing)

The variables were recoded and summed, such that a score of 4 indicates that the respondent felt all four should be prosecuted.

10. *WEAPONS*. This scale represents the number of listed weapons that the respondent feels are unnecessarily cruel. Seven weapons comprise the WEAPONS scale:

I am going to read you a list of weapons that have been used in some places, including Vietnam, by one or both sides. Please tell me which of these weapons you think is unnecessarily cruel.

(1) napalm (burning jellied gasoline which spreads all over)

(2) germ warfare

(3) chemical warfare

(4) plastic bombs

(5) dum-dum bullets

(6) mines and booby traps against civilians

(7) simple weapons which make treatment of victims nearly impossible and cause death or mutilation (like pungee sticks, poison spears, glass, and nail homemade bottle bombs).

The coded responses were:

(1) unnecessarily cruel

(2) not unnecessarily cruel

(3) not sure (coded as missing)

As with the other scales, these responses were recoded and added, with a score of 7 indicating the respondent felt all the weapons are unnecessarily cruel, and a score of 0 that none is unnecessarily cruel.

11. POWRIGHT. This scale deals with how one feels about treatment of prisoners of war and the rights they should have. It comprises five statements:

(1) Prisoners of war may not be treated better or worse on the basis of race or political beliefs.

(2) Prisoners of war must be permitted to contact their families and to write letters to them.

(3) Prisoners of war should not be forced to do work that directly supports war.

(4) Prisoners of war must be allowed to formally put their complaints against the administration of the camp in writing.

(5) Prison camp rules and punishments must meet the standards of international agreements.

The responses to these were:

(1) agree

(2) disagree

(3) don't know (coded as missing)

After being recoded, the item responses were summed: a score of 5 means the respondent agreed with all the statements, showing most concern for POWs.

Political Attitude Measures

Political Attitude Measures

Scale Name	# of Items	Alpha Total Sample	Alpha Vietnam Veterans	Alpha Era Veteran	Alpha Non-veteran	Alpha All Veterans
1. MILINT	2	.71502 (n = 1227)	.72924 (n = 320)	.67519 (n = 335)	.72750 (n = 572)	.70194 (n = 655)
2. VCNVA	2	.76707 (n = 1267)	.75756 (n = 323)	.78463 (n = 343)	.76751 (n = 601)	.76760 (n = 666)
3. ALIENGOV	7	.72162 (n = 1265)	.72082 (n = 339)	.72082 (n = 339)	.71718 (n = 596)	.72307 (n = 669)

ATTR: Attitude toward resisters

This measure was an open-ended item that asked the respondent how he felt about resisters who refused to serve during the war. The responses were content analyzed and coded 1–5:

(a) supported their action to opposed their action

MILINT

Description: Attitude toward U.S. military interventions in foreign countries scale

Scoring: 0 to 100; low score against intervention

high score favors intervention

Items: Send troops to Argentina

Sent troops to Africa

N.B. Don't knows in original items assigned a middle value.

No prorating

ALLENGOV

Description: Alienation (or lack of confidence/trust) from government scale

Scoring: 0 to 100; low score—low alienation

high score—high alienation

Items: Confidence in executive branch

Confidence in Supreme Court

Confidence in Congress
Public officials don't care what you think
How things are going in the country these days
How much of the time you can trust the government to do what's right
Government run for big interests/all the people
Missing Values Aliengov (–9)

NOTES

Notes to Introduction

1. The sites were Brooklyn, New York; southern Westchester County, New York; Bridgeport, Connecticut; Atlanta, Georgia; Los Angeles, California; Chicago, Illinois; South Bend, Indiana; the two rural counties adjacent to South Bend; Columbus, Georgia; and the two rural counties adjacent to Columbus.

Notes to Chapter 1

1. For a detailed description of period-of-service measure see methodology appendix.

2. For a more detailed discussion of our approach to this issue, see R. Laufer et al., *Legacies of Vietnam. Post-War Trauma: Social and Psychological Problems of Vietnam Veterans in the Aftermath of the Vietnam War*, vol. 3 of the Final Report to the Veterans Administration and Congress, Washington, D.C., Government Printing Office, March 26, 1981; R. S. Laufer, M. Gallops, and E. Frey-Wouters, "War Stress and Trauma: The Vietnam Veterans Experience," *Journal of Health and Social Behavior* 25 (1984):65–85; T. Yager, R. S. Laufer, and M. Gallops, "Some Problems Associated with War Experience in Men of the Vietnam Generation," *Archives of General Psychiatry* 41 (1984):327–33; R. S. Laufer, E. Frey-Wouters, and M. Gallops, "Traumatic Stressors and PTSD," in *Trauma and Its Wake*, ed. Charles Figley (Bruner/Mazel, 1985); R. S. Laufer, "War Trauma and Human Development: The Vietnam Experience," in *The Trauma of War*, ed. A. Blank, S. Sonnenberg, and J. Talbot (American Psychiatric Press, 1985).

3. The combat scale is composed of ten items. They are: 1) served in an artillery unit which fired on the enemy, 2) flew in an aircraft over Vietnam, 3) stationed at a forward observation post, 4) received incoming fire, 5) encountered mines or booby traps, 6) received sniper or sapper fire, 7) in a patrol that was ambushed, 8) engaged VC or NVA in a firefight, 9) saw Americans or Vietnamese killed, and 10) was wounded. The scale was coded in an additive fashion. Items 1 through 6 were given a value of 1 if true, items 7 through 10 were given a value of 2 if true. The value of each experience was added cumulatively. The maximum range on the scale was from (0) had none of these experiences to (14) had all of these experiences . The effective range of the scale in our sample was (0) to (13). The mean of the scale was 5.9; the median 5.7; and the standard deviation 4.1 (the characteristics of the weighted data). Nine percent of the sample saw no combat, 33% low combat (values 1 through 4), 31% moderate combat (values 5 through 9), and 27% heavy combat (values 10 through 13).

4. In measuring exposure to abusive violence we used a set of open-ended questions in which the veteran was asked whether he experienced the "dirty side of war" and if so, to describe the events in this category. We required that veterans had at least witnessed the event or to have seen its consequences soon after its commission and to have clearly known who had carried it out. To make the measure an indicator of objective experiences we eliminated any events of which they had heard secondhand. In our sample roughly a third (31%) reported they were directly exposed to at least one episode. The incidents most often cited were torture of prisoners, including pushing them from helicopters; physical mistreatment of civilians; use of napalm, white phosphorus, or cluster bombs on villages; death or maiming by booby trap; and mutilation of bodies. Most of the men who reported episodes described cases in which U.S. regulars were involved (78% of those exposed). Less than a third mentioned instances in which the Vietcong or NV regulars were involved (31% of those exposed). Another 13% reported cases in which ARVN or Korean (ROK) forces were involved. (These three figures do not sum to 100% since over a third of those exposed mentioned more than one episode.)

In previous work we tested a model that differentiated the effects of exposure to abusive violence by the perpetrator of the act. Our findings suggest that the traumatic quality of the experience is the imagery associated with it; the issue of who initiated the action was not significant if the veteran had only witnessed the event and did not participate in it personally. Consequently, the emphasis in constructing measures of abusive violence should be on the distinction between those who witnessed episodes and those who actively participated in them.

Exposure to abusive violence is related to the level of combat exposure but is not so strongly tied to it to justify the conclusion that these two measures reflect the same dimension of war stress. The mean level of combat for those who witnessed episodes of abusive violence is significantly higher than that of veterans not exposed (8.4 vs. 4.7). However, there is little difference on combat among those exposed between those who participated in and those who simply witnessed episodes (8.5 vs. 8.4).

5. See methodology appendix.

6. The percentages do not sum to 100% because the categories were derived from textual materials through content analysis and responses could be classified in more than one category, i.e., responses were not mutually exclusive.

7. The relationship was significant at (p lt. .10).

8. The relationship was significant at (p lt. .10).

9. This relationship was not statistically significant.

10. These relationships were not statistically significant.

11. This relationship was not statistically significant.

12. Laufer, "War Trauma and Human Development."

13. The findings discussed in this section are presented in statistical form in Laufer et al., "Traumatic Stressors and PTSD." In this volume, because we do not include multivariate tables, we summarize the results of the multivariate analysis presented in the paper cited above.

14. The occupational prestige of activists' parents is also significantly higher than that of the low activists. We do not present a table on this finding because the Duncan Occupational Prestige Index we use is linear and the cross-tabular presentation would not be very meaningful.

Notes to Chapter 2

1. Laufer et al., *Legacies of Vietnam. Post-War Trauma: Social and Psychological Problems of Vietnam Veterans in the Aftermath of the Vietnam War*, vol. 3 of the Final Report to the Veterans Administration and Congress, Washington, D.C.: Government Printing Office, March 26, 1981; Laufer et al., "War Stress and Trauma"; Yager et al., "Some Problems Associated with War Experience in Men of the Vietnam Generation"; Laufer et al., "Traumatic Stressors and PTSD"; Laufer, "War Trauma and Human Development: Vietnam."

2. See W. H. Eaton, "Research on Veterans' Adjustment," *American Journal of Sociology* 51 (1946):483–87; R. J. Havighurst et al., *The American Back Home: A Study of Veteran Readjustment* (New York: Longmans, Green, 1951); D. Becker, "The Veteran: Problem and Challenge," *Social Forces* 25 (1946):95–99; W. B. Brookover, "The Adjustment of Veterans to Civilian Life," *American Sociological Review* 10 (1945):579–86.

3. See M. Polner, *No Victory Parades: The Return of the Vietnam Veteran* (New York: Holt, Rinehart and Winston, 1971).

4. V. Fischer et al., *Myths and Realities: A Study of Attitudes Toward Vietnam Era Veterans* (Washington, D.C.: Louis Harris and Associates, 1980).

5. See methodology appendix.

6. See P. Fussell, *The Great War in Modern Memory* (New York: Oxford University Press, 1975).

7. S. Freud, *Beyond the Pleasure Principle* (New York: Hogarth Press, 1953 [1921]); R. J. Lifton and E. Olson, "The Human Meaning of Total Disaster: The Buffalo Creek Experience," *Psychiatry* 39 (1976):1–18.

8. M. J. Horowitz, *Stress Response Syndromes* (New York: Aronson, 1976).

9. Ibid.

10. N. J. Zilberg, D. S. Weiss, and M. J. Horowitz, "Impact of Event Scale: A Cross-Validational Study and Some Empirical Evidence Supporting a Conceptual Model of Stress Response Syndromes," *Consulting and Clinical Psychology* 50 (1982):407–14.

11. R. S. Laufer, E. Brett, and M. S. Gallops, "Dimensions of Post-Traumatic Stress Disorder Among Vietnam Veterans," *Journal of Nervous and Mental Health Disease* 173 (1985); R. Hough et al., "Natural History of Post Traumatic Stress Disorder," paper presented at the American Psychological Association, Anaheim, Calif., 1983.

12. G. Boulanger, C. Kadushin, and J. Martin, *Legacies of Vietnam*, vol. 4, *Long Term Stress Reactions* (Washington, D.C.: Government Printing Office, 1981).

13. Laufer et al., "War Stress and Trauma."

14. Laufer et al., "Dimensions of Post-Traumatic Stress Among Vietnam Veterans."

15. R. S. Laufer, E. Brett, and M. S. Gallops, "Post-Traumatic Stress Disorder (PTSD) Reconsidered: PTSD Among Vietnam Veterans," *Post-Traumatic Stress Disorder: Psychological and Biological Sequelae*, ed. B. A. van der Kolk (Washington, D.C.: American Psychiatric Press, 1984).

16. R. S. Laufer, E. Brett, and M. S. Gallops, "Symptom Patterns Associated with Post-Traumatic Stress Disorder Among Vietnam Veterans Exposed to War Trauma," *American Journal of Psychiatry* 142 (1985).

17. We focus on the psychological impact of witnessing abusive violence on whites because they show evidence of more long-term psychological scars from their experience than do their black counterparts. The reader should not infer from this that blacks were less upset than whites when they saw acts of abusive violence; or that many blacks who witnessed abusive violence do not have troubling memories—they do. In the aggregate, however, white witnesses seem to experience more long-term psychological traumatization than do blacks.

18. We examined variables tapping attitudes toward the war, toward the Vietnamese, of Vietnamese views of U.S. soldiers, of the effects of the war on Vietnamese civilians and society, toward the use of abusive violence, toward the treatment of civilians in war, toward actions against civilians, toward the use of destructive weapons in urban areas, and toward the treatment of captured guerrillas.

19. S. Leventman and P. Camacho, "The 'Gook' Syndrome: The Vietnam

War as a Racial Encounter," in *Strangers at Home*, ed. C. R. Figley and S. Leventman (New York: Praeger, 1980).

20. W. S. Gould, "Racial Conflict in the U.S. Army," *Race* 15 (1973):1–23; C. C. Moskos, "Surviving the War in Vietnam," in *Strangers at Home*, ed. C. R. Figley and S. Leventman, pp. 71–85.

21. L. Sloan and H. Phoenix, "The Quality of Race Relations in the Vietnam Era Military," paper presented at the annual meeting of the Society for the Study of Social Problems, Boston, 1979.

22. R. S. Laufer and M. S. Gallops, "Life-course Effects of Vietnam Combat and Abusive Violence: Marital Patterns," in *Journal of Marriage and the Family* (November 1985); Yager et al., "Some Problems Associated with the War Experience in Men of the Vietnam Generation."

23. The weighted percentages understate the differences between Vietnam and Vietnam era veterans, because they do not control for other characteristics of the veterans. In a regression model the Vietnam era veteran (b = .04) compared to the Vietnam veteran (b = .09) p lt. .01.

24. For a more detailed discussion of this issue, see Laufer, "War Trauma and Human Development."

25. G. Vaillant, *Adaptation to Life* (Boston: Little, Brown, 1977).

26. J. Adelson, "The Political Imagination of the Young Adolescent," *Daedalus* (Fall 1971); E. Erikson, *Identity, Youth and Crisis* (New York: W. W. Norton, 1968); K. Keniston, *Youth and Dissent* (New York: Harcourt, Brace and World, 1972); D. P. Hogan, *Transitions and Social Change* (New York: Academic Press, 1981); G. H. Elder, Jr., "Historical Change in Life Patterns and Personality," paper presented at the Eastern Sociological Meetings, Philadelphia, 1978; H. H. Winsborough, *The Transition from Schoolboy to Adult*, Center for Demography and Ecology, Madison, Wisconsin, Working Paper 76–13, 1976; Vaillant, *Adaptation to Life*.

27. Keniston, *Youth and Dissent*.

28. R. S. Laufer, and V. L. Bengston, "Generations, Aging and Social Stratification: On the Development of Generational Units," *Journal of Social Issues* 30 (1974):181–205.

29. Vaillant, *Adaptation to Life*.

30. C. C. Moskos, *The American Enlisted Man* (New York: Russell Sage, 1970).

31. J. P. Wilson *Forgotten Warrior Project, Part I*, "Identity, Ideology and Crisis: The Vietnam Veteran in Transition," report submitted to the Disabled American Veterans Association, 1978.

Notes to Chapter 3

1. For an authoritative source of information, see R. Falk, ed., *The Vietnam War and International Law*, vols. 1 and 2 (Princeton: Princeton University

Press, 1968 and 1969).

2. As stated in the introduction of *The Vietnam War and International Law*, vol. 1, p. 4. This introduction was prepared on behalf of the panel by Richard Falk.

3. See United States Department of State, Office of the Legal Adviser, "The Legality of United States Participation in the Defense of Viet Nam," 54 Department of State Bulletin. The memorandum was submitted by the Legal Adviser to the Senate Committee on Foreign Relations on March 8, 1966.

4. See, for example the view of the National Lawyers Guild as quoted by T. Taylor in *Nuremberg and Vietnam: An American Tragedy* (Chicago: Quadrangle Books, 1970), p. 96.

5. These arguments are expressed in such documents as the "Legal Memorandum on Vietnam War of Lawyers' Committee on American Policy Toward Vietnam," 1967, in R. A. Falk, G. Kolko, and R. J. Lifton, eds., *Crimes of War* (New York: Random House, 1971), pp. 189–202. Also R. A. Falk, "International Law and the U.S. Role in the Vietnam War" in *The Vietnam War and International Law*, vol. 1, pp. 362–401.

6. See, for example, Louis Harris and Associates, *Myths and Realities: A Study of Attitudes Toward Vietnam Era Veterans* (Washington, D.C.: Government Printing Office, 1980), pp. 52–72.

7. Our findings are similar to those in ibid. This study reported that 47% of their sample of Vietnam veterans (49% of all heavy-combat veterans) felt that we should have stayed out of the war as against 40% who argued that we did the right thing in getting into the fighting in Vietnam. They also found that only 5% expressed no strong feelings one way or the other, while 6% remained confused or not sure (see table III-3, p. 57).

8. In ibid., it is reported that while 37% of the heavy-combat veterans agree strongly that we could never have won the war, the majority are convinced that we lost the war because of a failure of the country's leadership to exercise the necessary political will. (See p. 58 as well as tables III-4, III-6.)

9. Our findings are similar to those in some earlier studies, such as H. Schuman, "Two Sources of Anti-War Sentiment in America," *American Journal of Sociology* 78, 3 (November 1972):513–36.

Notes to Chapter 5

1. See Article 13 of the Fourth Geneva Convention and Article 50 of Protocol I additional to the Geneva Conventions of 1949; also, International Committee of the Red Cross, *Draft Additional Protocols to the Geneva Conventions of 1949, Commentary* (Geneva, 1973), pp. 55–56.

2. M. Walzer, *Just and Unjust Wars* (New York: Basic Books, 1977), pp. 130–31, 135.

3. See Charles Fried's discussion of "Imposing Risks on Others," in *An Anatomy of Values; Problems of Personal and Social Choice* (Cambridge: Harvard University Press, 1970), ch. 2.

4. Quoted in D. Pike, *Viet Cong* (Cambridge: MIT Press, 1968), p. 242.

5. See G. I. A. D. Draper, "The Status of Combatants and the Question of Guerrilla War," *British Yearbook of International Law* 45 (1971).

6. See the study by F. Siordet, "Les Conventions de Geneve et la Guerre Civile," *Revue Internationale de la Croix Rouge* 32 (1950):104–22, 187–212; also H. Lauterpacht, on "Rules of Warfare in an Unlawful War," in *Law and Politics in the World Community: Essays on Hans Kelsen's Pure Theory and Related Problems in International Law*, ed. G. A. Lipsky (Berkeley: University of California Press, 1953), pp. 92–93.

7. Walzer, *Just and Unjust Wars*, p. 187.

Notes to Chapter 6

1. A. Cassese, "A Tentative Appraisal of the Old and New Humanitarian Law of Armed Conflict" in *The New Humanitarian Law of Armed Conflict*, ed. A. Cassese (Naples: Editoriale Scientifica, 1979), pp. 496–97.

2. G. Best, *Humanity in Warfare* (New York: Columbia University Press, 1980), p. 325.

3. See, for example, Protocol I, Article 51, paragraph 2; also International Committee of the Red Cross, *Draft Additional Protocols to the Geneva Conventions of 1949, Commentary* (Geneva, 1973), pp. 56–57.

4. See Protocol I, Article 51, paragraph 5; also *Commentary*, pp. 58–59.

5. The Hague Regulations Respecting the Laws and Customs of War on Land, 1899, provide in Article 25 that "the attack or bombardment, by any means whatever, of towns, villages, habitations, or buildings which are undefended is prohibited." At the Hague Peace Conference of 1907, the above regulations were adopted, reinforcing its principles. See also Protocol I, articles 59 and 60.

6. See especially the Hague Convention of 1907, the 1923 Draft Rules of Air Warfare, the Fourth Geneva Convention of 1949, the Hague Convention of 1954 and Protocol I.

7. Protocol I, Article 54.

8. Protocol I, Article 56, paragraph 1.

9. Ibid., paragraph 2; for a discussion of this principle see *Commentary*, p. 63.

10. See, for example, GAOR, resolution 3264 (XXIX), December 9, 1974; report: A/9910; and Protocol I, Article 55.

11. See Fourth Geneva Convention, Article 19 (1); also Article 6 of the Hague Convention No. IX of 1907; Protocol I, Article 57; for a discussion of precautionary measures, see *Commentary*, pp. 64–67.

12. These fundamental guarantees are found in a number of international legal instruments, including the Fourth Geneva Convention, Protocol I, and the International Covenant on Civil and Political Rights.

13. G. von Glahn, *The Occupation of Enemy Territory* (Minneapolis: University of Minnesota Press, 1957), p. 237.

14. Ibid., pp. 239–40.

15. Ibid., p. 236.

16. Protocol I, Article 51, paragraph 6, and Article 52, paragraph 1.

17. This article extends and supplements articles 16 and 27 of the Fourth Geneva Convention. See also the *International Covenant on Civil and Political Rights*, Art. 6(5).

18. Article 77 in Protocol I, paragraph 2. It is further provided that in recruiting among those persons who have attained the age of fifteen years, the parties to the conflict shall try to give priority to those who are the oldest.

19. See Article 77 in Protocol I, paragraphs 3, 4, and 5, and Article 68 of the Fourth Geneva Convention.

20. See Part II, Articles 8–32 in Protocol I; and *Commentary to Draft Protocols*, pp. 17–40.

21. Best, *Humanity in Warfare*, p. 328.

22. See, for example, the Preambles of the Hague Convention No. IV of 1907, the Geneva Conventions of 1949, and the Protocols Additional to the Geneva Conventions.

23. T. Taylor, *Nuremberg and Vietnam: An American Tragedy* (Chicago: Quadrangle, 1970), pp. 130–31.

24. As quoted in ibid., p. 135.

25. Ibid., p. 131.

26. For discussion of this issue, see, for example, J. Race, *War Comes to Long An* (Berkeley: University of Califiornia Press, 1972); D. Pike, *Viet Cong* (Cambridge, Mass., 1968).

27. See United States Military Assistance Command, Vietnam, Directive Number 513-23, dated May 1971 (unclassified contents), Documents 1 and 2.

28. For an account of the legal issues raised by the tactics and weapons used by the United States in Vietnam, see *Law and Responsibility in Warfare— The Vietnam Experience*, ed. P. D. Trooboff, published under the auspices of the American Society of International Law (University of North Carolina Press, 1975); see also books published by the Stockholm International Peace Research Institute (SIPRI), such as *Ecological Consequences of the Second Indochina War, Weapons of Mass Destruction and the Environment*, and *Warfare in a Fragile World: Military Impact on the Human Environment*.

29. See N. Chomsky, *At War with Asia* (New York: Random House, 1969), pp. 288–313; Race, *War Comes to Long An*; Walzer, *Just and Unjust Wars*, pp. 188–97; J. Schell, *The Military Half* (New York: Knopf, 1968).

30. As reported by S. Hersh, *Chemical and Biological Warfare: America's Hidden Arsenal* (Indianapolis: Bobbs-Merrill, 1968), pp. 151–57.

Notes to Chapter 7

1. For discussion of the use of unnecessarily cruel weapons, see, for example: Report of the Secretary-General of the United Nations, *Napalm and Other Incendiary Weapons and All Aspects of Their Possible Use*, United Nations publication, Sales No. E. 73.I.3; Report of the International Committee of the Red Cross, *Weapons that May Cause Unnecessary Suffering or Have Indiscriminate Effects* (Geneva, 1973); Report of the International Committee of the Red Cross, *Conference of Government Experts on the Use of Certain Conventional Weapons*, Lucerne, 1974 and Lugano, 1976; Stockholm International Peace Research Institute (SIPRI), *Incendiary Weapons* (Stockholm: Almqvist & Wiksell, and Cambridge: MIT Press, 1975).

2. A. Cassese, "Means of Warfare: The Traditional and the New Law," in *The New Humanitarian Law of Armed Conflict*, ed. A. Cassese (Naples: Editoriale Scientifica, 1979), p. 161.

3. Ibid., pp. 165–66.

4. Note G. A. Res. 2444 (XXIII), December 19, 1965; 2675 (XXV) December 9, 1970; and 3318 (XXIX) December 14, 1974.

5. Cassese, "Means of Warfare," pp. 170–71.

6. Ibid., p. 179.

7. Actually, the first codification of the laws of war was contained in the Lieber Instructions of 1863, a code of war conduct for the U.S. Army promulgated by President Lincoln. Although only U.S. forces were bound to its provisions, the code well represents the customs of war at that time. See the recently published *Lieber's Code and the Law of War* by Richard Shelly Hartigan for a discussion of the 1863 Instructions.

8. See Articles 22, 23a, and 23b. For other references to the use of poison, see Lieber Instructions, Article 70; Washington Treaty of 1922, Article 5; and the Treaty of Versailles, Article 171.

9. Protocol for the Prohibition of the Use of Asphyxiating, Poisonous or Other Gases, and of Bacteriological Methods of Warfare, June 17, 1925.

10. See, for example, G.A. resolutions 2932 (XXVII), November 29, 1972, and 3255 (XXIX), December 3, 1974.

11. See *Final Act of the International Conference on Human Rights*, United Nations publication, Sales No.: E.68.XIV.2, p. 18.

12. The protocol prohibits the use not only of poisonous and other gases but also of "analogous liquids, materials or devices."

13. See G.A. Res. 1653, 16 U.N. GAOR, Suppl. 17, at 4, A/5100; and further, G.A. Res. 2936 (XXVII), November 29, 1972, which links nonuse of force with the prohibition of the use of nuclear weapons.

14. Protocol I, Articles 35 and 36; see also Resolution 22, Follow-up Regarding Prohibition or Restriction of Use of Certain Conventional Weapons, adopted at the fifty-seventh plenary meeting of the Diplomatic Conference on the

Reaffirmation and Development of International Humanitarian Law Applicable in Armed Conflicts, June 9, 1977.

15. The name of the treaty is the Convention on Prohibitions or Restrictions on the Use of Certain Conventional Weapons Which May Be Deemed Excessively Injurious or to have Indiscriminate Effects. The attached protocols are: Protocol I—The Protocol on Non-Detectable Fragments; Protocol II—The Protocol on Prohibitions or Restrictions on the Use of Mines, Booby Traps and other Devices; Protocol III—The Protocol on Prohibitions and Restrictions on the Use of Incendiary Weapons.

16. Cassese, "Means of Warfare," p. 167.

17. For a more detailed discussion see M. Lumsden, *The United States Rules of Engagement in Vietnam as They Relate to the Use of Certain Specific Weapons: A Brief Survey and Analysis* (Stockholm International Peace Research Institute, April 1976).

18. *Congressional Record*, pp. S 9897–9905. They comprised the following documents: United States Military Assistance Command, Vietnam, Directive No. 525-13, Dated May 1971 (unclassified contents), including the following annexes: Rules of Engagement—Surface Weapons Excluding Naval Gunfire; Rules of Engagement—Fixed Wing Air Operations; Rules of Engagement—Rotary Wing Air Operations; Rules of Engagement—Naval Gunfire. Excerpts from various directives concerning rules of engagement and operating authorities for Southeast Asia: Regulation No. 525-4, 16 March 1968, Headquarters, American Division, APO San Francisco, Combat Operations, Rules of Engagement; Regulation No. 525-1, 30 January 1968, Headquarters, 11th Infantry Brigade, APO San Francisco, Combat Operations, Rules of Engagement, Change 1; Regulation No. 525-1, 10 April 1968, Headquarters, 11th Infantry Brigade, American Division, Combat Operations, Rules of Engagement, Change 1; Regulation No. 525-1, 9 February 1968, Headquarters, 11th Infantry Brigade, APO San Francisco, Combat Operations, Rules of Engagement.

19. Document 1, *General Rules*, 1971.

20. Document 1, Annex 2, 1971.

21. See J. B. Neilands et al., *Harvest of Death* (New York: Collier Books, 1962); Clergy and Laymen Concerned About Vietnam, *In The Name of America* (Annandale: Turnpike Press, 1968).

22. As quoted by L. C. Petrowski, in "Law and the Conduct of the Vietnam War," *The Vietnam War and International Law*, ed. Richard A. Falk, (Princeton: Princeton University Press, 1969), vol. 2, p. 503.

23. For a discussion of the M-16 rifle, see ibid., pp. 504–505.

24. S. Hersh, *Chemical And Biological Warfare: America's Hidden Arsenal* (Indianapolis: Bobbs Merrill, 1968), pp. 151–57; see also J. Lewallen, *Ecology of Devastation: Indochina* (Baltimore: Penguin, 1971).

25. As quoted by Petrowski, "Law and the Conduct of the Vietnam War," p. 506.

26. R. R. Baxter, "Humanitarian Law or Humanitarian Politics? The 1974 Diplomatic Conference on Humanitarian Law," *Harvard International Law Journal* 16, 1 (Spring 1975):26.

27. Our query was phrased as follows:

1. I am going to read you a list of weapons that have been used in some places, including Vietnam, by one or both sides. Please tell me which of these weapons you think are unnecessarily cruel and which are not unnecessarily cruel.

    1. Napalm (burning jellied gasoline which spreads all over)

    2. Germ warfare

    3. Chemical warfare (poisons and defoliants)

    4. Plastic bombs, the pieces of which cannot be found by X-rays

    5. Expanding dum-dum bullets

    6. Using mines or booby traps against civilians

    7. Simple weapons which make treatment of victims nearly impossible and cause death or mutilation (like pungee sticks, poison spears, glass and nail homemade bottle bombs)

2. Under which conditions do you think these weapons can be used?

    1. Anytime

    2. In urban areas for military reasons

    3. Only within the battle areas

    4. Never

Notes to Chapter 8

1. G. von Glahn, *The Occcupation of Enemy Territory*, (Minneapolis: University of Minnesota Press, 1957), p. 51.

2. For a discussion of the treatment of prisoners of war, see ibid., pp. 48–54; R. Baxter, "So-Called Unprivileged Belligerency: Spies, Guerrillas, and Saboteurs," in *British Yearbook of International Law* 28 (1951):323–45; I.P. Trainin, "Questions of Guerrilla Warfare in the Law of War," *American Journal of International Law* 40 (1946):534–62.

3. See Section II, Articles 43–48 of Protocol I; also *Commentary to Draft Protocols*, International Committee of the Red Cross (Geneva, October 1973), pp. 47–53.

4. Protocol II, Article 1.

5. See H. S. Levie, "Maltreatment of Prisoners of War in Vietnam," *The Vietnam War and International Law*, volume 2. ed. R. A. Falk (Princeton: Princeton University Press, 1969), p. 361–98.

6. See T. Taylor, *Nuremberg and Vietnam: An American Tragedy* (Chicago: Quadrangle, 1970), p. 148–49.

7. *New York Times*, International Edition, October 14, 1965.

8. Taylor, *Nuremberg and Vietnam*, p. 149.

9. Jean-Pierre Debris and Andre Menras, "Terror in Thieu's Prisons," Indochina Program, American Friends Service Committee, Philadelphia, 1971.

Notes to Chapter 9

1. For a Discussion of this principle, see G. von Glahn, *The Occupation of Enemy Territory: A Commentary on the Law and Practice of Belligerent Occupation* (Minneapolis: University of Minnesota Press, 1957), pp. 240–42; W. B. Cowless, "Trial of War Criminals by Military Tribunals," *American Law Association Journal*, 30 (1944):330–33, 362; J. W. Garner, "Punishment of Offenders against the Laws and Customs of War," *American Journal of International Law (AJIL)*, 14(1920):70–94; G. Manner, "The Legal Nature and Punishment of Criminal Acts of Violence Contrary to the Laws of War," *AJIL* 37 (1943):407–35.

2. International Committee of the Red Cross, Draft Additional Protocols to the Geneva Conventions of August 12, 1949, *Commentary* (Geneva, October 1973), p. 94.

3. The titles of the four Geneva Conventions are: First Convention—Geneva Convention for the Amelioration of the Condition of Wounded and Sick in Armed Forces in the Field; Second Convention—Geneva Convention for the Amelioration of the Condition of Wounded, Sick and Shipwrecked Members of Armed Forces at Sea; Third Convention—Geneva Convention Relative to the Treatment of Prisoners of War; Fourth Convention—Geneva Convention Relative to the Protection of Civilian Persons in Time of War. See Articles 49 to 52; 50 to 53; 129 to 132; 146 to 149. Also *Commentary*, pp. 94–95.

4. See Protocol I, Section II, Article 85.

5. T. Taylor, *Nuremberg and Vietnam: An American Tragedy* (Chicago: Quadrangle Books, 1970), p. 24.

6. Ibid. pp. 26–27; see also United States, France, Great Britain, Soviet Union, *Agreement for the Prosecution and Punishment of the Major War Criminals of the European Axis*, August 8, 1945, in *AJIL* 39 (October 1945), Supplement, pp. 257–64.

7. See Taylor, *Nuremberg and Vietnam*, pp. 27–28.

8. See *Law Report of War Criminals*, selected and prepared by the United Nations War Crimes Commission, vol. 4 (London, 1949); also Trials of War Criminals before the Nuremberg Military Tribunals under Control Council Law No. 10, Nuremberg, October 1946-April 1949 (Washington: U.S. Government Printing Office, 1949–1952), 14 vols.

9. G.A. Res. 95, 1 GAOR, U.N. Doc. A/64/ADD.1. The Tokyo Trials began in June 1946, and the judgment was given in November 1948.

10. See Yearbook of the International Law Commission, 1950. Also Parry, "Some Considerations upon the Content of a Draft Code of Offenses Against the

Peace and Security of Mankind," *International Law Quarterly* 3 (1950):208; Fenwick, "Draft Code of Offenses Against the Peace and Security of Mankind," *AJIL* 46 (1952):98; Johnson, "The Draft Code of Offenses Against the Peace and Security of Mankind," *International and Comparative Law Quarterly* 4 (1955): 445.

11. See, for example, the Fourth Geneva Convention, Articles 146, 147, 148, 149. For a commentary see H. Lauterpacht, "The Problem of the Revision of the Law of War," *British Yearbook of International Law* 29 (1952): 360–82.

12. A similar provision is found in the *United States 1956 Army Manual*, see *Field Manual 27-10, The Law of Warfare*, paragraph 501, p. 178.

13. R. S. Laufer, M. Gallops, and E. Frey-Wouters, "War Stress and Trauma: The Vietnam Veteran Experience," *Journal of Health and Social Behavior* 25,1 (March 1984); R. S. Laufer, E. Frey-Wouters, M. Gallops, "Traumatic Stressors in the Vietnam War and PTSD," *Trauma and Its Wake*, vol. 1, ed. C. Figley (Bruner/Mazel, 1985); R. S. Laufer, E. Brett, and M. Gallops, "The Relationship Between Stressors and Symptomatology in Post-Traumatic Stress Disorder among Vietnam Veterans," in *New Perspectives on Post-Traumatic Stress*, ed. B. van der Kolk, Clinical Insights Series (American Psychiatric Press, 1984); T. Yager, R. S. Laufer, and M. Gallops, "Some Problems Associated with War Experience in Men of the Vietnam Generation," *Archives of General Psychiatry* 41 (April 1984); R. S. Laufer "War Trauma and Human Development: The Vietnam Experience," *The Trauma of War, Stress and Recovery in Vietnam Veterans*, ed. A. Black, S. Sonnenberg, and J. Talbot, (1985).

14. See the Hague Convention on Land Warfare of 1907, Article 1; Geneva Conventions of 1949, (First, Article 47; Second, Article 48; Third, Article 127; and Fourth, Article 144); Additional Protocol I. Articles 82,83.

15. R. Lifton, "Beyond Atrocity," in *Crimes of War*, ed. R. A. Falk, G. Kolko, and R. J. Lifton (New York: Random House, 1971), pp. 18–22.

16. P. G. Bourne, "From Boot Camp to My Lai," in *Crimes of War*, ed. Falk, Kolko, and Lifton, pp. 464–465.

17. P. Karsten, *Law, Soldiers and Combat* (Westport, Conn.: Greenwood Press, 1978), p. 148. See also T. J. Farer, *The Laws of War 25 Years After Nuremberg* (New York: Carnegie Endowment for International Peace, 1971), p. 49.

18. As quoted by Karsten, *Law, Soldiers and Combat*, p. 148.

19. This argument has been made by many scholars. See, for example, Taylor, *Nuremberg and Vietnam*, pp. 20 and 41; Quincy Wright, "The Outlawry of War and the Law of War," *American Journal of International Law* 47 (1953):371; Lifton, "Beyond Atrocity," pp. 18–22; and M. Walzer, *Just and Unjust Wars* (New York: Basic Books, 1977).

20. The constructed scale of awareness of the rules governing warfare range from (0) No knowledge of any rules to (100) Full knowledge of all the rules. The mean of the scale was 59 and the standard deviation was 30. The scale

was collapsed into three categories as presented in tables 9.12 and 9.13. 0 to 40 was coded (1) Unaware of the rules of war; 41 to 79 as (2) Somewhat aware of the rules of war; and 80 to 100 as (3) Fully aware of the rules of war.

21. The main proponent of this view is Carl von Clausewitz, *On War*. He can now be read in the new translation by Michael Howard and Peter Paret (Princeton: Princeton University Press, 1976). For a discussion of the military necessity argument, see W. G. Downey, "The Law of War and Military-Necessity," *American Journal of International Law* 47 (1958):254–62; N. C. W. Dunbar, "Military Necessity in War Crimes Trials," *British Yearbook of International Law* 29 (1952):442–52.

22. Department of the Army Field Manual FM 27-10, The Law of Land Warfare, (Washington, D.C.: U.S. Government Printing Office, 1956), ch. 1, Basic Rules and Principles, Articles 1 and 7.

23. Ibid., Article 3

24. *Rules of Engagement*, Document 3, paragraph 4.

25. See LAOS, April 1971. Staff Report prepared for the use of the Subcommittee on United States Security Agreements and Commitments Abroad of the Committe on Foreign Relations, United States Senate. (Washington, D.C.: U.S. Government Printing Office, August 3, 1971).

26. Ibid., pp. 10–11; see also a later document: *Thailand, Laos, Cambodia, and Vietnam*, April 1973, a Staff Report prepared for the use of the Subcommittee on United States Security Agreements and Commitments Abroad of the Committee on Foreign Relations, United States Senate (Washington, D.C.: U.S. Government Printing Office, June 11, 1973).

27. *Field Manual 27-10, The Law of Warfare*, p. 182, par. 509, entitled "Defense of Superior Orders."

28. Ibid., par. 501.

29. S. Hersh, *Cover-Up* (New York: Random House, 1972), pp. 98–118.

30. Ibid., pp. 118–33.

31. See J. Goldstein, B. Marshall, and J. Schwartz, eds., *The My Lai Massacre and Its Cover-up: Beyond the Reach of Law?* (New York: Free Press, 1976).

32. Taylor, *Nuremberg and Vietnam*, p. 174, 182.

33. For a detailed discussion of this issue, see Falk, Kolko, and Lifton, eds., *Crimes of War*, pp. 419-577; see also M. Cohen, "Morality and the Laws of War," in *Philosophy, Morality, and International Affairs*, ed. V. Held, S. Morgenbesser, and T. Nagel (New York: Oxford University Press, 1974), pp. 76–78; Walzer, *Just and Unjust Wars*, pp. 304–305.

34. Similar arguments are found in the scholarly literature. See, for example, Taylor, *Nuremberg and Vietnam*, pp. 42–58; also Yoram Dinstein, *The Defense of Obedience to Superior Orders in International Law* (Leyden: A. W. Sijthoff, 1965).

35. J. Glenn Gray, "The Warriors," in *Crimes of War*, pp. 515,517,520–21.

Notes to Chapter 10

1. D. S. Surrey, *Choice of Conscience—Vietnam Era Military and Draft Resisters in Canada* (New York: Praeger, 1982).

2. See methodology appendix, Human Rights scales (INDWAR).

Notes to Appendix

1. The sites were Brooklyn, New York; southern Westchester County, New York; Bridgeport, Connecticut; Atlanta, Georgia; Los Angeles, California; Chicago, Illinois; South Bend, Indiana; the two rural counties adjacent to South Bend; Columbus, Georgia; and the two rural counties adjacent to Columbus.

2. Our sample also included 83 Chicanos interviewed in the Los Angeles area. This special population is excluded from the present analysis.

3. G. Rothbart, "General Methodology," in *Legacies of Vietnam*, vol. 1 (Washington, D.C.: Government Printing Office, 1981), pp. 79–97.

4. G. Rothbart, M. Fine, and S. Sudman, "On Finding and Interviewing the Needles in the Haystack: the Use of Multiplicity Sampling," *Public Opinion Quarterly* 46 (1982):409–21.

5. Prepared by Robert S. Laufer and Mary Lennon in consultation with Douglas Gurak.

6. Dohrenwend et al. (1980) lists the items in each scale.

7. This section is derived from Boulanger et al. (1981).

8. This question was omitted from the nonveteran questionnaire.

9. The items were originally used in the 1971 Harris Survey, "A Study of the Problems Facing Vietnam Era Veterans: Their Readjustment to Civilian Life."

SELECTED
BIBLIOGRAPHY

Selected Bibliography

Adelson, J. "The Political Imagination of the Young Adolescent," *Daedalus* (Fall 1971).

Baxter, R. R. "Humanitarian Law or Humanitarian Politics? The 1974 Diplomatic Conference on Humanitarian Law," *Harvard International Law Journal* 16, 1 (Spring 1975).

——"So-Called Unprivileged Belligerency: Spies, Guerrillas, and Saboteurs," in *British Yearbook of International Law* 28 (1951).

Becker, D. "The Veteran: Problem and Challenge," *Social Forces* 25(1946).

Best, G. *Humanity in Warfare* (New York: Columbia University Press, 1980).

Boulanger, G., Kadushin, C., and Martin, J. *Legacies of Vietnam*, Vol. IV, *Long Term Stress Reactions* (Washington, D.C.: U.S. Government Printing Office, 1981).

Bourne, P. G. "From Boot Camp to My Lai," in *Crimes of War*, ed. Richard A. Falk, Gabriel Kolko, and Robert Jay Lifton (New York: Random House, 1971).

Brookover, W. B. "The Adjustment of Veterans to Civilian Life," *American Sociological Review* 10 (1945).

Cassese, A. "A Tentative Appraisal of the Old and New Humanitarian Law of Armed Conflict," in *The New Humanitarian Law of Armed Conflict*, ed. A. Cassese (Naples: Editoriale Scientifica, 1979).

—— "Means of Warfare: The Traditional and the New Law," in *The New Humanitarian Law of Armed Conflict* ed. A. Cassese (Naples: Editoriale Scientifica, 1979).

Chomsky, N. *At War with Asia* (New York: Random House, 1969).

von Clausewitz, C. *On War*, trans. Michael Howard and Peter Paret (Princeton: Princeton University Press, 1976).

Clergy and Laymen Concerned about Vietnam. *In The Name of America* (Annandale: Turnpike Press, 1968).

Cohen, M. "Morality and the Laws of War," in *Philosophy, Morality, and International Affairs*, ed. V. Held, S. Morgenbesser, and T. Nagel (New York: Oxford University Press, 1974).

Cowless, W. B. "Trial of War Criminals by Military Tribunals," *American Law Association Journal* 30 (1944).

Debris, J.P., and Menras, A. "Terror in Thieu's Prisons" (Philadelphia: Indochina Program, American Friends Service Committee, 1971).

Dinstein, Y. *The Defense of Obedience to Superior Orders in International Law* (Leyden: A. W. Sijthoff, 1965).

Downey, W. G. "The Law of War and Military Necessity," *American Journal of International Law* 47 (1958).

Draper, G. I. A. D. "The Status of Combatants and the Question of Guerrilla War," *British Yearbook of International Law* 45 (1971).

Dunbar, N. C. W. "Military Necessity in War Crimes Trials," *British Yearbook of International Law* 29 (1952).

Eaton, W. H. "Research on Veterans' Adjustment," *American Journal of Sociology* 51 (1946).

Elder, G. H., Jr. "Historical Change in Life Patterns and Personality," Eastern Sociological Meetings, Philadelphia, 1978.

Erikson, Erik. *Identity, Youth and Crisis* (New York: W. W. Norton, 1968).

Falk, R. A., ed. *The Vietnam War and International Law* (Princeton: Princeton University Press, vol. 1, 1968; vol. 2, 1969).

Falk, R. A., Kolko, G., and Lifton, R. J., eds. *Crimes of War* (New York: Random House, 1971).

Farer, T. J. *The Laws of War 25 Years after Nuremberg* (New York: Carnegie Endowment for International Peace, 1971).

Fenwick, "Draft Code of Offenses Against the Peace and Security of Mankind," *American Journal of International Law* 46, 98 (1952).

Fischer, V., Boyle, J. M., Bucuvalas, M., and Schulman, M. A. *Myths and Realities: A Study of Attitudes Toward Vietnam Era Veterans* (Washington, D.C.: Louis Harris and Associates, 1980).

Freud, S. *Beyond the Pleasure Principle* (New York: Hogarth Press, 1953 [1921]).

Frey-Wouters, E., and Laufer, R. S. "The Vietnam War in the Post-war Era in the United States," in *Key Issues of Peace Research*, ed. Y. Sakamoto and R. Klaassen (Ontario: International Peace Research Association, 1983).

Frey-Wouters, E., and Laufer, R. S. "The Political Legacy of the Vietnam War," paper presented at the International Society of Political Psychology, Oxford University, 1983.

Fried, C. *An Anatomy of Values; Problems of Personal and Social Choice* (Cambridge: Harvard University Press, 1970).

Fussell, P. *The Great War in Modern Memory* (New York: Oxford University Press, 1975).

Garner, J. W. "Punishment of Offenders Against the Laws and Customs of War," *American Journal of International Law* 14 (1920).

von Glahn, G. *The Occupation of Enemy Territory: A Commentary on the Law and Practice of Belligerent Occupation* (Minneapolis: University of Minnesota Press, 1957).

Goldstein, J., Marshall, B., and Schwartz, J., eds. *The My Lai Massacre and Its Cover-up: Beyond the Reach of Law?* (New York: Free Press, 1976).

Gould, W. S. "Racial Conflict in the U.S. Army," *Race* 15 (1973).

Gray, J. G. "The Warriors," in *Crimes of War* ed. R. Falk, G. Kolko, and R. Lifton (New York: Random House, 1971).

Havighurst, R. J., Eaton, W. H., Baughman, J. W., and Burgess, E. W. *The American Back Home: A Study of Veteran Readjustment* (New York: Longmans, Green, 1951).

Hersh, S. *Chemical and Biological Warfare: America's Hidden Arsenal* (Indianapolis: Bobbs-Merrill, 1968).

Hogan, D. P. *Transitions and Social Change* (New York: Academic Press, 1981).

Horowitz, M. J. *Stress Response Syndromes* (New York: Aronson, 1976).

Hough, R., Gongla, P. A., Scurfield, R. M., Corker, T. M., and Carr, C. R. "Natural History of Post Traumatic Stress Disorder," paper presented at the American Psychological Association, Anaheim, Calif., 1983.

International Committee of the Red Cross. *Weapons that May Cause Unnecessary Suffering or Have Indiscriminate Effects* (Geneva, 1973).

—— *Draft Additional Protocols to the Geneva Conventions of 1949, Commentary* (Geneva, 1973).

Karsten, P. *Law, Soldiers and Combat* (Westport, Conn.: Greenwood Press, 1978).

Keniston, K. *Youth and Dissent* (New York: Harcourt, Brace and World, 1972).

Laufer, R. S., "War Trauma and Human Development: The Vietnam Experience," in *The Trauma of War, Stress and Recovery in Vietnam Veterans* (American Psychiatric Press, 1985.

Laufer, R. S., and Bengston, V. L. "Generations, Aging and Social Stratification: On the Development of Generational Units," *Journal of Social Issues* 30 (1974).

Laufer R. S., Brett, E., and Gallops, M. S., "Dimensions of Post Traumatic Stress Disorder Among Vietnam Veterans," *The Journal of Nervous and Mental Disease* 173 (1985).

Laufer, R. S., Brett, E., and Gallops, M. S. "Symptom Patterns Associated with Post Traumatic Stress Disorder Among Vietnam Veterans Exposed to

War Trauma," *American Journal of Psychiatry* 142 (1985).

Laufer, R. S., Brett, E., and Gallops, M. S. "The Relationship Between Stressors and Symptomatology in Post-Traumatic Stress Disorder Among Vietnam Veterans," in *New Perspectives on Post-Traumatic Stress*, ed. B. van der Kolk (Clinical Insights Series, American Psychiatric Press, 1984).

Laufer, R. S., Frey-Wouters, E., and Gallops, M. S. "Traumatic Stressors in the Vietnam War and Post-Traumatic Stress Disorder," in *Trauma and Its Wake*, ed. Charles Figley (Brunner/Mazel, 1985).

Laufer, R. S., and Gallops, M. S. "Life-course Effects of Vietnam Combat and Abusive Violence: Marital Patterns," *Journal of Marriage and the Family* (1985).

Laufer, R. S., Gallops, M., and Frey-Wouters, E. "War Stress and Trauma: The Vietnam Veterans Experience," *Journal of Health and Social Behavior* 25 (1984).

Laufer, R. S., Yager, T., Frey-Wouters, E., and Donnellan, J. *Legacies of Vietnam. Post-War Trauma: Social and Psychological Problems of Vietnam Veterans in the Aftermath of the Vietnam War*, vol. 3 of the Final Report to the Veterans Administration and Congress (Washington, D.C.: U.S. Government Printing Office, 1981).

Lauterpacht, H. "The Problem of the Revision of the Law of War," *British Yearbook of International Law* 29 (1952).

—— "Rules of Warfare in an Unlawful War," in *Law and Politics in the World Community: Essays on Hans Kelsen's Pure Theory and Related Problems in International Law* ed. George A. Lipsky (Berkeley: University of California Press, 1953).

Leventman, S., and Camacho, P. "The 'Gook' Syndrome: The Vietnam War as a Racial Encounter," in *Strangers at Home*, ed. C. R. Figley and S. Leventman (New York: Praeger, 1980).

Levie, H. S. "Maltreatment of Prisoners of War in Vietnam," in *The Vietnam War and International Law*, vol. 2, ed. Richard A. Falk (Princeton: Princeton University Press, 1969).

Lewallen, J. *Ecology of Devastation: Indochina* (Baltimore: Penguin, 1971).

Lifton, R, J. "Beyond Atrocity," in *Crimes of War*, ed. R. A. Falk, G. Kolko, and R. J. Lifton (New York: Random House, 1971).

Lifton, R. J. and Olson, E., "The Human Meaning of Total Disaster: The Buffalo Creek Experience," *Psychiatry* 39 (1976).

Lumsden, M. *The United States Rules of Engagement in Vietnam as They Relate to the Use of Certain Specific Weapons: A Brief Survey and Analysis* (Stockholm International Peace Research Institute, April 1976).

Manner, G. "The Legal Nature and Punishment of Criminal Acts of Violence Contrary to the Laws of War," *American Journal of International Law* 37 (1943).

Moskos, C. C. *The American Enlisted Man* (New York: Russell Sage, 1970).

—— "Surviving the War in Vietnam," in *Strangers at Home*, ed. C. R. Figley and S. Leventman (New York: Praeger, 1980).

Neilands, J. B. et al. *Harvest of Death* (New York: Collier, 1962).

Petrowski, L. C. "Law and the Conduct of the Vietnam War," in *The Vietnam War and International Law*, vol. 2, ed. R. A. Falk, (Princeton University Press, 1969).

Pike, D. *Viet Cong* (Cambridge: MIT Press, 1968).

Polner, M. *No Victory Parades: The Return of the Vietnam Veteran* (New York: Holt, Rinehart and Winston, 1971).

Race, J. *War Comes to Long An* (Berkeley: University of California Press, 1972).

Report of the International Committee of the Red Cross, Conference of Government Experts on the Use of Certain Conventional Weapons, Lucerne, 1974 and Lugano, 1976.

Schell, J. *The Military Half* (New York: Knopf, 1968).

Schuman, H. "Two Sources of Anti-War Sentiment in America," *American Journal of Sociology* 78, 3 (November 1972).

Secretary-General of the United Nations. *Napalm and Other Incendiary Weapons and All Aspects of Their Possible Use*, United Nations publication, Sales No. E. 73.I.3.

Siordet, F. "Les Conventions de Geneve et la Guerre Civile," *Revue Internationale de la Croix Rouge* 32 (1950).

Sloan, L. and Phoenix, H. "The Quality of Race Relations in the Vietnam Era Military," paper presented at the annual meeting of the Society for the Study of Social Problems, Boston, 1979.

Stockholm International Peace Research Institute (SIPRI). *Ecological Consequences of the Second Indochina War, Weapons of Mass Destruction and the Environment* (Stockholm, 1974).

—— *Incendiary Weapons* (Stockholm: Almqvist & Wiksell, and Cambridge: MIT Press, 1975).

Surrey, D. S. *Choice of Conscience—Vietnam Era Military and Draft Resisters in Canada* (New York: Praeger, 1982).

Taylor, T. *Nuremberg and Vietnam: An American Tragedy* (Chicago: Quadrangle Books, 1970).

Trainin, I. P. "Questions of Guerrilla Warfare in the Law of War," *American Journal of International Law*, 40 (1946).

Trials of War Criminals before the Nuremberg Military Tribunals under Control Council Law No. 10, Nuremberg, October 1946-April 1949 (Washington, D.C.: U.S. Government Printing Office, 1949–1952), 14 vols.

Trooboff, P. D., ed. *Law and Responsibility in Warfare—The Vietnam Experience*, published under the auspices of the American Society of International Law (University of North Carolina Press, 1975).

United Nations War Crimes Commission. *Law Report of War Criminals*, vol. 4 (London, 1949).

United States, France, Great Britain, Soviet Union. *Agreement for the Prosecution and Punishment of the Major War Criminals of the European Axis*, August 8, 1945, in *American Journal of International Law* 39 (1945), supplement.

United States Department of State, Office of the Legal Adviser. "The Legality of United States Participation in the Defense of Viet Nam," *Department of State Bulletin* 54, March 8, 1966.

Vaillant, G. *Adaptation to Life* (Boston: Little, Brown, 1977).

Walzer, M. *Just and Unjust Wars* (New York: Basic Books, 1977).

Wilson, J. P. "Identity, Ideology and Crisis: The Vietnam Veteran in Transition," *Forgotten Warrior Project, Part I*, report submitted to the Disabled American Veterans Association, 1978.

Winsborough, H. H. *The Transition from Schoolboy to Adult* (Madison: Center for Demography and Ecology, Working Paper 76–13, 1976).

Wright, Q. "The Outlawry of War and the Law of War," *American Journal of International Law* 47 (1953).

Yager, T., Laufer, R. S., and Gallops, M. "Some Problems Associated with War Experience in Men of the Vietnam Generation," *Archives of General Psychiatry* 41 (1984).

Zilberg, N. J., Weiss, D. S., and Horowitz, M. J. "Impact of Event Scale: A Cross-Validational Study and Some Empirical Evidence Supporting a Conceptual Model of Stress Response Syndromes." *Journal of Consulting and Clinical Psychology* 50 (1982).

INDEX